JEWISH LIBERAL POLITICS IN
TSARIST RUSSIA, 1900–1914

# Jewish Liberal Politics in Tsarist Russia, 1900–1914

## The Modernization of Russian Jewry

Christoph Gassenschmidt
*Research Fellow, Research Institute for the
History and Culture of Germans in Russia
Albert-Ludwigs-University, Freiburg, Germany*

 NEW YORK UNIVERSITY PRESS
Washington Square, New York

© Christoph Gassenschmidt 1995

First published in the U.S.A. in 1995 by
NEW YORK UNIVERSITY PRESS
Washington Square
New York, N.Y. 10003

Library of Congress Cataloging-in-Publication Data
Gassenschmidt, Christoph, 1959–
Jewish liberal politics in tsarist Russia, 1900–1914 : the
modernization of Russian Jewry/ Christoph Gassenschmidt.
p.   cm.
Includes bibliographical references and index.
ISBN 0–8147–3079–5
1. Jews—Russia—Politics and government.   2.   Russia—Politics and
government—1904–1914. 3. Jews—Russia—Emancipation.   4. Zionism–
–Russia.  I. Title.
DS135.R9G35   1995
947'.004924—dc20                                    94–38315
                                                      CIP

Printed in Great Britain

To Ritsa

# Contents

# Acknowledgements

First and foremost I would like to thank the Memorial Foundation for Jewish Culture, New York, and the Deutsche Akademische Austauschdienst (DAAD) for their financial help, without which this book would not have been possible. I am also very grateful for the substantial financial support I received from my mother, my parents-in-law, and especially from Georg and Elisabeth Gawliczek who helped me through a very difficult situation. My greatest gratitude goes, however, to my wife, Ritsa Panagiotou, who not only supported me for nearly three years, but also had to go through the agony of proofreading and correcting this work.

For the academic part, I am especially grateful to my academic guide and mental father of this work, Prof. Dr. Heinz-Dietrich Löwe. For their useful comments I thank especially Prof. Dr. Heiko Haumann, Prof. Ezra Mendelsohn, Prof. Jonathan Frankel, Dr. Eli Lederhendler, Dr. David Sorkin, Dr. Harry Shukman, and Prof. John Klier. My gratitude goes especially to Dr. Ralph Tuchtenhagen and Benjamin Nathans who provided me with aditional material. I also thank the staff of the YIVO Institute, New York, as well as the staff of the various libraries and archives who guided me through the mountains of material and led me to the essential documents.

Last but not least, I would like to thank my friends Bart, Kleanthis, Rolf and Saugata, who cheered me up and motivated me with their sense of humour and their positive thinking.

I am solely responsible for all the errors or mistakes which might occur in the book.

CHRISTOPH GASSENSCHMIDT

# List of Abbreviations

| | |
|---|---|
| Bund | Vseobshchii Evreiskii Rabochii Soiuz v Litve, Polshe i Rossiia (General Jewish Workers' Union in Lithuania, Poland and Russia) |
| EDG | Evreiskaia Demokraticheskaia Gruppa (Jewish Democratic Group) |
| EIO | Evreiskoe Istoricheskii Obshchestvo (Jewish Historiographic Society) |
| EKO | Evreiskaia Kolonisatsiia Organisatsiia (Jewish Colonisation Organisation) |
| EKOPO | Evreiskii komitet pomoshchi zhertvam voiny (Jewish Committee for the Relief of Victims of War) |
| ELO | Evreiskoe Literaturnoe Obshchestvo (Jewish Literary Society) |
| ENG | Evreiskaia Narodnaia Gruppa (Jewish People's Group) |
| ENP | Evreiskaia Narodnaia Partiia (Jewish People's Party) |
| Kadets | Konstitutsionno Demokraticheskaia Partiia (Constitutional Democratic Party) |
| KI | Kneset Isroel |
| KK | Kovenskii Komitet (Kovno Committee) |
| ND | National Democrats |
| ORPE | Obshchsetvo dlia rasprostranenie prosveshcheniia mezhdu evreiami v Rossii (Society for the Spread of Enlightenment among the Jews in Russia) |
| ORSE | Obshchestvo rasprostranenie pravilnykh svedenii o evreiakh i evreistve (Society for the Dissemination of True Knowledge on the Jews and Judaism) |
| ORT | Obshchestvo dlia remeslennago i zemledel'cheskago truda (Society for the Promotion of Artisan and Agricultural Labor) |
| OZE | Obshchestvo okhraneniia zdorovia evreiskago naseleniia (Society for the Improvement of the Hygienic and Health Condition of the Jewish People in Russia) |
| RSDRP | Rossiiskaia Socialdemokraticheskaia Rabochaia Partiia (Russian Social Democratic Workers' Party) |
| RSO | Rossiiskaia Sionistskaia Organisatsia (Russian Organization of Zionistists) |
| SD | Social Democrats (also RSDRP) |
| SERP | Sionistskaia Evreiskaia Rabochaia Partiia (Zionist Jewish Labor Party) |

SP      Soiuz dlia Dostizheniia Polnopraviia Evreiskago Naroda v Rossii (Union for the Attainment of Full Rights for the Jewish People in Russia)

SRN     Soiuz Russkago Naroda (Union of the Russian People)

SS      Sotsialisty Sionisty (Zionist-Socialist Labor Party)

TB      Tiferes Bokhurim

# Introduction

This study covers an important period of Russian-Jewish history in pre-revolutionary Tsarist Russia: Jewish 'Liberal Politics' from about 1900 until 1914. The analysis concentrates on the Jewish social and political activists who during the First Russian Revolution of 1905 founded the first Russian-Jewish political organization embracing Zionists, Nationalists, Liberals and non-party affiliated Socialists: the 'Union for the Attainment of Full Rights for the Jewish People in Russia' (Soiuz dlia Dostizheniia Polnopraviia Evreiskago Naroda v Rossii – SP). This organization represented a break with the past of Russian-Jewish history in two respects: first, in terms of its membership and organizational framework; and second of its political demands for equality of rights as well as national and cultural autonomy for Russian Jews. This combination of civil and national rights was supposed to prevent what West European Jews had offered in exchange for equality of rights: assimilation. The Union represented a milestone for the mobilisation and politicization of the Jewish masses in Russia, and it furthered the political differentiation among the non-orthodox socialists and non-socialists. Nevertheless, Jewish historiography, with few exceptions, focused mainly on the national participants of the Union, Dubnov's Autonomists and the bourgeois Zionists, but neglected, or only mentioned in passing – and only in connection with the two big Russian Jewish organizations at that time, the ORPE and ORT – the Liberals around the lawyers Maksim M. Vinaver and G.B. Sliozberg, and the 'Trudoviki' around Leon Bramson and M.A. Krol. Also, the study of Jewish Marxist Socialism, the 'Bund', as well as of Labour Zionism largely stops with the end of the First Russian Revolution. Scholars of Russian-Jewish history such as Alexander Orbach, Michael Stanislawski, Steven Zipperstein, Eli Lederhendler, or John Klier have only recently started to go beyond the description of Zionism and Bundism and events, groups and political activities after 1905–06 are still sadly underresearched. Generally speaking, Jewish Liberalism, nationally minded in its mainstream, has been neglected or wrongly lumped together with 'assimilationism'. For example, Goldscheider and Zuckerman, in their study on the transformation of the Jews, compare Russian-Jewish Socialism and Zionism with German-Jewish Liberalism as if there had been no Russian-Jewish Liberalism. Yet, Russian-Jewish Liberals – Jewish activists who were either members of the liberal Russian Constitutional Democrats, the Kadets, or, at least, supported their political programme – were the driving force behind the foundation and the activities of the Soiuz Polnopraviia. They were also active members of the Central Committees of various Russian-Jewish cultural and social organizations. In short, they were very active, important and, as will be shown, everything but assimilationists.

The scholars mentioned above have maintained that Jewish politics existed in Russia already before the rise of Zionism and Bundism. This implies a wide definition of politics as it basically includes all the various forms of Jewish representation ranging from the *Shtadlanim* – wealthy members of Russian-Jewish society who personally intervened with the authorities on behalf of Jewish interests – to the Jewish intelligentsia of the pre-1880s promoting inner-Jewish reform. In that respect, David Biale's statement, that Jewish politics always existed in one form or another, makes sense.

A somewhat different position, a narrower definition of politics is necessary. Not intra-communal relationship, not even the early phase of proto-Bundist activity constitute politics in any real or modern sense of the word. For our purpose, politics means participation in a political process. This process germinates with the first seeds of civil society and comes into its own with inter-community (ethnic) relationships, and with the appearance of parties interacting with the intention of influencing their respective constituencies as well as the rules of the political system. It also implies a political process geared to representative institutions. This study concentrates on what Jewish activists contributed to the development of some form of civic society within Jewish and Russian society and to the integration of Jewish political trends into the larger political process. This of course again had inner-Jewish implications, which – without the other aspects – will be focused upon for the period 1907 to 1914.

Jewish Liberal politics in Russia witnessed three main stages within the period from the 1890s until the outbreak of World War I: the phase of proto-liberal politics from the early 1890s until late 1904. During this period, Jewish Liberals followed up tactics still based on rather traditional patterns: Shtadlanut, propaganda activities to enlighten Russian society about the Jewish plight, and the organization of a legal defence bureau. The second phase witnessed the emergence of Jewish Liberal politics, culminating in the political struggle for the Jews in the First Russian State Duma (from the end of 1904 until summer 1906). Finally, reinforced by the Duma's failure and the government's hostile attitudes, the third stage of Jewish liberal Politics was characterized by a tactical shift from solely political (parliamentary) activities to organic work. Here, independent from the general political situation, Jewish Liberals in co-operation with their former partners aimed at modernizing the Jewish community, and thereby changing the Jewish plight fundamentally through a reform programme for the Jewish community itself. The vehicle to materialize organic work was the mobilization of Jewish national economic, educational, social and cultural forces.

From the beginning, Russian-Jewish politics in general, and Jewish-liberal politics in particular, was embedded in the context of the political situation and development in Tsarist Russia. Within the entire period under discussion, Russian-Jewish liberal politics followed and adjusted their tactics to the ups and downs of the political situation in Russia. They hereby became part of a phenomenon which characterized European history since the early nineteenth century: the struggle of the national minorities, particularly in the Habsburg Empire, Russia, and Germany-Prussia, for political independence or national-cultural autonomy. According to Miroslav Hroch, the struggle of national minorities, such as the Lithuanians, Estonians, Finns, Norwegians, Flemish, Slovaks or Czechs, went through three distinct phases. In a first phase a small circle of intellectuals, priests or students, influenced by radical ideas in the universities, started to take an interest in the history and culture of their own people. After this period of research, they went on to the second phase where they began to propagate a national consciousness among their fellow countrymen. Once successful, this small circle of intellectuals resulted in a national mass movement (third phase). Russian Jews were no exception. At the beginning, in the 1890s, a small circle of intellectuals, such as lawyers, doctors, journalists and students began with extensive historical work and spread their ideas through the Jewish press to the Jewish masses. Russian Jews discovered their history, literature, culture, and finally, their own national identity. In contrast to the nationalities mentioned above Russian Jews, however, reversed the sequence: first they demanded political rights and then national-cultural. On the other hand Jewish liberalism developed in parallel to Jewish nationalism, but not before, as had been the case in western and central Europe.

Yet another similarity lay in the way all the minorities readjusted their politics according to the political circumstances. After the refurbishing of the political order in 1849 in the Habsburg Empire or in Russia after 1863 and 1907, leaders of various nationalities altered their strategies to avoid open confrontation with the ruling majority. As the various nationalities could not expect equal rights, many of them began extensive organizational work from the grassroots. This is what the Poles called 'organic work', and practised after the failure of 1863. To counteract increasing economic and political pressure from the ruling governments in Russia, Austria-Hungary or Prussia, they strengthened their national cohesion and identity by forming their own cultural, economic and social institutions. After 1907, Russian Jews did exactly this when they shifted their priorities from parliamentary to organic work in light of continuing inequality and Stolypin's *coup d'état*, which made parliamentary work less promising. This did not mean political retreat, but – given the political circumstances – an increasing emphasis on self-reliance. Slogans such as self-help and self-protection illustrated the determination of these intelligentsy to find ways and means to improve the economic situation, to fight assimilation – by founding Jewish cultural and social institutions – and growing anti-Semitism. As the Poles before them, they set up organizations specifically designed for this purpose. A modernization process with all its side effects was instigated. The implicit secularization of the Jewish community meant that the Jewish intelligentsia once again challenged the traditional communal leadership and provoked a reaction of conservative religious elements that desperately defended their positions. Also, political dissent between various streams of the intelligentsy over how to modernize and secularize Jewish life became very much part of this period between 1908 and 1914.

As with other national minorities in Tsarist Russia, Jewish politics – as defined above – emerged within the wider political context. At first, until 1905, Jewish politics kept a low profile and followed traditional patterns of promoting Jewish interests. Jewish politics in a modern sense developed when in 1904–05 the general discontent within Russian society triggered the Revolution of 1905. The rise of the progressive forces of Russian society paved the way for Jewish activists to join in and to shift their strategy to a higher profile by participating in the liberation movement. Jewish Liberals not only took part, but followed the general pattern of creating a public space – their own public space – through the Soiuz Polnopraviia.

This study analyses the historical and intellectual roots, motivation and circumstances impelling Jewish Liberals and their partners in the SP to get involved in Russian and community politics. Chapter 1 is designated to this while the second deals with the Soiuz Polnopraviia, its activities and political position during the Russian Revolution of 1905 and its struggle for 'full' rights for Russian Jews. It is also necessary to shed some light on the disintegration of this first all-Russian all-Jewish organization. Why didn't the Soiuz Polnopraviia continue beyond the Revolution? Was the Jewish Liberal organization, the 'Jewish People's Group' (Evreiskaia Narodnaia Gruppa), really just an organisation to combat Zionism? This is too simple an explanation. Therefore, the foundation of various Jewish parties has been dealt with in greater detail in chapter 3.

Jewish politics after the dissolution of the SP was not the end of Jewish

Liberal politics and simply the ascendancy of Zionism. Liberals continued to play an important, perhaps the most important, role in Jewish politics. Central to this study are, therefore, the ways and means employed by Jewish Liberals and their opponents in the so-called 'Stolypin' years (1907–1911) and the so-called 'dark' years (1911–1914): organic work and its impact on Jewish society. In light of the general crisis of the political parties in Russia – which lobbies did Russian-Jewish activists use to realize the aims of organic work? To recall Biale: there was always some sort of representation of Jewish interests, and powerlessness was never really absolute in the diaspora.

Almost nothing has been written on Jewish politics during this period. This study, therefore, takes up events and topics only briefly touched upon so far: for instance, the Economic Conference (1908) and the Kovno Conference (1909) mentioned by Orbach, Janowsky, and Levitats. The fact that Jewish Liberals took a leading part in all Jewish cultural, social, economic, and educational organizations such as ORT and ORPE has never been addressed. Therefore, it seemed necessary to put the different mosaic stones together, in order to gain a clearer and more analytic picture of the Stolypin years in general, and of what we may call Jewish Liberal politics in particular. In short, this combines Jewish political history with excursions into the fields of Jewish education and economy. This book examines the policies and actions of these Jewish activists, their motives, ideas and differences. A thorough analysis of Jewish localities would, however, go beyond the scope of this study. Nonetheless, references to specific places will be made whenever it seems necessary to illustrate successes or failures of organic work. For this reason, chapter 4 and 5 are more voluminous than others.

Since Jewish Liberal politics addressed Russians as well as the Jewish communities all their activities have been recorded in Russian. Therefore it did not seem necessary to include Hebrew sources. Even the Zionists had their own Russian press throughout the entire period under consideration. All sources of immediate interest to this study were published in Russian, such as the annual reports of Jewish organizations such as ORT, ORPE, ELO, and EIO, the protocols of the Kovno Conference, the various memoirs of the most important Liberal figures, the Duma protocols, and most of the newspapers. Since Jewish Liberals turned to the community, many of their actions were also recorded in Yiddish, many sources are written in this language and they are also used for this study: the biggest Jewish daily 'Der Fraind', the left-wing Zionist press, memoirs of various Bund leaders and leaflets found in the Bund Archive in New York in Yiddish were also valuable for this study.

It remains to explain two technicalities: first, all dates are according to the Julian calendar which for the twentieth century was then thirteen days behind the Gregorian calendar of Western Europe; secondly, inconsistencies in the transliteration of names such as Dubnov or Dubnow, Jabotinsky or Zhabotinskii arise from the various systems used and throughout this study the endnotes give names in the way the quoted books or sources did.

# 1 The Emergence of Jewish Liberals in Russia: from Acculturation to Revolution

This chapter describes the socio-political background which let the Liberals re-emphasize their Jewish past and develop a new self-consciousness. This found expression in their first activities – in the organization of legal aid provided to Jews and the propagation of Jewish rights – and finally presented them as another interest group beside those already active (the Zionists and the Jewish Socialists, also known as Bundists). However, from the early 1890s until the eve of the First Russian Revolution in 1904, the Liberals pursued a strategy still mainly bound to the old methods of promoting Jewish interests, and can be described as a combination of *shtadlanstvo* and activities focused on protest and propaganda actions against anti-Semitic measures and acts of the Russian government. Therefore, according to our definition of politics, the first stage was characterized by a mainly non-political approach to the solution of the Jewish question in Russia.

## 1.1 JEWISH SOCIETY IN TRANSITION

Jewish Liberals appeared as a result of a process of transformation within Jewish society which took place during the reign of Alexander II.[1] His new approach to solving the Jewish question – which can be described as the traditional formula for emancipation, 'equal rights for Russification' – laid the basis for the Liberals' advent. Alexander II's policy towards the Jews had changed in two ways: in his attempt to break down what both he and his father Nicholas had called 'Jewish separateness', he no longer used repressive means and had given up all attempts at converting Jews to Christianity. His approach aimed at Russifying the Jews, and to this end he extended promises and even rewarded elements regarded as Russified. Along these lines merchants of the first guild, university graduates and artisans were granted the right to live everywhere in the empire, which was to be both a reward and in the case of the latter also an incentive. Large numbers of Jews responded by flocking into Russian schools and universities.[2] His policy found support among the successors of the late

1

Haskalah – the Jewish enlightenment movement – which became more influential towards the end of the 1860s in Russia.[3] These latter day 'Maskilim' propagated – along the lines of the emancipation pact – acculturation to Russian culture and life, and focused their efforts on the dissemination of secular education and on the spread of the knowledge of Russian among the Jews. This had found its institutional expression in the foundation of two organizations: the Society for the Spread of Enlightenment (ORPE) in 1863, and the Society for Promotion of Artisan and Agricultural Labor (ORT) in 1880.[4] These Maskilim regarded the knowledge of Russian as a means of entering and progressing in the wider world. Many young Jews followed the call of the Maskilim and began studying at Russian universities, where they got their degrees as lawyers, doctors or engineers; this is how a new strata within Jewish society emerged, the intelligentsia. The Jewish intelligentsia, and in some ways the merchants as well, represented a new generation of Jews which either tried to bring their religious belief into line with the secular world, or even left Judaism as a religion altogether. Through their study at Russian universities they were exposed to subjects representing the modern, secular and non-Jewish world, and were thus freed from the intellectual and psychological boundaries of the Jewish *Shtetl*. Their interest in Russian culture grew, contacts with their Russian fellow students of different political views encouraged many of them to turn their back on their old traditional Jewish world, and, as a result of this, tried to become acculturated to Russian society. As graduates of Russian universities they – especially the lawyers and doctors – belonged to the privileged circles not only of Jewish, but also of Russian society. With these professions and as journalists they entered key positions of Russian social life outside the realm of the state apparatus. These professions were advantageous in the sense that they guaranteed a relatively free life and provided overall and more analytical insight into the Jewish plight. These intellectuals started to think about solutions in a broader framework.

The changes, however, affected only a relatively small circle of Russian Jews, and as Michael Meyer has put it: 'it [the Haskalah] undermined the old way of life without providing a satisfactory new one'.[5] The Jewish masses distrusted the so-called 'Berlinchiki' – the Maskilim – and the intelligentsia as well as the measures pursued by the government, and persisted in their traditional way of life, which centred around Orthodoxy. The large masses of artisans, petty traders, *melameds* (traditional teachers), tenants, and also the *Luftmenschen*[6] rejected the assimilation that was propagated.[7]

Despite the Haskalah's failure on a large scale, the social and occupational structure of Jewish society had entered the first stages of a transformation which was to change Jewish politics as well as Jewish community life. Journalists in certain Jewish newspapers such as *Razsvet* (1860–61) and *Sion* (1861) started to challenge the traditional Jewish world by putting forward the first suggestions for a modernized Russian-Jewish community alongside the West European model: this included the modernization of the traditional education system, of the taxation system, the rabbinate, and a secularisation of the Jewish community structure. Although this stemmed only from a relatively small circle of intellectuals,[8] which was still part of the Haskalah movement, these were the first steps within Jewish society towards acting 'politically' and finding a solution for the Jewish question.[9] In fact, as will be discussed below, all these demands found wider acceptance within Russian Jewry when the target changed from Russification to Jewish 'nationalization'; when the intellectuals reacted to the fact that in the late 1870s and early 1880s the government began to shift its policy of integrating Jews by Russification to excluding them from Russian society. At this moment, Jewish Intellectuals were only left with the option of going back to the roots: instead of Russification, 'Nationalization', that is strengthening cohesion among Jews.

A major turning point for Russian-Jewish life and the political concepts pursued hitherto was the assassination of Tsar Alexander II in 1881 and the wave of pogroms which rocked the Pale of Settlement shortly after. This outbreak of violence not only ended a relatively peaceful time for the Jews in Russia,[10] but led the government to turn to a restrictive anti-Jewish policy.[11] At first, the government was as surprised and horrified by the pogroms as the Jewish population. Moreover, it regarded the pogroms as the work of the revolutionaries. Subsequent investigations could not, however, substantiate this theory, and the anti-Semitic press as well as the Minister of Interior, N.P. Ignatev put the blame on the Jews themselves, claiming that they had provoked the pogroms by 'exploiting the native population'.[12] Authorized by Tsar Alexander III in August 1881, Ignatev started to design an anti-Jewish restrictive policy which finally resulted in the so-called 'May Laws' of 1882. By imposing this restrictive legislation on Russian Jews, Alexander III not only broke with the policies of his ancestors who had tried to end Jewish separateness, but he set up a legal framework which aimed at restricting and isolating Russian Jews from the rest of the population.[13] This not only stopped the acculturation process which was under way, but condemned Russian Jews to live under appalling circumstances, from which no salvation was offered.

The pogroms of 1881 and the May Laws of 1882 provoked a process of reorientation among Jewish intellectual circles. Assimilation no longer seemed the appropriate way of solving the Jewish question. Other means and ways had to be found to improve the lot of Russian Jews: thus, the Jewish intellectual world split into various groups to evaluate the situation and try to formulate an answer. The general question was whether a better future was achievable in Russia: if this was the case, the question remained of how this could be achieved. Would it be worthwhile to stay in the country, and fight together with the revolutionary forces, which were still in their nascent stage? Or would it be better to leave the country and try to make it elsewhere?

These questions were discussed extensively in the Jewish newspaper *Razsvet* in August 1881, especially after Russia faced the first wave of Jewish emigration.[14] The debates saw two opposing sides: the 'Emigrationists' and the 'Integrationists'. The former – mainly composed of writers, journalists and poets – for the first time challenged the established leadership of the 'Integrationists' led by G.O. Gintsburg, Bakst and the conservative rabbis. The uprise of these Jewish intellectuals, caused by the 'Integrationists'' opposition towards emigration and the hopes which were created by the plans for a mass emigration by the first Jewish organizations abroad – among them the 'Alliance Israelite Universelle' – lasted, however, only until the spring of 1882. The new Minister of the Interior, Dmitrii Tolstoi, took the wind out of the 'Emigrationists' sails by stating that he would no longer tolerate any further pogroms. Furthermore, the Turkish authorities and the USA had revised their views of permitting further Jewish immigration; the advocates of this solution had therefore lost their ground.[15] Emigration was no longer regarded as the proper solution for the bulk of the Russian Jews, and seemed – due to the political changes – rather unrealistic. Even if it would have been manageable, it would not have been easy for five and a half million Jews to emigrate without provoking a rather restrictive immigration policy by the other countries in question, such as Germany, France and England.

After the wave of the pogroms, Leon Pinsker, a doctor from Odessa, publicly presented his pamphlet *Autoemancipation*.[16] His book was the final expression of the ideas which were already formulated by Moses Leib Lilienblum. He had realized that the reasons for the persecutions were the Jews' status as foreigners. As a solution he proposed that Jews cease to be foreigners and build a homeland of their own.[17] Despite the fact that Pinsker's pamphlet was an expression of early Zionist thinking which aimed at creating an asylum primarily for the poor Jews of Russia who were difficult to integrate, his concept of autoemancipation emphasized more strongly than ever the principal existence of a Jewish nation which has its own rights, and which should emancipate itself. Even more important was Pinsker's insistense that it made no sense to rely on non-Jews for a solution, but solely on the Jews themselves.[18] Under the shock of the pogroms, his idea of a Jewish home and autoemancipation, which was certainly not new, fell on fertile ground among those Jewish intellectuals who were desperately looking for solutions.[19] His booklet became known in the bigger cities in Russia and the first 'proto-Zionist' circles – such as 'Ahavat Zion' ('Brotherhood of Zion Society'), 'Kibbuz Niddehei Israel' ('Society for Gathering the Dispersed of Israel'), and the 'Hovevei Zion' ('Lovers of Zion') movement in 1884 with Leon Pinsker as its spokesman – came into being.[20]

However, the sphere of activity of these proto-Zionist groups was limited to the big Russian-Jewish centres such as Odessa, St. Petersburg and Minsk.[21] Furthermore, these intellectual circles were relatively small in numbers, politically unorganized and without any links to each other. Finally, since the Jewish press had not yet developed to the extent that it would some twenty-five years later, they had no possibility of reaching the Jewish masses.

The majority of the Jewish intelligentsia, including Pinsker, still saw Russia as their country, and the concept of 'National identity' – which was the catchword the proto-Zionists propagated – did not resound in the Jewish public before the 1890s. From the early 1880s until the mid-1890s, the majority of the Jewish intelligentsia, such as the Jewish students, did not show any particular interest in the Jewish question as such. During their studies at Russian or West European Universities, they joined the various radical revolutionary movements, especially the beginning Russian Social Democratic Movement and the terrorist 'Narodnaia Volia' ('People's Will') dominating the revolutionary spirit at the universities. Moreover, the minorities in general and the Jews in particular became the main carriers of the Narodnaia Volia in the 1880s. Five out of the seven major Narodovol'tsy leaders were Jewish (Abram Bakh, Boris Orzhikh, Natan Bogoraz, Zakharii Kogan, Khaim Lev Shternberg), Jewish membership among the Narodovol'tsy in the South and Southwest was approximately 35 per cent (1886) and 20–25 per cent (1885–1890). People like Shternberg or M.A. Krol who later joined the Jewish Liberals, from 1882 until 1884 were dedicated to both terrorism and unifying workers' circles in Odessa. Other Jewish Radicals such as Arkadii Kremer, Liidia Akselrod, Lev Iogikhes and Tsemakh Kopelson joined the Social Democrat Movement which by the end of 1894 had influenced the Russian underground in all the major cities of the empire. The turning point for the majority of these radicals came with the final collapse of the Narodnaia Volia in 1894, and with the fact that the proto-Zionist Movement made an increasing inroad in Social Democratic circles.[22]

The first Jewish socialist circles started their activities in 1890 in North-West Russia under the name of the so-called 'Vilna Group'. They approached the Jewish problem from a purely 'internationalist' point of view. According to their Marxist views anti-Semitism and the pogroms were merely a 'subordinate-contradiction' to the 'main-contradiction' of the capitalist system. As opposed to the proto-Zionist circles, they believed in a future, socialist Russia which would not recognize any differences among its constituent nationalities.[23] From the beginning they were linked to the Russian revolutionary circles: their basis for action was, therefore, different from that of the proto-Zionists. From the very beginning they were focusing on a change of Jewish society, which the Zionists had not yet envisaged. Their focus of attention was to work from the bottom and fight for the workers' rights. They were the third ones to challenge the old and traditional structures of the Jewish world from the roots. The early Bundists were active in the political as well as in the economic field. Very soon, however the Bundists were forced to compromise on their internationalist views, since in order to advocate their ideas they were forced to use the language spoken by the majority of Russian Jews, Yiddish.

In the early 1890s the proto-Zionist ideas spread all over the Pale and the concept of a Jewish national identity was further developed through Ahad Ha'am's propagation of 'Cultural Zionism' and Simon Dubnov's 'Autonomism'.[24] The Jews, at least some Jewish intellectuals, started to openly display the value of Jewishness.

At about the same time as the Bundists and the Zionists another part of the new Jewish intelligentsia raised its voice in St. Petersburg in the 1890s. The University graduates – especially the young Jewish lawyers – had to face the fact that they had been included in the anti-semitic policy of the Russian government which became much more repressive between 1882–1889, and restricted the Jews' economic, political and personal life.[25] Thus, *inter alia*, in 1889 the government had blocked the admission of Jewish lawyers to the Russian bar.[26] This was a major blow to the would-be Jewish lawyers who had become more or less acculturated – but not assimilated – to Russian society and already lived on equal terms with the Russian lawyers, and who, in short, were about to establish themselves. This frustration, as Alexander Orbach has pointed out, was exacerbated 'as a consequence of being denied that full measure of acceptance from the general society that they had been longing for'.[27] All their efforts towards achieving the elevated position they were striving for seemed to have amounted to nothing. Furthermore, they witnessed the worsening plight of their fellow Jews, and with it the idea of a politically reformed system.

This cannot, however, be the only reason why a group of acculturated and privileged Jews, who had lost direct contact with the Jewish masses, began emphasizing their Jewish identity. The new law could be one explanation: but a more convincing argument for this change can be seen in the fact that they had also been influenced by the ideas and conceptions raised among Jewish intellectuals to whom they had close contacts, such as Ahad Ha'am and Dubnov.[28] Secondly, as Gregorii Aronson has pointed out, 'the demographic processes, like internal migration, the decline of the small towns, the flight of the more prosperous elements to the cities, and the tendency to a rapidly increasing urbanization in the 1890s' had caused the Jewish shtetl's traditional and religious life to change or to deteriorate. The cities' modernized and secular life increasingly influenced Jewish society, a fact which 'threw many Yeshiva students into secular life, and many of them became also revolutionaries'.[29] Third, the Jewish intellectuals were already working in Russian-Jewish newspapers such as *Voskhod* ('Rise') under Landau's editorship and *Budushchnost* ('Future') under S.O. Gruzenberg's editorship,[30] and were thus already involved in Jewish 'activities'. Hence, a circle of young academics such as Jewish lawyers, as well as journalists and doctors, came together in St. Petersburg under the auspice of the well-known lawyer A.Ya. Passover. The members of this circle regarded anti-Jewish legislation as the decisive cause for the desperate economic and social position of the Jews in Russia. Attached to this group was also the historian Simon Dubnov, whose 'call for the systematic collection of source materials on Russian-Jewish history' (1891) – which he regarded 'as a necessary step for the writing of a solid and scholarly history of Russian Jewry'[31] – stimulated the very first actions of this circle to start research on the history of the Jews in Russia.

The lawyers – also discriminated against as Jews – in turn began to identify themselves with their fellow Jews. Exclusion did not only further cohesion, but developed a national consciousness among the lawyers which 'goes hand in hand with a growing interest in the past', in other words the history of the Jewish people.[32] As a consequence of this interest, Maksim Vinaver, one of the group members, together with Dubnov, founded the Historic-Ethnographic Commission in 1892 which gave this venture the framework needed.[33] Their research resulted in a two volume study about Russian Jewish history, entitled *Regesty i nadpisi* (*Digests and Inscriptions*), published by the Society for the Spread of Enlightenment among the Jews (ORPE) in 1899.[34] This group consisted of lawyers such as Maksim M. Vinaver, G.B. Sliozberg, M.I. Kulisher, O.O. Gruzenberg and others who had learnt their legal profession with Passover, the archaeologist S.M. Goldshtein, the historian Mark Vishnitser; they were joined by another lawyer, L.M. Bramson, and the historian Yulii Brutskus, who had been active in Moscow and moved to St. Petersburg after having finished their studies in 1891. All of them were born between the 1860s and early 1870s, but they came from all parts of the Pale and had diverse family backgrounds.[35] There was no apparent conformity among the members of the group, neither socially nor politically. From the very beginning, it was a group of persons who had neither a fixed ideology nor a common conception. The only thing they had in common was their immediate 'engagement' in Jewish affairs. Many of them, upon arrival, started working in organisations such as ORPE and ORT in St. Petersburg.[36] Here, they became familiar with the intelligentsia world and its traditional drive towards modernization of Jewish life: tackling Jewish backwardness, the lack of modern education and of religious reform, and the economic problems such as the high concentration of the Jewish masses in the cities, which – combined with the lopsided occupational structure of Jewish society[37] – had produced drastic impoverishment and a rapid increase in the demands on Jewish welfare organizations.[38] This group's location, St. Petersburg, was very advantageous, since the traditional way of promoting Jewish interests, that is Shtadlanstvo, was still very much in demand. The representatives of the Jewish communities were still using the metropolitan shtadlanim, such as Baron G.O. Gintsburg[39] – who financed many Jewish welfare, local or nation-wide organisations such as ORPE – or, after 1906 Moshe Ginzburg,[40] in order to put forward their requests to the authorities in St. Petersburg.[41] Furthermore, to a certain extent the Jewish community of St. Petersburg was a trend setter for all the reform-oriented Jewish communities in Russia. Most of the cultural, commercial and philanthropic organizations were initiated in St. Petersburg and were imitated in the provinces.[42]

This group, which appeared publicly from 1900 under the name 'Defense Bureau' ('biuro zashchity'),[43] through Baron Gintsburg had the financial support of a personality known by almost every Russian Jew, and who was also a recognized and influential figure in Russian circles. Even more important were his connections to Jewish bankers in France and England, the Rothschilds and Montefiores, which they could use in order to achieve 'international' recognition.

The trigger for this group's decision to start a systematic activity – to set up an organization like the Defense Bureau – was apparently the infamous Blondes case in Vilna (1900–1902) in which a Jew was accused of ritual murder. The Defense Bureau realized that this dimension of anti-Semitism needed organized counteraction, which had to be conducted on a wider basis than just Blondes' defence which had been taken over by the

Russian lawyers V.D. Spasovich and Mironov and their assistants Maksim Vinaver and O.O. Gruzenberg.[44]

The legal aid activities were complemented by a second dimension: an information campaign within Russia, in order to spread correct knowledge about Jewish life in Russia and the causes of the Jewish plight.

For this the bureau established two sub-organisations covering the major areas of activity: a press bureau in charge of the information campaign, and a legal advice bureau responsible for defending the pogrom victims. In order to influence Russian public opinion they decided, in addition to the usual intervention in Russian government circles, to win the support of personalities with a good name in Russian society such as the writers Maksim Gorkii, Leo Tolstoi, Vladimir Solov'ev and Vladimir Korolenko.[45] Their approach was a major departure from *Shtadlanut* policy as with the public figures an open campaign was pursued, in contrast to backstage manoeuvring aimed at powerful courtiers or bureaucrats. Still, among their activities, interventions with the ministers in charge remained important.[46] From 1900 to 1903, the press bureau actively produced pamphlets and information brochures about the situation of the Jews.[47] However, it was not successful in spreading their ideas to really broad circles. An organization similar to the Defense Bureau was set up in Moscow, where well-known representatives of the Jewish community such as V.V. Gorkov, A.F. Fuks or rabbi Jacob I. Maze were active; but co-operation with them did not take place, as they had no permanent organization. Since the Defense Bureau did not manage to set up an organizational network beyond St. Petersburg, for instance in Kiev or in Odessa – according to Sliozberg due to the very strong propaganda of Zionism and Bund which strongly influenced the youth[48] – it remained concentrated in St. Petersburg. The Bureau still addressed a mainly Russian audience, and the material was still written in Russian. The Yiddish-speaking Jewish masses were not yet the main aim of their activities, and they thus remained still somewhat isolated. The Defense Bureau, in a way, needed a spectacular event in order to make itself known to a wider public.

Their hour came with the pogroms in Kishinev (1903) and Gomel (1904). These provoked the transformation of the Defense Bureau into an interest group decisively breaking with the traditional policy of Shtadlanut. The Bureau now entered the active struggle for Jewish rights by defending the pogrom victims at court while at the same time stepping up their propaganda campaign abroad. The actual trial was used by the Bureau as a conscious step to enter the political arena. Furthermore, Jewish liberals profited from strategic weaknesses of the other two major Jewish parties which were already very active within Jewish society: the Zionists and Socialists – called Bundists.

## 1.2 THE CRISIS OF THE 'ESTABLISHED' JEWISH PARTIES: THE BUND AND THE ZIONISTS

From 1900 to 1903, political circumstances and inner-party disputes between party factions, as well as problems with the 'basis' which occurred in both parties, had led both the Bund and the Zionists into a political impasse. By 1903 the Zionists – like the Bundists – were declared illegal, and were thereby threatened by persecution from the Russian police. This situation resulted in the increased political isolation of the Zionists – due to the failure of their politics – and the Bundists – due to their bad strategy.

The workers' Zionists – 'Poalei Zion'[49] – which were founded two years after the Russian Organization of Zionists (1898)[50] in Ekaterinoslav in 1900, within two years had achieved a position among Jewish workers which allowed them to compete seriously with the Bund. The main reason lay in their programme which focused primarily on the economic, trade unionist struggle, rejected any 'engagement' in Russian politics,[51] and rather strived for the formation of a socialist system in an own state and not in Russia with its anti-Semitic features.[52] Furthermore, Poalei Zion was advocating the preservation of the Jewish community,[53] which coincided with the wish among Jewish workers to keep in touch with Jewish life and its regulations.[54] Finally, the Bund played into the hands of its opponents when it decided at its fifth Congress (1903) to give the revolutionary and political struggle priority over the economic struggle for better salaries and a shorter day of work. This led to dissatisfaction among the workers as they did not accept the intelligentsia's (Bund leaders) predominance. Poalei Zion branches increasingly appeared between 1901 and 1902 in many Russian or Russian-Polish cities.[55]

The Poalei Zion became a real alternative to the Bund through its co-operation with the 'Independent Jewish Labour Party' founded by Sergei Zubatov, the head of the Okhrana in Moscow.[56] Zubatov had realized that the discriminatory legislation had driven the Jews into the arms of the Revolution. In order to turn the situation around and to successfully fight the socialist movement, he proposed to give the Jewish workers – as well as the working class in general – a recognized place in a modern Russia ruled by a benevolent Tsar.[57] For this, economic, trade-union-based struggles had to be legitimized by the government and perhaps supervised by the police. His argument that 'the Bund had used the economic struggle primarily as a means of stirring the masses, while the improvement of the economic status of the workers came only second', met with sympathy among some leading Bundists who were in his custody.[58] In practice the police now often supported workers against employers and Zubatov himself publicly berated the employers. Moreover, Zubatov organized trade unions and public lectures for workers.

The Independents' movement had started in Minsk with the help of Vasilev, the head of the Guberniia's police administration who was influenced by Zubatov. The party was granted its own printing press which enabled it legally to edit a newspaper[59] through which the Independents propagated – as opposed to the ideological language of the Bund – the catchy slogan 'bread and knowledge', combining the revolutionary trade unionist struggle with self-education. The active interference by Vasilev during some strikes[60] convinced many Jewish workers to join the movement, which had found an ally in the Poalei Zion – which, like the Independents, was not interested in revolutionary politics[61] – and widened its influence from Minsk to Odessa and Moscow.[62]

However, after a short and very successful period in which the Bund's predominance was shaken in many cities in the Pale of Settlement,[63] the Independents' movement collapsed. This failure was precipitated when a strike organized by the Central Committee got out of control and actually developed into one of the biggest strike waves ever witnessed in South Russia. Subsequently the Prime Minister lost confidence in this experiment, ordered Zubatov to put a stop to it, and moved him to St. Petersburg where he could control him. Pleve's decision may also have been caused by the decisions of the Zionist congress which took place in Minsk in 1902, during which the Zionists articulated the Jews' claim for their own culture, organizations and independent nationality in Russia. This induced Pleve to revise his outlook. Pleve, who until this point had probably tolerated the Zionists because of their target of advocating the emigration of vast masses of the Jewish population and their declared 'non-engagement' in Russian politics, declared the Zionists illegal and prohibited further experiments in the field of police supervised trade unionism.[64] Zubatov's idea of a peaceful co-existence of the workers' movement and autocracy finally collapsed with the pogrom of Kishinev in 1903. Under these circumstances, the Independents saw no reason to preserve a party which was in a semi-legal position: they therefore dissolved the party at its last conference of July 3 1903.[65]

From then on the Zionists were – like the Bund – exposed to repression and were not able to pursue their activities as before. The Russian Zionists, finally, had to face an even deeper crisis when world Zionism split into two factions (1903): the Territorialists (advocates of any territory, for instance Uganda) and the 'Palestinophiles' (Palestine as the future Jewish state).[66] This rift deeply affected the Russian Zionist movement as well: Dr. Nachman Syrkin walked out on the Poalei Zion and founded the territorialist Zionist-Socialist Labour Party – called SS for short, due to its Russian name 'Sotsialisty Sionisty'.[67]

The failure of the Jewish branch of the Zubatovshchina and Pleve's change of mind had pushed the Zionists into illegality. As they still kept a distance from any involvement in Russian home affairs, the Russian Zionists now found themselves isolated. This resulted in a disorientation which did not end until the Zionist congress in Helsingfors in December 1906.

The Bund – the 'General Jewish Workers' Union in Lithuania, Poland and Russia' ('Vseobshchii Evreiskii Rabochii Soiuz v Litve, Polshe i Rossiia') – which was founded in 1897 had been the dominating force on the streets, especially among the Jewish workers, until the appearance of the Independents.[68] However, the popularity they achieved among the workers by promising a socialist future, by organizing many more workers' 'kassy' – rudimentary trade union groups – and by founding libraries and translating political and non-political books into Yiddish, was very soon challenged.[69] The workers did not always follow the Bund leadership and its ideas of organized trade unionist work,[70] and instead were interested in fast improvements, such as better salaries and working conditions. The Bund was thus very often confronted with spontaneous strikes.[71] Furthermore, it had to deal with the peculiar Jewish economic structure of small entrepreneurs, where a master could easily be forced to close his shop and hire himself out and where a worker often set up his own small independent workshop. This hindered the Bund from pursuing the Marxist theory of exploitation, since an exploited worker could easily become an 'exploiter' himself. The Bund also had to face competition on the streets by the emergence of the Independents and the Poalei Zion. In order not to loose its dominant position among the workers, at its Fifth Congress in 1903[72] the Bund had integrated national demands in its programme, such as the national-cultural autonomy, an idea already promoted by the famous historian Simon M. Dubnov.

The Bund's reorientation of 1903 met, however, with strong resistance within the general Russian organisation, the RSDRP, to which the Bund belonged organizationally. At the Second Congress of the RSDRP, the Russian Social Democrats did not accept the Bund's claim to be the sole representative of the Jewish workers, and reproached the Bund for having raised national demands which they considered inappropriate for a Marxist, internationally-oriented organization. For them, the class struggle had priority over advocating national demands which in any case would be solved by the overthrow of the political system. As the Bund insisted on its autonomy in propaganda and organizational affairs, it left the RSDRP on its Second Party Congress in 1903, which to some degree isolated them from the general workers' movement.[73] This may have been a handicap for the Bund. During this temporary split it was no longer possible for the Bund to work within the framework of the Russian movement, which had hitherto made it easier to propagate the Bund's ideas.[74] During the breakaway period which lasted for four years (1903–1906), the Bund had to deal with an increasing competition embracing the Zionists, the bourgeois nationalist, the radical liberal and the non-party socialist intelligentsia; the wish for more trade unionist oriented work among its rank-and-file; and finally the separation from the Russian umbrella organization which had provided it so far with a basis in Russian society.

## 1.3 THE MOVE TOWARDS AN OPEN DEFENSE OF RUSSIAN JEWS

Despite the fact that both groups – Socialist Zionists and Bundists – had to suffer some setbacks in their political activities, both organizations still maintained a strong position among the Jewish workers. The percentage of genuine industrial workers within Jewish society, however, was very small.[75] This meant that the majority of the Jewish population – which consisted of traders, artisans, tavern keepers, merchants and so on – remained unrepresented. The Jewish society in its complex form needed a representative which would embody the interests of all strata of the Jewish population, and offer solutions adequate to their specific problems.

Exactly at this time, as both the Zionists and the Bundists were very much in a crisis, the Defense Bureau grabbed the chance to enhance its public standing by raising its voice on behalf of the Jewish people as a whole. The situation of the horrifying pogroms of Kishinev and Gomel imperatively demanded that someone, some group, stood up in defense of Jewish interests. These outrages propelled Jewish political groups into action. The impression shared by almost all Jews that nothing had been done either by Russian society or the government, and that the policy pursued by the existing Jewish organizations had not achieved any results, led to the realization that the Jews had to take their fate in their own hands and could no longer rely solely on the Russian government, which in light of the pogroms had given no indication of a change in policy towards the Jews. On the contrary, the situation seemed to be worsening: the thinking among some circles of the high bureaucracy towards the Jewish question was clearly illustrated in a memorandum Pobedonostsev, overprocurator of the Holy Synod, had given to the minister of the Interior, Pleve.[76] Thus, a certain radicalization took place among the Jewish lawyers participating in the Defense Bureau. As M.A. Krol put it in his memoirs: 'the general situation and the development of the Jewish community had made it necessary to approach the Jewish masses'.[77]

The shift towards an active defense of Jewish interests which happened within the Defense Bureau was an expression of a growing interest within the Jewish middle class to engage in Jewish politics, which became evident in the increasing numbers of people joining the Defense Bureau. The growing flood of anti-Semitic literature, the increasingly anti-Semitic course of some elements of the government towards Russian Jewry, the general political instability, as well as the desperate state of the economic and social situation of their fellow Jews forced more and more Jewish middle-class intellectuals to participate.[78] In a first step after Kishinev, they focused on spreading the knowledge about the real situation of the Jews in Russia as well as abroad.[79] For this purpose, the Defense Bureau contacted the Jewish organizations abroad, above all the 'Hilfsverein der deutschen Juden', which functioned as a mediator between the Eastern and Western organizations in Paris, London and America. With the support of the most influential person in the Hilfsverein, Paul Nathan,[80] the Defense Bureau founded a special section in Berlin which was conducted by Leo Motskin. This section published and disseminated a bulletin in order to inform the public in Germany, Austria and England about the economic, social and legal predicament of the Jews in Russia.[81]

The objective was to put pressure on the Russian government by the foreign press and foreign public opinion and by Jewish representatives such as the Rothschilds, in order to force the government to re-evaluate its policies and to improve the situation of Russian Jews. In other words, international diplomacy was used as a means in the political struggle the Jewish intelligentsia had now engaged in. Expanding the scope of its work, the Defense Bureau established another news bulletin in Paris edited by Solomon V. Pozner, who was the foreign correspondent of the Russian-Jewish periodical *Voskhod* in Paris. The Defense Bureau had also more or less regular relations with the Anglo-Jewish Association[82] through one of its main activists Lucien Wolf – the historian and editor of the English-Jewish newspaper *Jewish Chronicle* – although its official leader was Claude Montefiore. In the following years, the public in Western Europe and especially England was kept informed through his newspaper, the *Jewish Chronicle*.[83]

This activity on the international level was complemented by activity on the national, Russian level, as the Defense Bureau pursued a propaganda activity in Russia parallel to what was being pursued abroad. Due to the political circumstances, however, the press bureau conducted by Alexander I. Braudo, chief librarian at the Rossica Department of the St. Petersburg Public Library, had to work totally under cover; it could not, therefore, risk revealing its direct connection to the Defense Bureau itself, in order not to discredit it.[84]

As a direct reaction to the Kishinev pogrom, in 1903 Yulii D. Brutskus published an appeal in *Voskhod* to all Russian Jews, urging them to form self-defense units. That the police confiscated this copy did nothing to turn around the swing among the Jewish intelligentsia towards more radical politics and an active defense. At the same time, a group of writers in Odessa, among them Dubnov, Ahad Ha'am, Rovnitskii, Ben-Ami and Bialik also appealed to the Jewish people to organize such units.[85] As this time the appeal was not published in a newspaper, but sent directly, in hundreds of copies, to the Jewish communities, the effect was enormous. It had – as Krol called it – an 'electrifying' effect among the Jewish youth; since this appeal also coincided with the Bund's expansion of self-defense activities, it resulted in the formation of self-defense units in many cities in the Pale of Settlement in 1903–04 which consisted of young people from all different political backgrounds, but remained independent of the Bund.[86]

The transition to an active defense of Jewish rights and of Jewish life and property was also evident in the Defense Bureau's approach towards the pogrom trials: it did not aim at financial compensation for the pogrom victims – this was considered almost impossible to achieve – but focused on background inquiries and the exposure of those guilty. The lawyers – such as Karabchevskii, Gruzenberg, Zarudnii, Kal'manovich and Vinaver – who had been sent by the Defense Bureau to represent the Jewish interests fought tooth and nail in the courtroom by presenting witnesses and preports which implicated the authorities, incriminating even the vice-governor of Bessarabia, Ustrugov. Despite the evidence, however, the court resident refused to extend the inquiry towards possible culprits in official-dom. Krol interpreted the court president's refusal as stemming from his fear of government reprisals, should an investigation reach this level.[87] Due to this conduct of the court president, the plaintiffs and defenders of the Jews drafted a protest resolution, read it in the open courtroom and walked out.[88]

During the Gomel pogrom trial of 11 October 1904 the Jewish lawyers[89] pursued the same methods and practices they had in the Kishinev one. This time the trial was conducted without the public and the prosecution – the anti-Semitic lawyer and attorney of the pogromshchiki, Shmakov and his assistant Pogozhev – was allowed throughout the trial to reproach the Jewish people with all sorts of anti-Semitic accusations; a normal conduct of the trial was thus impossible. Therefore, this time the Jewish lawyers delegated a protest resolution to Vinaver – similar to that in Kishinev – which he recited in public in the courtroom.[90]

Through the publicity which these trials received within Jewish society, these lawyers, and especially Vinaver, had established their names among the fighters for the Jewish cause. These declarations not only demonstrated the lawyers' disagreement with the conduct of the trial, but also served as an announcement by this very small group of socially successful, acculturated Jews to the Jewish public that they also identified themselves as Jews and as a group which would stand up for the Jews' rights and would challenge the Russian government. They thereby offered themselves as another representative group of Jewish interest: independent of Zionists and Bundists, more mainstream than those and therefore potentially more successful. Simon Dubnov's statement bore witness to the fact that they succeeded with their first target of making themselves known within Jewish society: he claimed that Maksim Vinaver's reputation grew with the declaration he had made in the courtroom and that his name became very well known within Jewish society as one of the lawyers who had not only defended pogrom victims, but had stood up for the rights of the Jews as a suppressed minority. He became the hero of the Jewish masses.[91] He experienced the same popularity as Oscar Gruzenberg would some years later, as the attorney of Mendel Beilis (1911–1913).[92]

Despite the fact that the Defense Bureau did not succeed in obtaining a verdict of guilty for the pogromshchiki, its approach of exposing pogrom activists, and publicizing the alleged and real participation of officials in the pogroms was very successful. The pogrom trials of Kishinev and Gomel led to the politicization of the Defense Bureau in general and the lawyers in particular. These lawyers were to become the spearheads of a new Jewish movement embracing the intelligentsia hitherto not affiliated to neither Socialist Zionism nor Bundism,[93] and were to establish themselves as another political force within Russian-Jewish society which would not only challenge the already existing parties or groups but also influence them. The influence on the Zionists of basic Liberal thoughts and ideas was particularly evident when the former presented their famous political programme, called 'Gegenwartsarbeit', in 1906.

The Liberals had achieved recognition among the Jewish masses. This was a very important step for their subsequent activities as publicity was necessary in Jewish society which so far had been largely impervious to modern political and social activity, but which was now looking out for new ways of improving their situation. Herein, they profited from the fact that they had conquered some strategic positions in society. They dominated the legal Jewish press and monopolized the few spheres of legal activity which were open to the Jews. In these positions they had become figures in Russian and Jewish society alike. The Jewish community leaders and the Jewish masses had realized that there was another group working on behalf of the Jews other than the Zionists – who at this time just favoured emigration – and the Bundists – who limited themselves to the workers' case and had nothing to offer to those Jews who were still very much bound to a more traditional Jewish life. Furthermore, the Defense Bureau was supported by the big *shtadlanim* such as Baron G.O. Gintsburg, the Poliakovs, and the 'sugar-baron' Brodskii who all had connections and access to government circles – an additional means of influence. Through these *shtadlanim* the Bureau also had the opportunity to further familiarize itself with leadership groups locally and to learn even more about the needs and wishes of the Russian-Jewish communities. They were able to make the demands of the broader strata of the Jewish people their own, to represent their case wider and better than the Bundists and the Zionists did, but they also were increasingly successful in spreading their own values, ideas and to expand their organization.

However, in order to establish themselves as another force among the Jewish political parties and groups, the Liberals had realized that the Defense Bureau with its legal aid and propaganda activity was neither sufficient to improve the legal and social positions of the Jews, nor enough to exert influence on the Russian political scene. In order to disseminate their ideas successfully and win support among the Jewish masses an approach different from that of the Bureau was required. The opportunity to choose a new form of political action with a higher profile was given to the Defense Bureau activists by the dramatically changing political situation in Russia: Russian society was just as much dissatisfied with the autocracy and the Russian government as the minorities in general and the Jews in particular. After Pleve's assassination on 15 July 1904 the revolutionary movements which until then had been underground came to the open demanding the overthrow of the autocracy and a change of the political system. Thus, the emergence of the middle-class Jewish intellectuals in Russian-Jewish politics practically coincided with the deep dissatisfaction of the outer world of Russian society. The increasing protest movement of Russian society met so to speak with that of the privileged and acculturated Jews in a time when they were looking for ways to change their approach. The new spearheads of Jewish society could combine their forces with the propagators of liberal and democratic politics in Russia, the bourgeois and liberal forces of Russian society which were reform-oriented and striving for a system of participation. The general liberation movement in Russia coincided with a desire within Jewish society to organize broadly, to represent itself and create a democratic Russia which would give the Russian Jews an equal place among all the other members of Russian society.

The emergence of Jewish 'liberal politics' witnessed two major steps. The setting up of the Defense Bureau illustrated the rise of a new strong sense of Jewish self-consciousness of the very part of Jewish society which had become acculturated to Russian society. This first step was accompanied by taking advantage of those modern means of communication and conducting politics which these groups were well placed to do by their very character. With the organization of the press bureau they had realized the press's increasing importance and influence. They no longer based their activities solely on ameliorative actions but they had discovered the value of information as a political weapon within a rapidly changing and modernizing Russian society. The second important step in Jewish liberal politics happened with the pogroms and the pogrom trials, which hardened the resolve among the lawyers to transform the newly-achieved Jewish self-confidence into something durable – with organizational and also otherwise practical consequences. This resolve was stiffened by the pogrom trials, and the sense of urgency for the creation of a constitutional system was sharpened. Only such a constitutionally structured regime could bring a guarantee of equal rights for Jews. In the informational booklets they published and distributed in Western Europe and in Russia as well, they only accused the Russian authorities and government, but not Russian society. This indicated their belief in Russian society and in a better future for all the citizens of Russia, including the Jews. Based on the progressive forces within Russian society this approach seemed to be promising, and could in the long run bring a future for Russian Jews which could become an alternative to the way the Zionists and Bundists propagated.

# 2 The Revolution of 1905 and the Struggle for Legal Emancipation

The second phase of Jewish liberal politics witnessed the breakthrough from traditional forms of representing Jewish interests to modern politics. The Russian Revolution of 1905 and its key player, the Russian intelligentsia, paved the way for the Defense Bureau members to shift their approach from welfare and legal aid activities to politics, and provided them with the possibility to claim legal emancipation for Russian Jews. Thus, in order to enforce the democratisation of the country, and to create a legal political opposition in Russia, the intelligentsia initiated the banquet campaign, the petition's movement and finally founded the Union of Unions in 1905. Jewish Liberals perceived the creation of a public space as the opportunity to join the Revolution, and bring forward specific Jewish demands more effectively. To this end, Jewish Liberals founded the Soiuz Polnopraviia, an organization which was open to all political groups within Jewish society, and thus served as a public space for Jewish society. The SP in turn enabled Jewish Liberals to spread their political standing to wider strata of Jewish society, and to mobilize and politicize the Jewish masses. Moreover, in addition to the struggle for a democratisation of the country, the Liberals widened their efforts among the leaders of the Jewish communities in Western Europe and America, and added to constitutional reform within Russia external diplomatic pressure on the Russian government.

This new approach, which was followed up from early 1905 until mid-1906, proved extremely important for the further course of Jewish Liberal politics. The political activity from the grassroots – among the Jewish masses – and ideological disputes with the other groups participating in the SP, forced the Liberals to crystallize their own political programme, and finally transformed them from a group of Jewish intellectuals whose primary interest was Russian domestic affairs, into a pressure group for Jewish national interests.

## 2.1　THE NEW STRATEGY: THE CREATION OF A SURROGATE FOR RUSSIAN JEWS

The entire process which transformed Jewish community leaders from political indifference to a new political self-awareness was triggered by a political event which 'served as a catalyst to awaken' the Jewish masses.[1] In the case of the Russian Jews, this catalyst was the beginning of the Russian Revolution of 1905.

The turning point for the revolutionaries' activities came with the assassination of Pleve on 15 July 1904, and the beginning of the so-called 'thaw' with the appointment of the more tolerant Prince P.D. Sviatopolk-Mirsky as Minister of the Interior. The intelligentsia circles around the Zemstva and the constitutionalist 'Union of Liberation' used the new freedom – especially the relaxed censorship and the permission for several new national newspapers to be published – to bring their demands for a constitutional change of the political system to the open.[2] Since it was not known how far the new government's 'tolerance' would go, by the end of 1904 the oppositional circles started to organize a public campaign in order to form a broad anti-Tsarist front and to enforce concessions from the government. To this end, the radical liberal Union of Liberation (Soiuz Osvobozhdenia – SO) initiated the so-called 'banquet' campaign, which was accompanied by the 'petitions' movement' spreading all over Russia and attracting Zemstvo activists as well as broad segments of the intelligentsia – especially lawyers, doctors and journalists – to its ideas and into its rank.[3] Moreover, it mobilized the masses when the news about the heavy defeats of the army in the Russo-Japanese war reached the Russian public, and many strata of Russian society joined the Russian Liberation movement in its struggle for radical reforms and for a constitutional Russia. During the banquet campaign of late 1904, the SO moved to the next step, the organisation of the intelligentsia in professional unions. Hereby, the intelligentsia not only mobilized almost the entire Russian society, and developed an organizational framework which went beyond the dimension of private meetings, but created a public space for all the oppositional forces not organized hitherto. The first Unions (Soiuzy) were founded in March–April 1905, and in May 1905 they organized a central organization, the so-called 'Union of Unions' (Soiuz Soiuzov) whose task was to coordinate the struggle of the various Unions' work for political freedom.[4] Each union sent two representatives to St. Petersburg where the umbrella organization had its central committee.[5]

The 'banquet' campaign and the foundation of the Unions served as the catalyst which allowed the Jewish Liberals to enter Russian politics.[6] The general Russian movement provided the radical Jewish Liberals with the possibility to raise specific Jewish demands on a dimension with a higher profile, within the scope of a nationwide revolutionary movement. Therefore, the Defense Bureau decided, as M.A. Krol put it, 'that the right moment had come for us to raise our specific Jewish demands, and to come forward with a programme which includes all the reforms necessary to end Jewish inequality'.[7]

Thus, within the scope of the petitions' movement, in late 1904 the leaders of thirty-two Jewish communities sent a letter to the government demanding political, social and educational equalization for the Jewish people in Russia.[8] The arguments on which they based their letter – *inter alia* that the Russian economy would benefit from giving the Jews equal rights – could not, however, persuade a government which to a considerable extent was suspicious of the industrialization and modernization process initiated by its own Ministry of Finance. They regarded the Jews as the creators of a new economic phenomenon – capitalism – which was particularly resented by the representatives of old, pre-industrial and agriculturally-structured Russia, that is the landowners and large parts of the aristocracy.[9] The petition, therefore, understandably remained without success. In fact, none of the signatories had expected anything else, as the petition had a completely different function: to propagate a political platform on which the widest possible circles of Jewish society could converge.[10] Along these lines, a few weeks later, in March 1905, the Liberals and former members of the Defense Bureau – such as Vinaver and Sliozberg – organized an illegal gathering with sixty-seven leading Jews in Vilna in order to set up an independent Jewish organization among all the other Unions.[11] The growing interest of the Jewish social activists in general political affairs was evident in the fact that Jewish representatives of thirty-one cities followed the Liberals' initiative.[12] The participants represented four distinct political trends within Russian Jewry: the Zionists with Ahad Ha'am and Shmarya Levin, the left-wing but mostly non-Marxist socialist Jewish Democratic Group with its leader Leon M. Bramson (later Trudovik),[13] the Autonomists with Simon Dubnov, and finally the Radical-Liberals such as Vinaver, Sliozberg, Sheftel and others, who were also to play a vital role in the Constitutional Democratic Party, the Kadets (founded in October 1905). Strictly speaking, there was even a fifth group present at the conference which was, however, neither organized nor acted as such: rabbis such as the conservative Hirsh Rabinovich (Kovno) and the liberal state rabbis Jacob Maze (Moscow) and Temkin (Ekaterinoslav).[14] This meeting was the starting point for the involvement of these Jewish 'middle-class' activists in Russian politics. For the first time in Russian history, representatives of the Jewish communities, together with the leaders of the various political groups within Jewish society, met in order to create a public space for Russian Jewry. The resolutions of this first congress of the Union for the Attainment of Full Equality for the Jewish People in Russia ('Soiuz dlia Dostizheniia Polnopraviia Evreiskago Naroda v Rossii') reflected the new approach by its initiators, the Jewish Liberals: the political struggle for a democratic Russia within the general Russian Liberation movement, through which equal rights and autonomy in community, cultural and educational affairs were to be achieved.[15]

The political platform of the Soiuz Polnopraviia represented a combination of Dubnov's Autonomism and ideas which were based on the demands of the Russian Liberation movement, and indicated its intention to co-operate and fight with the Union of Unions for a constitutional democratic system, with a parliament elected by the people.

> The Soiuz Polnopraviia is convinced that the realization of its task is possible on the basis of the inviolability of the person and property, the freedom of the word and the press, of unions and meetings, and the participation in the people's representative body which will be elected on the basis of the general, equal, direct and secret right to vote.[16]

Shortly after the Vilna congress, the Soiuz Polnopraviia joined the Union of Unions, thus openly entering Russian politics. Thereby, the SP established itself organizationally as the independent Jewish representative within the Soiuz Soiuzov, which at that time represented the major element of the oppositional movement, and commanded wide support within Russian society.[17]

This new strategic concept supported by the Liberals in the Soiuz Polnopraviia met, from the very beginning, with resistance from Simon Dubnov, the spokesman of the Nationalist/Zionist camp within the organization. During the Vilna congress he insisted that the national demands of Russian Jewry should not be neglected during the political struggle. In principle, the Liberals' definition of the Jewish people was very similar to Dubnov's. The Liberals' leaders, Vinaver and Sliozberg, like Dubnov, regarded Russian Jews as a nationality which was part of the Imperial Russian 'body politic'.[18] However, the Liberals' priority was to achieve a democratic and constitutional system in Russia, and therein to realize national-cultural autonomy for Russian Jews. As they argued 'during the struggle for emancipation in Western Europe such national demands were not put forward and to raise them now would endanger the Union's political struggle', and therefore 'the priority should be to achieve civil emancipation, since national rights could be pushed through more easily in a Russia in which the Jews had achieved legal emancipation'.[19] This did not, however, convince the majority of the congress. Dubnov's request was accepted, and the national demands were included in the platform of this organization.[20] The SP's cohesion was secured for the moment, but Dubnov's insistence on the priority of Jewish national demands was conflict-prone. Two groups arose within the Union: the Radical-Liberal camp, which gave the political side priority over the national, and the Nationalist/Zionist bloc that insisted on reverse priorities.

The resolutions concerning the organizational structure of the Soiuz Polnopraviia indicated the Union's will to base its activity on wide strata of Jewish society. The twenty-two members of the Central Committee – with its seat in St. Petersburg – included eleven from the provinces. Although the Central Committee assumed the day-to-day conduct of the Union's affairs, the congresses of the representatives of the local groups gathering periodically served as the highest organ.[21] The most prominent members elected to the Central Committee represented various political trends, and underlined the Soiuz Polnopraviia's openness to any Jewish democratic group: Vinaver (later Kadet), Sliozberg (later Kadet), Bramson (Trudovik), Shmarya Levin (Zionist), Dubnov (Jewish Nationalist) and Mark Ratner (Social Revolutionary).[22] Furthermore, the membership fee – which at 50 Kopeks was the lowest within the Soiuz Soiuzov – as well as the regulations of membership – anyone over twenty-one years, without any distinction of sex who agreed to the Vilna platform, and who was recommended by two members[23] – underlined the Union's will to become an organization with a broad basis within Jewish society, and to mobilize and politicise the Jewish masses. The aim was to lead them out of their social and political isolation into a better future within a democratically structured Russia, where discrimination would no longer exist.

## 2.2 THE SOIUZ POLNOPRAVIIA ESTABLISHES ITSELF IN THE RUSSIAN LIBERATION MOVEMENT

The SP entered Russian and Jewish-national politics on two levels at the same time: from March until August 1905 it lobbied for Jewish rights within the Soiuz Soiuzov and Russian society, and propagated the Vilna platform among the Jewish masses; from August–September 1905 onwards it mobilized the Jewish voters. During this time, the Liberals pursued a new strategic concept, that is the propagation of Jewish rights and the mobilization and politicization of the Jewish masses.

Since the SP was established neither among the Jewish masses nor the Russian political parties or groups, its first activities were focused on spreading its political programme and winning public support for its demands and political ideas. The Central Bureau started its propaganda and organizational activities by sending speakers to the provinces, producing printed material en masse and thus disseminating the Vilna platform among Russian Jews across the country.[24] On the other hand, two representatives – the lawyers L.M. Bramson and A.D. Margolin[25] – had been elected by the first congress of the SP to join the Central Committee of the 'Union of Unions' – founded in Moscow on 8 and 9 May 1905.[26]

It was very well understood by the Vilna congress that support had to be achieved among the Russian revolutionaries, so that in case of a successful revolution Jewish interest would not be neglected.[27] Therefore, the SP followed up a strategy which aimed at winning resonance within the unions for specific Jewish demands such as the equality of rights,[28] and by using the publicity effect of the Soiuzy to reach the Jewish masses. The most important union in this respect was the Union of Writers and Journalists' as it dominated public opinion and its central nerve system more than any other union, and thus was the main conductor of the publicity campaign. Therefore, the SP sent a representative, Leopold Sev, to the congress of writers and journalists in St. Petersburg in May 1905. In his speech, Sev pointed to the discrepancy between the Union's demand for equal rights to all Russian citizens regardless of their nationalities and the anti-Semitic articles still found in Russian newspapers. Consequently, he called upon the journalists to report on the real situation of Russian Jews,[29] and to publish a declaration in favour of Jewish rights. This, he argued, 'would advance the publicity effect of the SP among the Jewish masses still indifferent to the Liberation Movement and would thus help the SP to gain support within Russian Jewry'.[30] The prospect of winning over large masses for the Liberation Movement on the one side, and the general striving for democratic reform and demands on the other, led the congress finally to announce a declaration in which it condemned anti-Semitic actions, emphasized national rights and supported the equality of rights.

> The congress considers it necessary first to set up the demands for civil and political emancipation of the Jews and the right of the Jewish people for national-cultural self-determination. Second, the congress expresses the desire that the press organs should concisely illustrate the Jewish question in order to guarantee that the demand in point one can be realized.[31]

Since many SP members, especially the leading figures, were lawyers, engineers, doctors and journalists, they had also joined their respective professional unions where they advocated emancipation and cultural autonomy for the Jewish People in Russia.[32] In fact, all the unions, including the roof-organization, Soiuz Soiuzov, adopted the demand of equal rights for the Jews in their programmes. In this context, SP representatives such as L.M. Bramson, Yakubson and I.V. Gessen were particularly active, the first two at the meetings of the Union of Peasants[33] and the latter in the Union of Zemstvo Activists.[34] The first step of Liberal politics, to establish the Jewish question as one point among the reforms to be aimed at by the Liberation Movement, was achieved. The SP had lobbied successfully for the Jewish cause, and from then it was clear that the demand of the Unions for civil equality for all nationalities applied also to the Jews.

The Soiuz Polnopraviia made another step forward in its political activity in the context of Bulygin's Duma project.[35] The Soiuz Soiuzov as well as the entire Russian society were opposed to the Bulygin Duma, as its functions were essentially consultative and the suffrage excluded major parts of the population, especially the intelligentsia and industrial workers.[36] The Soiuz Polnopraviia protested especially strongly when rumours were spread that the Jews were also to be excluded from the elections to the Duma. This was the moment when the SP left the path of pure propaganda activity and changed from the theoretical claim of being the representative of the Jewish masses to real political work. The Central Bureau of the SP had realized that all its efforts would come to naught unless the right to vote was assured; this was crucial for the future of the SP, since its main political target was participation in parliament. The SP reacted impetuously and called on the Jewish town councillors to leave their posts. This action was successful as many followed suit, and when they announced their resignation they also publicly demanded the emancipation for the Jews in municipal affairs. This action was accompanied by protests of numerous communities against the exclusion of the Jews from the Duma elections.[37] However, during the vote concerning the question of the participation in the Bulygin Duma – at the third congress of the Soiuz Soiuzov which took place in St. Petersburg from 1 to 3 July 1905[38] – the SP abstained from its vote; this was most likely due to tactical reasons, as its next action clearly indicated its will to participate in the Duma. The SP sent a delegation – consisting of the lawyers Sliozberg and M.I. Kulisher – to Count Vitte in order to win his support for the Jewish cause.[39] This action succeeded, as the Council of Ministers deleted the paragraph denying Jews the right to vote. The draft was submitted and with the support of Vitte and the Minister of Finance, Kokovtsev approved at the Conference of Ministers and the Tsar at Peterhof; hence, the right to vote was also granted to the Jews.[40] Vitte's motive for intervening on behalf of the Jews was probably not primarily due to humanistic sentiments but had been based on rather practical premises: according to Krol a secret memorandum had fallen into the hands of the SP, which stated that the government's main intention was to counteract the revolutionary tendencies among the Jewish youth by granting Russian Jews the right to vote.[41]

The SP delegation to Vitte was no longer the typical shtadlanim intervention which usually aimed at the mitigation or the withdrawal of some anti-Jewish restrictions. For the first time in Russian Jewish history, this intervention was not one of a Jewish oligarch intervening for some Jewish individual or community's interests, but one of delegates sent by a Jewish organization which claimed to be the political representative of Russian Jewry. It was a political action which was part of the general activities of this organization and of its fight for Jewish rights. It was the end of a long transformation process from the typical *shtadlanim* activity – based on individual lobbying – which had been predominant in the pre-1881 years, towards political action based on general and party activity in 1905.

Further evidence of this shift can be seen in the fact that after the Tsar had made another concession to the Revolution by granting autonomy to Russia's universities – and 'thereby removed these institutions from the jurisdiction of the police'[42] – the SP used this new sphere of freedom to join openly the Revolutionaries' demands at the universities.[43] Finally, when the law concerning the Bulygin Duma[44] was published on 6 August 1905, the SP took immediate action and followed up their next target of mobilizing the Jewish masses, although the future political system was uncertain. They ran inquiries in the various constituencies about the chances of sending Jewish deputies into the parliament. The results were promising and the election of some Jewish members seemed feasible. It was only a question of organization and mobilization of the Jewish vote.[45] In this context, the SP issued a call to Russian Jews to participate in the elections, propagated co-operation with progressive elements 'who pledged themselves to support equal rights for Jews', and gave the first tactical instructions to the Jewish voters: 'we warned against partisan party-splintering at the polls and altogether against boycotting the elections.'[46] The expectations rose even further when the Tsar, forced by the increasing political protest which resulted in a general strike that paralysed Russian public life, published the October Manifesto in October 1905.

## 2.3   THE SOIUZ POLNOPRAVIIA IN THE ARENA OF RUSSIAN CONSTITUTIONAL POLITICS

The October Manifesto became the turning point for all revolutionary and oppositional groups and parties, including the SP. Since the Tsar had promised an elected legislative chamber and certain basic civil liberties, they had to redefine their future aims and strategies.[47] Some groups were satisfied with what was achieved, but others had to ask themselves if the offer to participate in the parliament should be taken up and how they could fight from within the Duma for reforms and for extending and securing the constitution. For instance, the newly-founded Constitutional Democrats, the Kadets, decided to participate in the parliament in order to exploit the first major breach in the enemy's – Tsarism's – defence.[48] Most socialist groups, and the Bundists in particular, at first boycotted the Duma as they wanted to proceed from political to social revolution. They still believed in the possibility of overthrowing the government, and hence advocated an armed uprising.[49] Nonetheless, the elections seemed like a good opportunity for agitation on a legal basis: therefore, the Bund declared its 'active' election boycott.[50]

The SP also had to map out its course at this political watershed. Until then, in terms of its general political outlook, the SP had seemed homogeneous; however, with the Manifesto the differences between the political tendencies within the SP surfaced. Until October–November the Liberals, led by Vinaver and Sliozberg, commanded the majority within the SP. However, with the progress of the revolution and its first achievement, the Manifesto, the SP had grown in terms of members as well as branches in the provinces.[51] This in turn influenced the composition – seventy delegates from thirty cities representing 5,000 members – of the Second Congress which took place from 22–25 November 1905 in St. Petersburg under the shock of the October pogroms.[52] Since this congress had to determine the future course and strategy of the SP, two different views clashed: further co-operation with the Liberation Movement promoted by the Liberals and parts of the left-wing, or political retreat and concentration on a Jewish national policy supported by the Nationalists and Zionists. This debate first occurred during the discussion on the pogroms which had followed the October Manifesto, and second on the discussion on the future strategy of the SP. The pogrom wave which had swept the country appeared to be a particular blow to the newly-born Jewish self-consciousness.[53] The Autonomists (Dubnov) and the Zionists (Levin, Ussishkin) interpreted the pogroms as the outcome of an anti-Semitism rooted in Russian society and which included the Liberation Movement. This view was supported in light of the reaction of the Socialist parties to pogroms on a local basis,[54] and the Zemstvo's positive but late statement towards the Jewish question which appeared after the pogroms.[55] The Liberals in turn held the government and the local authorities responsible, and could refer to their allies, the intelligentsia and the radical Zemstvo people, as having relatively 'white sheets' regarding the Jewish question.[56] Finally, the congress not only agreed with the Liberals but followed their standing that future anti-Jewish outrages could only be prevented by depriving the old upper class and the bureaucracy of their power. This was illustrated in the radical democratic demands for investigating the pogroms, compensating the pogrom victims by the government, putting the police under the control of the city councils which in turn were to be democratised by granting Russian Jews equal rights as well as the suffrage, and finally handing over the outstanding parts of the Korobka tax to the pogrom victims.[57]

The conflict between Zionists/Nationalists and Liberals resurfaced the next day when the SP had to determine its future strategy. Within the course of the discussion, the conflict turned into a vote of no confidence of the National camp towards the strategy championed by the Liberals and hitherto pursued by the SP: the co-operation with and activity within the Liberation Movement. It started with criticism raised by some provincial delegates that the Union's organization was too centralized and that its Liberal leaders were too occupied with other affairs.[58] The critics' primary concern was not the 'engagement' of Liberals such as Vinaver and Sliozberg in the Kadet party, but the main issue of the future strategy of the SP. The Nationalist/Zionist camp demanded a new, more nationally-oriented strategy which implied the retreat from the Russian Liberation Movement.[59] By referring to the pogroms they argued that the SP should not waste its energy on a Russian society which had just proven its attitude towards the Jews, and instead should concentrate on activities within Jewish society. Finally, Vladimir Zhabotinskii (Zionist) proposed what he regarded as the only possible political representation of the Jewish people in Russia: the all-Jewish national assembly.[60]

> . . . We turn our back to the external world which has turned its back to us a long time ago, and we turn ourselves to the internal, national Jewish policy. It is not necessary to write Manifestos to Russian society but to our own, Jewish people in order to wake them up to a new life and to encourage them to take their fate in their own hands. The assembly of this Jewish parliament will be the turning-point in the history of the Jewish people.[61]

However, the Zionists and Nationalist failed to convince the majority. They succeeded in preventing the organisational fusion of the SP with the Kadets – similar to the Bund's to the RSDRP – but not the close leaning of the SP to the Kadets. The Liberals still commanded a too strong position within the SP. Moreover, the Liberals' policy of co-operating with the Liberation Movement had brought them two allies, the Kadets and the

Trudoviki, who were willing to participate in the Duma, and consequently in the elections. Since the SP leaders – the Liberals Vinaver, Sliozberg, Sheftel and Iollos – were also members of the Kadets, and L.M. Bramson, Krol and Yakubson of the Trudoviki – founded shortly before the opening of the Duma – the question of whether or not the SP should participate in the Duma was no longer controversial. More importantly, with the achievement of the right to vote for the Jews, the Liberals had given Russian Jews a political perspective. Therefore, doubts voiced concerning the pogroms were artificial. The SP was, in a sense, forced by popular demand to keep going on. Finally, due to this promising perspective the all-Jewish national assembly seemed unnecessary. The Liberals' approach of tackling the 'actual and urgent tasks', such as raising civil, and not national, demands and thereby participating in the Liberation Movement was more convincing. The Trudovik M.A. Krol illustrated to the congress the only way which could promise any success to the SP:

> After this last battle the Jewish people will be free. Our place is in the first row of the fighters for the Russian Liberation Movement, and therein to fight shoulder to shoulder together with the Jewish revolutionary proletariat.[62]

The decision against the 'Ghetto' – in the political sense – and in favour of the further 'engagement' in the Russian Liberation Movement was taken. The congress included the National Assembly in the final resolution, but it had no direct consequences for the further political strategy of the SP. It seemed to have been a concession by the winners – the Liberals – to the losers – the Zionists and Nationalists.[63]

Nonetheless, at the end of the congress it was made clear to the Jewish public that to participate in the Duma did not mean to co-operate with the government. Thus, the SP made a propagandistic attack on the government, which was widely believed to have been involved in the pogroms. Since Vitte, as the Prime Minister, was the symbolic figure of the government, the congress reproached him with having been at least jointly responsible for the outrages, although he was the one who some weeks earlier had ensured the Jews the suffrage. Therefore, in a special resolution the SP renounced further negotiations with the present government.[64]

The congress decided to continue the work in the Liberation Movement and to proceed with the election campaign by sending information material regarding the October Manifesto to the provinces, by registering Jewish voters and making the Jews aware of their right to vote and of the fact that by voting they could take their fate in their own hands. The SP also intensified its propaganda activity against anti-Semitism in Russian society and among the Russian political circles and parties.[65] For this purpose, the SP elected a committee which was to investigate the pogroms and another one which was to organize Jewish self-defence everywhere.[66]

In this context, the SP achieved a major success, both on the national and international level. As far as the international level of its propaganda activity was concerned, the Russian Revolution of 1905, the pogroms following the October Manifesto and the foundation of a non-socialist Jewish organization such as the SP had led to a change among the West European and American Jewish leaders' approach towards solving the Jewish plight. In light of the latest pogroms and the failure of negotiations and talks between Paul Nathan, Oscar Straus, Jacob Schiff and Vitte at the end of 1905, assimilation seemed to be inopportune; a solution of the problem by the Russian government was not to be expected either.[67] Emigration of five and a half million Russian Jews was considered to be impossible. Therefore, the Jewish leaders abroad, especially Jacob Schiff, changed their course and favoured political reform within the Russian system as advocated by the moderate revolutionaries, such as the constitutionalists and Liberals.[68] This made it possible to support a revolutionary organization like the SP, since it propagated the transformation of Russia into a democracy of the West European or American model which would guarantee the emancipation of the Jews; this, subsequently, would bring about a solution to the Jewish question in Russia.[69] In this context, Baron Edmund de Rothschild and the Jewish Colonization Association subsidized the Russian liberal newspaper *Rech'* in order to 'influence public opinion in Russia in favour of Russian Jews'.[70] The connections which were set up with the West-European leading Jewish activists also brought the first results. In 1905 Lucien Wolf and Paul Nathan had founded three journals in order to publicize the information sent from Russia about the real situation of the Jews: the *Russische Korrespondenz* in Berlin, the *Russian Correspondence* in London, and the *Correspondance Russe* in Paris.[71] They used the information about the realities of the autocratic regime to put pressure on their governments. This was particularly true after 1905 whenever the Russian government was seeking a loan from the Jewish bankers abroad such as Lord Rothschild, or from the American government. The acceptance of the request for a loan was always bound to a demand to the Russian government to emancipate the Jews or, at least, lift some of the anti-Jewish restrictions.[72] For instance: although in 1905 the Russian government was able to float a loan with some French-Jewish bankers, thus preventing Russia's bankruptcy, Jacob Schiff's campaign among West European bankers against a Russian loan – and in favour of loans to Japan – had a lethal political effect as it not only enabled Japan to carry through the war and achieve victory over Russia, it also established its position in the international financial markets.[73]

Secondly, the SP continued to be successful on the national level by achieving another resolution by the major revolutionary or oppositional organization on behalf of the Jews: by the Soiuz Soiuzov. The October Manifesto had also forced the Soiuz Soiuzov to clarify its future course of action. Since this organization consisted of unions representing various groups of Russian society and a large spectrum of interests, the interpretation of the Manifesto, that is the pros and cons of the Duma, caused the homogeneity of the Union to crumble. Some unions had already decided to go their own way and participate in the Duma, no matter what the umbrella organization would decide. This also affected the composition of the Central Committee of the Union of Unions which witnessed the departure of the Liberals and former Osvobozhdentsy such as Miliukov and Vinaver and the taking over by more radical elements. Since the Soiuz Soiuzov had radicalized itself – it promoted the socialists' aim of an armed uprise[74] – it was not surprising that the Soiuz Soiuzov announced an appeal to the Russian people at the end of its congress in November 1905 in favour of the emancipation of the Jews, which they saw guaranteed by a change of the political system for which they were working. This was a similar point to that of the Russian Socialists, which saw the political and economic system as the main source of anti-Semitism and pogroms as its direct result. Therefore, the Soiuz Soiuzov directed an appeal to the Russian public not to follow any pogrom agitation in the future and to fight against it, as those outrages were being used by the autocratic regime to fight the Liberation Movement and the democratization of the country.[75] With this appeal the SP had achieved another success in its struggle against anti-Semitism in Russia. From now on, the pogroms were considered – at least, among the opposition, the revolutionaries and the intelligentsia – as a weapon which the government tried to turn against the Liberation Movement, especially since intellectuals and workers were also attacked during the pogroms.[76] Furthermore, the two major political forces participating in the elections, the Kadets and the Trudoviki, had adopted the demand of the equality of rights for all nationalities into their programmes.[77]

The SP had been successful in instigating the country's progressive forces to stand actively for the equality of rights. These appeals have to be considered as a success beyond the mere declamatory. They supported the Liberals' short-term tactics of co-operation with non-Jews and their long-term approach to the solution of the Jewish question through the introduction of a constitutional regime. Their approach seemed to be more promising than the unrealistic approach of their Nationalist/Zionist opponents to concentrate exclusively on activities and organizational work among Jews. The Liberals had advocated parliamentary work, fought with passion in the second congress of the SP for the continuation of its struggle for the constitution as Jewish emancipation could only be achieved through legislation and within a constitutional Russia based on democratic principles. In contrast to the Soiuz Soiuzov, Jewish Liberals interpreted the Duma and the elections as the best weapons in fighting for a constitution. This was also a clear negation of further revolutionary upheavals and as yet publicly declared breach with the socialist parties. Therefore, the Liberals fought tooth and nail against the Zionists/Nationalists' attempt to pull the SP away from the Liberation Movement, and went ahead with the election campaign and the mobilization of the Jewish people and its vote.

## 2.4   THE MOBILIZATION OF RUSSIAN JEWS INTO POLITICS

As mentioned above, the Soiuz Polnopraviia had started its election campaign before the October Manifesto. The Union's most talented speakers, such as Vinaver and Zhabotinskii, had been sent to the provinces to propagate its programme and to encourage Jews to participate in the election. To that end, election committees were founded in all the major cities of the Pale of Settlement.[78] Information brochures[79] were distributed in order to inform the Jewish voters about the Duma and the elections. The practical work at the grassroots, that is among the Jewish voters, was taken over and conducted independently by those election committees which were usually run by the most influential people of the respective Jewish community that, however, took their clues from the SP.[80]

Despite the positive results of the first inquiries regarding the situation in the respective constituencies, such as the balance of power between the various political groups and parties, it was necessary to make sure that as many progressive candidates as possible went through.[81] This aim, however, could only be achieved by combining the Jewish vote with that of other groups or parties. Therefore, alliances with the Kadets – as the strongest party in Russia – and representatives of other minorities had been arranged in those constituencies where neither part had a clear majority.[82] Locally, it was agreed between those parties and groups to set up joint election committees to decide upon the most promising and best candidate possible, and to support him with united force. These alliances included the Ukrainian Democratic Party and the Kadets in Poltava,[83] a common election committee consisting of thirty members with the Kadets, the SP and ten representatives of the Jewish population in Vilna,[84] and an alliance between SP and the Kadets in St. Petersburg.[85] In addition to professional people, Jewish candidates included rabbis and merchants.[86]

However, although a Jewish organization such as the SP could propagate its ideas more openly than the Bundists and was less harassed by the police,[87] it had to face a whole series of problems in conducting the election campaign: these had various roots such as anti-democratic behaviour or outright repression by local authorities, machinations by the landowners and aristocrats, growing anti-Semitism among other minorities such as the Poles, and a certain indifference among Jewish voters.

One example of anti-democratic behaviour fired by ethnic prejudice was the fact that the local authorities used every means to prevent individual Jews from going to the polls.[88] Quite often the authorities did not inform the population about the details of the elections, and the SP had to spread leaflets among Jewish voters to make good for this.[89] To avoid further disruptions by the local authorities the SP exploited the centralized government system and received generalized permission of the St. Petersburg Gradonachalnik to hold meetings.[90] This was the most persuasive means of securing the meetings which were essential for a successful election campaign. Similar action was taken in cases when polling stations had been set up at a great distance from Jewish quarters; the SP engaged the governor in order to change the location to facilitate the right to vote.

Despite the fact that the elections witnessed a wide participation of Jewish voters, securing the SP twelve seats in the First Duma,[91] it cannot be denied that in some areas the Jewish population showed a certain indifference to the elections. The reasons were manifold and ranged from the still considerable influence of conservative and religious Jews in the South of Russia who were opposed to any political activity, to a certain fear of repressions from the authorities, and a lack of political experience.[92] Furthermore, once the SP had actually managed to organize a meeting of Jewish voters, it had to face the bullying tactics of the Bund: this essentially meant making an appearance at meetings it had not called, propagating the boycott and then dispersing the meeting with physical force.[93]

Apart from all these problems, which could be counterbalanced or neutralized by the SP to a certain extent, there was a basic anti-Semitic tendency among certain strata of Russian society, as well as a growing nationalism in Russian Poland against which nothing could be done in the short time-span of the elections. For instance, a possible alliance between peasants and Jews – which was not unthinkable at that time[94] – was undermined by the machinations of the united block of Polish nobles and Russian landowners in Volynia.[95] A possible alliance with the peasants in

Podolia failed as the SP nominated the landowner Baron Gintsburg, one of the most prominent members of Jewish society; he was not acceptable for the peasants as they had formed an alliance in order to prevent the election of privileged persons.[96] In Russian Poland, the Jews failed to promote a single Jew into the Duma, as during a critical phase of the election campaign the Polish National Democrats used anti-Semitism as a political means to defeat their opponents – the Polish allies of the Kadets – which were supported by the Jews.[97] As a consequence, one and a half million Polish Jews remained without a single representative of their own, that is a Polish-Jewish Duma deputy. This was not, however, caused by the bad conduct of the SP, but rather by a misinterpretation of the situation in general and of the intentions of the National Democrats in particular. Unlike the Russian-Jewish community leaders, Polish Jews had not recognized the need for a separate Jewish organization, since the Polish politicians had made known that they would speak for all the nationalities in Poland, and advocate equality for all the suppressed nationalities.[98] Thus, they did not anticipate that the National Democrats would play the nationalist and anti-Semitic card once they faced the serious challenge by the Polish Kadets in Warsaw.[99] The consequence was that they suffered a serious defeat, which did not, however, lead to a change in their general view; Jewish-Liberal politics, therefore, remained a Russian phenomenon.

Despite these setbacks, the election campaign proved to be very successful as the Jewish masses went to the polls despite the Bund's active boycott. Moreover, the Bundists had to admit the failure of their boycott strategy, and grudgingly recognized the success of their opponents, the SP. For example, the Bundist Aleksandrov stated that 'the Jews had gone to the polls as if they had gone for a pilgrimage'.[100] The Socialist Zionist newspaper *Evreiskii Narod* estimated the Jewish participation in the elections in Vilna and Romno as high as 97 per cent and 96.7 per cent respectively; and on the national level the figure was 75–80 per cent as opposed to 50–60 per cent among the non-Jewish population.[101]

During the election campaign the Union was forced to leave the salons, that is the theory, and had to organize meetings of the Jewish voters in the provinces; in other words, it had to engage in practical political work within an increasingly changing Jewish society. As Isaac Shneerson, later State Rabbi in Chernigov and Kadet member (1906), put it: 'new dimensions had come to the Jewish masses. It was no longer only the struggle between Mitnagdim and Hasidim. New slogans had entered the Jews' mind such as class struggle, emancipation, equality of rights, an own national territory, consciousness of the proletariat and so on.'[102] The election campaign and the SP's interference with the local authorities to ensure the Jews' right to vote let the SP activists discover new connotations which most likely triggered a kind of psychological experience of re-embedding'.[103] This national self-consciousness among the SP members and the Jewish Duma deputies was reflected in the growing demand for the convocation of an all-Jewish national assembly and a national representative Jewish Duma group. These two demands were to be read increasingly in the Russian-Jewish newspapers.

The SP profited from this growing interest in politics – as its membership grew from 5,000 in 1905 to 7,500 in January 1906 – as did the bourgeois Zionists. The latter suddenly found themselves within a new political framework in which they could articulate their political views and propagate them to a nationwide audience. Moreover, the Zionists realized their chance to re-emphasize their claim for the national priority and seriously challenge the Liberals' political leadership of the SP. The Zionists' and Nationalists' hour had come when the SP, at the end of the election campaign and briefly before the elections, organized its Third Congress in St. Petersburg from 10 to 13 February 1906, two months before the opening of the First Russian State Duma.

The main points on the agenda were whether or not the SP should finally participate in the elections and in the Duma, and if so, which tactics should be pursued. The first two issues, the final participation in the Duma, won a clear majority among the congress participants for various reasons: first of all, this motion commanded the support of the majority of the congress; second, the SP's main strategy was to achieve equality of rights through the legislation, and therefore, a boycott of the legislative body, the Duma, would have been inconsequent; third, and even more important, the SP had successfully mobilized the Jewish masses for the election campaign, and a subsequent Duma boycott would have been hard to explain to the Jewish constituencies. Therefore, the propagators of a Duma boycott such as the Trudovik M.A. Krol, was not able to challenge the Liberals' pro-Duma stand. Krol's doubts concerning the credibility of the Duma and the Kadets as well as his argument that with the participation in the Duma the SP would be supporting a government which was in its form despotic and only represented the ruling strata and nationality did not convince the congress.[104] Instead, the Kadet and chairman of the Soiuz Polnopraviia, Vinaver won the majority in favour of the Duma, and the congress decided to participate in the Duma by 38 votes to 22.[105]

Nonetheless, in the further course of the congress, the Zionists and Nationalists used every occasion to challenge the Liberals' leadership. The conflict surfaced especially on the issue of the appropriate ally during the actual elections, not the election campaign. In this context, Ahad Ha'am, as one of the spokesmen for the Liberals' opponents, tried to discredit the Liberation Movement and especially the credibility of the progressive elements. To support his argument, he mentioned the Narodnaia Volia's – the terrorist movement of the late 1870s and early 1880s – approach of having used the pogrom as a means to divert the people's anger into a general revolution. In his opinion the Narodovol'tsy's tactic was still practised by the Russian Liberation activists. Consequently, he demanded to concentrate on Jewish national activities.[106]

At this point, the Liberals received the support of the SP's left-wing and especially the Trudovik Bramson,[107] and were able to win the majority to accept an alliance with the Kadets during the elections. The Nationalist/ Zionist camp did not, however, give up its attempt to make the Soiuz Polnopraviia adopt a more national line. Since the Zionist Ahad Ha'am's 'vote of no-confidence' towards the Liberation Movement had failed, they attempted at least to force the future Jewish Duma deputies to pursue a nationally-oriented activity. In this context, the Nationalist Dubnov put forward his idea of a Jewish Duma group which was to have a binding group discipline on all the issues affecting the Jews.[108] The Liberals as well as the left-wingers opposed this proposal impetuously. For instance, Sliozberg pointed to the fact that due to double-membership a nationally-oriented Jewish Duma group would bring the Jewish Duma deputies into conflict with the Russian parties, the Kadets and Trudoviki; furthermore, the Jewish Duma group would be too small to be a serious factor in the parliament.[109] Finally, the Zionist and Social Revolutionary Mark Ratner found a compromise formula which excluded group discipline, and which due to its vague and non-committing formula was acceptable to the Liberals.

> Jewish deputies who have their place within the parties and act collectively in questions concerning Jewish affairs are much more useful for the national group than a Jewish group.[110]

The political conflict within the SP could once more be contained, in particular because the Russian political situation seemed promising. Moreover, the Soiuz Polnopraviia and its Liberal leaders showed their confidence and belief in the forthcoming Duma by addressing a proclamation to the Russian-Jewish population which once again called them to go to the polls:

> Brother Jews, use your right and participate in the elections to the State Duma! The proximity of elections to the State Duma is forcing people who share the same ideas to unite into political parties and unions. We

stand on the side of only those parties that represent the equality of all without differentiation according to nationality, the equality of all citizens before the law, the complete realization of political freedoms and a right of universal franchise. However, in such an important moment, we believe that above all we should unite into one whole in order to give all our votes to those future representatives in the State Duma who will swear to you to advance the question of Jewish equality before all else and to defend it in the Duma on our behalf.[111]

## 2.5 THE STRUGGLE FOR LEGAL EMANCIPATION IN THE FIRST STATE DUMA

The Duma which had opened on 27 April 1906 seemed to be promising in terms of its political constellation: the Constitutional Democrats with their 180 deputies and the 84 Trudoviki commanded a majority in the parliament of 497.[112] The Jewish Liberals with their leader Maksim M. Vinaver, saw their political approach succeeding: a progressively-oriented Duma had been elected, and the party to which the Jewish Liberals belonged was the biggest within the Duma and, therefore, its major force. Based on their support, the legal changes, which would solve the Jewish question, could be pushed through by law. The First State Duma, however, was mainly concerned with general Russian issues such as the Agrarian Question. Furthermore, briefly before the opening of the parliament, the Tsar had published the Fundamental State Laws on 23 April 1906 which left the army, fleet, foreign policy, the right to declare war and to call and dissolve the Duma and the State Council in the hands of the Tsar. The latter had been set up as a second chamber by the Tsar in February 1906, and was geared towards counterbalancing the influence of the Duma as half of its members were appointed by the Tsar, and the other half elected by more conservative elements and traditional social institutions of Tsarist Russia, for instance the Zemstva. In fact, the Duma's efficacy became very much limited in its legislative power as both Tsar and State Council had the right to veto.[113]

Nevertheless, since equality of rights was one of the very basic demands for the future democratically-structured Russian state, it had been given priority by the Duma. Furthermore, some very prominent Kadet members such as Vinaver and Joseph Akchurin, the leader of the Muslims, also represented their respective nationalities. To a great extent the Kadets owed their victory in the elections to their tactics of setting up alliances with the minorities.[114] This in turn meant that they had an obligation to promote the demands of their inter-ethnic members. Furthermore, as the national question was also brought forward by the Polish bloc, the Kolo, the Duma could not ignore national demands.

By the time of the Duma's dissolution, however, the aspirations of Russian Jews were disappointed and the SP and Jewish Liberals had to face the left-wing's campaign defaming the Duma. The critics blamed the failure on the Liberals and especially on their activity in and support of the Russian party, the Kadets.[115] This criticism, however, does not hold once we follow up the activity of the First State Duma and the attention which was given to the Jewish question. First of all, Jewish Liberals did not fail because of the failure or mistakes in Kadet strategy. Rather, the dissolution of the Duma was a reflection of the demise of the Revolution and partly because the revolutionaries and radicals – not so much the KD – had overplayed their hand. Besides, neither the progressive parties nor the nationalities had achieved anything. We have to look more closely at the Jewish deputies' activity in the Duma and the way the Jewish question had been dealt with. First of all, the Liberals' tactics of lobbying for Jewish rights through the Kadets was logical as this party had the majority of seats in the Duma. Indeed, whenever the question of the minorities arose, the Jewish deputies were always supported by the Kadets and the Trudoviki. Second, Jewish Liberals regarded equality of rights as a fundamental issue on which they would not compromise. On the contrary, they confronted and reproached the government and the respective ministers for their anti-Semitic policy, and demanded that they accept responsibility for the pogroms. They learnt to behave like modern politicians who knew the way to achieve their political aims in parliamentarian politics. But they also stuck tenaciously to their belief that the Jewish question could only be solved through the legislative channels, and finally, by a constitution which was promoted by all the progressive parties within the Duma. Parliamentary work in the Duma had, however, to pass the necessary level of the Duma Commissions which were to draft the respective bill. This was, in turn, a political activity which was not very much appreciated by the Jewish revolutionaries and the critics of the SP, both full of expectations. Nevertheless, the activity of the Jewish Liberals in the Duma was the climax of Jewish Liberals' work during the Revolution of 1905.

The Jewish question was raised in the Duma on four occasions: in the speech which Vinaver delivered as an answer to the Tsar's throne speech; in connection with the Bill of the Equality of Rights; within the scope of an interpellation about police involvement in printing inflammatory material addressed to the Minister of the Interior, Stolypin; and finally, during the stormy session concerning the Belostok pogrom on 2 June 1906.

Until the outbreak of the pogrom in Belostok, the Jewish Kadets such as Vinaver, Iollos and Frenkel worked primarily within the Russian party, and through their influential position in the party tried to promote Jewish interests.[116] Moreover, since they belonged to the very top of the Kadets, they did not need to form a separate Jewish Duma group. However, from the very first moments of the Duma the Jewish Kadets made clear that they were not only members of a Russian party, but also representatives of the Jewish people. For instance, Vinaver raised the Jewish question in the speech which he gave as a response to the Tsar's throne speech.[117] Therein, Vinaver protested against the fact that the Tsar had not uttered a single word concerning the Jewish question, as if the Jewish people did not exist. Therefore, he made clear to Duma, Tsar and government that the Jewish people now had their representatives who would fight for their cause. Furthermore, Vinaver reproached the Tsar and the government for their anti-Semitic policy and he made clear that this would no longer be tolerated by the Duma; there would be no peace in the country as long as there was no equality of rights for all the citizens in Russia. This speech was the first appearance of a Jewish politician in a Russian political institution, demanding in public the abolition of all restrictions and the equalization for the Russian Jews. It is most likely that by describing the Jewish plight and the real situation of the Jews, he informed many deputies for the first time about the Jewish question.[118] The Duma, however, did not take any measures during the next days and went back to the general Russian problems.

A couple of days later, however, Vinaver's speech and work within the Duma witnessed its first success: a motion for a bill concerning civil equality, signed by 151 deputies, was brought into the Duma. After a brief discussion the bill was referred to a special committee which was to discuss it.[119] Thus, the bill went into the committee stage of the Duma commissions which to the critics of the SP smacked of political defeat and failure.

The Kadets raised the Jewish question and the pogroms using them as a means of attacking the government and unmasking its anti-Semitic and reactionary policy. Pointing to Tsarism's Jewish policy they denounced the political system in Russia as obsolete and which ought to be abolished.[120] Thus, the Jewish question was raised for the third time when the Duma confronted Stolypin on 8 May 1906, with an interpellation regarding the involvement of some officials of the Ministry of Interior in printing inflammatory material against the Jews.[121] Not only the Kadet leaders Petrunkevich, Kokoshkin and Miliukov, but also the Trudovik leaders Ryzhkov, Zhukovsky and Aladin attacked the government.[122] The Jewish question, however, was only one of many and not the most important problem the Duma had to deal with. General Russian problems such as the Agrarian Question came back into the focus of attention. The Jewish deputies and the Kadets had done their utmost to promote the cause of the Jews in the parliament; at this time, there was not really much more they could have done.

Nevertheless, the Jewish Kadets had to face harsh criticism for their tactics in the Duma during the fourth congress of the Soiuz Polnopraviia, which gathered from 9 to 12 May 1906 in St. Petersburg. Two major issues arose during this conference: the organizational structure of the SP, and the tactics in the Duma. In both respects, the Liberals again had to face challenges from the left and from the Nationalist-Zionist camp. The first reproached them of centralism and undemocratic conduct of SP affairs while the second tried to take over the leadership. The congress which now witnessed a shift in power in favour of the Liberals' opponents, however, came to agreements regarding the organizational structure: from now on the local committees should conduct their political activity more independently. The link to the centre in St. Petersburg was improved by the setting up of so-called information bureau. These were to inform the population about political events, to gather material regarding the relation between Jews and non-Jews together with general information, and to send it to St. Petersburg. This was to enable the Central Bureau to promote Jewish interests better and more effectively. The organizational structure was democratized by abolishing any quota or limit for SP members from the provinces. From now on, any member could be elected to the Central Bureau.[123]

These changes, however, did not particularly interest the Zionists who were not concerned about the organizational structure and the question of whether or not it was democratic. The Zionists' challenge went beyond this and had the sole purpose of claiming the leadership within the SP. Their target was not the actual tactics of the Liberals in the Duma, but their wider political conception and their conduct in advancing the Jewish cause in general. Now, with the majority of the congress behind them, they felt comfortable enough to raise the issue of the Jewish Duma group once again despite the fact that the Duma was already working on the bill for the equality of rights, and had just started an inquiry regarding the police's involvement in the pogroms. This underlines Alexander Orbach's view that the Zionists were looking for a way to enter Russian politics, and had realized that at this moment of crisis within the SP the opportunity had come for them to present themselves as the real representatives of Russian Jewry.[124] The Zionist delegates, especially Zhabotinskii, seemed to believe that only Jews could defend Jewish interests and therefore a Jewish Duma group was obligatory.[125] The Zionists therefore rejected a compromise formula by the Liberals G. Landau and Frumkin to organize meetings on a voluntary basis, where the particular course of action regarding Jewish problems could be coordinated.[126] Instead, the discussions went on for two days, and reached the point at which the Liberals threatened the congress with their immediate departure, as no compromise was foreseeable.[127] The fact that in the end the Zionists renounced their demand for binding discipline within the Duma Group did not prevent the various parties and groups of the SP from losing faith in the future of that organisation.[128] The Zionists proved unable to take over the leadership of the SP, and the Liberals realized that the SP as a united force had reached an impasse. Impatience, disunity in the decisive political moments and the search for quick fixes characterized not only the general revolutionary movement but also the majority of the Jewish parties and groups. The gap between the two opposing sides had become so wide that any compromises in terms of their different approaches seemed to be impossible, although the First Duma was still in existence and the failure of the Liberals' political approach was not yet foreseeable.

On the contrary, some eighteen days after the SP's fourth congress, the Jewish question was put before the plenum of the parliament for the fourth time. As opposed to the first three occasions, this time the Jewish question had been raised by events outside the Duma: by the outbreak of a pogrom in Belostok. Almost the entire Duma as well as the Russian press[129] reacted with indignation, as the pogrom happened while the Duma was actually in session. Since the Duma believed in the government's, or at least the higher administration's involvement – even if the first was never proven – this was interpreted by many deputies as another attempt by the authorities to suppress the revolutionary movement, and its first big achievement, the State Duma. This was seen not only as contradictory to the idea of democracy, but primarily as an attack against the very existence of the parliament. This was the reason why this time the Jewish question received most support among the Duma deputies and resulted in a resolution in favour of the emancipation of the Jews. It also prompted, on 9 June 1906 the setting up of a committee consisting of thirty-three deputies – among them 5 Jews – which was ordered by the Duma to draft the bill for civil equality.[130] The discussions illustrated the support and the sympathy given by the Duma majority to the Jews. Thus, immediately after the news had reached the Duma on 2 June 1906, the Kadets reacted promptly by asking Stolypin directly how he intended to stop the pogrom and protect the Jews.[131] The Jewish deputies such as Shmarya Levin and Rozenbaum,[132] as well as the famous Kadet leaders Kokoshkin and Petrunkevich, raised their voices and showed their disgust with the pogrom and the regime which still let this happen, and demanded the equality of rights for the Russian Jews. The right-wing parties, which had reacted with their stereotypical anti-Semitic arguments,[133] could not influence the Duma's favourable attitude towards the equalization of the Jews. The Duma demanded an official statement from the government concerning the pogrom, the punishment of those guilty and guarantees that this would not happen again.[134] Finally, after impetuous discussions in which Stolypin rejected the government's responsibility, the former vice-Minister of Interior and governor of Bessarabia, Prince S.D. Urusov totally discredited the government by describing in detail the machinations of the government in a police department of St. Petersburg.[135] Thereafter, the Duma set up another committee which was to investigate the circumstances of the pogroms. This committee selected three Duma deputies, among them the Jewish deputy and Trudovik Yakubson, and sent them to the various localities.[136] This was the first time the Duma took immediate action to protect the Jews and to find the guilty persons. The Jewish deputies had achieved moral support by the Duma's majority and a tangible success in the form of the committees which included Jewish deputies. This meant that for the first time in the history of Russian Jews their democratically-elected political representatives were given the opportunity to influence a law which was meant to bring equality of rights to Russian Jews.

However, the Tsar dissolved the Duma on 9 July 1906. Generally speaking, the Duma proved to be too radical for Stolypin's reform project and the convocation of a Second Duma with a rather left-wing, but also stronger right-wing oriented composition seemed to be more promising for both the Tsar and the government.[137] The committee for the Equality of Rights had not finished its work by the time the Duma was dissolved. The Jewish question was again postponed and referred to some uncertain point in the future. As far as changes of the legal status of the Jews were concerned, nothing – apart from the suffrage – had been achieved. However, the debates concerning the Jewish question in the Duma indicated the willingness of the majority of the Duma to give the minorities in general and the Jews in particular the equality of rights. Furthermore, the Duma's approach to Jewish emancipation was more than what could have been expected. The Jewish question came before the plenum of the Duma four times. The commissions meant a loss of time for the legal solution of the Jewish question. The dissolution of the Duma signalled the final decline of the revolutionary movement which had already suffered some major setbacks: the split of the Liberation Movement after the October Manifesto, the suppression of the peasants' revolts and the Moscow uprise in December, 1905. In short, the Tsar and the government were regaining control in a decisive manner.

The general political approach of the Liberals, to achieve the solution of the Jewish question with the help of the Russian progressive parties through the legislative process, had failed for now. Their activity within Jewish society through the Soiuz Polnopraviia, however, was successful in many ways and served as a learning experience in the field of practical politics. First, they had succeeded in setting up a Jewish umbrella organization, embracing all the Jewish non-Marxist parties and groups which worked successfully for nearly one and a half years. They had managed to keep this organization alive despite the fact that due to the different political views the organization was very problematic from the very beginning; something they shared with all the other Unions. Second, the SP also initiated a process of politicisation and mobilization among Russian Jews, which can be seen through the very existence of the election committees which were set up in the capitals as well as in the provinces. During the election campaign, these organizations were very active, especially regarding the formation of alliances with other minorities and the progressive Russian parties; this activity secured the Russian Jews twelve Duma deputies. Third, the very existence of the SP was also responsible for the change in the approach of Jewish leaders abroad towards the solution of the Jewish question in Russia.

The Liberals had succeeded on the international level as well. Through their activity as the SP's leaders the Liberals had made their names known within Jewish society, won followers in the provinces through the SP's branches, and established themselves as another political force within Russian Jewry. It was a basis on which the Liberals could continue their political struggle for equality of rights and an improvement of the conditions under which Jews had to live. The fact that the Duma had been dissolved and the attempt to revive it with the Vyborg appeal had failed, made a review of the political situation necessary.[138] The Liberals especially suffered from the consequences of the failed Vyborg appeal, since their leaders, such as Vinaver, were deprived of their suffrage, and some of them had to face persecution and ended up spending two months or more in prison. Since all the twelve Jewish deputies had signed the appeal, the SP suffered a major blow. As mentioned above, the approach of the Liberals to create a public space for Russian Jews was successful and the Jewish masses showed a great deal of enthusiasm. However, neither the political struggle in the Duma, nor the pressure from the Jewish community leaders abroad, had brought the solution of the Jewish question any closer. Another watershed was reached and a new approach was needed in order to find a way out of this impasse. Here, considering the success of their activities it seemed most promising to reorganize on the local level and, at the same time, to speed up reform and modernization within the Jewish community. However, this approach, which was materialized after Stolypin's *coup d'état* of June 1907, was overshadowed for one year by a reorientation process among all Jewish groups hitherto participating in the SP.

# 3 The Road towards Self-Determination: New Elections, the Second State Duma and the Search for a New Approach

The dissolution of the First Duma and the failure of the Vyborg appeal necessitated a re-evaluation of the political situation and of tactics to be applied. The political approach pursued by Jewish Liberals – to combine all Jewish groups and parties with the exception of the orthodox Marxist factions in a central organization – had reached an impasse. The ideological gulf between Zionists and Liberals had become so wide, especially on the issue of Jewish political representation, that a further co-operation between these two political camps became impossible. With the First Duma's dissolution, the Liberals had lost support among their nationalist and Zionist partners, and a process of differentiation took place, transforming the main political streams which had participated in the SP into parties. The entire Jewish political body was affected by this process, and by the end of 1906 the representation of Jewish interests had developed into a kaleidoscope of groups and parties: the Zionists were split into a bourgeois (the RSO) and a socialist camp (SS, Poalei Zion, SERP); the Jewish middle-class was represented by the ENP (Evreiskaia Narodnaia Partiia – Dubnovtsy), the ENG (Evreiskaia Narodnaia Gruppa – Vinaver, Sliozberg, etc.) and the EDG (Evreiskaia Demokraticheskaia Gruppa – Bramson); and finally, the Socialists (Bundists).[1]

This chapter deals with the period from the dissolution of the First Duma in July 1906 until the convocation of the Third Duma in November 1907, which was to see the ideological and practical development of the new approach of Jewish Liberal politics, that is Autonomism (national programme) combined with Constitutionalism (political, economic reform). The key factors for this shift were the growing reactionary trend in the country, the surging nationalism among certain nationalities – for instance the Poles – and especially the appearance of the bourgeois Zionists in the political arena. The Liberals answered the Zionists' challenge by presenting

45

a programme, based on the Vilna Platform, which went beyond political demands, offered an economic and national programme as well as the call for self-help. The Liberals' main emphasis on political activity was substituted by a combination of lobbying for the Jews in the Duma, propaganda activity among Russian society, and organic work – here with the main emphasis on the modernization of Jewish society and community life. In short, it was the final shift of Jewish Liberal politics towards Autonomism.

### 3.1   THE ELECTIONS TO THE SECOND DUMA: THE LIBERAL-ZIONIST CONTROVERSY, OR 'NATIONALISM' VERSUS 'INTEGRATIONISM'

The forthcoming elections to the Second Duma forced all political parties to reassess the situation. During this period, two decisions were to influence this process decisively: first, the Social Democrats' decision to participate in parliamentary work, and second, the Third Russian-Zionist Congress with its decision to appear as an independent political party – both in November 1906. These events were to start two processes which were partly linked to each other: a rapprochement between parts of the RSDRP and the Kadets; and a differentiation process of the former member-groups of the SP.

The process of re-evaluation among the Socialist parties was decisively influenced by the political circumstances of the time: the decline of the revolutionary movement due to the exhaustion of the masses, and the revival of the reactionary forces in the country. Furthermore, in light of the forthcoming elections, the government's decision – as a consequence of the Vyborg appeal and the persecution of the signatories – to prohibit the Kadets to hold their Fourth Congress in Russia created an awareness among the Socialists that the forthcoming elections were mainly to develop into a struggle between conservatives and the opposition; this created a solidarization between some left-wing oppositional parties, especially between the Mensheviki and the Kadets. Another key factor for the SDs' re-evaluation of the Second Duma was the fact that its rank-and-file, the Moscow workers, had already decided to set up an alliance with the Kadets; they thus forced their party finally to participate in the policy making of the country.[2]

The tactical turn of the RSDRP towards participation in parliamentary work could already be witnessed during its Fourth Congress which took place in April 1906 in Stockholm. Here, the Mensheviki – who at that time commanded the majority in the Central Committee – were able to push through their resolution against the boycott and in favour of a participation of the SD in the next Duma. This decision was finally materialized in the SD's congress in Tammerfors, Finland, in November 1906. Here, in light of the forthcoming elections, the Mensheviki, together with the Bund, also pushed through a resolution advocating co-operation with bourgeois forces. Ideologically they justified their decision to participate in the elections as well as in the Duma with a re-evaluation of the revolution. They argued that despite the fact that the First Duma was dominated by the Kadets, the Duma had proven to be a democratic institution which could be used as the new tribune for the revolution and socialist agitation. As a consequence of this, the congress decided to agree to alliances with the Kadets in order to avert the election of a conservative candidate.[3]

In fact, political reality in Russia as well as public opinion left the SD no other political alternative than to join 'parliamentary' work. The Bund, for instance, had to face serious problems due to the electoral law which left its candidates only a slight chance to win a seat in the Second Duma, as its traditional clientele – workers who were working mainly in factories with less than fifty employees – was disenfranchized.[4] Furthermore, as opposed to the last elections, a Jewish public had come into existence in form of a wide range of Jewish newspapers of various political views.[5] In fact, all these newspapers now demanded the participation of their respective parties in elections and Duma. For instance, the Socialist-Zionist organ *Evreiskii Narod* stated that the boycott tactic had proven ineffective, since during the last elections the Jews had gone overwhelmingly to the polls, thus confirming once more the tremendous success achieved by the SP. Consequently, it followed the Mensheviki's demands to participate in the elections, as the Duma could be used as a mighty centre for the organization of the people, and it propagated the new Socialist slogan for the elections: Alliance.[6] Since the three Zionist Socialist parties (SS, SERP, Poalei Zion) had followed the general move towards parliamentary work and decided to participate in the elections, the Bund could not stand aside.[7]

The integration process of all oppositional parties into parliamentary work was, however, paralleled and to some degree countermanded by a differentiation process within the Jewish political mainstream which had carried and supported the SP. At first, the election campaign followed the call of the Zionist newspaper *Evreiskii Golos* which stated that 'all the parties had realized that an even greater struggle between the reactionary and the progressive elements will take place in the forthcoming elections, and therefore, the Jews should go again to the polls unitedly'.[8] In fact, the SP branches immediately started the election campaign according to the patterns of the last elections: organizing and mobilizing the Jewish vote within the scope of the Jewish election committees, and setting up alliances with their traditional allies, the Kadets and other nationalities.[9] Furthermore, the leaders of many Jewish communities set up independent non-affiliated election committees, thus indicating that a mobilization of the Jewish vote independently from the political parties had taken place at the grassroots.[10]

However, the fact that the Zionists now ran the election campaign independently, caused a split of the broad Jewish political movement. Only the Liberals and Bramson's EDG still acted within the scope of the SP, preserving its Central Committee. As a consequence, former leaders of the SP were now competing with each other for a Duma ticket in many constituencies in the Pale of Settlement such as in the gubernii of Kovno and Kherson, as well as in the cities of Vilna and Vitebsk.[11] Finally, the political struggle between the bourgeois Zionists, the Russkaia Sionistskaia Organisatsiia (RSO) and the Liberals surfaced. The Zionists not only terminated the co-operation with the Liberals, but also felt confident enough to challenge their former partners by pursuing politics as a political party, as they had decided at their Third Congress in Helsingfors at the end of November 1906. Here, the chief RSO ideologist Zhabotinskii won the majority for his idea of going it alone. However, for their so-called 'Gegenwartsarbeit' the Zionists adopted the SP's Vilna platform, that is a co-operation with the Russian Liberation Movement in its struggle for the democratization of the political system in Russia; they thus vindicated their competitors' tactics with hindsight, as well as the Autonomists' demand for the foundation of an all-Jewish National Assembly. Furthermore, the Helsingfors platform aimed at the democratization of the Jewish community, an amelioration of the Jewish economic situation and emigration. In short, the 'Gegenwartsarbeit' was the decision by the Zionists to enter Russian politics as an independent force.[12]

The fact that the Zionists appeared as an independent political party made Jewish Liberals such as Vinaver, Sliozberg, Kulisher and Sheftel abandon the idea of the SP. In response to the Gegenwartsarbeit, the Liberals founded the 'Evreiskaia Narodnaia Gruppa' (ENG – Jewish People's Group), and set up their own press organ, the *Svoboda i Ravenstvo* ('freedom and equality') in St. Petersburg. In light of the election campaign, an ideological struggle arose in the street as well as in the Jewish press between the 'Integrationists' – who advocated promoting Jewish national interests within the framework of a co-operation with their respective Russian partners, the political parties – and the 'Nationalists', who favoured a purely national policy focusing on the representation of

Jewish interests according to the model of the Polish parliamentary group, the 'Kolo'.[13]

The importance which was given to the Zionist challenge can also be seen when one considers that none of the Jewish parties involved had recorded the fact that in October 1906 Stolypin had come up with a proposal to grant some concessions to Russian Jews. In fact, his initiative won acceptance in the Council of Ministers, which actually worked out the proposals and submitted them to the Tsar; the Tsar, however, vetoed the initiative in December 1906.[14]

As the Zionists' bid for supremacy within the Jewish community was made in the midst of the election campaign, they did not take a stand on Stolypin's initiative. Rightly, Liberals and Jewish populists (Bramson) perceived this as an open challenge to their tactics of representing Jewish interests, and felt compelled to counteract. Shortly after the foundation of the ENG, the Liberals issued an appeal to Jewish voters in *Der Fraind* in December 1906 which aimed at warding off the Zionists' attempt to seize political leadership.[15] In this appeal, the Liberals did not attack Zionism as such, but the Zionists' new policy and their uncompromising stand on raising Jewish national demands through an independent Jewish party. Since the Liberals believed that emancipation could only be achieved in cooperation with the Russian Liberation Movement, they regarded the Zionists' action as a step towards political isolation; moreover, it was seen as being contradictory, since the Zionists had maintained their ultimate aim, emigration to Palestine.[16] To the Liberals, the Zionists' decision to set up a political party in a country from which they intended to emigrate clearly made no sense. The Liberals regarded a Jewish Duma deputy as a representative of both Russians and Jews, and therefore rejected the new Zionist 'Gegenwartsarbeit' as utopian, called the Zionists 'emigrants in principle', and finally called on Russian Jews not to follow them as their new programme would endanger the political struggle for Jewish emancipation in Russia.[17]

This appeal was followed by three other appeals of which the fourth especially provoked a heated controversy. In this appeal, which was addressed to Jewish voters, the Liberals called upon them not to vote for the Zionists, since due to the Zionists' present position 'every Zionist deputy represents a danger for us [Jews]'.[18] These two appeals forced the Jewish political groups and parties to take a side in this struggle. For example, the newly-founded nationalist Jewish People's Party (Evreiskaia Narodnaia Partiia) with its leaders S.M. Dubnov and M.N. Kreinin dissociated itself from the ENG and its appeal.[19] Due to their programme[20] which was very similar to the 'Gegenwartsarbeit', that is to emphasize primarily Jewish national demands, they took the Zionists' side. The only difference was that the 'Dubnovtsy' rejected emigration in principle, and promoted national autonomy for Russian Jews as a target, unlike the Zionists who regarded it as a training ground for the future Jewish state in Palestine. However, their agreement on the level of the principle of raising national demands made them the Zionists' allies.[21]

Bramson's left-wing-oriented Jewish Democratic Group (Evreiskaia Demokraticheskaia Gruppa) was also pulled into this struggle. The EDG's left-wing position, which had great similarities to Russian populism, brought it close to the liberal ENG, especially its 'integrationist' approach. However, Bramson's (Trudovik) left-wing views had always led him to emphasize a more democratic conduct of SP affairs, and he was thus open to a new experiment that might water down what he regarded as the bourgeois character of Jewish politics, for which he believed the Liberals stood. This brought the EDG closer to the Zionists and to their intention of running Jewish affairs with a new approach, claiming to be the real national and democratic representation of Russian Jewry. However, apart from St. Petersburg, the EDG played a minor part in the election campaign.

The Zionists answered the ENG's appeals with broadsides in their press organs, in which they portrayed the Liberals as old-fashioned *Shtadlanim*. The Zionists rejected the Liberals' attacks of being 'emigrationists', and praised themselves as the new and really democratic force on the Jewish street, representing Jewish national interests properly.[22]

Since at the same time the 'Nationalists' also launched a campaign against the Bund,[23] a rapprochement between Liberals and the Bund took place. The Bund, due to its 'integrationist' ideology – like the Liberals they advocated national-cultural autonomy and cooperation with their Russian allies – regarded the liberal ENG as an ally in its traditional struggle against Jewish Nationalism and Jewish conservatism. Since the Liberals had openly turned against the Zionists, Bund and ENG had one thing in common: the Zionist opponent. Despite the fact that Bundist ideologists such as Medem and Litvak still kept an ideological distance from the Liberals,[24] on the practical level of the election campaign, the Bund decided to give the struggle against nationalism priority over the class struggle. During the election campaign, both Bund and ENG put the ideological differences aside and fought together against the representatives of Jewish nationalism, bourgeois and socialist alike. Consequently, a wide range of alliances between Bund and ENG was set up in Vilna, Minsk,[25] Rostov/Don, Kremenchug, Poltava, Sevastopol, and Kovno.[26] Other alliances embracing the Bund, Mensheviki, Kadets, SP and a block of left-wing and non-party affiliated voters was set up in

Ekaterinoslav,[27] or in Romno where a coalition was formed between Kadets, Jews, Ukrainians, Social Democrats and the Bund. Finally, the Mensheviki and the Bund announced in the press their general approval of alliances in the first stage of the elections: the election of electors.[28] The struggle between 'Integrationists' and 'Nationalists' was reported from many constituencies during the election campaign. Since the ENG as well as the Zionists appeared relatively late in the election campaign, the main target for both was to impose their respective political views on the already existing non-party-affiliated Jewish election committees. This resulted in heated confrontations in some constituencies, such as in Belostok, where the fact that the Zionists had taken over the Jewish election committee caused the organization of a second committee by Territorialists, Bundists, Kadets and non-party affiliated Jews.[29]

The rapprochement between Bund and Liberals (ENG) became also evident in some articles which appeared in the Liberals' organ *Svoboda i Ravenstvo* ('Freedom and Equality') within the course of the growing polemics by the 'Nationalist' camp (ENP, EDG, Zionists). In one of these articles the Liberals expressed their sympathy with the Bund due to its 'integrationist' approach. Furthermore, it was emphasized that there were only some principal differences between ENG and Bund.[30] Generally speaking, whenever the Bund was mentioned in *Svoboda i Ravenstvo*, the tone was rather moderate, and criticism towards the Bund on the ideological level disappeared for the time being from the Liberals' political vocabulary.

The bourgeois Zionists' chance of success in the election campaign in turn was questionable from the beginning, as they also had to struggle against their competitors within the general Zionist movement, the socialist Zionist groups. In contrast to the Bund, the various Zionist Socialist factions such as Poalei Zion, SS and SERP still ran the elections along the lines of the class struggle. Therefore, they still regarded the RSO as reactionaries – as they were bourgeois – and therefore, as opponents of the Jewish workers' interests.[31] The bourgeois Zionists (RSO) such as D. Pasmanik in turn reproached SS and SERP for having betrayed their national ideology.[32] Since the workers' 'Nationalists', such as the SERP organ *Di Folksshtime*, also criticized the Bund for its 'Integrationist' approach, both Zionist camps, the RSO and the Zionist Socialists, became completely isolated in the elections. This became evident in the newspapers' complaints that the Bund had joined the ENG's struggle against Jewish Nationalism and Zionism to the extent that it had preferred alliances with the Liberals instead of the representatives of the Jewish proletariat, the Zionist-Socialist parties.[33]

The elections to the Second Duma resulted, finally, in disappointment for all Russian-Jewish political activists. Nonetheless, considering the political circumstances, the election of four Jewish deputies cannot be seen as a disaster as these elections had not only brought greater competition with the participation of the Socialists, but also saw national gerrymandering by the authorities, which was particularly directed against the Jews. Furthermore, in contrast to the first elections, the general conditions were now less favourable, the revolutionary movement had abated and the government had been able to regain the initiative with a somewhat more reactionary course.[34] Also a certain indifference occurred among the voters stemming from various factors, such as political tiredness, disappointment with the First Duma's work and consequently a certain pessimism with respect to the Second Duma.[35] Further unfavourable factors were the increasing anti-Semitic activities led by the ultra-reactionaries,[36] manipulation by the local authorities during the campaign,[37] machinations by landowners and the clergy to undermine an alliance between Jews and peasants,[38] and finally, the anti-Semitic election campaign by the National Democrats (ND) in Poland, which led to Polish Jews again not being represented in the Duma.[39]

The general political situation and the particular conditions of the elections had made it extremely difficult to return a considerable number of Jewish deputies. It has to be concluded therefore that the election of only four deputies was not caused by the inner-Jewish dissent alone, as the Zionist press claimed.[40] With respect to the RSO's failure in the election campaign it has to be stated that its new concept did not find sufficient support at the grassroots level; the Liberals' approach still seemed much more promising to Jewish voters. This was documented by Zhabotinskii's brief and frustrated summary of his election campaign in Volynia in which he stated that despite the fact that the Zionists promoted Jewish national demands, the Jews voted for the Kadets.[41] Furthermore, the Zionist press reported that some local Zionists had ignored the directives of the Central Committee and had set up alliances with the Liberals.[42]

## 3.2   THE ENG: THE LIBERAL VERSION OF AUTONOMISM

The ENG's activities can be separated into two phases: the first phase witnessed the Liberals' efforts to establish the ENG, by promoting their views, winning wider support, and fighting their main political opponent, the Zionists; the second phase was characterized by drafting a programme, combined with first actions to materialize it.

In the first phase the ENG followed the patterns of the SP's political activities: they used the 'freedom of assembly' guaranteed by the October Manifesto in order to organize a series of so-called organizational congresses in St. Petersburg at the end of January 1907. Since these congresses were open to anyone interested, they were to fulfil a special purpose: first, to explain the reason for the foundation of the ENG to the audience; second, to present the new approach; third, to recruit new members. Since the 'Nationalists' regarded these congresses as a good opportunity to challenge the Liberals and undermine their efforts, these congresses became another 'battlefield' between the 'Integrationists' and 'Nationalists'.

On 17 January 1907, the first organizational congress of the ENG took place in St. Petersburg, at which 124 out of the 160 invited people appeared. In his opening speech, the chairman Vinaver justified the foundation of the ENG by referring to the Zionists' uncompromising stand on the Jewish national Duma group, and the fact that the Zionists had given their claim for leadership the frame of the Helsingfors programme. As far as the ENG's political nature was concerned, Vinaver gave evidence to the fact that the Liberals were still envisaging a Jewish umbrella organization similar to the SP. Thus, he stated that the ENG aimed at embracing representatives of all parties and views which accepted the Vilna platform and, therefore, it would not consider itself a political party. Furthermore, he pointed especially to the ENG's national programme with its particular emphasis of developing the national culture of Russian Jewry, and at the same time improving the economic situation of the masses. In this context, Vinaver made clear to the audience that the ENG intended to organize and mobilize the people for self-help in the economic and national-cultural field. In general, the ENG aimed at organizing the Jewish masses for the struggle for civil equality and Jewish national rights. Vinaver had shown that the Liberals' new approach was a new version of Dubnov's autonomism, with the main emphasis, however, on politics which seemed promising in Tsarist Russia of that time.[43] The basic frame for Liberal Autonomism was given by Liberals such as M.L. Goldshtein, M.I. Sheftel, and L.Ya. Shternberg – one of the ENG's chief ideologists – who announced to the congress that the ENG would follow politically the tradition of the Vilna platform – to fight for the democratization of Russia – but at the same time promote the development of Jewish national culture. Within this struggle, however, they rejected a further co-operation with the Zionists due to the ideological differences, and their uncompromising stand towards the Liberals.[44]

Since this congress took place just a few weeks after the ENG had issued two appeals against the Zionists, a charged atmosphere still prevailed.

For instance, the Zionist Yanovskii stood up and attacked the ENG as being a creation of dishonest people, called the appeal a 'pure lie', and finally reproached the ENG of intolerance towards other groups such as the Zionists. However, Yanovskii's attack proved to be ineffective as all the other attendants followed Vinaver's call, and joined the ENG at the end of the congress.[45]

This first congress was followed by a second[46] – which was not, however, recorded in the press – and a third, which took place on 29 January 1907 in St. Petersburg, again under the chairmanship of M.M. Vinaver. It followed the same patterns as the first. Thus, various prominent ENG leaders such as Vinaver, M.V. Pozner, G.B. Sliozberg, L.Ya. Shternberg and M.L. Trivus, as well as Zionist and nationalist activists such as Idelson, Bubkov (both Zionists) and S.M. Dubnov were present. Instead of Vinaver, M.V. Pozner gave the 'ideological' speech in which he justified the ENG's foundation along the same lines as Vinaver, and assured the audience that the Liberals had more to offer than just the struggle against Zionism. On the contrary, he pointed out that the new approach combined the struggle for civil rights with that for a spiritual perfection of the Jewish people in Russia. Therefore, the ENG's main target was to create an atmosphere favourable to Jewish life and its development based on legal and democratic grounds.[47]

The Zionists (Idelson, Bubkov) and the Nationalists (Dubnov) appeared at the rostrum in the same way as in the first congress: first, to discredit the ENG as a proper Jewish organization due to its 'integrationist' approach, and to stress once again the necessity of a party promoting 'real' national demands such as the foundation of an all-Jewish national assembly; at the same time they called upon the audience to join their parties. Dubnov tried to calm the storm by referring to the fact that the Zionists had gone their independent way already before the Helsingfors congress, and therefore it only sanctioned what had already be decided. He called on the audience to end the disputes and work for the Jewish cause in an unemotional way. Finally, he used the opportunity to familiarize the audience with the ENP's programme and called upon them to join the ENP, as this organization would advocate a broad programme with regard to Jewish national interests – as opposed to the ENG's minimal programme.[48]

The ENG leaders in turn were eager to show the congress that the Nationalists' reproaches were unjustified, and that the ENG acted according to the exigencies of political reality. In this context, Sliozberg rejected Idelson's criticism in particular, and the Zionists' attacks in general. He pointed out that if 'we were really assimilationists, as you say, then you [Zionists] would have won the elections'. Reminding Idelson of bitter realities he added that the Zionists had lost the elections due to their 'isolationism'.

Vinaver's response to Dubnov pointed not only to the roots of the conflict between 'Nationalists' and 'Integrationists' at that time, but also underlined the similarities to Dubnov's Autonomism. Thus, one point of conflict was the concept for the reorganization of the Jewish community. Here, the Liberals shared Dubnov's views. However, while the ENP advocated a national, centralized union of Jewish communities with the principle of enforcement, the ENG favoured a free and decentralized union of democratized communities based on a pluralistic structure. In this context, Vinaver particularly rejected Dubnov's concept of a 'national-secular' community as it excluded the interests of the religious elements of Russian Jewry. The Liberals' 'engagement' on behalf of the religious elements was not based on the rejection of the secularization of Jewish community life *per se*, as the envisaged modernisation would automatically imply secularization. It seemed that the Liberals' refusal to exclude the religious elements from community leadership was based on the fact that it still commanded, as shown during the elections, a significant influence. In fact, the Liberal organ *Svoboda i Ravenstvo* sharply rejected the secularization of the Jewish community at that time as 'the religious needs have priority for the Jewish masses and they base their life on this ground which includes also the cult'.[49]

Shternberg supported Vinaver's arguments regarding the reorganization of the Jewish community, and highlighted the Liberals' ideology of 'a policy oriented towards the realities of Jewish life in Russia' in one sentence, by restating what he had written in an article in *Svoboda i Ravenstvo*:

> The ENG is advocating a synthesis as it believes in the revival of Jewry, and not in utopias such as our own country, or the creation of a Jewish-national *Seim*.[50]

As a consequence, Dubnov's defense of his concept, and his assurance that the Nationalists would not interfere in the freedom of religious persons, did not bridge the differences. His offer for co-operation, in case the ENG appeared with a national programme, was rejected by Vinaver at the end of the congress.[51]

After these congresses had fulfilled their purpose of establishing the ENG, the Liberals used their press organ *Svoboda i Ravenstvo* to present a programme of action by addressing appeals either to the Jewish public or the ENG's local branches. In these appeals they pointed to the first target for the reorganization of the Jewish community: the legalization of the Jewish community within the scope of the reform of local and municipal self-government. Since they expected this reform to be one of the first issues discussed in the Duma, the ENG called upon its members in a circular to discuss this issue by including, if possible, all the democratic elements who had not yet joined the ENG. This way, the ENG's final decision in this question could be based on the needs of all the people.[52]

Furthermore, the St. Petersburg committee of the ENG published an appeal in which it announced its intention to start the reform of the Jewish community in St. Petersburg, meaning the reorganization of Jewish welfare, cultural and educational organizations on a democratic basis, and the establishment of a body of lawyers providing the Jewish population of St. Petersburg with juridical help.[53] As is discussed below, the reform of the Jewish organizations meant to democratize ORT and ORPE.

Finally, the ENG published a more general appeal to the Jewish people which clearly stood in the tradition of the Liberals' activity inside the SP. It called upon Russian Jews to continue their political activity, to organize themselves in local ENG branches, discuss all the actual needs of the masses, and finally, announce the results to the envisioned advisory board in order to supply the Jewish deputies with sufficient information. They thereby envisaged the same co-operation between the Jewish representatives inside the Duma, and organized groups outside with connections to the grassroots, which they had already promoted during the First Duma.[54]

### 3.3   THE ENG'S PROGRAMME OF ACTION: MODERNIZATION OF JEWISH LIFE AND THE DEMOCRATIZATION OF ORT AND ORPE

The second phase started with the convocation of the ENG's first congress, which took place in St. Petersburg at the end of February 1907. Here, the Liberals offered a programme which went beyond solely political demands, and at the same time started a new period of Jewish Liberal politics. The programme accepted at the congress reflected a combination of the political demands of the Vilna platform and the newly-developed autonomist view: 'the struggle for our civil, political and national rights, the development of the economic and spiritual forces of Russian Jewry, as well as the organized struggle against anti-Semitism'.[55] On the level of internal reform of the Jewish community, despite the struggle with Zionists – and to a certain extent with the Dubnovtsy – they still aimed at a joint organization of all democratic Jewish elements.

The envisaged modernization of the Jewish community followed the patterns already outlined during the organizational congresses: first, the community administration was to be put on a democratic basis, embracing all elements of the Jewish community; second, the taxation system was to be reformed, by substituting the traditional but obsolete Korobka and Candle taxes with a progressive income tax.[56]

The chief ideologist of the ENG, L.Ya. Shternberg highlighted the main train of thought of the ENG's programme. His report showed two basic points: first, the participation in parliamentary work, through which among others the reform of the Jewish community would receive legal sanction; second, the necessity of self-help independent from the Duma, as a counter-action to the growing anti-Semitism in Russia and nationalism in Poland. In this context, the Liberals' new slogan became 'self-protection'; this was described first as securing the legal grounds for cultural-national rights, including the right to use one's own language in school, and second as putting the community on a secure financial basis, which was to be achieved within the scope of the democratization of local self-government. Within this reform the Jewish community was to be freed from the local Russian administration, and be reorganized on a democratic basis. This way, the Jewish community would become the representative of Jewish society. Self-protection included an economic concept to help those strata of Jewish society which were not yet represented by any party – artisans, petty traders, the 'Lumpenproletariat' and so on. Here, Shternberg argued, since Socialists represented only the workers' interests, and Zionists primarily aimed at emigration, the economic renaissance of Russian Jewry must be pursued through an interaction between the local population – which was to provide us with the exact information about the local economic needs – and the Jewish leadership. In parallel to the economic, the ENG aimed at the spiritual and national rebirth of Russian Jewry through a reorganization of national education on the basis of Jewish national-ethical ideals, and the complete integration of the masses into the general culture.[57]

The central focus of the new programme was the growing economic anti-Semitism in Russia as well as in Poland. The ENG's perception of the new economic anti-Semitism as a serious threat to Jewish life which needed an organized Jewish reaction was also reflected in an article in *Svoboda i Ravenstvo*. The article stressed that the only way to fight this new dimension of anti-Semitism was to organize an economic counter-boycott and to work for an amelioration of the general conditions and competitiveness of the Jewish population. In short, the author, as well as the ENG, now demanded more than propaganda activity: they wanted active counter-action, since to overcome an economic boycott needed more than publishing booklets and information brochures.[58]

The ENG's concept of active 'self-protection' put the lever on the democratization and decentralization of already existing Jewish organizations such as ORPE and ORT. Furthermore, new organizations, such as professional unions and Saving and Loan Co-operatives, were to be founded which were to enable the Jewish traders and artisans, as the bulk of the Jewish work force, to compete with their Russian fellows. Finally, the programme included other Jewish fields such as health service, education, welfare and even some economic demands for the Jewish workers.[59] In short, the ENG's programme focused on the modernization of Jewish life on all possible levels.

The ENG's statute underlined the Liberals' will to base their activity on wide strata of Jewish society, as the condition of membership was kept open, the fee was fixed at sixty kopeks a year, and the ENG was defined as a non-political organization which like the SP aimed at embracing all the various political groups and parties. The organizational structure was very much the same as the SP: the general congress was to set the overall direction, while the Central Committee (fifteen from St. Petersburg and fifteen members from the provinces) in St. Petersburg was to conduct the ENG's general affairs, and the local branches were to run the day-to-day work based on periodical guberniia or regional congresses.[60]

However, despite the fact that the ENG had in principle joined the autonomist camp by drafting this wide-ranging programme, the 'Nationalists' either questioned te legitimacy of the ENG-congress as an all-Jewish congress,[61] or reproached the ENG that it had not produced anything new,[62] but had merely gathered the programmes of other parties,[63] or ridiculed the ENG's plan to pursue its educational programme within the scope of ORPE.[64]

Nevertheless, the ENG went on to realize its programme within the framework set by the concept of 'self-protection'. Within the scope of the ENG's organized struggle against anti-Semitism, the St. Petersburg committee of the ENG decided in its meeting of 28 March 1907 to organize a series of lectures concerning the Jewish question in order to familiarize wide circles of Russian society with the legal and economic situation of the Jews in Russia. Two weeks later a special commission[65] began implementing the decision: Sliozberg delivered the first lecture about the legal situation of the Jews in Russian in the Tenishevskii school in St. Petersburg.[66] On 15 May 1907, M.M. Kovalevskii lectured on 'How the Jewish question had been solved in the West'.[67] By the end of 1907, the Liberals founded a special publishing house called 'Razum' (reason). In the following years various books, brochures and booklets on various aspects of the Jewish question appeared. It served as a means for the Liberals to back up their lobbying for Jewish rights in and outside the Duma.[68]

In pursuit of organizational expansion and in preparation for the regional congresses, the ENG continued to organize meetings and gatherings in various cities of the Pale. Here, they propagated their new programme, and proposed to set up organizations such as a Society for Emigration ('Obshchestvo razseleniia i emigratsii'), a Society for the Promotion of Loan and Co-operatives ('Obshchestvo sodeistviia kreditu i kooperatsii') and so on.[69] At these meetings, the Liberals were able to find wider support, to recruit new members and to set up an organizational framework. ENG branches were founded during meetings in cities such as Belsk (25 members), Yurburg (42), Gomel (250),[70] Keidana (gub. Kovno – 60), Brest-Litovsk (120), Kovno (70), Vidza (gub. Kovno), Surazha,[71] Anan'eva (gub. Kherson), Lukashevki (gub. Kiev),[72] Vilna (45), Perm' (26), and Disna (gub. Vilna). In all these branches a committee had been elected immediately which in turn elected delegates to the ENG Conference of the North-Western region, the next step in the Liberals' efforts to win wider support.[73]

An indication of the ENG's success was given by its opponents who tried to discredit the members of these branches as old-fashioned and undemocratic, as they were not elected by the Jewish people. In practical terms this meant that the ENG won support among the traditional community leaders and the local intelligentsia. For instance, in the context of the foundation of a ENG branch in Moscow, an article was published in *Der Fraind* in which the author claimed that the Liberals were only able to mobilize some rich Jews and *shtadlanim*, whom he did not consider the real representatives of the Jewish people.[74]

Since all the Jewish parties had raised the issue of Jewish Community reform in their programmes, many gatherings of Jewish self-help, welfare or educational organizations were attended by the various parties' representatives. This helps to explain why, despite the ideological struggle, most parties and groups achieved a minimum degree of consensus enabling them to co-operate in 'organic' work. For example, in an article in its organ *Nasha Tribuna* in April 1907, the Bund called on its supporters to participate together with other parties in social work.[75] In this context, a general gathering of the ORPE took place on 9 May 1907 in St. Petersburg in which the ENG was represented with G.B. Sliozberg as the chairman, and the EDG (Bramson) and the ENP (Khoronzhitskii) by some of their leaders. In this gathering the ENG's will to push through parts of its programme, such as the decentralisation of already existing Jewish institutions, met with a reform element within ORPE that already at a general ORPE conference in December 1906, in St. Petersburg had announced a forthcoming reform of the organization.[76] Now ORPE undertook the first steps towards democratization and decentralisation through a change in the framework of the ORPE's activity and in the statutes: first, it was decided to expand ORPE activity to cover education outside schools; second, in a break with the founding purpose of ORPE, the final decision on which language was to be used in the reformed education was left open in order not to endanger co-operation from the beginning; third, the membership fee had been decreased from 10 to 3 roubles in order to attract more members; finally, the leadership of the ORPE had been decentralized from St. Petersburg to the general congresses of the ORPE to which representatives of its fifty-two branches should be elected. The resolutions altogether covered a wide range from the foundation of institutions of Jewish learning, libraries, lectures, courses for Jewish teachers, museums, exhibitions and so on. Finally, it had been decided to collect material concerning the situation of Jewish education, the support of already existing institutions of education and of individual students, and the publication of various works and studies by ORPE.[77]

In the same context, a general ORT gathering took place in St. Petersburg in May 1907 under the chairmanship of the Autonomist Dr. Zalkind. During this gathering, in which B.D. Brutskus (RSO), G.B. Sliozberg (ENG) and I.M. Berger (RSO) outlined the targets and duties of ORT, it had been decided to reorganize the organization. The decision to fix the annual membership fee at 3 roubles proved that the basic point of this democratization was to attract new members, a fact which in turn would widen the basis for the ORT's work among Russian Jews.[78]

Consensus was found among Jewish intellectual circles also with respect to the necessity of setting up new organizations for various other needs of Russian Jews. In this context, the Society for Scientific Jewish Editions (Obshchestvo dlia nauchnykh evreiskikh izdanii) had been founded on 25 March 1907 in St. Petersburg, which planned to edit a Jewish encyclopedia in Russian.[79] In Moscow, the Society for the Dissemination of True Knowledge on the Jews and Judaism (Obshchestvo dlia rasprostraneniia pravil'nykh svedenii o evreiakh i evreistve) was founded whose main target was to fight anti-Semitism by organizing lectures, public meetings, editing scientific analyses on the Jewish question, journals and newspapers.[80]

The ENG continued its efforts to win wider support for its organic work by convening the so-called 'Congress of the ENG for the North-West region', which took place from 18 to 20 May 1907 in Vilna. The Central Committee members Vinaver and Sliozberg participated as well as representatives of various cities from the gubernii Vilna, Kovno, Grodno and Mogilev. On the agenda were issues such as educational work, struggle against anti-Semitism, relations with the SP, question of housing, local activities of the ENG, the amelioration of the situation of Jewish petty traders and the legalisation of the ENG. The decisions taken by the congress showed that the ENG proved able to find further support. The congress called upon the ENG members in the provinces as well as the local communal activists to start with the active struggle against anti-Semitism, and to participate in 'organic' work, by working in all the communal institutions and organizations and connecting them with each other. In practical terms, the congress proposed to reorganize the system collecting the Korobka and the Candle tax by basing it on an elected body, instead of leasing it to private tax-farmers. Also, the congress suggested as another part of organic work the amelioration of the housing situation by either providing new facilities or, at least, the accommodation for the poor.[81]

The ENG called upon its local ENG branches to run organic work independently under the new slogan 'self-protection'. The decision to embrace wide strata of the population was further tribute to the realities of Jewish life, meaning that it was impossible to impose on the various communities a solution which might have been suitable for St. Petersburg but due to the different conditions would have been worthless for other localities. Therefore, the congress proposed to the ENG branches to consult on and elaborate the conditions for setting up loan and credit institutions which could support the Jewish shopkeepers as well as the local population. On this level, the ENG's efforts met with those of another Jewish organization, the EKO, which had already started a large-scale expansion of Saving and Loan Co-operatives; it thus supported this movement both financially,[82] and ideologically, by disseminating brochures in Russian and Yiddish about 'small credit' and statutes for Loan and Credit Co-operatives.[83]

However, as long as the Second Duma still existed and a political solution to the Jewish question seemed within reach, the Liberals also pursued another pattern of the SP, that is to achieve the equality of rights for the Jews, or at least the basic legal grounds needed for the reorganization of the Jewish community within the scope of parliamentary work.

## 3.4 THE JEWISH QUESTION IN THE SECOND DUMA

For various reasons, the Second Duma was less promising for the ENG's political approach than the First Duma. Despite the fact that the Second Duma was dominated by the opposition,[84] the political constellation of this

parliament had changed. With 99 out of 520 deputies, the Kadets – on
which their Jewish members, the ENG, had based their hopes – still remained the strongest party in the parliament, but had lost the commanding
position they possessed in the First Duma. The Second Duma was characterized by a rather balanced representation of the opposition consisting
of Socialists, Liberals, and the right-wing minority.[85]

Due to the experience of the dissolution of the First Duma, and the re-
evaluation of the Duma by the Socialists,[86] the opposition's tactics in the
Duma differed from the one pursued in the First Duma. The entire opposition changed its tactics from an open confrontation with the government
towards a rather cautious approach, which became evident in the opposition's main slogan: 'Preserve the Duma'. This cautious approach in turn
affected the handling of various issues or projected laws. The Kadets as
well as the Socialists preferred not to debate controversial issues such as
the Jewish question openly in the Duma and to deal with them within the
scope of general reform projects or bills such as the 'bill for equality of
rights', the 'bill for freedom of conscience', and the 'bill for the inviolability of the individual'.

The Second Duma comprised only four Jewish deputies representing
three different Jewish groups: the ENG members and Kadets Dr. A.G.
Abramson (gub. Kovno) and the engineer L.G. Rabinovich (gub.
Ekaterinoslav), the Zionist-Kadet Ya.N. Shapiro (Courland), and the Social Democrat Dr. V.E. Mandelberg (Irkutsk).[87] However, the fact that the
KD Duma faction included three other deputies such as O.Ya. Pergament
(Odessa), I.V. Gessen (gub. St. Petersburg) and V.M. Gessen (city of Pet)
who declared their nationality as Jewish, but of Christian faith, strengthened the Jewish representation in this party and raised the Liberals' hopes
that lobbying for the Jews' case could still be promising.[88] Still, the fact
that in the Duma plenum attention was mainly given – as in the First
Duma – to general Russian issues such as unemployment, the desperate
situation of the peasants, martial law and the agrarian question, meant that
the question of the emancipation of the Jews was tackled primarily on the
level of the commissions.[89]

On this level, the Jewish Liberals worked systematically for equal rights.
The Liberals' belief in the possibility of moving towards democratization
in Russia, and with it in working within the framework of Russian party
politics, made work on the prospective bills or laws the main task. For this
purpose, the ENG set up two commissions: one to review all the bills
introduced in the Duma by either the government or the Duma parties, and
a second one for the budget.[90]

When the Kadet faction set up a special Duma commission on 'national and religious equality', consisting of fourteen Kadet deputies with Jewish Kadets A.G. Abramson, I.V. Gessen, V.M. Gessen and O.Ya. Pergament and with representatives of other national minorities among them Moslems, Latvians, Lithuanians the ENG seized the opportunity to lobby on behalf of Jewish interests. The ENG regarded this commission as the centre for Jewish activity in the Duma, in which emancipation would be achieved within the wider scope of civil rights including all the various nationalities living in Russia. Thus, among the non-Duma members invited to participate – such as the former Duma deputies S.A. Kotliarevskii and L.I. Petrazhitskii (both Kadets) – were the ENG leaders, the lawyers M.I. Kulisher and G.B. Sliozberg. Vinaver, the former Jewish deputy, ENG leader and one of the most prominent Kadet leaders, was elected chairman of the commission.[91]

The ENG representatives reported on the legal position of the Jews in order to provide the commission with adequate information. Since in law Jews were only defined as a religious group the commission decided in accordance with the KD Duma faction that the appropriate place to address Jewish equality would be the 'Bill on the freedom of conscience'. The decision to act on the level of this commission, and not in the plenum of the Duma, also had practical reasons: this way the Jewish question would be immediately discussed and solved once and for all, by abolishing all the restrictions which were imposed on members of various religions. Finally, fruitless debates in the Duma could thus be avoided.[92]

That the Kadets had not forgotten the Jewish emancipation is shown also by the fact that the Kadet Duma faction set up a special sub-commission on the Jewish question with the Kadet Teslenko as chairman including the Jewish deputy Abramson. Teslenko was also chosen to report for the Kadets on the Jewish question in the Duma. 'The work on this bill was going so well that if the Duma would have existed two or three weeks more, the Jewish question would have been brought into the plenum of the Duma'.[93] Abramson's report to this commission on Jewish disabilities – for example concerning the right of residence – met with success. After the commission had examined all anti-Jewish restrictions in trade and industry on 21 May 1907, it recommended to abolish all these restrictions.[94]

Further action had been taken by the Jewish deputies Abramson and Rabinovich at the session of the 'commission on the inviolability of the person' on 16 May 1907. Here, they proposed to include the abolition of all restrictions on the right of residence of Jews outside the Pale in the Bill.[95] The issue of equality of rights won wider support when two projects on the abolition of all restrictions regarding political and civil rights in connection with religion and nationality had been brought to the Duma's review: one was signed by 173 members of the opposition, while the second one was signed by 42 members of the SD Duma faction.[96]

However, the attempts by the opposition to get down to the nitty gritty of parliamentary work and to keep the Duma alive failed because of various reasons: first, real parliamentary work and keeping a low profile proved very difficult as the right-wing tried *inter alia* to provoke the dissolution of the Duma throughout its existence by staging incidences; second, the opposition was divided into the Social Revolutionaries, the two Social Democrats (Bolshevik and Menshevik) camps, the Kadets, Trudoviki and the Polish Kolo, which due to the ideological differences made a unified oppositional policy impossible; and finally, when Stolypin realized that he would not be able to pursue his agrarian reforms with this Duma, he pushed for its dissolution and the Tsar dissolved it on 3 June 1907.[97] None of the bills – including the 'Bill on the Freedom of Conscience' or 'Bill on the Inviolability of the Individual' – was ever fully discussed, and Russian Jews as well as the Liberals were left with empty hands, as had been the case after the First Duma's dissolution.

## 3.5  THE ALL-JEWISH NATIONAL ASSEMBLY: ANOTHER LIBERAL-ZIONIST CONTROVERSY

The question of whether to create an all-Jewish organization had moved again into the focus of attention with the opening of the Second Duma. The Zionist press regarded the few Jewish deputies as accidently elected, and their work not as a proper representation of the Jewish people.[98] According to the Zionists only a Jewish Duma group would have been the appropriate representation for the Jewish people. Yet, with only four Jewish deputies, this was now impossible. As they questioned the efficacy of the representation of Jewish interests through Russian parties, the Zionists showed from the beginning a negative attitude towards the Second Duma. The fact that the Second Duma did not openly discuss the Jewish question but dealt with it within the scope of the general projects, intensified the Zionists' dissatisfaction. Therefore, they advanced two proposals which were to guarantee a proper Jewish representation: the election system had to be changed towards a proportional suffrage, which would give the minorities a better chance to promote their candidates; and a Jewish representation outside the Duma had to be created, the all-Jewish national assembly which should take Jewish interests in its own, Jewish hands.

The first demand, the Zionist press declared, could be satisfied within the scope of the 'Bill on a new and democratized suffrage' planned by the

Kadet Duma faction, in which proportional suffrage was to ensure the nationalities an appropriate representation in the parliament. According to the Zionists, this was not guaranteed by universal suffrage as Jews represented neither the relative nor the absolute majority in any of the gubernii. During the entire period of the Second Duma's existence the Zionist press pointed to the importance of this Bill for the nationalities in general, and the Jews in particular.[99]

As proportional suffrage never materialized, the second point, the all-Jewish national assembly, moved into the centre of a Zionist newspaper campaign. Within this context the Zionists rediscovered the SP as a platform which could temporarily serve as a surrogate until the Jewish national assembly would be elected.[100] In fact, Zionist and Liberal interests met in terms of re-activating the SP, at least, in the capacity of an advisory board to the Jewish Duma deputies, and the Central Committee of the SP (dominated by the ENG) set up a special commission for this task.[101] This raised hopes among the Zionists and Autonomists for a general revival of the SP. The reason for the Zionists now to advocate a continuation of the SP was that they did not manage to set up a similar organization of their own. Neither did they have a political lobby in Russian society, such as an allied Russian organization on which they could base their activities, as the Liberals with the Kadets or the Bundists with the RSDRP. Therefore, on 25 March 1907, the St. Petersburg branch of the SP (dominated by the bourgeois Zionist RSO, Dubnov's ENP and Bramson's EDG) organized a special meeting with the Zionist Dr. Zalkind as chairman, which was to discuss the further role of the SP. Against the votes of the ENG representatives the majority of the meeting decided to follow the proposal by M.L. Kreinin, V.R. Idelson and O.O. Gruzenberg to preserve the SP.[102] The meeting finally elected a new committee consisting of representatives of the three parties (RSO, ENP, EDG) such as O.O. Gruzenberg, L.M. Bramson, M.L. Kreinin, V.S. Mandel, S.E. Veisenberg, A.I. Rapoport, A.V. Zalkind, B.D. Brutskus, N.Ya. Lunts, G.Ya. Frumkin, and B.E. Flaks.[103]

The Liberals on the other hand had lost confidence in the SP. They argued that with the appearance of four Jewish parties the SP had lost its *raison d'être* of being an unpolitical umbrella organization. The liberal ENG which still commanded the majority in the SP's Central Committee rejected a revival of the SP as it saw the Zionists' attempts at reviving the SP as an attempt to hijack it for their own political aims.[104] The Zionists in turn attacked the Liberals' unwillingness to revive the SP and called them 'National Assimilationists'.[105]

Nonetheless, a last effort to find a compromise was made in May 1907 by the Central Committee of the SP which convened a meeting of two representatives of each of the four SP parties. But in light of the political differentiation within the SP, a compromise concerning the future of the SP could not be achieved. The Liberals wanted a loose discussion, while Dubnov's ENP and Bramson's EDG wanted to preserve the SP in its previous form. The Zionists' proposal to transform the SP into a nationally-oriented organization whose decisions were to be binding on all the parties, did not win the majority. A compromise became impossible and the Zionists walked out of the SP. The SP, which since the dissolution of the First Duma had only shown some activity at the top level of its St. Petersburg and Vilna branches as well as the Central Committee, ceased to exist.[106] Despite some articles in the Jewish press which tried to keep the idea of the SP and the organization as such alive, the only part of the SP that continued functioning was its Zionist/Nationalist dominated branch in St. Petersburg. A revival of the SP was, however, no longer feasible, and not even some references to the popularity of the SP in the province could prevent its final dissolution.[107]

At the time when the revival of the SP was discussed, the RSO's chief ideologist Zhabotinskii advanced a new concept of a future Jewish representation. Since he rejected a revival of the SP in its old form, he proposed instead to create a neutral centre which was to have two functions: to serve as a proper advisory board to the Jewish Duma deputies, and to become a Jewish national authority. This neutral centre was to be established by a 'congress of Jewish electors' which would win more consensus among the various parties since all the Jewish political parties would be represented in it, and would therefore provide the organization with the authority needed.[108] The Jewish daily *Der Fraind* welcomed the idea, and proposed that due to the desperate state of the Jews' economic situation, this body could also elaborate a plan on internal Jewish reform regarding Jewish education and the creation of the necessary institutions and organizations.[109] In light of the dissolution of the Second Duma, and Stolypin's *coup d'état* of 3 June 1907 – he had changed the electoral law to favour the conservative forces in the country, the landowners, the orthodox clergy and Russians – this theory gained in importance as all the Jewish parties and groups were once again confronted with the issue of Jewish representation. The low expectations regarding the forthcoming elections to the Third Duma and its anticipated right-wing constellation, as well as the failure to revive the SP as an all-Jewish organization, made Zhabotinskii's proposal of a representative organization outside the Duma, such as the congress of electors, worth considering. Consequently, the four Jewish parties, the Zionists, ENP, EDG, and ENG, organized a meeting in order to discuss the ways and conditions to set up such a congress.[110] During this meeting, however – which took place in November, 1907 – the differences between Zionists and ENG imperilled the venture from the beginning. The majority of the meeting reached a compromise by accepting the ENG's view regarding the future organization of the congress of electors: first, instead of all, only half of the electors of all the three elections were to be elected to the congress; second, the future all-Jewish organization was to take over a wide range of responsibilities in line with the ENG's programme of 'self-protection';[111] third, an organization committee consisting of two representatives of each of the four parties as well as six neutrals was to be set up. However, a final agreement among all the four parties was not reached as the Zionists hesitated to agree to these decisions, and made their participation dependent on the approval of their Central Committee.[112] Therefore, this project, which had been brought up by the Zionists themselves, reached an impasse due to their uncompromising stand, and never materialized.

## 3.6 THE ELECTIONS TO THE THIRD STATE DUMA AND THE FINAL SHIFT TOWARDS 'ORGANIC WORK'

The election campaign was considered worthwhile in terms of politicising the Jewish masses and propagating political ideas. Despite the fact that the Jewish political parties did not expect anything from the elections, and that Russian Socialists heatedly debated a boycott,[113] all of them decided to participate. In fact, for many parties such as the Socialists – being illegal – an election campaign was the only opportunity to propagate their ideas openly.[114]

Stolypin's *coup d'état* did not change the Liberals' appreciation of the political value of the next elections. Therefore, at their congress in St. Petersburg on 13 June 1907 which enjoyed considerable provincial participation, the ENG decided to take part in the elections, thus continuing a policy adopted in the first two elections.[115]

All the Jewish political parties agreed that with the new electoral law a right-wing, conservative Duma would emerge.[116] Consequently, after the political mobilization and education of the Jewish public, the main target was to 'limit the damage', that is the number of ultra-right and conservative Russian deputies. The tactics of each Jewish party was dominated by the will to fight tooth and nail against reactionary candidates. This was very difficult as Stolypin had weighed voters in such a way that workers lost most of their influence on the elections, and the peasant share in electors was also limited considerably in favour of the landowners. The number of cities which elected their deputies directly to the Duma was reduced from 25 to 7.[117] The city curiae were divided in two, the first of which – with the richer townspeople – commanded a greater influence.[118] Finally, on the first level of the elections, the election of electors, the voters were separated according to their respective nationalities in order to favour the Russian voter.[119] In short, Stolypin had designed the electoral law to achieve a conservative Duma which would be more willing to co-operate with the government, in particular with respect to the Agrarian Reform.[120]

As a consequence of the worsening political situation and the increasing repressions and persecutions,[121] first signs of a general shift among Jewish religious elements towards 'organic work', implying inter alia, reform of the Jewish Community, were emerging.[122] However, in the political arena of the election campaign, that is on the ideological level of Jewish politics, the 'Nationalist' – 'Integrationist' dispute resurfaced on the local 'battlefield' in St. Petersburg. In its tenth circular the RSO announced the Zionists' participation in the elections along the lines of Helsingfors, by running the elections under their own flag.[123] The RSO also repeated its demand for a Jewish-national parliamentary group,[124] while the Bundists and the Liberals (ENG) fought again shoulder to shoulder against such a plan.[125] This brought a repetition of attacks in the Zionist press against the Liberals as enemies of national autonomy or of a Jewish territory.[126]

The conflict between Liberals and Zionists broke out in St. Petersburg when the local branch of the SP consisting of RSO, EDG and non-party-affiliated Jews decided to run the election campaign to the Third Duma along Zionist lines; for example it changed its tactics from pursuing a coalition with non-Jewish parties to swinging the Jewish vote behind individual candidates sympathetic towards Jewish demands. To this end, it sent representatives such as S.E. Veisenberg, M.N. Kreinin, Khoronzhitskii to various Duma candidates such as Count I.I. Tolstoi (non-party-affiliated), Miliukov, Koliubakin and Ushakov (all Kadets) to hear from them about their proposals for a solution to the Jewish question.[127] The interview with Miliukov provoked a controversy between Zionists and ENG, as the SP representatives accused the KDs of not having raised the Jewish question in the first two Dumas, and criticized some of their leaders, such as Struve and Shchepkin, for their assimilationist views. They maintained that as a consequence of these policies, the Jewish voters had lost confidence in the Kadets.[128] This 'interference' in liberal 'business' provoked a strong reaction from Vinaver, the ENG leader. He described the interviews as being tantamount 'to letting the KD candidates take their political exams' despite the fact that 'everybody knows their favourable stand towards the Jewish question and the right for cultural self-determination'.[129] He also wrote a letter to the KD leader Miliukov to assure him that those who interviewed him were not the leaders of the Jewish people, and expressed his confidence in the KDs and their programme.[130] Furthermore, the ENG addressed an appeal to the Jewish voters in St. Petersburg, in which it condemned the interviews by the local SP branch, and called upon Jewish voters to vote for the opposition candidates. In this appeal the ENG announced that it would set up an election committee to organize and mobilize the Jewish vote, which was realized a couple of days later.[131] Finally, the ENG organized a meeting of Jewish voters in St. Petersburg on 7 October 1907, in which Sliozberg condemned the interview action. At the same time, he assured the Kadets of the loyalty of the Jewish voters, and gave the KD candidate the opportunity to defend the Kadets' Duma tactics. Here, Koliubakin assured the public that the Kadets' tactics were only adjusted to the present political situation, and would change when the times changed. His statement did not, however, convince the Nationalists – for instance G. Landau (EDG), and the Duma candidate, the Russian lawyer A. Zarudnii – who held the Kadets responsible for the fact that the Jewish question as such was not raised in the two Dumas; they therefore argued that the Jews should vote for the left-wing parties. Finally, the Nationalist M. Kreinin defended the SP action, and stated that the ENG did not have the monopoly of running politics.[132] Afterwards the Zionist press and *Der Fraind* attacked the ENG's and Vinaver's unconditional support for the Kadets[133] and the fact that the St. Petersburg election committee was not elected; it was therefore considered as undemocratic as the entire Liberal organization which – the Autonomist Kreinin maintained – was only a place for Gevirim and had no support in the provinces.[134]

As was to be expected, despite the efforts of all opposition parties, Jewish or not, a right-wing Third Duma could not be prevented. This was due to several reasons: first and foremost, the electoral law weighing votes; second, the repressions and machinations by the administration had reached their peak; third, the new election had inter alia discouraged Jews to exercise their right to vote[135] – especially since the voters were arbitrarily separated into national curiae by the administration – quite often due to the machinations of local reactionary elements and the anti-Semitic 'Union of the Russian People' (Soiuz Russkago Naroda – SRN).[136]

The Zionists' approach of running politics independently had failed once more. The two Jewish deputies who had been elected to the Third Duma, Niselovich and Fridman, were both Kadets and had co-operated with the ENG. Furthermore, the Russian senate declared all Zionist organizations illegal as they 'call on the Jewish people to fight actively against the general conditions of life which had been set by law. This would create a hostile relation to the local native population'.[137]

Furthermore, the pre-conference of the Russian Zionists gathering for the general conference of Zionists in the Hague showed that the decision of the Helsingfors programme to run politics under their own flag had become controversial. Prominent former supporters of this decision, such as Dr. Pasmanik, Klauzner, Dr. Brutskus, Leo Motskin, B. Goldberg, as well as the former Zionist Duma deputies Sh. Levin, Yakubson, Rozenbaum, Dr. Katsenelson and Dr. Bruk now rejected it. Dr. Pasmanik and Motskin argued that as during the Second Duma elections Zionists would always be forced to compromise and that Zionist politics could therefore not be pursued to their full potential. Brutskus and others considered Zionism not yet strong enough to act independently; Yakubson even accepted the ENG's argument that the Zionists would isolate themselves. The 'go it alone' camp with its main protagonist Zhabotinskii, the well-known Zionist leaders N. Syrkin and Ussishkin, and delegates Grinberg and Galenki, could no longer command a majority; the main point of the Helsingfors programme – making the RSO an independent political party – lost majority support; from then on, Zionist politics concentrated primarily on Palestine.[138]

Inter-Jewish conflicts during the last election campaign saw only losers. The Zionists managed to send only one candidate to the Second Duma, and were declared illegal. The Liberals' efforts to achieve legal emancipation through the Duma had failed once again. The Bund entered a deep crisis facing persecution by a reinvigorated government to the extent that most members were forced to quit political activity, to emigrate or to engage in the field of non-political, cultural and organic work. The majority of the Bund leaders such as Leib Blekhman, Vladimir Medem, Arkady Kremer, Mark Liber and Bronislaw Grosser chose by 1908–09 the first two options. As a consequence of this crisis, the membership of, for instance, the Bund (1906 – 33,890), and the Poalei Zion (1906 – 25,000) dropped drastically in 1908 to 800 and 300 members respectively. The other Socialist-Zionist organizations such as SERP and SS were dissolved, and their more energetic members joined organic work.[139] Although the political enthusiasm of the First and the Second Duma periods was severely dampened,[140] broad segments of the Jewish population displayed a great energy in creating and participating in the new cultural, economic and educational organizations. The absence of political leadership was substituted by self-initiative on the community level. The Liberals' new approach met with a new determination among wider strata of the Jewish population to help oneself and get organized and was also matched by a strategic re-orientation by the other Jewish political parties such as the Bund, RSO, EDG and ENP.[141]

With the opening of the Third Duma in November 1907, a new era of Russian-Jewish politics began. Since purely political work was no longer promising, or simply impossible, members of all Jewish parties turned to the new field of activity: organic work. The Duma still received attention but the main focus was now on reorganization and modernization of Jewish community structures, on self-help, welfare and cultural activities. The ideological struggle between the various Jewish political parties was substituted by cooperation on the level of the organizations and institutions of an emerging Jewish society in Russia.[142]

# 4 Jewish Liberal Politics from 1908 to 1911: Reorganization, Determination and the Beginning of 'Organic Work'

As Stolypin's *coup d'état* had finally crushed hopes based on the Duma, that now consisted largely of aristocrats, landowners and clerics, the only solution was to rely on internal forces and abilities. In short, Russian-Jewish social and political activists affected the same shift towards internal politics as the Poles in Prussian Germany, and the Czechs in the Habsburg Empire.[1] This position was taken up by all Jewish political leaders. Following the Jewish Liberals' slogan of 'self-protection', coined in the ENG's platform of 1907, all the Jewish political parties started to co-operate on the level of organic work from 1908 to 1914. Within these six years, two periods determined by the political situation can be distinguished: the first phase of organic work, that is the Stolypin years, from 1907–08 until his assassination in 1911, and the second phase from 1911 to 1914. This chapter will deal with the first period which witnessed the reorientation of most Jewish political activists to organic work. Over the catchwords of the nineteenth century, the modernization and secularization of Russian-Jewish life, the 'old battle' between 'reformers' – all the Jewish political middle-class intellectuals including Zionists and Bundists – and 'conservative elements' – consisting mainly of Hasidic rabbis and *melameds* of the traditional Heder – was rejoined. While the former pushed for modernization and secularization by setting up cultural, economic and educational organizations,[2] most representatives of the latter fought both, as they felt threatened by this dual process.

During this period, Jewish Liberals played a major role in shaping organic work. In fact, most of the efforts of organic work were initiated by, or at least greatly influenced by, Jewish Liberal and Autonomist thoughts. On the cultural and educational level, the Autonomists Dubnov and Kreinin co-operated with Vinaver and Sliozberg. In the economic and social field, Liberal thoughts met with the will of the left-wing – among others Bramson – to democratize Jewish organizations, such as ORT and ORPE, and by democratizing and decentralizing them to put organic work on a broader basis.

## 4.1 BACK TO THE ROOTS: JEWISH HISTORY AND SELF-INITIATIVE AT THE GRASSROOTS AND THE ADVENT OF ORGANIZED ORTHODOX RESISTANCE

Due to the positive results of the years preceding the Revolution of 1905, the first steps of the Jewish middle class activists of all colours within organic work were characterized by a certain concentration on the field of Jewish scholarship and secondary or higher education. The trend towards co-operation among the former 'opponents' became evident as early as January 1908, when a group of activists of different political backgrounds – including Baron David G. Gintsburg, the ENG members M.I. Kulisher and G.B. Sliozberg, as well as the founder of the ENP, Simon Dubnov – organized Jewish Higher Education Courses for Oriental Studies in St. Petersburg.[3] Dubnov's and Sliozberg's statements indicated that co-operation in this field reflected the common interest of these circles to entrench Jewish national conscienceness among the young, and at the same time, to found bodies and institutions of Jewish scholarship and historiography. Sliozberg described the primary target as 'preserving Jewish cultural and historical heritage in order to maintain it for the young and a better future', while Dubnov regarded the courses as the first step towards a scholarly Jewish historiography; as he put it, 'these courses are to deepen and strengthen Jewish scholarship which will have a great effect on the self-consciousness of the people'.[4] Both regarded them as part and parcel of the envisaged self-help and self-protection on the level of higher education. Thereby, the Jewish youth could be given a chance to get higher education (self-help), and at the same time, would be taught in the past and their cultural and historical roots, that is their Jewishness (self-protection). As Sliozberg put it:

> Therefore, it was about time to open such courses which are to give the possibility to create and develop the Jewish ideals which lay in our past. This will bring us great benefits in the future, and above all wealth.[5]

These courses, eventually attended by many Jewish students, served as a substitute for university education for many Jewish would-be students. True, they never went beyond the limits given to a private institution located in St. Petersburg. Nonetheless, at the very least, the courses served as an experiment and represented the forerunner of the wider plan to set up a Jewish university – an idea which became the focus of the educational part of organic work after 1911, when the government took an extremely repressive course. Soon, however, the courses of higher education became a source of controversy, spurred by Dubnov's increasing dissatisfaction with the programme; Dubnov accused the sponsor of these courses, Baron David Gintsburg, of dilettantism, as he supposedly did not take this venture seriously but rather regarded it as a private hobby to give his interest in Jewish scholarship the frame of a discussion group.[6] The Jewish middle class activists realised that the only way to achieve any significant changes would be to leave the mere walls of Gintsburg's salon, and foster the values of Jewishness through nationwide Jewish organizations. This approach materialized shortly after the release from prison of former Jewish Duma deputies such as Vinaver, Bramson, G.Ya. Bruk, Sheftel, Dr. Katsenelson and M. Rozenbaum – who as signatories of the Vyborg Appeal were sentenced to three months imprisonment[7] – between August and October 1908.[8] Three months after Vinaver's release, Liberals and Autonomists (Dubnov) put the cultural and historical part of organic work on a firm basis, and gave it a wider framework by founding the Jewish Historiographic Society (Evreiskoe Istoricheskii Obshchestvo) and the Jewish Literary Society (Evreiskoe Literaturnoe Obshchestvo).[9] The first congress of the EIO which took place in St. Petersburg on 16 November 1908 confirmed the major trend towards co-operation. Like all the other Jewish organizations of that time, EIO membership not only included all the major Liberal figures such as Vinaver, Kulisher, Gornfeld, M.B. Syrkin, M.L. Trivus and L.Ya Shternberg – all of whom were elected in the organization's Committee – but represented a conglomeration of Jewish intelligentsia such as A.I. Braudo, M.L. Vishnitser, I.I. Gessen, S.M. Goldshtein, the ENP leader S.M. Dubnov, and L.L. Sev.[10] Of course, co-operation did not preclude conflict, due to the different concepts of how a historical-scientific organ should be run, or stemming from different political views. It was not surprising that the first organs set up, the monthly *Evreiskii Mir* as well as the *Perezhitoe*, in both of which all big names initially participated, soon faced internal conflicts. In the case of *EM*, co-operation became impossible as the Zionists reproached the editorial board, namely Vinaver, for anti-Zionist tendencies, and Dubnov criticised the fact that *EM* did not pay enough attention to Polish and Russian-Jewish history and ethnography. This caused Dubnov, Vinaver and their ilk to quit the co-operation, and to set up their own historical weekly *Evreiskaia Starina*.[11]

The differentiation of political opinion had by 1910 led to the fact that the common interest in Jewish history and science was represented by two press organs. Still, both journals aimed at fulfilling the intentions of virtually all Jewish intellectuals to raise the prestige of Jewish history, culture and values. The same applied to the new organizations ELO and EIO founded by 'Autonomists' and Liberals. Both organizations did not reflect the pressing short-term economic, social or political needs of the day but more long-term concerns of self-preservation and ethnic or national identity. They also were an expression of the common interest among the Jewish intelligentsia to develop, similar to the efforts of German-Jewish activists in the nineteenth century, the 'Wissenschaft des deutschen Judentums', a serious scholarship of Russian Jewry.[12]

The difference between EIO and ELO lay in the fact that the former was a rather centralized scholarly organization in which the St. Petersburg activists played the major role, while the latter was based on loose discussion groups all over the Pale that attested to an increasing interest in a modernized version of Jewish culture in general and in Jewish literature in particular. The ELO gained considerably in popular support in its three years of existence from 1908 to 1911. An indication of this was given by *Razsvet*, which reported constantly on the foundation of new branches in the provinces; already after half a year of existence, the ELO had received requests to set up branches from more than ninety places.[13] Despite this great success, however, the ELO was confronted with the problem of how to organize, co-ordinate, and above all, to finance its activities. Therefore, when the ELO leaders drew a first resumé of the organization's activities at an ELO meeting on 15 November 1909, they valued that the organisation had already forty branches in the provinces with seven hundred members from various strata of Jewish society. However, they criticised the lack of adequate financial means due to which ELO was not able to go beyond organizing lectures, and fulfil the other tasks such as publication of books and support of Jewish writers. Furthermore, the Revision Commission criticized the inactivity in raising funds. Despite the fact that the Central Committee member, the Autonomist M.N. Kreinin, was able to dismiss the reproaches,[14] it foreshadowed the conflict between a Central Committee largely based on St. Petersburg members, and the new members in the provinces who were setting up local branches of all Jewish social organizations; a conflict with the grassroots activists out for more independence, who refused to bow to traditional St. Petersburg leadership. Financial problems, as it turned out, did not endanger the development of the ELO, as its branches acted on the basis of their own finances. As will be discussed below, however, the financial issue became a serious problem in organizations where finances granted real power such as ORT and ORPE; especially when the Bundists and Zionists began to reorganize themselves in these institutions for the purpose of imposing their ideas on them.

The conflicts and internal problems of the various Jewish organizations should not, however, be overestimated. Russian-Jewish society tried to reach for new shores. The rise of a whole new range of initiatives and organizations attests to this fact. The task of moulding and modernizing Jewish society on all its levels found more and more local support; the ENP leader Kreinin described the mood of the moment in an article in *Der Fraind*, claiming that belief in political work was substituted by a wide range of initiatives from below and activity among Russian Jews.

> . . . One has started to take care of [Jewish] national education in places as far away as Astrakhan, Tsaritsyn, Voronezh, Kursk and so on. People organize schools, libraries, and there are people everywhere who become concerned about the people's needs . . .[15]

Without going into details, it may suffice to mention some of the many new local cultural and educational organizations or initiatives to highlight a general trend: a society for the support of Jewish teachers and *Melameds* of the city of Kiev was set up ('Obshchestvo vspomoshchestvovaniia evreiskim uchiteliam i melamedam g. Kieva i cherty evreiskoi osedlosti') and legalized in September 1908;[16] the Society for the dissemination of reading and writing among the Jews in Riga ('Obshchestvo rasprostraneniia gramotnosti sredi evreev g. Rigi') was founded as early as February 1908;[17] the Society for Literature and Art ('Literaturno-artisticheskoe obshchestvo') in Minsk in March 1908; a society of Jewish art, called Betsalel and the Society for Jewish folklore music ('Obshchestvo evreiskoi narodnoi muzyki'), both founded in St. Petersburg in June 1908.[18]

In contrast to Jewish organizations in the nineteenth century, these cultural organizations aimed at raising Jewish national consciousness, popularizing a secular Yiddish and Hebrew culture and literature, and at the introduction of general and secular subjects into the syllabus of any Jewish educational institution, be it primary, secondary or higher education. They thereby interacted with and supported the efforts of major Jewish public figures to strengthen not only Jewish culture and to develop a historical consciousness, but they represented the social base for major social change. Thus, due to the Russian Jews' hunger for education and their growing wish to break the mental boundaries of the ghetto, the Jewish intelligentsia and the middle-class leadership found the support their predecessors, the maskilim, had sought in vain, in order to achieve the modernization of Russian Jewry. Influence was not a one-way road. A certain interaction took place between the grassroots, the demands of the various new Jewish political groups, and the traditional leadership circles in St. Petersburg. This became especially evident in the two most important fields of organic work: educational and economic reform, being the two fields in which Jewish liberal politics concentrated its efforts, as is discussed below.

The modernization process reopened an old front which became typical for the period of organic work: the struggle over the separation of 'church and state', that is the secularization of Jewish society, the common aim of the Jewish intelligentsia activists. This provoked the reaction of the religious elements which since 1908 started to organize themselves in order to defend the religious basis of the Jewish community and their positions in it. The appearance of an organized conservative movement was helped along by the Ministry of Interior's announcement – in its circular no. 83 – to convoke a Rabbi Congress either by the end of 1908 or beginning of 1909.[19] Preparations for this commission quickly gathered full speed. Rabbis everywhere discussed the issues of the forthcoming Rabbi Commission, for instance, in Kiev, Kherson, Ekaterinoslav, Vilna and Minsk.[20]

At around the same time, the conservative elements moved beyond mere gatherings by giving themselves an organizational framework in the 'Kneset Isroel', registered in April, 1908, and the 'Tiferes Bokhurim' – both establishing headquarters in Vilna. Both organizations proclaimed the same anti-reformist stand: to preserve the traditional values of Judaism. The statutes of the KI stated as its main target the fight against educational secularization which since about 1902 had become evident in the appearance of Yiddish secular schools and the reformed 'Metukan Heders'.[21] Both school types aimed at modernizing Jewish education by giving secular subjects priority over religious ones. The KI planned to set up Jewish primary schools for poor children 'according to the rules of God', to set up reformed Talmud Torah and Yeshivoth, as well as orphanages, evening and Sunday schools for adults.[22] The Tiferes Bokhurim headed in the same direction, that is the education of the young in accordance with the spirit of religion. This organization addressed an appeal to Jewish society in which it mentioned the poor moral education of the Jewish workers and shop assistants as the main reason and basis for the desperate situation of the Jews. Finally, it asked for support for the evening school for adults, clerks and workers, which had been founded by the Tiferes Bokhurim in order to instruct the latter in the basics of the Jewish religion.[23] While the TB remained limited to Vilna, the KI gained wider support mainly in the small towns of the Pale. Branches were founded in Slutsk (Gub. Minsk), Talsen (Courland), Miastkovo, Kossovo (Gub. Grodno), Raduno and Ivo (Gub. Vilna).[24] A petition by the St. Petersburg Hasidim to the minister of interior, asking for permission to set up their own Hasidic community, illustrates that even the ultra-conservative religious elements tried to expand to the bigger, more secularized Jewish communities.[25]

Surely enough the appearance of the religious elements was attacked by secular 'reformers' as a threat to a successful modernization of Jewish society. For instance, the Zionist A. Davidson called the Kneset Isroel a 'politically reactionary organization whose only aim is to get the power over the Jewish people out of the hands of the government in order to fight sedition (kramola)'. The KI's programme confirms Davidson's judgement, as the rabbis claimed the right to prosecute legally any insult towards Jewish religion, orally or written, the right to confiscate brochures and books which could cause damage to the morality and traditional forms of Jewish religion as well as to punish their authors and editors. This would have affected almost any publication by the reform-minded Jewish intelligentsia.[26] However, Davidson's criticism of the rabbis should be regarded with caution as it was part of the ideological struggle between secular and religious elements, in which certain codewords substituted for reality. Moreover, Davidson did not reflect on the conflict among the religious elements themselves, which were split in three: the reform-minded orthodox rabbis (the reform rabbis), the orthodox, and anti-reformist ultra-orthodox (the Hasidim). While the KI's programme was certainly an expression of conservative thinking, a gathering of twenty communal and state rabbis of Volynia province in Zhitomir reflected the awareness of their opponents, the reform rabbis, to the problems facing Jewish community life. Instead of opposing reforms in principle, these rabbis discussed issues such as the reorganization of Jewish community structures, taxation as well as the syllabus of the traditional Jewish and vocational schools. These issues came very much into the focus of the intelligentsia's reform plan.[27]

## 4.2 THE ECONOMIC CONFERENCE OF 1908: THE ARTISAN AS THE BASIS FOR SOCIAL CHANGE

The Liberals were, of course, well aware of the fact that spiritual regeneration alone was not enough and could not satisfy people in dire poverty. Furthermore, the ideological struggles had to be overcome as the Jewish masses needed above all practical, fast and efficient help. In fact, the call for reform by the reformers and the intelligentsia received wide acceptance from the grassroots. For one, if the report of *Razsvet* of March 1908 can be taken as symptomatic, provincial Jewish activists and leaders had started independently with the modernization and re-organization of Jewish community structures by setting up revision commissions and community councils in order to improve the financial situation of the community and to form a representation of the community. Such cases were reported from Rostov/Don,[28] Vitebsk, Odessa, Simferopol, and Ekaterinoslav.[29]

Second, and even more important for communal restructuring, the call for self-help was taken up in the communities by the Jewish traders and artisans who increasingly joined the Saving and Loan Co-operatives. These organisations became extremely important, if not essential, for the reform process as they provided especially Jewish artisans with the financial means to modernize their workshops and survive economic competition. Originally, these institutions of small credit started off on a local basis in many Jewish communities since the mid-nineteenth century. The first credit organizations, known as the 'kassy', were, however, limited in scope, gave only occasional support and the creditees usually took loans in order to cover the needs of everyday life. Moreover, they were rather short-lived as they depended on locally raised money, and legislation proved difficult. They reached, however, wider dimensions when the Russian government introduced a new model-statute for co-operatives in 1897. The new statute made it easier to establish co-operatives as they only needed the approval of the Ministry of Finance, and no longer that of the Ministry of Interior, which had been traditionally hostile towards any Jewish activities. Finally, in 1904 the Ministry of Finance completely liberalized the law. These credit co-operatives became totally independent from the Korobka tax, and thus free from outside interference by either local authorities or orthodox elements of Jewish society. After 1905, the Jewish intelligentsia discovered them as a new field of activity and organisations such as the EKO and ORT started regular attempts to establish and propagate Loan and Saving Co-operatives. Furthermore, since these organizations played an important role in the 'nationalities' struggle' at that time – for instance among the Poles in German-Poland[30] – and were encouraged by the government, the state bank and the Zemstva, from around 1907 the co-operative movement in Russia enjoyed a general upswing. All over Russia Saving and Loan Associations, Credit Co-operatives, Consumer Co-operatives, and societies for mutual credit mushroomed.[31]

Jewish Saving and Loan Associations now started to appear in almost all cities and towns. Carried by the local intelligentsia, these co-operatives operated with contributions from their members. They attracted wider strata of Jewish society as the minimum sum of 10 roubles to be deposited was deliberately kept small, and loans could be covered as non-Jews and the intelligentsia used these institutions as a bank to deposit their savings. The statistics which were provided by EKO for 1909 indicate that the system worked so well that more than 90 per cent of the credits granted were paid back within the same year. This meant that these Loan and Credit Associations stabilized themselves, and the basis for a loan system had been established by 1909.[32] Therefore, these institutions could easily form the backbone of organic work.

Naturally, both the reform activities in the communities and the Loan and Saving Associations still lacked organization and above all coordination. As this needed a united effort of all the Jewish groups, the ENG leaders Vinaver and Sliozberg convoked an 'Economic Conference' in St. Petersburg on 8–9 March 1908. The conference was to serve 'as a preparatory session for the larger task of moving ahead with communal restructuring in order to stabilize the community',[33] as a forum to discuss various possibilities for economic reform, and as a tool to unite various groups of Jewish society for organic work. Seventy people were invited to this gathering, 38 ENG members, one Zionist, two EDG, five non-party-affiliated participants, ten delegates from Moscow, two from Vologda, one from Tula and eleven from the Pale of Settlement. Even if none of the participants explicitly put it in these terms, reform efforts had to begin with the artisans 'because of their peculiar preoccupation with 'productiveness': the artisans were the only Jewish element in economic life that had strong roots in the sphere of production'.[34] Therefore, Vinaver suggested to improve the artisans' economic situation by setting up a 'joint-stock company' which was to take over the regulation of economic life of the Jewish artisans in the Pale; as M.I. Kulisher put it, it was to provide Jewish artisans with cheap tools and raw material, as well as to sell and distribute the goods.[35] The discussions which followed the opening speeches produced a kaleidoscope of options on the means to realize the envisaged aims. For instance, Bramson promoted 'internal migration' – the resettling of Jewish artisans outside the Pale – as a solution. This proposal received much attention but proved not applicable under Russian realities. In the end, the envisaged marketing organization was approved by the majority, and thus, the first and very basic step for economic reform was taken. A commission was formed to work out the statutes and collect funds. The conference also demanded to look into means of how public opinion could control the work of the marketing organization. In addition a technical information bureau was created.[36]

In spite of the growth of many-sided undertakings – for instance, the opening of the first 'Commercial school' in Kherson on 1 September 1908, as well as the foundation of many Labour organizations, such as the Vilna Society of Labour Aid ('Vilenskoe obshchestvo trudovoi pomoshchi') in

Vilna[37] – Jewish Liberals realized that the modernization process could only succeed if a multifaceted approach was attempted. Here, economic and educational reform became interlinked. In fact, one lever was found in vocational training for artisans who at that time almost all lacked proper training, since a system of apprenticeship did not exist. In light of this situation a joint effort with ORT was made in December 1908, to pressure for reforms in vocational training. To this end, ORT organized a congress of the administrators of the Jewish artisan schools in Vilna under the chairmanship of G.B. Sliozberg, who described the new approach of Jewish Liberal Politics as a multiple one which would still aim at the ultimate target of achieving legal emancipation, but in light of the social anti-Semitism would give priority to measures against the anti-Jewish economic boycott. Since Jews were still required to live within the Pale of Settlement, the only things to be done were to improve the quality of the work of Jewish artisans, and to organize the sale of products all over Russia. For the first, schools for Jewish artisans were necessary.[38] The congress spent considerable time debating the causes for the small numbers of enrolment, and on finding the means to change this. Katsenelbogen (Kherson) and Kaletskii (Belostok) insisted that a solution ought to be applicable to the difficult social and economic conditions of the Jewish artisans. Therefore, in order to attract more young Jews to the artisan schools, education for Jewish apprentices had to be improved so that they could pass the educational census required to enter artisan schools, the hours of teaching to be reduced, the apprentices to be provided with clothes and a basic salary, and finally jobs to be found for the graduates. Only these changes could prevent them from dropping out. After rather short discussions the congress almost unanimously suggested the following measures: the census was to be solved by introducing preliminary courses for general education at the artisans' schools, and by engaging Jewish teachers from other institutions for these courses; societies supporting the students financially were to be set up at the schools. To propagate the idea of these schools, parents' gatherings were suggested, through which the parents could familiarize themselves with the schools and thus become convinced of the advantages of vocational training for the young. Finally, a special bureau was to be set up to provide graduates of vocational schools with jobs inside and outside the Pale.[39] The congress also wanted the quality of work to be enhanced by encouraging the artisans to join the evening courses for Jewish artisans which already existed in Odessa, Mogilev, Warsaw, Vilna and other places.[40] The link between economic and educational reform was emphasized by the congress' recommendation that in all these courses artisans should receive general education as well as technical training. In short, they envisaged a modern type of Jewish artisan who combined technical skills with a general education which would enable him to compete successfully in a modernizing Russian economy. With respect to the controversial question, which language was to be used, the congress' majority voted for the formula advocated by Liberals and Autonomists, not to exclude or to give priority to any of the languages (Russian, Polish, Yiddish, Hebrew). The language used would be the language spoken by the majority of the students.[41]

The Economic Conference and the congress of the administrators of the artisans' schools had laid important foundations for modernizing Jewish economic life. Moreover, by focusing on the Jewish artisan the intelligentsia looked for a partnership with the stratum within Jewish society which was most desperate, and therefore most willing to cooperate. To this end, plans were made for reforming the education and training for both apprentices as well as Jewish artisans. The idea of setting up a marketing organization for Jewish artisans' products met with wide support. The marketing organization materialized a year later when the trade-industrial society 'TRUD' became legalized. In the first paragraph of its statute, it stated as its tasks 'to provide artisan and industrial institutions with equipment, to organize the purchase and sale of artisan machines, material, tools and products, respectively'. The founders justified the new organization with the argument that although the Bund had done much to increase the artisans' conscienceness within its trade unionist struggle, it had taken neither steps towards improving the Jewish artisans' skills, nor their technical equipment and thus did not contribute to a fundamental improvement of their economic situation.[42]

However, it became quite obvious that all these reform plans could only be implemented once wide strata of Jewish society would be induced to co-operate. The nationwide framework of Jewish organizations such as ORT and ORPE seemed singularly suited to attract more and more people interested in reform. For this, their organizational structure had to be democratized and their approach widened. From this background, the EDG leader and Trudovik Bramson started his attacks on the structures and the approach of ORT and ORPE. He focused especially on what he saw as their merely charitable function, which for him as a left-wing activist, as well as for the Liberals was an intolerable situation. During an ORT meeting on 30 March 1908, he first raised his voice for an expansion and systematization of ORT activity in a democratic and unbureaucratic way in order to affect structural changes that should enable Jewish artisans to maintain their position in spite of rapid industrialization. The Central Committee member Sliozberg, while not denying Bramson's points in principle, was able to convince the majority that the latter's attacks betrayed an untimely impatience. He blamed the supposed indifference among Jewish society towards ORT on the fact that organic work on a nationwide basis had just started, and consequently could not yet have reached the masses to the degree desired.[43] However, a month later, at ORT's next meeting, Bramson's demands for action finally won a majority. Furthermore, the meeting's final resolutions illustrated the impact of the two conferences mentioned above on ORT decision-making: five committees were set up to activate and regularize organic work. One committee was to inquire into various questions of vocational education, one to examine the economic situation of the Jewish artisans and workers, one for the Saving and Loan Co-operatives, another one to settle Jews outside the Pale and find employment for them, and finally a committee charged with improving ORT's financial situation.[44] At its next general meeting, ORT paid its tribute to the increasing amount of Saving and Loan Co-operatives by deciding to organize a congress of the Co-operatives in order to co-ordinate the activities, to publicize these institutions by editing a special newspaper, to re-organize the artisans' schools, to start an inquiry into economic questions in the Pale etc.[45] At the next congresses in March, April and May 1909 the disputes surfaced again. The question was whether ORT should pursue its aid programme in a charitable way, by giving aid to single persons or organizations, or undertake a systematic approach. The Committee members Sliozberg and Ya.M. Galperin stood for the first approach and the 'opposition' – or, as Shapiro called them 'Young Turks' – consisting of Bolotin, Bramson and B.D. Brutskus supported the latter. The conflict was aggravated at the next meeting of 16 April 1909, in which the 'opposition' proved able to revolutionize future ORT activity by concentrating on nationwide efforts regarding the development and improvement of Jewish agriculture and handicraft, based on the principle of economic self-help. Thereafter, the Committee members Sliozberg, Galperin, D. Feinberg, the engineer S.I. Meerson, and I.I. Shafir offered their resignation from the Committee. The disunity within ORT, however, was solved during the next meeting on 3 May 1909. Here thirty-two members drew up a resolution to re-evaluate the decisions taken at the last meeting regarding ORT's future activity. The congress rejected this request, but a compromise was achieved when it was agreed that the sum of 1,500 roubles of the last statement of accounts was to be given to single artisans. After this compromise, the retired Committee members rejoined the Committee and thus the financially important support of Jewish notables like the Gintsburg family, the Brodskiis and Poliakovs was secured for the future.[46]

In the educational field, ORPE's intention to become the instigator of educational reforms met with problems similar to ORT. In order to attract wider strata of Jewish society to ORPE's plans to modernize Jewish education in general, and the Jewish school system in particular, ORPE had to overcome its reputation as a mere tool of the Haskalah of the nineteenth century. To this end, ORPE activists had to go themselves to the various cities and towns in order to propagate and start the organization's activity.[47] Moreover, ORPE leadership had also to deal with rebellious local activists out for more independence. This became evident when at a ORPE meeting on 17 November 1908 a dispute arose between St. Petersburg and the provincial delegates over the finances. The conflict reached its peak when the St. Petersburg Committee proposed that the provincial branches contribute financially to general ORPE activities run by the Central Committee. The provincial representatives refused to do so, and the conflict was carried to the next meeting on 11 January 1909. Here, another dimension entered the conflict: Zionist and Liberal candidates competed with each other by presenting their respective candidates for the chairmanship of the congress. This time, the Zionists proved able to push through their candidate Gordon, and the ENG candidate Sliozberg failed. This conflict should not, however, be overestimated as ORPE had developed into a multi-party organization, and therefore certain conflicts were unavoidable. Furthermore, at this time various disputes concerning elections could be observed in all Jewish organizations. More important was the fact that the EDG leader L.M. Bramson stood up in the conference and demanded fast and decisive changes within ORPE, including the necessity to speed up the general conduct of ORPE.[48]

Bramson's desire for action was shared by Jewish Liberals who not only intended to win wider support for their approach in organic work, but who also aimed at taking the steam out of the religious elements' resistance against the envisaged modernization process. This was the basic motivation for convening a congress of representatives of the various political groups, Jewish communities and Jewish organizations. The congress was originally supposed to take place in Kiev, but due to the impossibility to get permission, it finally took place in Kovno, in November 1909.[49]

However, the convocation of the Kovno conference was also politically motivated, as the Liberals had never abandoned political efforts in the Duma. An indication of this was Maksim Vinaver's initiative in 1908 to put pressure on the Kadets to openly support the two Jewish Duma deputies in their efforts. Supported by the Moscow Kadets, Vinaver and the leader of the Moscow Kadets, Dr. Chlenov, urged the Central Committee to gather a special meeting in Moscow in order to evaluate the Kadets'

Duma tactics. During the meeting in January 1909 in Moscow, Vinaver and the Moscow Kadets pressured the Central Committee for a shift towards oppositional work and an open defense of Russian Jews. By painting a dark picture of a loss of confidence among Kadet voters and of serious political damage unless a change of tactics was undertaken, the venture met with success: the Central Committee of the Kadets nominated the Duma deputies Karaulov and Nekrasov to speak on behalf of the Jews in the name of the Kadet Duma faction.[50] How successful Vinaver's move was became evident in the fact that from early 1909 onwards Kadet leaders such as Rodichev and Maklakov not only defended Russian Jews against the right-wing anti-Semitic outbursts in the Duma,[51] but also became active outside parliament by meeting Jewish community leaders for feedback and material to defend Russian Jewry appropriately.[52] Vinaver continued his campaign on behalf of Russian Jews within the Kadet party in order to make it actively adhere to its own programme of 1906, which granted equality of rights to all minorities.[53] The Kadets' shift to a more openly conducted oppositional policy in the Duma, now made it easier for the two Jewish deputies to represent Jewish interests. To ensure the best representation possible, however, it needed a common Jewish organ which would act as a representative of Russian Jewry outside, and at the same time as an advisory board for the Jewish Duma deputies.

## 4.3 THE KOVNO CONFERENCE OF NOVEMBER 1909: THE SECULARIZATION AND MODERNIZATION OF THE JEWISH COMMUNITY

This conference was an important milestone of organic work for two main reasons: first, it witnessed the second attempt – after the failure of the Soiuz Polnopraviia – to act collectively by giving some form of co-ordination and co-operation to the reform efforts hitherto pursued; second, it signalled the next step in the efforts to reform Jewish society, the modernization and democratisation of the Jewish community structure in Russia. The opportunity seemed to arise just at the time when the Kovno conference was in its preparatory stage, a bill was being introduced in the Duma, which aimed at the legalization of denominational societies, religious unions and communities of a different, non-Christian faith. The initiators of the Kovno conference, the ENG, and the Jewish Duma deputies in particular, perceived this bill as an opportunity to combine the two points mentioned above: to bring about a better co-operation and co-ordination of organic

work, and to organize the Jewish community on a firm legal basis and
thereby to take another step towards normalization and democratisation of
Jewish life in Russia.[54]

At the same time, given the ideological differences and struggles of the
various Jewish groups and parties of the last three years, the bill touched
upon the sensitive issue of Jewish political leadership. Against this background, the initiative of a single group like the ENG to convoke the Kovno
conference was bound to be perceived by its opponents, the Zionists and
Bundists, as an attempt to usurp political leadership. Their suspicions were
reinforced by the fact that the initiators had convened the conference by
inviting, rather than electing the participants.[55] The criticism of the Kovno
Conference as being an 'undemocratic gathering'[56] whose organizers had
deliberately excluded representatives of certain communities such as
Vologda and Belostok,[57] represented, however, nothing else than a typical
pattern of Russian-Jewish political culture at that time which did not let
one party recognize the value of another party's initiative. On the ideological level, the Kovno Conference was heavily criticised, but – as with the
controversies of the past – representatives of all Jewish parties participated
as it seemed an opportunity too good to miss to put their claims forward.
While Bund leaders such as Vladimir Medem and A. Litvak disapproved
of the composition of the conference and also of its 'bourgeois' aims and
background, the Bund had to recognize its significance,[58] and consequently
sent its observers – among them A. Litvak.[59] The same applied to all the
other Jewish political groups: the Zionists were present with Dr.
Katsenelson, Chlenov, M. Ussishkin and Yulii Brutskus, the EDG with
Bramson, the Autonomists (ENP) with Dubnov, Kreinin, as well as Baron
D.G. Gintsburg.[60] Due to the forthcoming Rabbi Commission, the participants also included important state rabbis such as rabbi Maze of Moscow,
rabbi Aronson from St. Petersburg, and rabbi Shneerson of Chernigov as
it seemed important to win their support. All in all, 120 delegates from
forty-six cities in and outside the Pale of Settlement appeared at Kovno.[61]
In fact, the Kovno Conference became the first common congress of all
the Jewish political groups since the last congress of the Soiuz Polnopraviia
in May 1906.

Three main issues or problem areas appeared: first, the already mentioned bill; second, the future Jewish community in a broader sense with
all the questions pertinent to it such as leadership, special taxes for Jews
(such as the 'Korobka'), membership, its future organizational structure
and some detailed religious questions. The third area of contention concerned more practical questions which were connected to the economic
and general welfare of the Jewish masses, such as the improvement of

the loan and credit co-operative system for Jewish artisans and traders. Another topic touched upon was the lack of intelligentsia interest in Jewish community affairs which had been criticized in the Jewish press.[62]

To summarize the problems: The paradox of the present situation of the Jewish community lay in the fact that as a governing body in a legal sense it no longer existed (it was formally abolished in 1844); yet as far as the fiscal duties of the community were concerned, the government still addressed its claims to the 'Jewish community' – which, as far as the administration was concerned consisted of Jews 'honoured by the community and of independent means' – and not to the Jews as individuals.[63] Beyond this, the definition of the Jewish community raised key issues such as the questions of membership and leadership and the Korobka tax. Who should belong to the Jewish community? Only the Jews who had registered with the prayer houses or all Jews living in the area? What would the position of the rabbis be? Should they play the same important role as before? These issues were essential as they were part of the struggle over the modernization and secularization of the Jewish community.

The issue of the Jewish community's fiscal duties can be distilled down to the basic question of how to make sure that the special taxes imposed on Russian Jews such as the Korobka tax – a tax which was only paid by Jews, as it was levied on 'kosher' meat – were used for Jewish purposes exclusively, and to find a more just tax. Originally, this tax was earmarked by law for special Jewish purposes such as welfare and charity, the maintenance of synagogues, and for education. The collection of taxes which the Jews had to pay, came under the control of the gubernia administration, which, for instance, leased the Korobka tax to an entrepreneur who had the right to charge the 'kosher' meat with a tax and could prohibit the import of meat from outside the community. This opened the door to all kinds of malpractice and to the exploitation of the masses. Furthermore, the administration abused the Korobka tax for paying, for example, the police, for the construction of streets or street-lighting.[64] Therefore there were good reasons for abolishing the tax in the name of more equality and of lightening the burden of the poor.

The Congress went straight into the most important and most controversial issue: the reorganization of the Jewish community structure. Here, Sliozberg gave his version of the ideal future community structure on which most of the participants could converge in one or the other way. At first, Sliozberg painted a dark picture of the present state of the Jewish community which came closer to the ideas of the rabbis than to his fellow Liberals. He also criticized the Jewish youth and intelligentsia as they showed a certain indifference to the Jewish community from the moment they received access to Russian schools of higher learning – to gymnasia and universities. Thus, the Jewish intelligentsia had gone its own way, and the moment unity was needed Jewish society witnessed a split between the Orthodox and the Intelligentsia. As Russian Jewry faced ever more aggressive anti-Semitism, Sliozberg called upon the two sides to end the conflict as it had a destructive effect on community life, and instead to co-operate in the reform of the Jewish community as the only possible answer to anti-Semitism. Sliozberg envisaged a Jewish community organized with an obligatory membership and an administration elected by the prayer houses. Every Jew had to register with a synagogue. As far as the reform of the taxing system was concerned, he supported the reformers' demand to introduce a progressive income tax, instead of the unjust Korobka tax.[65]

However, since Sliozberg's proposal did not satisfy either of the two sides – neither the rabbis nor the reformers – it triggered long disputes about many aspects of the Jewish communities, such as the qualification for membership, the Korobka tax and especially the leadership. Broadly speaking, in all these discussions the old controversy over 'secularization', over the division of 'church and state' at the grass roots, respectively of 'religion and society' resurfaced. The left-wing reformers, especially Bramson and Saker, wanted to transform the old elitist and religious structure of the Jewish community into a more democratized and secularized one, in which the rabbis' responsibilities would be limited to the religious sphere.[66] Administration of 'business' affairs, like schooling and welfare, and the leadership of the community would be turned over to a council of Jews which should be elected by all Jews whether they be religious or not. The rabbis in turn defended the traditional structure of the Jewish community, based on integralist institutions without a separation of the religious from the non-religious, as well as the rabbis' dominating position.

Not surprisingly, the conflict over the secularization of the Jewish community reached its peak within the scope of the re-organisation of the Jewish community and the issue of membership. Both sides, reformers as well as traditionalists (the rabbis) stood by their position. While the first unconditionally voted for secularization by any means, the latter doubted whether secularization would be in accordance with their interest of preserving the traditional values of Jewish life. This can be seen clearly within the general discussion on the bill itself. Here, the Zionist Yulii Brutskus, realizing the political value of the bill, welcomed it as an 'opportunity to legalize our community and to get the rights which we still lack', and showed no compromise over the issue of reform by stating 'if the Hasidim disagree they should organize their own organization within the community'.[67]

The rabbis – by no means Hasidim themselves – in turn demonstrated strong reservations about the bill and the direction the reformers wanted to take. Their spokesman, rabbi Ya.I. Maze, rejected the very idea of a bill regulating the affairs of the Jewish communities, claiming that no bill could stop or even reverse the trend of a growing non-belief.[68] Here, he was supported by the reformer V.O. Garkavi, who pointed out that the aim of unifying the community was endangered by a clause which allowed every twenty Jews to elect their own rabbi. The result, he argued, could be the existence of thirty or forty rabbis in a city like Vilna, Kovno or Grodno. This way the new law would not lead to unity but to an atomization of the Jewish community.[69]

The same front line between rabbis and reformers occurred on the issue of membership. Here, the rabbis defended the traditional structure of the Jewish community, which was based on the assumption that there could be no separation of religion and more secular affairs. Consequently, Maze concluded that membership of the Jewish community could only be based on the affiliation to Judaism, or as he put it: 'A Jew can not be a Jew when he does not profess to the Jewish religion'.[70] Adherence to religion was and was to remain the sole criterion for determining who was a Jew and who was not. Therefore the rabbis advocated the registration of the members with the prayer houses as the only basis for membership in the Jewish community.

The reformers, on the other hand, fought for a community which was no longer determined by an adherence to Judaism as a religion and to the observance of its precepts of daily life. Against such demands the reformers invoked the freedom of conscience – the concept of basic human rights. For example, Freidenberg insisted that 'every Jew should decide for himself if he wants to practise the faith or not. On the contrary, the community should be organized by all parts of society. Affiliation to the prayer houses is irrelevant'.[71] He suggested that all Jews who were members of a Jewish organization or institution or of a prayer house and were thereby professing their Jewish national identity should be a member of the future all-embracing Jewish community. The Trudovik L.M. Bramson also applied his demands for complete democratisation of Jewish organizations to the Jewish community through the principle of 'one man, one vote', or as he put it: 'each member of the community should have the right to vote. Direct elections mean equality and this is a main principle of democracy'.[72] In short, for the reformers, secularization implied democratization which in turn meant the break from traditional leadership.

At this point, Sliozberg was able to calm the storm by reminding the audience of the main task of the conference – the achievement of unity:

Religious or secular community is not the point. We are here to unify Russian Jewry, to create a central Jewish community and this should be done either through the new bill or the existing laws.[73]

He managed to convince both sides that nobody wanted to exclude the other part, to leave the hammering out of a compromise formula to a commission and to pass over to the next issue, the Korobka tax. This was not as controversial as the membership question, for example.

Here, the rabbis showed the same attitude as the organized anti-reformist Orthodox in their first activities in 1908: resistance to reform of Judaism or traditional Jewish education, but openness towards reform efforts in fields where the economic situation of Russian Jewry could be improved. This line became evident when on the one side they voted for the preservation of the Korobka tax as a cornerstone of the existing informal community structure, and against an income tax in place of the Korobka as a danger for the cohesiveness of the community. An income tax, they argued, would only be paid by a quarter of the Jewish community. Others pointed to the conditions of the small communities where only the Korobka tax would bring enough income to cover expenses, and others regarded the tax on 'kosher' meat as an element signifying the importance of religion for the coherence of the community.[74]

On the other side, since many delegates had shown the rabbis that the Korobka tax no longer covered the community's expenses on its welfare, social and health organizations,[75] most of them agreed to the necessity to reform the tax on 'kosher' meat, and especially the form of farming out. Many even agreed to substitute the Korobka with a new tax, and as a compromise the conference agreed that the Korobka tax should only be abolished when the new Jewish community had been founded. This way those elements of the Korobka tax that tended to reinforce cohesion inside the Jewish community would be preserved until the new law could provide a basis for the unity everybody was striving for.

As opposed to the controversies over the forms of reorganization, membership and so on, the conference achieved a general consensus on the third main issue: economic reforms. Here, L.G. Rabinovich, the spokesman for the secular social organizations and for the Jewish organization 'TRUD', voiced the concerns of his organization, and restated the reformers' call for self-help and the establishment of self-help organizations, especially for artisans. He pointed to a general deterioration of the economic situation of Russian Jewry, reflected in a sharp increase of unemployment among the Jewish population.[76] He added that the number of persons who would normally be able to support the Jewish community with donations was decreasing. Only the few comparatively well-off could continue to do so. Pauperization had reached such a peak that many artisans could not even afford to buy their tools any more. Profit margins had dropped and artisans had to travel extensively to sell their products.[77] Under these circumstances, the introduction of a marketing organization which was to buy and sell through co-operatives could make an obvious contribution to a piecemeal improvement.

The conference agreed to the proposals of Rabinovich's report, which was identical to the 'TRUD' programme and the Liberals' intentions to set up a network for the already existing loan and saving co-operatives, which could help the artisans modernize their workshops and organize the sale of products and the purchase of raw materials. On the other hand, specialist training would have to be improved by schools for artisans which would teach craftsmen how to increase their productivity and to improve the quality of the goods produced.[78]

The resolutions at the end of the conference showed that an agreement could be reached on all questions involved. The future Jewish community was to be governed by a Council of the community elected by direct vote. The Council in turn would elect the executive of the community – to consist of between seven and ten members – which was to be the governing body of the community. Every Jew of eighteen years and above, who had lived in the community for not less than one year, would belong to the community. A Jew was defined as having been born a Jew and not having converted to a non-Jewish denomination. All members should have the right to vote and to be elected. Affiliation to a prayer house as the condition for membership was rejected.[79]

A progressive and obligatory income tax was to replace the Korobka tax when the new community would be in existence. Poor Jews, however, who were living below a certain income minimum would not be charged. A special commission had to regulate all taxation affairs. The Administration was to give an annual account of its activity to the Council.[80]

The Jewish community as envisaged can be considered as a democratic and modernized organization which would have allowed all elements of Jewish society to participate. Despite the fact that the position of the rabbis was not yet defined, the rabbis present at this congress – of whom many had received a secular education or even had acquired a 'doctor-grade' from a Russian or foreign university – were willing to accept the platform proposed by this assembly.[81]

The conference which had dealt mainly with the internal questions of the Jewish community was also successful in political terms. The Liberals succeeded in forming an advisory board assisting the Jewish deputies in the Duma through the creation of the 'Kovenskii Komitet' by the conference. This committee consisted of representatives of the four main Jewish parties, and included all the members of the advisory board which was working until then.[82] The KK started its activity in February 1910, by organizing a gathering including their provincial members. The main issues pointed to the next and actual targets of Jewish Liberal politics such as the bill on the abolition of the Pale in the Duma, as well as the forthcoming Rabbi Congress. According to the newspaper *Der Fraind*, the KK decided to introduce the bill into the Duma. Regarding the Rabbi Commission it decided to send a questionnaire to the provinces which testified to the interest of the KK members to find an appropriate solution for the rabbis' position in the future Jewish community. The KK wanted to base its advice to the Rabbi Congress on the results of the questionnaire.[83] By March 1910, it was reported that the KK had worked out a project regarding the organization of the future Jewish community, and had sent it to the local social activists to be discussed.[84]

At that time the government finally convened a Rabbi Commission – two years after it had originally been announced, and the first one for seventeen years – in order to 'improve the spiritual condition of the five and a half million Jews residing in Russia'.[85] The formulation with which the government justified the convocation might suggest that it was trying to rekindle the old partnership with the Jewish religious elements in order to combat the modernization process within Jewish society; this approach was consistent with the growing tendency to look for conservative support in an all-Russian context. In any case, the government made clear that the commission would only be allowed to discuss religious questions such as family affairs, the rabbi question, the Jewish community, etc.[86]

Since the convocation of the Rabbi Commission coincided with a period when the entire Jewish public was discussing plans for a future reformed Jewish community structure, this Commission had an enormous significance for both the reform-minded middle-class and the opponents of reform, such as the conservative Hasidim. Since the Rabbi Commission was a body usually convened by the government to assist Russian legislation in dealing with certain issues related to religion, it was perceived by the two opposing sides as an opportunity to influence it according to their ideas. Therefore, the Liberals, that is their moderate wing including Sliozberg and the Notables Gintsburg, Poliakov and Brodskii as well as the Hasidim, led by the rabbi of Liubavich, Shneerson, participated in this gathering. The congress was essential for the former in terms of the implementation of reforms, and for the latter in terms of securing an important position for the conservative rabbis in Jewish society in general, and the community in particular, as well as organizing the religious forces against the reformers.[87]

## 4.4  THE RABBI COMMISSION OF 1910: REFORMING ORTHODOXY AND ITS QUEST FOR MODERNIZATION

The heated atmosphere over the problems of modernizing the Jewish community could be observed in the elections to this congress. The Kovno resolutions in favour of the secularization of the Jewish community had added additional fuel to the fears of the Hasidim of losing further ground within Jewish society. The Hasidim especially complained that the Jewish youth was forgetting its Jewish religious heritage, by going increasingly to Russian gymnasia and universities where they were educated in secular subjects and consequently Jewish education was becoming secularized.[88]

The conservative rabbis' fears were also based on the very existence of the double rabbinate, which added a second dimension to the conflict between the orthodox but reform oriented rabbis and Hasidim, that of the state versus the communal rabbi. The state rabbi was created by the government as the official representative of the Jewish community to the authorities. The fact that not only did he have all the administrative functions in his hands, but in most of the cases did not even have a religious education, created a horror vision for conservative communal rabbis of a rabbi degraded to a pure registrar without any qualifications required for this post. Thus, it could be no consolation for the communal rabbi that his rabbinical and religious education was very much appreciated and commanded the respect and authority within Jewish community.[89]

The state rabbis had, however, witnessed a certain revalorization within Jewish society as more and more qualified persons, and even communal rabbis moved into the position of state rabbis. These rabbis represented the modern type of a rabbi who was secularly educated, spoke Russian, and came into close personal contact with the secular community leaders now pressing for reforms. These modern rabbis first appeared in the big cities where they became familiar with the political struggle of the Jewish middle-class intellectuals, and their efforts to mitigate the Jewish plight. They realized the necessity of political, economic and social reforms and in many cases had already begun to support many aspects of the reform process. In fact, these 'modernizing' rabbis such as Temkin (Ekaterinoslav), Maze (Moscow), Aizenshtat (Rostov/Don; later St. Petersburg), G. Bruk (Vitebsk) and Isaac Shneerson (Chernigov) had overcome community boycott and thus the restricted position of many state rabbis as pure registrars,

and due to their 'engagement' in communal work had won an increasing
popularity within Russian Jewry, and became the ally of the reform minded
secular elements during the Rabbi Congress.

By organizing a reception at Baron Gintsburg's house in St. Petersburg
before the opening of the Rabbi Commission on 28 February 1910,
Sliozberg tried to calm the heated atmosphere between communal and
state rabbis, and to win understanding for the Kovno Conference and its
reform plans. Sliozberg insisted on the necessity of reforms as they would
improve Jewish community life, and at the same time, assured the rabbis
that the Kovno conference did not intend to interfere in religious affairs,
nor to exclude them from the reform process. Instead, he called upon the
rabbis to co-operate in the commission towards a reform adequate for the
future Jewish community.[90] Three days later, on 3 March 1910, the Rabbi
Congress of forty delegates elected by the Jewish communities in Russia
and Poland opened in St. Petersburg. Stolypin, as minister of Interior,
chose three state and three communal rabbis who were in charge of presenting the resolutions taken by the Rabbi Congress to the government.[91]
Baron D.G. Gintsburg was nominated as the chairman of the Rabbi Congress and G.B. Sliozberg as its secretary.[92]

During the course of the congress, which was in session for four weeks,
it became evident, however, that Sliozberg's and the progressists' intentions to calm the storm was not successful. On the very essential issues
of the rabbinate, the future position of the rabbi, the educational census
required for the rabbi and of the future structure of the community,[93] the
discussions between the opposing sides became very heated. In the course
of the deliberations the spokesman for the ultra-conservatives, rabbi
Shneerson of Liubavich, feeling encouraged by the fact that the progressive elements were nominally in the minority,[94] fired a broadside against
the reform plans, especially with respect to the most controversial issues.
Surprisingly, however, the desire and the arguments for a reformed Jewish
community structure, reinforced by practical considerations proved stronger
and more convincing, and the reform-oriented rabbis won the majority.

Therefore, on the issue of the rabbinate and the rabbis' qualifications,
the congress did not follow the conservatives' proposal to legalize the
communal rabbinate. Rather, in light of the impossibility and impractica-
bility of legalizing the traditional rabbinate, Sliozberg convinced the majority to accept a logical solution which would give traditional rabbis the
possibility to become state rabbis. He had argued that since the government only recognized the state rabbi, and demanded a minimum of general
education – the knowledge of Russian with a Russian school certificate –
it would be more realistic to strive for a diminution of the census. By

making at least the knowledge of Russian obligatory for all the rabbis, the communal ones included, they would be able to enter the state rabbinate and communicate better with the Russian administration. To ensure that the respective rabbi would be qualified from a religious point of view, a collegium of rabbis would examine the various candidates on their religious knowledge and ability to lead a community.[95] This solution was acceptable to the majority, and since Shneerson was unable to come up with alternative proposals,[96] the majority agreed to this logical proposal which was both realistic and would still provide the rabbis with some control.[97]

The tendency of the congress' majority to follow proposals applicable to the realities of Russian Jewish life continued with all other crucial issues. For instance, regarding the rabbi's position in the future Jewish community, the congress rejected the conservatives' desire to keep it on a firm religious basis. Rabbi Maze (Moscow), for instance, claimed that there were also people in the communities who commanded a greater authority in theological learning than the rabbis, and convinced the majority for his solution: the rabbi's position as an advisor for general and religious affairs.[98] By defining the rabbis' position in the future Jewish community in this way, the congress filled the gap the Kovno Conference had left in its resolutions. The position as an advisor within the future Jewish community leadership did not signify a loss of influence, given the Jewish society's respect for the excellent capacity of rabbis as advisors. On the contrary, they still would have the opportunity to influence any decision taken by the community leadership.[99]

Despite the fact that the ultra-orthodox rabbis objected to the future community structure envisaged by the Kovno conference – once again raised by Sliozberg and supported by Isaac Shneerson and Vladimir Temkin – the congress followed the path of reform.[100] Here, the majority agreed on the necessity of the legalization of the Jewish community and also 'that it would be advisable to create a central authority to manage Jewish religious affairs'.[101] Finally, the congress not only accepted the community reform plan but agreed on almost all the other points – allowing for slight alterations – with the resolution taken by the Kovno Conference.[102] The membership question was only slightly altered in terms of the age of the future community member: every Jew who lived more than one year in the community and was twenty-one years old. All the members of the community who payed taxes could participate and could be elected to the Council and the executive.[103]

The congress also adopted the same attitude to the Korobka tax as had the Kovno Conference. Although the progressists such as the lawyer Mazor,

Temkin, Brushtein and Frenkel demanded its abolition, the congress did not follow them for the reasons the Kovno Conference had not: since the existence of the welfare and educational institutions was based on the Korobka tax and there was no alternative tax in sight, it would be sustained until the future Jewish community was established.[104] The congress did not ignore the fact that the tax was abused in many cases. It followed the Liberals' demand – raised in the ENG's programme of 1907 – and suggested to take the farming of the tax out of the hands of the private tax-farmers, and put it under the control of the community. This solution proved to be applicable to Russian-Jewish life even without special legislation, as in the following years various Jewish communities adopted this suggestion, and thus increased the funds so essential for successful organic work.[105]

With the issue of education and the introduction of secular subjects, above all Russian, into the Jewish schools, the conservatives were only able to limit the 'damage' to their cause: the congress left the choice of whether or not to introduce secular subjects and Russian into the syllabus of the Heders and Talmud Torahs to the respective communities.[106] This decision did not, however, solve the problem, it sharpened conflicts locally. A community dominated by orthodox elements could keep its traditional education, while more progressive communities were now officially sanctioned to teach both traditional and secular subjects.

Despite the fact that the congress tended to change the traditional forms whenever it observed intolerable abuses, as with the rules governing engagements,[107] or agreed to the overall reform plan, a limit of reform-mindedness showed itself in many issues, such as whether to open the Heders to Jewish girls or to change the requirements for circumcision. In both cases, the conservatives were successful.[108] However, in all the decisions related to the future reform of Jewish community structures, the congress proved favourable to the progressists' proposals. As for the implementation of these decisions, however, it had become obvious already during the congress that the government was not willing to co-operate: when during the second week, a deputation consisting of the Notables Baron Gintsburg and Poliakov, and the rabbis Tsirelson, Shneerson, Maze, Soloveichik, Grodzenskii, Polinkovskii and Khein was sent to Stolypin in order to inform him about the progress and the decisions already taken,[109] Stolypin received them in a rather hostile fashion, and told them quite frankly that he was not prepared to make any concessions at the moment. Apparently, Stolypin repeated the stereotyped lines of his predecessors that 'a better economic situation will automatically come with the improvement of the spiritual situation of Russian Jewry. The situation of the

Russian Jews in general, however, could only be improved slowly and in the future. The basis for a change could be made by the Jews themselves by showing their loyalty to the Tsar'.[110] The reason for this hostile reception – which was heavily criticized in the Jewish press[111] – might have been the fact that Stolypin became negatively influenced by the congress of the United Nobility gathering at the same time in St. Petersburg – March 1910 – and in its final resolution regarded the Jews as the chief culprit for the side-effects of a modernizing Russian economy.[112] This interpretation is further supported by the *Jewish Chronicle*'s report in May 1910 in an article published in the government's organ *Rossiia* which officially assured the Black Hundreds that the ministry would not allow the Jews to establish an administrative organization, and that the Conference only provided for a religious body. It concluded: 'the Cabinet will also scrutinize the resolutions of the Conference and reject those which are not in conformity with the interests of Russia'.[113]

In the end, the congress elected a Committee consisting of Baron Gintsburg, the orthodox rabbis of Liubavich and Sokol as well as the rabbis Khein (Nezhin), Grodzenskii (Vilna), Modievskii (Khorol) and Rabinovich (Ponevezh) to summarize the various resolutions and hand them over to the Minister of the Interior.[114] In July 1910 the Committee submitted a complete report of 104 pages to the government. Five months later, in December 1910, the Ministry of Interior agreed to a vague possibility for rabbis to become state rabbis if those without the required census could show recommendations from the respective governor. This remained, however, the only concession the government ever made and thus can only be seen as the government's endeavour to fill the empty posts of state rabbis.[115] However, as we shall see, these two congresses – the Kovno conference and the rabbi congress – were to have a great impact on the course of organic work as many of their decisions were either carried out, or were developed further.


## 4.5  THE IMPACT OF THE KOVNO CONFERENCE AND THE RABBI COMMISSION ON 'ORGANIC WORK', ORT AND ORPE


The efforts of the Jewish Liberals were successful in so far as the Kovno conference as well as the rabbi congress confirmed the direction, and gave a boost to the organic work envisaged by the Liberals. In fact, the ideas brought forward in both congresses bore fruit in the following period from 1910 until 1914. Therefore, the impact of these congresses on organic work and the modernization and secularization of Jewish community life should not be underestimated. Nonetheless, the increasing differentiation of Jewish political opinion made sure that Liberal initiatives in general, and the Kovno conference in particular, were heavily criticized by the Bundist and Zionist press. Both parties clung to rigid ideologies, which made it difficult for them to recognize the potential value of the political, economic or cultural reforms spearheaded by their political opponents, the Liberals.

Despite the fact that, for instance, various Zionists participated in the 'Kovenskii Komitet', the Zionist press rejected the Kovno Conference and its political brainchild, the Kovenskii Komitet, because it was initiated by the Liberal ENG and therefore interpreted as the Liberals' attempt to arrogate the political leadership of Jewish society to themselves.[116] The same applied to the Bundists, who attacked the Kovno conference because of its 'bourgeois' complexion and supposed ignorance of the interests of the masses. Like the Zionists, the Bund's observer, A. Litvak, questioned the Conference's legitimacy on the ground that it was not democratically elected and would only be used by the ENG to further its own ends. However, they had to acknowledge a paradox that took the edge off their criticism: the conference, by captivating the public imagination, furthered the mobilization of the Jewish population and thereby contributed to the democratization of the Jewish community. They also had to acknowledge the importance of the Kovno Conference in having raised many problems concerning the daily life of the Jews.[117]

The Hasidim were also caught in the web of their 'ideology': their struggle against secularization and the intelligentsia. They could not accept the Liberals' politics within and around the Kovno conference as they interpreted the 'Kovno call' for unity as the Trojan horse of secularization. Through a proclamation to the Jewish people in Russia, shortly after the conference, the Ultra-Orthodox tried to diminish the impact of the Kovno conference on the provinces. They, in particular, rejected Vinaver's definition of Jewry as a nation, which was a secular concept, and not primarily as a religion.[118]

Given these officially negative reactions it could not surprise that the Liberals' efforts to win understanding for their actions cut no ice either with the Hasidim[119] or their political opponents, the Bundists and Zionists.[120] This was even more true of the politics of the Rabbi Congress. In light of the fact that they had already objected to the reform effort of the radical Liberals, the Kovno Conference, reform proposals by a congress run by rabbis, moderate Liberals and Notables proved to be the ultimate nightmare for Zionists and Bundists.[121] At least one Bund-leader, Vladimir Medem, however, showed some understanding for the rabbis' desire to achieve a legalized status. Finally, he joined the liberal *Evreiskaia Nedelia* response to Litvak's criticism by trying to win more understanding among secular elements for the rabbis, and he maintained that one should appreciate the fact that the rabbis had taken decisions in accordance with the Kovno reform plans. Both Liberals and Medem shared the opinion that Russian Jews could only profit from a unified community structure which included the religious elements.[122]

Despite all this criticism coming from the top level of the various party organs, the ideas of the two congresses found wide acceptance on the grass roots. Many cases were reported in *Novyi Voskhod* whereby the Kovno Conference resolutions met with a considerable interest in the communities; moreover, it was pointed out that the delegates had familiarized their constituencies with the existence and the programmes of organizations such as ORT, ORPE and others, which although in existence for a long time, were still unknown to many.[123] This venture proved very successful as ORT as well as ORPE witnessed an influx of new members between 1909 and 1911, which allowed the overall membership of these organizations to rise from 1,037 to 1,556, and 4,700 to 7,000 respectively, and consequently increased their budgets considerably.[124]

This growing interest in organic work, however, forced different Jewish political groups, even the Zionists and Bundists, to participate and to act through these organizations which really had been the Liberals' domain. Ideological purity had to be preached on one level, but on the practical level the lead given by their opponents had to be followed. This became especially evident in the further course of the ORPE congresses where Bundists pressured for a secular Yiddish school, while the Zionists favoured the secular and national Hebrew school.[125] These conflicts, far from hampering organic work, brought wider circles to participate in Jewish organizations for example in Odessa where the membership of the local ORPE branch moved up to 1,700 in 1911.[126]

The language dispute came into the open when in a meeting in February 1910, after a new Central Committee was elected – which, among others, consisted of Vinaver, Dr. Katsenelson, Sheftel and Goldberg – ORPE decided to go ahead with educational reforms.[127] The reform of the Jewish school system as such moved into the focus of attention. ORPE efforts to modernize Jewish education had hitherto been limited to Jewish teachers, in the form of the Grodno Teachers' Courses.[128] To this end, and in order to secure ORPE unity as a basic condition for successful educational work, a conference concerning educational reform was organized by ORPE activists, and took place in St. Petersburg from 25–28 March 1910. This conference was able finally to end the conflict between the Central Committee and the provincial branches. After both sides had once again raised their claims for more participation and independence, the majority agreed to a decentralization of ORPE by granting the branches more independence, but leaving the general conduct to the Central Committee. Branches responsible for the respective district were to be set up in the bigger cities that had to take care of cultural work by carrying their activities into all Jewish educational institutions of the respective rayon. In exchange for independence in local matters, the branches were obliged to send reports about their activities to the Committee to give it the appropriate information for a proper overall conduct. The Central Committee remained, however, in charge of educational work in cases where no local branch existed. Unity was secured. As the solution for the financial problems involved in educational reform indicated, for the first time the congress implemented ideas developed by the Liberals and approved by the rabbi congress: Dr. Mandelberg succeeded with his resolution to create a steady source of income for educational matters by taking the Korobka tax away from the private tax-farmers.[129] The organizational framework of ORPE was finally set up; furthermore, in order to tie the provincial branches and the committee even closer, from November 1910 onwards ORPE published its own journal, which acquired a wide readership all over the Pale.[130]

However, differences at the conference occurred once again as – within the discussion of the envisaged school reform – the Zionists started to impose their claims for a nationally oriented school on the meeting. The dispute over the appropriate language was triggered by the Zionists' claim to publish the envisaged special journal not in the 'language of assimilation', but in one of the two national languages, or at least add a supplement in Yiddish or Hebrew. Here, however, the Committee – with its members Kreinin, Sliozberg and Garkavi – won the day with a final vote of 24 votes to three in favour of Russian. They had argued that the journal was to fulfil a special purpose, and that it was not intended to be a journal for the ordinary Jew but dedicated to a special circle of people who would not understand Yiddish.[131] No compromise, however, was achieved on the issue of the future type of school. Dr. Eiger's report on the Jewish elementary school envisaged a modern type of elementary school including girls and boys, the teaching of secular and religious education, with Jewish subjects such as Yiddish, Jewish literature as well as general subjects; his report, however, triggered long and fruitless discussions on the language to be used, as his plan had excluded Hebrew.[132] This was especially inconceivable for Zionists such as Rozenbaum (Minsk), Syrkin, and Grinbaum who all insisted on the introduction of Hebrew as the proper national language, and attacked Russian as the language of assimilation. Integrationists such as Dr. Eiger and Garkavi, as well as the teacher Spivak rejected the idea of a nationally-structured elementary school, as they felt that the school should be practically-oriented and be based on general education, for which Russian was necessary. For them, a decision in favour of Hebrew or Yiddish would be purely political and ideological and would not help the children. Spivak offered a compromise accepting Jewish subjects as long as those did not endanger general educational targets. These differences could not be bridged and the conflict dragged on to the next ORPE meeting.[133]

Although the ENG was able to keep the control within ORPE's Central Committee,[134] the next general ORPE meeting, in January 1911, did not reach any compromise. Instead, the language dispute escalated within ORPE as the Yiddishists began demanding more efforts from the Central Committee on behalf of Yiddish.[135] These controversies were sharpened by a bill on national education discussed in the Duma which made the setting up of a Jewish secular primary school seem within reach.[136] It was not surprising, therefore, that at the next ORPE meeting in April 1911 these tensions erupted in a great blow out. After S. Ginzburg had delivered a report on ORPE activity – in which he held provincial ORPE branches as well as the authorities' increasing intransigence responsible for any lack of progress – the opposition moved straight into the controversial area of school reform.[137] The Yiddishists, such as the left-wing group consisting of Shapiro, Okun, Slutskin, and the Bundist Rafes (Vilna), and the Hebraists or Zionists such as Kogan, Brumberg, Khaikin, Polonskii and Ginzburg aggressively put their demands forward. The former – in keeping with their left-wing convictions – demanded a Jewish school based on Yiddish only and otherwise free of any nationalist tendencies, while the latter defended their concept of a Jewish-national school. While the Yiddishists attacked the teaching of Hebrew and the bible as useless ballast, the Zionists – like N. Pines (Vilna) – declared it a *conditio sine qua non* of Jewish national culture; against the background of growing assimilatory tendencies and difficult political conditions, they saw the nationalization of the school as 'our weapon'. The middle position was taken by the Committee member, M.N. Kreinin who supported a compromise of a syllabus consisting of Hebrew, the bible, and to a certain extent Yiddish as the language of teaching.[138] Eventually, the Committee was able to break the deadlock with a general formula for the reformed Jewish elementary school to which all the groups, at least for the moment, agreed: it was to be a secular school including boys and girls with a syllabus consisting of general subjects, Yiddish and Hebrew literature, Jewish history and the teaching of the Bible; the teaching of the basics of religion was left to each school's own decision, while the language of instruction would be chosen according to the mother tongue. As the majority of the pupils spoke Yiddish, it had to be Yiddish for all practical purposes. Taking these realities into account, it was decided to publish school books in Yiddish, including a short history of the Jewish people. To popularize the new school, the Committee proposed to set up model schools in some districts, as well as branches in the smaller towns.[139] In order to improve the teaching of general subjects such as Russian, natural science, geography, mathematics, physics and chemistry, plans were laid down to raise a pedagogical personnel that would be up to its tasks.[140] In the end, the demand to get the Korobka tax into the hands of the community was raised again by Vainshelbaum (Kiev), who referred to the negotiations between the Kiev ORPE branch with the governor. While he showed himself optimistic, the Odessa delegate pointed to an increasing unwillingness on the part of the authorities to co-operate, and mentioned as an example the fact that the governor of Odessa, Tolmachev, had not even given permission to the Odessa branch to hold its annual meeting.[141]

To sum up, ORPE had overcome its initial organizational problems, and despite the fact that the language dispute had entered its congresses, it proved able to find a compromise formula defining its future activity as the modernization of the Jewish educational system in general and the Jewish elementary school in particular, and the strengthening of Jewish national culture among the Jewish masses. The method by which the educational reforms were to take place was determined, and with the compromises reached the Kovno conference's call for unity in organic work was fulfilled.

While the impact of Liberal initiatives on ORPE was obvious in unifying its activities and in advancing practical solutions to real problems, the impact of Liberal ideas on the economic field of organic work became even more evident. The basic pattern of Jewish Liberal politics to achieve wider reforms through lobbying in and outside the Duma became a firm part of ORT activity. This was due to the Liberal belief that it was necessary to counteract further restrictive policies, and even to explore the ground of possible support for a policy of dismantling anti-Jewish legislation. The shift of ORT from a philanthropic society to an organization which openly defended political, social and economic interests of Russian Jews became evident for the first time when the Duma was discussing a law on the Sunday rest; a law trying to restrict the economic role of religious minorities like Muslims and Jews by making them less competitive. When the second all-Russian congress of artisans was called together by the Society for the promotion of Russian industry and trade ('Obshchestvo dlia sodeistviia russkoi promyshlennosti i torgovle') for the purpose of working out a new statute for the craft industry, ORT perceived this as a good opportunity to fight against the envisaged law on the one hand, and at the same time to lobby for other Jewish interests.[142] ORT gained Jewish representation at this conference, and at the same time assured an organized Jewish approach by setting up three sections: one for the professional organization of the artisans, one for the question of the Jewish apprentices and journeymen, and finally, one for the ecnomic needs of the artisans.[143] The main aims were to achieve a resolution which not only left the non-Christian artisans to select the day of rest themselves, but one that advocated an abolition of anti-Jewish legislation. Finally, ORT's most cherished dream was to widen economic reform work by achieving the right for artisans to organize themselves on a wider scale. In short, the target was to secure the inclusion of Russian Jews in forthcoming reforms, and thus, to give them a place in a modernized future Russian economy.

This venture succeeded in so far as the general desire for reforms within Russian society became evident in the composition of the Congress which – in contrast to the first in 1900 – consisted of a majority of reformers, and was therefore more tolerant and less nationalistic.[144] Indeed, the conference, which began on 15 January 1911, proved to be unconcerned with competition by non-Christian artisans and prepared to free the Russian economy from any restrictions by demanding equal rights to all artisans. The tactics of the Jewish delegates, among others Kaplan, Sliozberg, D.I. Khienkin and B.D. Brutskus, were to inform the congress of the problems for Jewish artisans, and of the dangers caused by an unclear legislation which had hitherto served local authorities as an excuse for abuses. Therefore, the target was to illustrate to the conference that only a statute which eliminates all possibilities for anti-Jewish restrictions would guarantee a free development of handicraft. Most important for the Jewish artisans were freedom of occupation for all artisans, freedom of movement, a free handicraft system based on self-organization instead of the guilds, and the right to celebrate Shabbat as the day of rest. Therefore, they assured the congress that the new post envisaged by the new statute, the artisan inspector would provide the solution for the first three points if he – instead of the guilds – would be in charge of the professional certificates needed to assure the right of residence. To them the guilds were one of the major obstacles as they quite often denied Jewish artisans the certificates. Furthermore, the obligatory registration into guilds should be abolished, and instead a self-organization of all the city's artisans be introduced. The Jewish representatives also pointed out that the congress' position on Sunday rest – to consider Sunday as the official day of rest, but allowing the city councils the possibility of choosing an alternative day – carried the risk that Russian nationalistic interests were favoured at the expense of the minorities' interests. The Jewish representatives demanded a guarantee allowing Jewish artisans to celebrate Shabbat (Saturday) as their day of rest. Finally, during the debate on the apprentices, the Jewish delegate Rosentsvaig (Gomel) demanded the abolition of the Pale of Settlement, which he considered to be the main cause for the desperate situation of the Jewish artisans. His speech triggered several anti-Semitic outbursts, inter alia from the delegate of the Odessa artisans, who demanded that Christian apprentices be forbidden to learn and work with a Jewish master. However, the Jewish delegates received the support of the workers' delegate from Lodz, Chemeriskii, whose proposal – to allow the artisans to choose their day of rest, for example Muslims on Friday and Jews on Saturday – finally won the majority of the congress.[145] The final resolutions passed by the conference were a major success for the Jewish activists, as the conference acknowledged the principle of full equality for all the members of all artisans' organizations, including the free choice for Sunday rest.[146]

The fact that more and more ORT activities followed the Liberals' approach is also shown by the fact that after the artisans' conference ORT made use of the presence of the remaining sixty Jewish delegates[147] and organised on 30 January 1911 a conference to get some feedback for further reforms. Here, based on the results of the Artisans' Congress, and anticipating that the congress would positively influence Russian legislation, Leon Bramson proposed that ORT assume a new policy aiming to reduce the competition among Jewish artisans: 'internal migration', by settling Jewish artisans in the gubernii outside the Pale of Settlement. Although some reactions were favourable, the probability of its failure was also pointed out. In principle most artisans accepted Bramson's proposal, especially the delegates from outside the Pale (Vologda and Novgorod), who on the basis of their positive experience and their successful integration into their cities approved of such suggested activities. However, they also pointed to the basic problem involved, which was that artisans had to receive papers from their guilds – something which could prove extremely difficult to achieve. Nonetheless, optimism dominated within the ORT leadership and among the artisans, and despite the fact that delegates such as Ginzburg (Berdichev), S. Margolin, and Vysotskii (Vilna) questioned the value of such a move, and rather wanted ORT to concentrate, for instance, on dissemination of know how, the majority of the conference approved Bramson's 'internal migration'. Thus, ORT undertook a project which, given Russian realities, seemed doomed to failure. Nevertheless, two months later, ORT took the next step to realize this plan by setting up a commission for the settlement of Jewish artisans outside the Pale, which was to collect further information on this topic.[148]

Immediately after the conference this new venture's future was already questionable: an anti-Semitic delegation of fourteen, led by Khuzhkov, went to Prime Minister Stolypin in an attempt to diminish the impact of the Artisan congress. They demanded to restrict Jewish competition by forbidding Jewish artisans to open workshops outside the Pale and to reintroduce the old artisans' administration that would be a further means to reduce the importance of Jewish craftsmen. This foreshadowed a future more restrictive course and ended all hopes in a free development of the Russian economy.[149]

## 4.6 JEWISH POLITICAL LOBBYING IN THE THIRD STATE DUMA, THE 'POLISH PROBLEM' AND THE BACKLASH OF ANTI-SEMITISM

As members of the Kadet Duma faction, the two Jewish deputies of the Third Duma, L.N. Niselovich and N.M. Fridman declared from the beginning their complete independence and freedom of action with regard to the Jewish question. Moreover, Niselovich stated that the tactics pursued in the first two Dumas had their value at that time, but since nothing had been achieved, the Jewish question needed to be raised separately and independently. To this end, in April 1908, he sounded out the leaders of various Duma factions concerning a bill on Jewish equality into the Duma.[150] Since the result was, however, discouraging, he shifted his policy towards achieving a gradual improvement of Jewish rights. A month later, in May 1908, during his activity in the Duma commissions, he came to conclude that 'the issue of Jewish equality would not be promising indeed, but according to talks with various Duma deputies, a bill on a part of the Jewish question such as the abolition of the Pale of Settlement could find wider support'.[151] Encouraged by various achievements of his and Fridman's efforts at the level of various Duma commissions such as the budget, finances, the reform of jurisdiction and so on, the probability of winning support for the introduction of an independent Jewish bill,[152] seemed to him only a matter of familiarizing the Duma deputies with Jewish problems, as 'reason of state and the wealth of our common fatherland demanded a positive solution to the Jewish question'.[153]

At this time, Niselovich's confidence in the Duma and the Octobrists was shared neither by the Jewish press nor the various Jewish political groups. For instance, in September 1908 the Zionist Davidson reproached Niselovich of only raising vain hopes with his optimism. In reality, he claimed, the 'Octobrist-Black Hundred Duma had a negative attitude towards the Jewish question, and the only way to protest against this would be that the Jewish deputies leave the Duma as there was no hope for a positive solution.'[154] This criticism seemed to be justified in light of Niselovich's and Fridman's unsuccessful efforts to defend Russian Jews, the former having spoken out in September 1908 against the bill to exclude the Jews from the post of Justice of the Peace,[155] and the latter with his speech on the numerus clausus for Jewish students in May 1909.[156] Niselovich maintained, nevertheless, that the majority of the Duma deputies were positive towards the envisaged bill on the abolition of the Pale.[157] Indeed, in November 1909, Niselovich's policy seemed to bear fruit when he once again sounded out various Duma leaders. In fact, they reassured him that if the Jewish deputies would not press for emancipation in the Duma but would concentrate on partial improvements – such as the abolition of the Pale of Settlement – they would find support among the right.[158] Vague promises were made by the Duma's president N.A. Khomiakov who regarded partial solutions such as the abolition of the Pale as possible and desirable. Similarly, the Octobrist leader A.I. Guchkov resisted promoting equality in general but promised the Octobrists' support of the right of residence to all the citizens without any exceptions. Even the leader of the moderate right, P.N. Krupenskii was prepared to make concessions, despite the fact that he wanted to confine the right of residence for the Jews outside the Pale to the cities, as in his view the Jews would revolutionize the peasants. More concrete was the Kadet leader Miliukov who not only stated that the Kadets would do everything to mitigate the Jews' situation, but went so far to promise parliamentary action: the Kadets intended to raise the demand for the abolition of the Pale within the context of the bill on the inviolability of the Individual.[159] Finally, 155 deputies – among them 27 Octobrists – indeed signed the bill but the Jewish deputies postponed its introduction due to the Jewish Kadet-members of the Kovno Committee who informed the Jewish deputies that the Kadets were not prepared to introduce the bill on the inviolability of the individual at that moment.[160]

Thereafter, Niselovich used the Jewish press to pressurize the Kovno Committee into finally agreeing to the action. He argued that Jewish inequality ought to be raised in the Duma even if this did not promise any success. As an interview with Niselovich in *Razsvet* on 28 February 1910 indicated, Kadet leaders such as Maklakov, Rodichev, Karaulov, Bobrianskii were finally prepared to give up their reservations concerning the bill on the abolition of the Pale. The party agreed to tackle this question within the context of the bill on the inviolability of the individual and its paragraph 15, which in its still valid version stated that every Russian citizen had the right to move freely, with the exception of those cases mentioned by law. As the exceptions included the Jews, the target was to delete the supplement and thus to widen the right of residence to everybody. This had been discussed extensively in the Duma commission on the bill on the inviolability of the Individual throughout 1909, but without results.[161]

Finally, another reform discussed in the Duma brought the Pale bill into the plenum: the introduction of municipal self-government in the former kingdom of Poland.[162] Here the Jewish Liberals were confronted by the problem that Polish Jews did not share their intention to secure equality of rights for Jews in that bill. The reason for this important difference between Russian and Polish Jewish activists lay in the fact that the Polish-Jewish middle class in particular believed that since the Poles were as suppressed a nation as the Jews, Poles and Jews had the same opponent, the Russian government. Therefore, the only solution feasible seemed to support Polish efforts for more autonomy and independence, all the more so as Polish Jews desperately wanted to avoid a further increase of tensions in an already difficult relationship between Poles and Jews. In order not to provoke Polish nationalism minor concessions were not sought, as they might have been accompanied by special Polish disabilities. This is also explained by the fact that in contrast to Russian Jews, the 'assimilationist' movement remained a firm factor within Polish Jewry well into the time of the new Polish Republic; these circles felt predominantly Polish.[163] For Russian-Jewish middle class activists on the other hand, giving equal rights to Jews was a matter of principle also when exemplified by comparatively small matters as Jewish participation in the envisaged municipal self-government in Poland. In November 1910, these two different concepts of the Jewish question clashed when Polish-Jewish delegates Nathanson and Dikshtein – who belonged to the acculturated circle around Bergson and the Warsaw newspaper *Izraelita* – came to St. Petersburg to talk to the Polish Duma deputies and the Russian-Jewish Duma deputies Niselovich and Fridman, to convince them not to act on behalf of Polish Jews and their participation in the future municipal self-government, as this would aggravate the already difficult situation. During these talks, Nathanson and Dikshtein demanded that the Kadets should not interfere, and that the Jewish deputies should not defend Jewish rights in Poland. This stand was, however, unacceptable to all the St. Petersburg Jewish activists. Vinaver, as the advocate of Jewish rights, protested sharply in *Der Fraind* against this action. He dissociated himself from the Polish-Jewish delegates, stressed that Russian Jews would never give up their struggle for equal rights, attacked the delegates as assimilationists, and asked them 'what had given them the right to ask us to shut up when our enemies were getting prepared to restrict our rights even further?'.[164] Finally, Vinaver, Sliozberg and Russian-Jewish intellectuals published a joint declaration protesting against Dikshtein's and Nathanson's intervention claiming that it had been harmful for Jewish interests. They stated their intention to ignore the talks and continue their struggle for full equality. They also repeated their demand for equal rights with regard to municipal self-government in Poland.[165] Sliozberg and Vinaver also attempted to mobilize Polish Jews – Vinaver even went personally to Warsaw – to protest against the *Izraelita* circle and the delegation in order to show the Polish Kolo in the Duma that these people did not truly represent Polish-Jewish opinion. The Liberals finally succeeded: a meeting of 1,400 Warsaw Jews condemned the action, Polish-Jewish workers from Lodz sent their protests to the Social Democrats' Duma faction, and many further protests reached St. Petersburg, for example from the Jewish teachers of Warsaw and from the Polish-Jewish community of Samoshch.[166] However, the Duma commission on the bill on municipal self-government in Poland decided with a vote of 11 to 4 that Jews would not be allowed to be elected to the posts of president, mayor, vice-president and secretary. Fridman demonstrated his disagreement with the decision by leaving the room immediately after the vote.[167] This defeat, together with others – for instance in the question of Sunday rest, where the Duma did not follow the minorities' demands of a free selection of their day of rest – increased the pressure on the Kovenskii Komitet. When *Razsvet* and *Der Fraind* questioned the KK's value, reproached it of secretiveness – as its work was not published – and finally put the blame on the latest anti-Jewish decisions on the inactivity of the KK, the KK responded by publishing parts of its protocols and by agreeing to move the bill into the Duma.[168] Thus, the bill that would have abolished the Pale of Settlement was introduced into the Duma. In accordance with the Kadet Duma faction and with the support of some Octobrists, it was referred to the Commission of the bill on the inviolability of the individual.[169] The Jewish deputies Fridman and Niselovich declared as the next and most important target the collection of appropriate material which would support the demand for the abolition of the Pale in the commission. They were realistic enough to see that success was most uncertain, but they favoured the discussion of the issues in the Duma at the earliest date possible.[170] The material was indeed produced with the help of the ORSE (Obshchestvo dlia rasprostranenie pravilnykh svedenii o evreiakh i evreistve) and communal activists like Bikerman and Yulii Gessen.[171] The bill, however, was buried by a hostile majority in the commission and the prospect of abolishing the Pale was never mentioned again. On the contrary, the right-wing press such as *Novoe Vremia* and *Zemshchina* immediately started an anti-Semitic press campaign to nip in the bud any attempt at partly dismantling Jewish disabilities.[172]

Even worse, in March 1911, the SRN instigated an anti-Semitic campaign in connection with the Yushchinskii murder in Kiev. Various notoriously anti-Semitic newspapers, including Men'shikov's *Russkaia Znamia* started an intensive inflammatory anti-Jewish campaign which changed a simple homicide to a blood libel against the Jewish people as a whole. As early as April 1911, the right-wingers brought an interpellation into the Duma in which they asked the parliament whether it was known that a Jewish sect existed which used Christian blood to bake their Matse, and if this was the case, they demanded the prohibition of the sect. Despite Niselovich's efforts – in alliance with the Duma factions of the Trudoviki, the Social Democrats and the Kadets – to prevent the acceptance of this interpellation, the Duma referred it with a vote of 108 against 93 for further investigation into a commission where, however, it was buried for good.[173] The government also shifted towards an increasingly anti-Semitic course, which was expressed in various ways: through an increase of expulsions of Jews from outside the Pale, the fact that ORPE branches – for instance in Kishinev and Kursk – were more and more hampered in their activities,[174] the closure on 1 July 1911 of the Jewish Literary Society (ELO), which was the most successful Jewish cultural organization with a total of 122 branches in and outside the Pale,[175] and finally, through an increasing reduction of Jewish students at Russian universities.[176]

Anti-Semitism became a much more prominent part of the government's policy – or at least that of certain ministries – when Stolypin was assassinated in Kiev in 1911, and when the new Prime Minister, Kokovtsev faced increasing pressure from the main protagonists of the blood libel, minister of justice Shcheglovitov and minister of interior Maklakov. The change of the political climate became clear when during the debates on Stolypin's assassination and the Kiev branch of the Okhrana failure to protect the prime minister, the Octobrist leader Guchkov did not miss the opportunity to point out that Stolypin was killed by a Jew.[177] This provoked strong protests by Niselovich and led him to conclude with a pessimistic statement that nothing could be achieved any more in the Third Duma, and only a unification of all Jewish forces would enable the Jews to fight the enemies.[178]

The increasing anti-Semitic tendencies within government and Duma, the closure of the ELO, increasing restrictions for Jews, as well as the forthcoming elections to the Fourth Duma, marked a watershed for organic work and Russian-Jewish politics. Answers to the new problems facing Russian Jews had to be found, and new grounds – especially regarding higher education – had to be explored in order to continue and widen organic work.

# 5 The 'Dark Years' after Stolypin: Anti-Semitism, Co-operation and the Peak of 'Organic Work'

Despite the growing anti-Semitism in Russia and Poland, the beginning of the Beilis Case, governmental repressions such as widespread expulsions, the closing down of the Jewish Literary Society in July 1911, and other restrictions on the cultural activities of Russian Jews, Jewish social activists continued their struggle for education, economic self-help, as well as their political efforts. It seemed that further restrictions only spurred on the activists, and led to a creativity in organizations like ORPE and ORT which sometimes, however, left Russian realities far behind, but which, nevertheless, was to become the basis for further development after World War I in the resurrected Polish Republic.[1]

Obviously, the work of Jewish activists had to affect a certain shift towards the struggle against anti-Semitism, but the main emphasis still lay on the search for modernization of Jewish society and on improving the Jewish lot. Surprisingly, it was during the so-called 'dark period' of Russian-Jewish history, between 1911 and 1914, that Jewish creativity witnessed its peak. Now the grassroots of Jewish society responded to the growing anti-Semitism with an ever increasing participation in all forms of economic and cultural self-help. At the other end of the social pyramid, on the top levels of ORT and ORPE Jewish social activists widened the scope of their activities, improved their efficiency, and thus took organic work another step forward. In general, the period witnessed an important increase in joint activities by all Jewish political groups. The highlights of this period were the inner-Jewish reform efforts through ORT and ORPE, as well as their efforts to gain recognition for these reforms on the general Russian level, that is at various All-Russian congresses such as the co-operatives and on national education. Furthermore, during the election campaign to the Fourth State Duma they fought Polish anti-Semitism and actively encouraged Polish Jews to follow the Russian Jews' struggle for equality. Due to the threats posed by the Beilis Case and the latest anti-Semitic actions by the ultra-right in parliament, the first actions of the

Liberals had to be directed against the blood libel and at organizing the struggle against the increasingly anti-Semitic course of both Duma and government.

## 5.1 THE STRUGGLE AGAINST BLOOD ALLEGATIONS AND ANTI-SEMITISM

The latest anti-Semitic events in the Duma, as well as the increasing number of anti-Semitic articles in the right-wing Russian press, brought about a policy which was a combination of a return to the tactics adopted before the 1905 Revolution and the newer form of social activities, organic work. Anti-Semitism was again fought through 'diplomacy' and an attempt to mobilize Jewish and Russian public. The means were on the one side fighting anti-Semitism by informing the Russian public of the realities of Jewish life, and thus improving the understanding of Jewish efforts to attain full civil rights; and on the other, educating Russian Jews with respect to Jewish history, philosophy, and culture. Various Jewish organizations were instrumental in these undertakings: most notably the Society for the Dissemination of True Knowledge on the Jews and Judaism (ORSE) which a few months later even started its own newspaper;[2] the Jewish Historic-Ethnographic Society, which through the lectures and seminars it held throughout the period also served the purpose of fighting prejudices and blood allegations;[3] other newly-founded organizations included the Jewish Scientific-Literary Society ('Evreiskoe nauchno-literaturnoe obshchestvo'), founded by S.M. Ginzburg and the St. Petersburg rabbi Dr. Aizenshtat, and the Society for the Promotion of Jewish Science ('Obshchestvo pooshchreniia evreiskoi nauki') founded by M.M. Vavelberg, A.D. Gintsburg and G.B. Sliozberg.

All these organizations were characterized by this double purpose: on the one side, to provide Russian Jews with a forum to discuss issues concerning Jewish history, philosophy, and cultural life, and to develop Jewish scholarship and literature; on the other, to acquaint broader circles in Russia who were present at these discussions, through the presentation of Jewish topics. Surely enough, these organizations were mainly concentrated in St. Petersburg and the authorities restricted their activities to this city. This especially applied to the successor organization of the ELO, the ENLO, which – given these limits – could never reach the popularity and spread of the ELO.[4] Nonetheless, these restrictions did not hinder the dissemination of ideas which were carried to the provinces by the Jewish press of St. Petersburg. Newspapers such as *Razsvet, Novyi Voskhod* or the

Yiddish daily *Der Fraind* (since December 1909 in Warsaw) reported frequently and in detail on all the congresses and activities of these organizations. By providing the province with this information, organizational framework was substituted by a network of information on the modernization efforts.

The first steps in the campaign against the inflammatory anti-Semitism of many right-wing organs – which tried to portray the Yushchinskii murder as a ritual murder and use it for their own purposes – was the organisation of Jewish and Russian public protest. Within Russia, the Jewish social activists of all colours mobilized the rabbis – as the official leaders of the Jewish community – to expose the blood libel as a concoction of the anti-Semitic press, and to undermine the attempts of the right-wing to present the Jews as a clandestine sect plotting against the Russian state. This action met with full success as rabbis from all parts of Russia sent protest letters against the blood libel by emphasizing that neither a blood ritual, nor a specific Jewish sect exercising it existed.[5] They also had considerable success in convincing Russian public opinion to join them in their struggle against this newest form of governmental anti-Semitism. The political opposition in the country, above all the Kadets and the Socialists of all colours reacted positively as this trial could easily be turned against the government to demonstrate its backwardness and utterly reactionary complexion. Consequently, all oppositional forces in Russia protested against the fabrication of the Beilis Case by anti-Semites within and outside the government. Towards the end of 1911 a joint declaration of Russian writers, scholars, and politicians was published carrying the signatures of 66 Duma deputies, six members of the Russian State Council, and famous writers such as Vladimir Korolenko, Fedor Sologub, Aleksander Blok, aristocrats like Counts I.I. Tolstoi and Aleksei Tolstoi, professors A. Zhizhilenko, M. Tugan-Baranovskii, Ervin-Grimm, L. Petrazhitskii, P. Chubinskii, and Kadet-leaders Struve, Petrunkevich, Miliukov and V.D. Nabokov.[6] Finally, articles written by Russian and Jewish intellectuals, such as Vladimir Korolenko, S. Elpatevskii or M. L'vovich, or the Bundist Vladimir Medem and the Zionist Vladimir Zhabotinskii appeared in Russian newspapers. The Russian intellectuals condemned anti-Semitism as a shame for a civilized country and as 'a means used by the Counter-Revolutionary forces to combat the progressive forces'. They called on the Russian public to consider the Jewish question as a general Russian problem to be dealt with by everybody.[7] While Medem repeated once again the Jewish social activists' and Bund's demand for national-cultural autonomy and the right to satisfy one's cultural needs freely, Zhabotinskii emphasized the need for a structural change in Russia: without a federation of independent nationalities there would be no equality of rights for the nationalities, no progress, and thus, no future for anybody.[8]

The protest also reached the international level. Letters of public protest from France, England, Germany and Austria carrying the signatures of the most prominent figures of the respective country were sent to the Russian government and were published in Russian newspapers. Furthermore, Lucien Wolf's newspaper *Jewish Chronicle* constantly and precisely informed the British reader about the restrictive and anti-Semitic course of the Russian government. The attempts of 1905–06 to put pressure on the Russian government through diplomacy and foreign public opinion culminated between 1912 and 1914 with the edition of a special supplement called *Darkest Russia*.[9] Other West European and American-Jewish activists such as Jacob Schiff, Louis Marshall and Paul Nathan had been lobbying since the Revolution of 1905 and the emergence of Jewish Liberal forces with the Soiuz Polnopraviia within their respective governments for a tougher course towards the Russian government because of its anti-Jewish attitudes. Also, whenever the Russian government was seeking loans in Western countries, many Western Jewish bankers would step up the pressure by making the availability of funds dependent on a relaxation of the government's policy towards its Jewish citizens.[10] The Yushchinskii or Beilis case therefore not only damaged the Russian government's reputation abroad, but also had a serious impact on Russian-American relations. With respect to the so-called passport question the US Government came increasingly under pressure from American-Jewish leaders. Due to the fact that American citizens were directly affected – the Russian government did not differentiate between a Russian Jew and a Jew holding a US passport, and consequently applied restrictive legislation to American Jews visiting Russia – Louis Marshall's campaign in US government circles for anti-Russian measures was finally successful: in December 1911, the American government decided not to extend the Russian-American trade agreement which expired at that time.[11]

Finally, all the efforts by the ministers of Justice and Interior to make the case against Mendel Beilis by bribing witnesses, setting up a jury favourable to this end, and so on – which were increasingly disapproved of even by Russian conservatives – came to naught: Mendel Beilis was acquitted in the trial which took place in Kiev in the autumn of 1913.[12]

However, the regime's unwillingness to accept the verdict and instead to launch an even more restrictive course became evident in its reactions to the protest movement sweeping the country. As Miliukov pointed out, '102 penalties were directed against the press, including the arrest of six editors, and 120 professional and cultural-educational societies were either closed or declared illegal'.[13] On top of this, in May 1914, 25 lawyers were put on trial for their protests against the Beilis Case, including EDG leader Leon Bramson, D.I. Khienkin and ORPE activist G.A. Goldberg who were all sentenced to six months' imprisonment.[14]

Surprisingly, even during this period, the struggle against blood libel and anti-Semitism was not, and never became, the main concern of Jewish-Liberal politics. Organic work and the modernization of Jewish society remained more important. Here, Jewish social activists continued to pursue their efforts through ORPE and ORT – the only legal Jewish organizations which were allowed to hold congresses and meetings on a wider scale – to carry the modernization of Jewish life in Russia further, and to fit a modernized Jewish society into the wider framework of a modernizing and industrializing Russia. This approach was to be reinforced by the composition of the new Duma which was again dominated by reactionaries. Political efforts were now redirected from lobbying within the Duma, to lobbying through general all-Russian congresses convened in the following period for the discussion of various economic and educational reform plans.

## 5.2   THE ELECTIONS TO THE FOURTH STATE DUMA AND THE END OF PARLIAMENTARY POLITICS

Since at that time the elections to the Duma offered the only legal opportunity to propagate political ideas nationwide and to mobilize the Jewish voters, they once again triggered hopes among the Jewish political groups for a political change. If with respect to the government this might have been hope against hope, there still could be gains expected for the inner Jewish situation. Therefore, former alliances between all oppositional parties, aiming at outvoting the conservatives, were reinforced. Jewish Liberals called the Jewish voters to participate in the elections, and to vote for the most progressive candidates.[15] The Jewish population responded positively, and the general trend towards co-operation among Jewish social activists of all colours continued. The old demands of previous elections – such as the demand for the convocation of an all Jewish congress[16] – resurfaced, but were not insisted upon with the same intensity. Therefore, common election committees were easily formed in Vilna, Kovno, St. Petersburg and in many other places. The St. Petersburg Committee again assumed some kind of leadership role. It consisted of all the members of the Kovno Committee, and two representatives of each of the

Jewish political groups, that is the ENG, EDG, and Zionists. In the constituencies, the Jewish Duma candidates consisted mainly of lawyers, doctors, engineers, state rabbis, bankers and local social activists.[17]

All hopes, however, for a fair election campaign were soon crushed by a regime which went to great lengths to secure a conservative Duma. Local authorities once again meddled into the campaign and seriously disadvantaged and hampered the oppositional parties on all levels and with all possible means: manipulations at the polls, falsifications of the voters' lists,[18] arbitrary division of the minorities into separate curiae[19] and so on. Finally, the Senate reduced the number of Jewish voters by excluding all Jews with only a conditional right of residence outside the Pale, dependent on the exercise of a certain profession. This excluded among others all Jewish artisans outside the Pale.[20] All this was topped by ultra-rightist pogrom threats,[21] which discouraged many Jewish voters to go to the polls or led to indifference.[22]

It could be no surprise that the election campaign in Odessa, the citadel of the Black Hundreds – where Jewish voters commanded half of the votes, and where therefore all the Jewish newspapers had been optimistic – resulted in a right-wing 'victory'. Sadly, Jewish Liberals had overestimated the strength of the Jewish vote in the first city curia, as had Zionists and Nationalists, who, falsely encouraged by the news that some conservative Russian candidates had withdrawn their candidature,[23] put forward their own candidates for Odessa's second curia, the lawyer Shapiro and Vladimir Zhabotinskii, against the Kadet candidate and Duma deputy Nikolskii.[24] The fact that Jewish Liberals had set up an alliance with the Kadets[25] and had advanced Sliozberg as the common candidate, had triggered off the 'old battle' between Liberals and Nationalists[26] – although Sliozberg in his campaign adopted an autonomist position.[27] In the end, both sides were outmanoeuvred by the ultra-right which used all possible means of intimidation in order to secure the victory of their favourites in both curiae: in the first, the principal of the university, Levashev, and in the second, bishop Anatoli.[28]

Jewish aspirations were also dashed after the triumph of their favourite, the worker Yagiello, in the Warsaw elections as Polish Nationalist retaliated with an intensified anti-Jewish economic boycott. In Warsaw, nerves were frayed by the fact that the Russian government had restructured and increased the electoral districts in Warsaw from twelve to fifteen in a way that gave Jews a majority in eight of them, with Jewish and Polish votes being equal in two others. In light of already existing tensions, Warsaw Jews had decided to forgo the nomination of a Jewish candidate,[29] to no avail: as their negotiations with the National Democrats – in which they even offered Jewish support on the condition that the ND candidate would openly support Jewish equality – failed, they then set up a Jewish election committee which started discussions on which candidate to support instead.[30] Since the circle of acculturated Jews around Nathanson and Dr. Herts still called on the Jews to vote for Polish candidates,[31] Russian-Jewish Liberals interfered. First, Vinaver cabled a telegram to the Warsaw daily *Haint* in which he supported the Nationalists' position by stating that the Jews should not vote for a candidate who did not support Jewish equality, but he still thought it wise not to exploit their majority of votes. Instead, he suggested to encourage the Polish Progressists to nominate their own candidate with a platform of equal rights. Vinaver also activated Kadet leaders such as Miliukov, Petrunkevich and Rodichev who publicly came out in support of his views. Finally, when the Social Democrats nominated the worker Yagiello, Vinaver called on Warsaw Jews to vote for him as the only candidate standing for the principle of equality. Vinaver argued that with the election of Yagiello the anti-Semitic outrages in Poland would come to an end, and the relations between the two nations would normalize. This is how Vinaver expressed the Jewish Liberal ideology as applied to Polish conditions:

> Poles and Polish Jews are politically one nation, but the Jews may hope for the right of cultural self-determination. Polish Jews must be united with the Poles as far as general political ideas are concerned. They must even now share the enthusiasm for Polish autonomy. Therefore, Polish Jews ought to co-operate with the Polish parties for general Polish political ideals. The condition for this co-operation is, however, the Poles' recognition of the Jews as citizens with equal rights in the country. . . . In case the progressive part of the Poles would try to impose the election of an anti-Semite, Polish Jews would be forced to take their fate in their own hands, that is to create those conditions without which a co-existence between the two peoples, which politically build one nation would be impossible.[32]

Warsaw Jews apparently shared Vinaver's views as Yagiello was finally elected with their support. However, as far as peaceful co-existence was concerned, Vinaver proved to be wrong. The Poles followed the ND's call for an economic boycott of Jewish shops as a reaction to the Jewish support for Yagiello.[33]

The Duma elections resulted in three Jewish deputies: the first and only Jewish Duma deputy ever elected in Poland, Dr. Bomash (Lodz), Gurevich (Courland), and the re-elected Fridman (Kovno).[34] However, the Fourth Duma elections did not bring about the overwhelming conservative majority anticipated by Tsar and government, and feared by the opposition. Despite all the machinations, restrictions, manipulations, pogrom threats, exclusions of masses of voters etc, the ultra-right parties suffered an unexpected defeat as the Duma witnessed only a slight increase of right-wing seats.[35] This temporarily raised hopes among the Kadets for a more conciliatory attitude within the government. The Jewish deputies did not, however, share this optimism, nor did they expect anything from the Duma. As early as November 1912 the new deputy Bomash stated that the main task of Jewish deputies must be the defence of the Jews against anti-Semitic outrages in the Duma and he insisted that more attention should be paid to 'extra-parliamentary' work. Since no other Jewish advice board existed, he consulted the Kovenskii Komitet, which supported him with the slogan of Jewish defense in the Duma and intensification of the efforts outside it – that is organic work. This view was partly shared by the other new deputy, Gurevich, who also advocated a defensive approach as the general direction of the Duma was not yet evident.[36] Nonetheless, Fridman, the third Jewish deputy, took a more active line demanding from the Kadets to introduce a separate bill requesting the abolition of all anti-Jewish restrictions.[37] His action succeeded insofar as the Kadets agreed to include a special paragraph in their draft bill on civil freedom.[38] For a short time Fridman pursued his independent policy, protesting in the Duma in December 1912 against the fact that in Kokovtsev's government's declaration, the Jewish question was not mentioned with a single word. Three days later, he held another speech in which he reproached the government for its reactionary tendencies, making Jewish life even more intolerable. He concluded his speech by demanding from the government finally to fulfil the promises of the October Manifesto of 1905.[39]

However, soon after this short period of political offensive, hopes gave way to reality and the Jewish deputies implemented the Kovno Committee's advice to play a rather defensive part. In the following period, the Fourth Duma was too preoccupied with general Russian problems, and therefore lobbying for Jewish rights became less and less promising. The political situation grew worse, and the prospects for a move such as the introduction of a pro-Jewish rights bill became hopeless. Moreover, the minister of interior Makarov was dismissed in December 1912, and was replaced by the hard-liner Maklakov, the former governor of the gubernia of Chernigov. One of his first actions was to withdraw Makarov's decision to convene another Rabbi Commission, which made it obvious that not the slightest hope for reforms was justified.[40] Furthermore, in late 1913 Maklakov denied the request of St. Petersburg Jewish social activists to convene a Jewish congress which – similar to Kovno – was to discuss the social, cultural and religious affairs of Russian Jewry, and to set up a representative Jewish body.[41]

The belief in the Duma as the place through which Russian Jews could ameliorate their situation faded away as the bill on civil liberties introduced into the Duma by the Kadets in February 1913, did not even entail a special discussion on the Jewish question.[42] The growing frustration with the Duma among Russian Jews in general and some Jewish Liberals in particular became evident when in March 1913, the Liberal Sliozberg in desperation approached the Russian Prime Minister Kokovtsev with his demand to do something for Russian Jews by invoking article 87 of the Basic Law, by excluding the legislative bodies.[43] Sliozberg's action was a lonely act of frustration, not based on any agreed policy. He may not have believed in it himself. The Jewish national press condemned his action, reviving the old shibboleth of the undemocratic shtadlan.

Jewish politics in the Duma ended in March 1914, after Fridman had introduced a bill abolishing the percentage norm for Jewish assistant attorneys signed by seventy-six Duma deputies.[44] One month later, the last pro-Jewish action before the War took place when the SD Duma faction introduced a bill removing all disabilities for minorities, the Jews included. The SD Duma faction's mouthpiece *Put Pravdy* explained that the SDs introduced the bill because nationalities as the Jews had become the victims of exploitation and repression in the same way as the workers. Anti-Jewish actions, such as pogroms and the Beilis Case, had grown to an unacceptable extent which forced the organized Marxists to pay more attention to the Jewish question. The Social Democrats did not expect anything from the 'nationalistic-Purishkevich Duma' – as they called the parliament – but stated: 'the working class felt obliged at least to raise its voice, and especially against national suppression the voice of the Russian worker must be raised'. Finally, it called on Russian workers to support the bill energetically by official resolutions.[45]

## 5.3  ECONOMIC REFORM PLANS: IDEALS, UNFULFILLED DREAMS, THE ORT

The productivization of Jewish labour remained the red thread and basis of ORT activity. The ways and means to realise this depended, however, to a great extent on the options left by a regime hampering many Jewish efforts and suspicious of modernization. Nevertheless, Tsarist Russia was in midst of economic modernization, regardless of whether or not the regime, in this case the Tsar and the ministry of interior, accepted them.

Instead, Russia's modernization imperatively demanded political, administrative and social change;[46] institutionally, the Ministry of Finance represented such need for reform in the interest of industrialization and modernization.[47] For instance, it was the Ministry of Finance which in 1904 paved the way for a modern co-operative movement by liberalizing and deregulating the setting up of co-operatives which not only resulted in a vast explosion of loan and credit associations, but also provided Russia with a rather well functioning system of co-operative credit.[48] Concomitantly, Russian economic bodies and institutions became increasingly aware of the fact that, to move ahead economically, free development was needed. Therefore, restrictions against minorities in general, and Jews in particular, came more and more under fire. Russian economic organizations increasingly interceded with the government whenever it announced further restrictions on Russian Jews which – like the mere existence of the Pale – could only damage the overall economy.[49] In spite of the anti-Semitic backlash in the Third Duma, the parliament remained the place where economic and educational reforms were discussed. And although the clamour for 'nationalization' of Russian trade and industry[50] led to intermittent anti-Jewish acts such as the exclusions of Jewish traders from Russian fairs, the Duma and its reform projects could still be influenced by Jewish activists, as such plans were usually submitted to the consideration of all-Russian congresses for further recommendations. Against this background the Russian government could not pursue its repressive course as thoroughly and coherently in the economic sphere as in the field of education. The industrialization and modernization of Russia, therefore, provided a niche from which ORT could continue its efforts to enable Russian Jews to preserve or find for themselves a place in a modernized Russia; this trend of ORT activity became increasingly evident in the years from 1911 to 1914.

This policy of ORT, to link their efforts on behalf of Russian Jews with the modernization process of Russia was made possible by the positive results of industrialization and the overall modernization of Russian economy. As Arcadius Kahan has pointed out, especially the 'process of industrialization and the commercialization of agriculture, as well as the urbanization had created new wants, a demand for new kinds of goods, new skills and new types of services. New opportunities arose which made the employment of large groups less dependent upon the local markets and more dependent upon the organization of the national market'.[51] Within the scope of this process, two factors increasingly played an important role: the Jewish entrepreneurs and the co-operative movement.

These two were especially important as the policies of the regime and the local administrations with their expulsions of Jews living in the country-side, accelerated the urbanization process of Russian Jews. Despite the fact that EKO had set up a more efficient system to help those that intended to emigrate – and as the statistics show many Jewish artisans and traders indeed chose this option[52] – Jewish centres such as Warsaw, Lodz, Odessa, Vilna and Ekaterinoslav witnessed an explosion in numbers.[53] This also meant increased competition among Jews in a field where Jews not only had a virtual monopoly, but where numbers were already far in excess of economic demand. The new hope was now that with industrial-ization, the Russian peasant's purchasing power had increased and Jewish handicraft would profit from this. With the discovery of the Russian peasant as a consumer, Jewish handicraft met with the interest of Jewish merchants and traders interested in expanding their ventures. The loss of mobility – due to urbanization and expulsions – was counterbalanced by initiatives of traders and by the co-operative movement, both of whom undertook the marketing of goods over long distances.[54]

Moreover, Jewish artisans started independently to organize themselves locally and to market their products. For instance, Jewish artisans initiated two producer co-operatives in Kishinev in October 1911, one for tailors' products, and one for shoemakers' products. In November 1911, the Jew-ish furniture workers of Zhitomir followed this example.[55] To encourage these grass root initiatives, ORT subsidized the two newly-founded even-ing courses for joiners in Belostok and Bobruisk, and granted a loan of 1,500 Roubles to the 'Communal warehouse for joiners' products in Bobruisk'.[56] Furthermore, it subsidized furniture warehouses in Zhitomir and Ekaterinoslav. Publications were also deemed very important, and included books on models of economic self-activity of artisans in Russian and Yiddish.[57] An interaction between grass roots and the centres took place in which ORT not only gained increasing support but its reputation as an institution for economic and educational activity grew. For instance, Jewish community activists from Berdichev asked ORT to open a local branch as they intended to set up a cultural organization which at the same time would aim at improving the technical skills of the artisans and the economic situation.[58] Due to these positive signs at the grass roots ORT unanimously decided to set up new branches in the gubernia of Mogilev and in the town of Mir (gubernia Minsk).[59]

In light of a great response to activities from the centre and of independ-ent initiatives at the grass roots which led to a mushrooming of Jewish organizations, ORT regularized – or at least subsidized – all the efforts at integrating the Jewish work force into the process of modernization in Russia. Jewish societies pooled their resources and co-ordinated their efforts.

ORT co-operated with locally-based organizations such as the Society of Labour Aid ('Obshchestvo Trudovoi Pomoshchi') in Vilna, the Odessa-based Society Labour (TRUD), the Society for the Development and Promotion of Productive Work among the Jews in Russia ('Obshchestvo dlia razvitiia i pooshchreniia proizvoditel'nago truda sredi evreev v Rossii') – initiated by M.I. Varshavskii, B.A. Kamenka, and M.I. Vavelberg – in St. Petersburg, the Society for the Building of Cheap Houses which existed in Belostok (formed in September 1910), Dvinsk (form July 1911) and Vilna;[60] ORT co-ordinated its activity with the EKO as in many cases their activities overlapped.[61] In close collaboration with these organizations, ORT aimed at expanding any promising activity in the field of production within Jewish society. In some cases ORT even spearheaded general Russian reforms. For instance, since 1909 ORT was organizing and subsidizing courses for electricians at the Vilna artisans' school – which according to Leon Shapiro, preceded the 'city-projected introduction of an electrical street car system' – as well as courses for automobile mechanics in St. Petersburg.[62] With the same intentions, and by adjusting to the new demands of the market, the Vilna Society for labour aid founded, a couple of months later, an artistic workshop for ladies' skirts. The workshop which had admitted twenty Jewish seamstresses was provided with the newest technical and hygienic equipment.[63]

On top of this, ORT set up a special commission in September 1911 with the intention of finding work for the graduates of artisan schools and vocational courses and to convince more and more Jewish parents to register their children with schools and courses in order to make the intended system of vocational training take root in Jewish society.[64] Here, ORT anticipated the recommendations of M.L. Bolotin who at an ORT conference one month later in St. Petersburg reported on the lack of students in the artisans' schools – a fact which was already well known to the ORT leaders.[65] Bolotin's criticism was borne out by local reports, published in 1911, and carried the disconcerting message that only a small percentage of apprentices finished the courses. However, the facts showed also the success of the courses and artisan schools, and proved that ORT's concentration on vocational training was heading the right way. For instance, the 231 artisans who graduated between 1895 and 1910 from the Vilna artisan school – founded in 1892 – had stayed in their profession and became 'multiplicators' as they could educate others. Furthermore, within the period from 1903 to 1913, the Vilna-based Society for labour aid had trained almost 2,000 artisans who 'won several medals at important exhibitions'.[66]

Finally, the evening courses became especially important for Jewish women as a means of achieving an education which the traditional Jewish school system had refused them, as girls were not admitted to the Heder. Thus, the struggle for general education and against illiteracy among Jews – especially among Jewish women – showed its first positive results.[67]

ORT agreed to the Kovno Conference's proposal that besides vocational training the most important step to improving the lot of the craftsmen would be the creation of a nationwide marketing organization, which was to sell their products on the market as well as to provide them with modern tools and machines; it thus immediately realized that both targets could ideally be achieved through the credit co-operatives which at that time were spreading all over the Pale. The Jewish Credit Societies, as well as the Saving and Loan co-operatives, did not only increase – while the former grew to 132 (at 1 January 1912), the latter increased from 166 before 1907 to 680 in 1911 – but also became financially independent from EKO by a constant growth of their turnover, and thus ran almost self-sufficiently.[68]

As had been the case with their fellow Russian activists, ORT activists realised, however, that a further development of the co-operatives' movement needed a nationwide network with an organization which could co-ordinate efforts and swap resources. The opportunity to propagate this idea, and at the same time to raise the demands for equality of rights, came when an all-Russian Congress of the Co-operatives was organized on 11 March 1912 in St. Petersburg to discuss a new proposed bill on small credit. The opportunity presented by the congress was also used by ORT and EKO to gather Jewish delegates from all over the country, which was increasingly difficult to arrange as the presence of provincial delegates needed the permission of the Tsarist administration. One of these gatherings was presided by G.B. Sliozberg, and attended by prominent ORT leaders such as Braudo, S.O. Margolin (St. Petersburg), Morgulis (Lodz), and by new men such as Solomonov (Kishinev) and Levin (Gomel).[69] In accordance with the representatives of the Central Committee of the EKO and ORT, it was agreed at this meeting that the Jewish delegates would demand that 'the opening of loan institutions should also be allowed to petty traders, the administration should no longer have the right to shut down existing Loan and Saving Co-operatives, and that fewer new credit institutions should be founded'.[70] As experience had shown, the credit co-operatives faced the problem that since the local authorities could not control them, they often shut them down quite arbitrarily. Therefore, Jewish members of the 'legislative section' of the all-Russian congress, I.A. Blium, L.S. Zak and S.B. Ratner suggested an addition to the draft law to the effect that a credit co-operative could only be shut down by a regular court. Zak, who also was chairman of the credit section, promoted ORT's suggestion of a nationwide organization including all credit co-operatives, Jewish and non-Jewish alike, and of opening up the co-operative movement to all the professions, as he regarded this as necessary for the further successful development of the credit co-operatives. The Jewish delegates achieved their target at least partially as the congress indeed recommended that everybody could become a member irrespective of social status or profession.[71] Finally, from 1913 onwards the ORT activists saw their wish for a unification of local co-operatives under regionally-based umbrella organizations become a reality. Under the pressure of World War I, the government opened the gates completely, and until the Revolution of 1917 six huge regionally-based consumer co-operatives appeared, embracing nearly 691,000 members; and the same applied to the Russian credit co-operatives which underwent the same concentration.[72]

The framework of Jewish organic work within ORT was finally completed in mid-1912. Shortly after the co-operative congress, reports on a strike movement in the textile industry and on problems caused by the modernization process in that branch of industry became frequent in the Jewish press. At the same time, reports on promising results of Jewish agricultural ventures reached the ORT leadership. Since ORT was interested not only in finding new fields of employment for Russian Jews and in dismantling the unnatural occupational structure, but also in seeking to integrate the Jewish work force into a modernized Russia, it was not surprising that ORT leaders immediately took up these fields. Encouraged by the success of committees set up locally by masters and social activists in convincing some Jewish entrepreneurs in the textile industry to employ Jews in modern factories with mechanized looms – for instance in Lodz, Tomashevo and Zdunskaia Volia[73] – in April 1912 ORT sent a representative, accompanied by a specialist, to Zdunskaia Volia in order to explore the local conditions of the weavers, and the best means of how to help the local weavers' attempts to switch from manual to mechanized looms.[74]

Furthermore, at ORT's general meeting of 30 September 1912, B.D. Brutskus convinced ORT to increase efforts in one of its former main targets: Jewish agriculture. In his report he referred to the successes achieved by Jewish farmers in the tobacco industry (government of Bessarabia), vegetable gardening (governments of Minsk and Grodno), hop-culture (government of Volynia), viticulture, cattle-breeding and processing of milk products, in all of which Jews played a major role. Brutskus demanded two things as the basis for success: funds and experts. Encouraged by Bramson's reference to earlier ORT successes in the field of agriculture the meeting agreed to the proposed expansion of ORT activity. The financial question, which remained ORT's biggest problem due to its small budget, was to be solved by 'engaging' the flourishing credit co-operatives in these agricultural ventures. Additional funds were to be collected by widespread propaganda within Jewish Society. Experts also had to be mobilized if the initiative was to get off the ground.[75]

In both cases, however, ORT had to take special problems into account. With respect to integrating Jewish weavers into the modern textile industry, ORT had to face the problem that the class struggle cut across inner Jewish solidarities. Additionally, growing tensions between Jews and Poles made it difficult to bring Jewish workers into modern factories. In many cases Jewish entrepreneurs and factory owners gave priority to their interests as employers and thus undermined ORT's efforts to secure Jewish weavers their place at the mechanized looms. They preferred non-Jewish workers, for the obvious reason that they could not afford to stop the production for two days – as the Russian government did not recognize Shabbat as the day of rest. ORT activists appealed to Jewish employers with some moderate success, and a certain number of them began to employ more Jews at their modernized factories.[76] As no official data are available for this period, it is hard to measure the success in this field.

With agriculture ORT soon realized that it was up against insurmountable forces, among them legislation preventing Jews from settling in the countryside and local authorities expelling Jews even without legal basis. And in light of the permanent lack of funds, ORT had to limit its activity to fields which were most promising. For example: ORT's annual report for 1913 showed an overall budget of 54,023 Roubles, which it invested only into those ventures which proved most promising. Consequently, the lion's share of the budget went into vocational training such as the artisans schools, the support of the electro-mechanic courses in Vilna, the propagation of artisans' instruction, granting stipends to students of the artisan schools, support for the co-operatives, and finally some funds for the newly discovered vegetable gardening. The trend towards scientifically-based work can be observed in the fact that for the first time funds for statistical surveys of particular handicrafts appeared on ORT's balance sheet.[77]

Given these financial and political limits, Jewish social activists decided to base future organic work on projects whose suitability could be proved rather than on ideals: ORT increasingly employed surveys which it ran in co-operation with the newly-founded 'Jewish Society for Statistics' in Vilna on 23 April 1913.[78] In other respects, ORT decision-making was also based on first-hand information. In May 1913 ORT extended the statistical surveys already started among the Jewish artisan workshops in Kovno to a regional level. To get more feedback from local activists ORT organized regional meetings, for instance, in Vilna, Minsk and Bobruisk.

Local Jewish community activists supported these endeavours.[79] A special conference called by ORT in July 1913, with the participation of the provincial delegates, was to help in deciding future activities.[80]

The opportunity to convoke such a conference, and to continue the work for the co-operatives and for equal rights presented itself with the Second All-Russian Co-operatives' Congress which took place in the beginning of August 1913, in Kiev. As the congress was of very progressive, not to say radical complexion, the major target of the Jewish delegates – a pro-Jewish declaration – was already reached after the first day. This showed itself in other fields too. The 'credit section' announced that the congress would recommend to Duma and State Council a law which would grant co-operatives more freedom and would allow a nationwide network of co-operatives.[81] Since the number of Jewish delegates was considerable – out of 1,200 delegates, 200 were Jewish, representing 600 Jewish Loan and Saving Co-operatives – ORT organized a Jewish conference at the Co-operatives' congress. During this conference – where 85 of the 200 Jewish delegates appeared – the main issue was the question of whether the credit co-operatives should be run independently (implying that they no longer needed the EKO's tutelage). This claim for more independence, raised by the spokesman of the co-operatives, Jacob Leshchinskii, reflected the fact that by 1913 the co-operatives (now numbering 680) had achieved major successes: their total capital had reached the amount of 40 million roubles (compared with the 1911 figure of 11 million) and the total of registered members had reached 450,000. Given the fact that only one family member could join a co-operative, the co-operatives probably provided around 40 or 50 per cent of the Jewish population with loans and credits. The reliability of the debtors was very high. For instance, in 1909 only 2.5 per cent of the loans were outstanding.[82] Taking these numbers into account, it was understandable that Leshchinskii rejected further meddling by St. Petersburg activists. Heated disputes ensued between him and the EKO delegates. The conflict was defused by concentrating on practical decisions. At the second session, the conference agreed to set up a committee which was to disseminate information on the co-operatives within Jewish society, and to set up a bank for mutual credit for the Jewish co-operatives. An organizational compromise between the representatives of the Jewish co-operatives and the EKO delegates was reached as the conference elected a joint committee, consisting of twelve representatives of the co-operatives and the EKO leaders, in order to achieve a better co-ordination. Finally, the propagation of the co-operative idea was to be pursued by a new journal in Yiddish.[83] The last decision was realised when the book-keeper of the trading company for mutual credit in Minsk, Tseitlin, received the permission to edit a journal called *Der Kooperativer Kredit in Mayrer Kant* ('the co-operative credit in the North-West Region') which was published four times a month.[84] These decisions of the Jewish conference were summarized in a final resolution, reported by M.B. Ratner to the general Russian congress, which approved it on 7 August 1913.[85]

Despite this success, however, due to its limited budget and the restrictions imposed by the legislation, ORT was forced to take stock of its activity at its meeting which took place on 14–15 February 1914 in St. Petersburg, under the chairmanship of G.B. Sliozberg, Bramson, Blank and so on. During this meeting, a re-evaluation and a sorting out of realistic and unrealistic projects took place resulting in the decision to give handicraft absolute priority over agricultural work, and to concentrate on fields less affected by outside interference such as small production. Acknowledging realities ORT also withdrew from the project of resettling Jewish artisans outside the Pale; this project had been pursued by ORT since the Artisans' Congress in 1911, and was still strongly supported by Bramson, but branded by his fellow Young Turks, L.V. Frenkel (Vilna) as not applicable to real life, and by B.D. Brutskus as an impossible and undesirable venture.[86]

It was the provincial delegates that were able to push through their views with the help of the information based on inquiries. For instance, Bolotin, B.M. Velikovskii and I.S. Voltke demanded more concentration on vocational training for both apprentices and instructors, on the basis of an inquiry made in 1913 among joiners, furniture workers and tailors, as well as on an inquiry on all Jewish handicrafts in Bobruisk. The reports reinforced present predilections as they seemed to convey a threatening message: they described a decrease in the number of apprentices, an increase of non-Jewish apprentices in Jewish workshops, and an increase of non-Jewish journeymen and masters in handicrafts which were hitherto regarded a Jewish domain. The report attributed this decline to technical backwardness, which also brought with it lower salaries in handicraft production. Therefore, the more capable elements looked for employment outside handicraft, or like the majority of the apprentices joined the big industry. To prevent future drop-outs, the reports advocated the improvement of production technique, more evening courses for adult artisans, and the edition of further books and manuals on handicraft technic.[87]

Another report by S.E. Sistrin on the statistical inquiry into the field of small production convinced the congress to continue and even widen the statistical surveys in this field,[88] as the two reports by I.V. Gurevich and Dr. Arkin on the 'assistance to the marketing of handicraft products in the Pale' had convinced ORT to continue in this field. ORT set up another special commission for further elaboration, and organized local regional conferences of the activists interested in the marketing of products of their regions.[89]

Two months later, a few weeks before the outbreak of World War I, a last general congress of the ORT took place on 27 April 1914 which did not, however, alter the decisions taken at the last congress. Sliozberg, speaking in the name of the Central Committee, once again called on the participants to increase their efforts, and referred to the fact that without sufficient support from the province, all the best intentions of the Central Committee could not succeed.[90]

## 5.4  ORPE AND THE REFORM OF THE JEWISH SCHOOL SYSTEM

In the field of education, many new Jewish organizations sprang to life around 1911 indicating that in fact Jewish social activists became particularly more determined the more restrictions and fences the government set up. It also supports the argument which claims that 'the greater the inequality, the greater the cohesiveness among Jews', a statement applicable to other national minorities at that time too, for instance, the Poles.[91] This phenomenon became particularly evident at all levels of education, especially in higher education. From 1910 until 1914, ORPE focused its activity on the nationalization and modernization of Jewish education by raising the professional standard of Jewish teachers, setting up new schools or reforming traditional ones, and supporting Jewish university students. Special efforts were also made to reorganize and modernize Jewish libraries in Russia. Originally such libraries were often used by the Bund to revolutionize the Jewish workers, but ORPE leaders regarded them as an important part of Jewish cultural work.[92] The libraries met with great success. An ORPE survey of 1904 claimed that the 105 libraries in existence satisfied a growing demand for general education.[93] In 1912, Dr. Zalkind called for more efforts in legalizing Jewish libraries and improving the quality of their holdings.[94] Due to budget constraints, ORPE decided that new libraries should be financed through other channels than its own budget. In fact, in accordance with widespread practise in Russia, the Saving and Loan Co-operatives increasingly stepped in by reinvesting parts of their surplus into all kinds of educational institutions.[95] On a local basis, ORPE continued its 'engagement' on behalf of the Jewish libraries and proved to be successful: the Jewish library in Vilna, for instance, witnessed a substantial increase in readers, while the budget and holdings of the ORPE-subsidized Gintsburg Library in St. Petersburg were growing strongly and steadily.[96]

Looking at ORPE's general records throughout this period, the lion's share of the budget went into the pedagogical courses in Vilna, the setting up of new schools, providing stipends to Jewish students and so on. The attractiveness of ORPE became evident in terms of an increasing amount of members as well as branches. As the statistics for 1913 indicate, ORPE's budget substantially exceeded that of the ORT: while ORT had a budget of 54,000 roubles, ORPE had more than 1.3 million.[97]

However, despite the fact that ORPE had a far bigger budget than ORT, this did not guarantee success, nor did it facilitate decision-making. The reason lay in the fact that activity in education involved many more internal and external conflicts than economic activity. ORPE activities were burdened by conflicts with religious and conservative elements, who fought tooth and nail – denunciation included – against any attempts to modernize traditional schools, as this implied secularization.[98] Such cases were reported for example from Balta (Podolia) and Kiev, where melameds and orthodox rabbis either denounced reformed schools as 'Zionist' to the authorities or simply demanded their closure.[99] This made ORPE's work for reform more difficult, and it could therefore pursue its activities only step by step since the local authorities usually gave only short term permissions to ORPE ventures, and dealt with each request separately.[100] Finally, the language dispute split the secular and reform-minded forces – within Russian Jewry in general, and within ORPE in particular – into three groups: the Autonomists who favoured a 'multiple solution' with 'equal rights' to all the languages possibly involved (Russian, Yiddish, Hebrew, Polish, German and so on), the Hebraists – mainly Zionists – and the Yiddishists – mainly Bundists.[101] This dispute led to serious dissensions between Autonomists and Zionists, for instance, in the important ORPE branch in Odessa. Here, in 1911 the Zionists demanded that the ORPE board dominated by Autonomists should allow a minimum of two-fifths of all hours to be spent on Jewish national topics in all schools subsidized by ORPE. Despite the fact that in the end the board made considerable concessions to national demands, the conflict between Autonomists and Zionists continued.[102] Given this complexity, the reform of the traditional Heder, for instance, was postponed again and again, and was only resolved when two of the three groups, the Autonomists and Hebraists, won the majority at an ORPE meeting on 23 March 1912 in St. Petersburg. Here, ORPE restated for the third time – after 1863 and 1873 – its will to reform the traditional Heder.[103]

ORPE decided to reform the existing Heder first and foremost because, 'given the magnitude of the task (the reform of the entire Jewish school system), money was always in short supply. This way it seemed possible to achieve a maximum effect with a minimum of means'.[104] Second, previous efforts to reform the traditional Heders into Metukkan Heders had not made the traditional Heder and Talmud Torah vanish quickly. These schools could only be reformed where there was strong enough support from Jewish society. But this often presupposed social change that had not yet taken place among the poverty-stricken Jewish masses, especially in the *shtetl*.[105] Only in bigger cities like Vitebsk, where the reformers dominated the community, a 'reforming orthodoxy' arose which adopted to the social changes by founding reformed Talmud Torahs whose syllabus included subjects such as Russian, arithmetic, Russian history, Jewish secular subjects, Pentateuch, bible, prayers and Hebrew.[106] Moreover, in other Jewish centres such as Vilna, Warsaw and Berdichev, Jewish children increasingly flocked to secular Jewish and Russian schools, and the amount of officially registered traditional Heders decreased. Nonetheless, the Heder still remained a factor within the Jewish educational system.[107] By drawing them in the wider frame of the Russian school system, the activists hoped to enforce modernization and secularization upon the traditional Jewish school system from above.

At a general members' meeting in January 1913, Dubnov, Bikerman and the teacher Shapiro were able to proceed with the decision on the reform of the Heder against the Yiddishist and SERPist, M.B. Ratner. While the former regarded the traditional Heder as part of the Jewish education system and appreciated its value for primary education, the latter completely rejected the Heder as it represented an obsolete school type favoured by conservatives, and therefore, was not compatible with his idea of a modernized and secular Jewish education system based on Yiddish as the language of instruction.[108]

After the proponents of the reform of the Heder had won the battle within ORPE, they concentrated on giving the reform the legal framework needed. Here, it is interesting to observe that the reformers obviously still intended to instrumentalize the state in their efforts at reform. Or perhaps they did not believe that the state would ever accede to such demands; but they put these forward because of their mobilizing effect on Jewish life and as an utopia which at least could serve as a compass in day to day activities.

The prospects for the convocation of the first All-Russian Congress for National Education in the end of 1913, finally provided ORPE with the opportunity to advance its new policy. As the Fourth Duma showed a reactionary constellation, ORPE could at least try to exert some influence through an all-Russian congress in order to secure reform proposals that would grant Russian Jews more opportunities for Jewish national education and especially an autonomous Jewish educational system. ORPE strove for proposals that would guarantee a legalized status for Jewish elementary schools, to be subsidized by the government and integrated in the Russian school system like the other schools, with the right to use the mother tongue as the language of instruction. As ORPE intended to include into such a system the Talmud Torah and the private schools, it became obvious that it planned to give old-fashioned Jewish schools the kiss of death. In order to represent Jewish interests at the all-Russian congress, it was necessary to come to an agreement about the basic question of the ideal structure of the reformed school, to define the language of instruction and other controversial issues hitherto not decided. Therefore, on the eve of the all-Russian congress on 23 December 1913, ORPE organized a preparatory meeting. Here, in fact, ORPE was able to find a common platform despite the heated discussions caused by the language dispute. After the Central Committee's report on 1913 covering a wide range such as the school question, the development of the ORPE journal *Vestnik Obshchestva*, the vocational training for teachers, the positive feedback from the teachers,[109] the Yiddishists mounted a frontal attack on the general conduct of ORPE with the intention of finding a majority for their idea of a secular Jewish school at the congress. The left-wing Yiddishists like A. Slutskii (Kiev), argued along the same lines as they had in former ORPE congresses by rejecting the reform of the traditional Heder as an outdated and reactionary venture. Instead, the Yiddishist Leshchinskii demanded more attention for the development of Yiddish in the Grodno teachers' courses. The Autonomists, the travelling representatives of the ORPE, Kh.Kh. Fialkov, M.N. Kreinin, and the Hebraist B.A. Goldberg, however, won the battle by referring to the fact that the schools with the subject of teaching Yiddish – for instance the evening courses for adults – were indeed subsidized by ORPE, that Jewish literature was fully taught as part of the Grodno courses and that steps had been taken by the Committee to edit school books in Yiddish.[110]

In the end, both sides had to acknowledge Russian-Jewish realities regarding the language of instruction and the teaching of religious subjects. In accordance with the decisions on the Jewish elementary school taken at the ORPE meeting of April 1911, it was confirmed that Yiddish was to be the language of instruction and the syllabus was to include religious subjects. The resolution demanded the right of elementary education for all Jewish children of school age, the right to open Jewish elementary schools free of tuition fees, with the mother tongue (Yiddish) as language of instruction and a syllabus consisting equally of general and Jewish subjects, in all places with more than fifty Jewish children of school age; finally, the integration of all Jewish schools such as elementary schools, Talmud Torah and private schools into the school net.[111]

The first All-Russian Congress for National Education which took place in St. Petersburg from 23 December 1913 until 3 January, 1914, vindicated the new approach: by approving of Jewish rights in the realm of education it confirmed the general trend within Russian society – as opposed to the government – towards more tolerance *vis-à-vis* the minorities. This congress confirmed the general determination to push for reform and the willingness to go forward without the government which could already be observed during the congresses of the co-operatives and the artisans. Not surprisingly, official distrust was pronounced, in particular with respect to Jewish participants. Only forty Jewish delegates (more than 600 delegates were present) received the right of temporary residence in St. Petersburg. ORPE therefore renounced its official participation, but it pursued its decision at least to report on the Jewish schools in the 'inorodtsy section'. At the session of 27 December 1913, G.A. Goldberg reported on the legal situation of the Jewish schools and described the increasing – mostly illegal – restrictions on Jewish pupils, the authorities' abuse of taxes assigned to educational matters, and tried to hammer it in that only the abolition of all the discriminatory laws could give Russian Jews the educational system they needed. Goldberg succeeded. The congress adopted a resolution demanding to scrap all legal disabilities for Jews and stated that such laws only demoralised Jews and Christians alike, and were harmful from a general as well as a pedagogical point of view. Kh.Kh. Fialkov's report on behalf of the Jewish elementary school was also a success. The congress accepted all reported points at the preparatory ORPE meeting, such as the necessity of setting up Jewish schools in the mother tongue, subsidies for Jewish schools by the Ministry of Education, and the right to introduce Jewish national subjects; the congress also recognized the need for qualified Jewish teachers, and recommended teachers' seminars and other training courses. Last but not least the congress condemned anti-Semitism in the schools and called on all to fight it.[112] On the whole, prospects for making elementary education general – for which the year 1922 was set as a target – were extremely good, had they not been disrupted by the war. The Yiddish national school – which could have materialized, since in June 1914, the Duma adopted a law which 'granted the peoples of Russia the right to choose the language of instruction in private educational institutions' – met the same fate.[113] Thus, the suggestion for such a new system of minority education – which of course presupposed the acceptance of multinationality by the state – came to nothing.

ORPE, like ORT, had succeeded in achieving pro-Jewish rights resolutions from an all-Russian congress. However, it remains difficult to measure the success of ORPE activity within the period from 1911–14 as the above-mentioned achievements had no time to show what they were worth because of the disruption of World War I. It is nonetheless significant that the basis for possible changes had been laid, as all of these congresses approved the reform proposals brought forward by Jewish activists. At the grass roots, organic work was often very successful mainly because many governors and authorities were prepared to back up reforms as long as communities or other organisations could prove that their respective activities were not based on politics. An example for this was the governor of Chernigov, N.A. Maklakov, a known anti-Semite, who granted almost all requests of the liberal rabbi Shneerson to reform the Jewish community itself, but expelled him temporarily when Shneerson demanded from the governor to stop the expulsions of Jews from his province.[114]

Generally speaking, some authorities or governors were indeed open to the arguments on which Jewish social activists based their requests, while others simply maintained their anti-Jewish posture. For example, the Kishinev city administration granted the Jewish community the farming out of the Korobka tax, arguing that the Jewish community had gathered in the last year 17,000 roubles more than the private tax-farmers before.[115] The same argument convinced the Kiev authorities to give permission to the Jewish community to use certain sums of the Korobka tax for education.[116] In other places, for instance Odessa, the Jewish community suffered a setback as the Black Hundred-run city administration leased the farming out of the tax to a private person, the 'tax farmer king' Tsimbolist, and not to the Jewish community.[117] Furthermore, it was widespread practise that local authorities used the tax for all kinds of purposes: in the case of Volynia, for instance, the Jewish community was to contribute with 10 per cent of the Korobka funds to the costs of gubernia administration.[118]

Furthermore, Jewish organizations in general, and ORT and ORPE in particular, increasingly faced problems as some local authorities refused to co-operate and often undermined reform efforts. For instance, ORPE's request to open further courses for teachers in Kiev based on the Vilna model was turned down by the Kiev 'Curator of the Educational District' with the argument that he would have given the permission if the programme of the courses would have been in accordance with the model of the Christian teachers' courses. Another example of such arbitrariness is the fact that although the joiners' co-operative in Mogilev had developed very well and enjoyed an increase of activity, it was shut down by the administration without any reason.[119]

Nevertheless, Jewish social activists unremittingly proceeded with organic work, and the years 1913–14 witnessed special efforts in two other fields which were both linked to the modernisation process of Russia, that is urbanization and higher education. For instance, in February 1912, Jewish social activists were able to get permission to found another nation-wide organization which dealt with the side effects of increasing urbanization, such as the danger of epidemics in the densely populated Russian cities and in particular in their overcrowded Jewish quarters. The Society for the Improvement of the Hygienic and Health Condition of the Jewish people in Russia ('Obshchestvo okhraneniia zdorovia evreiskago naseleniia' – OZE)[120] started its activity at the end of 1912, concentrated mainly on an information campaign on health and hygienic matters connected with the demands of big city life. OZE branches were founded in many cities of the Pale, and consequently OZE had already fully developed its nationwide organizational framework before the outbreak of World War I.[121] During the war OZE became the second big centre of Jewish organizational activity, together with EKOPO ('Evreiskii komitet pomoshchi zhertvam voiny' – the Jewish Committee for the Relief of Victims of War).[122]

In the field of higher education, Jewish social activists had already set up the Society for the Dissemination of higher Learning among Jews in 1911, which supported Jewish students financially.[123] The tightened anti-Jewish legislation with respect to higher education had made it necessary to go beyond financial aid, especially since large numbers of Jewish youths were ever more determined to enter higher education.

Due to the restrictions, Russian-Jewish students were left with three options: to wait for one of the official places, to go abroad, or to convert in order to be admitted to Russian universities. In fact, the second option was increasingly taken up by the majority of Russian-Jewish students, while only a few chose the third. As Zvi Halevy put it, this was 'due to the strong reactions against converts within the Jewish community'.[124] From 1911 onwards, some activists, like Tsinberg, published articles in the Jewish press condemning the conversions.[125] In 1913, in light of the emergence of anti-Jewish tendencies in French universities – after the same had happened in Germany – fears rose among Jewish social activists that Jewish students might now increasingly choose this option.[126] In July 1913, therefore, Jewish writers and community activists published a joint declaration against actual and would-be converts drafted by Simon Dubnov.

Dubnov saw inequality as the main reason for most conversions, but he specifically rejected career reasons as motivation for conversion.

> You are taking a step which will cut yourself and your grand children from your nation. You may achieve civil rights but you will lose the great historical privilege of belonging to a nation which is fighting for its fate and future, which makes its past valuable.[127]

Many activists now believed that a restrictive course in other countries, such as Belgium and Switzerland, was only a matter of time. Since these were, however, the only places for Russian Jews to receive higher education, they came to conclude that the only solution to the problem would be an independent Jewish university.[128] To finance such a venture, the Kovenskii Komitet in 1912 advocated an Educational Fund ('Prosvetitel'nyi Fond'). To discuss this a circle of people, among them Vinaver, Shternberg, R. Blank, Dubnov, the engineers Kanegisser and Press, met in St. Petersburg.[129] The KK had already succeeded in setting up a Technical Institute: in 1911 the Institute for Mining was founded and legalized in Ekaterinoslav with the engineers L.G. Rabinovich – former deputy to the Second Duma – and V.O. Garkavi as principals. Now in 1912–13, the Kovenskii Komitet found considerable support for the idea of a Jewish university, but not with respect to the location. The great dividing lines of internal Jewish politics made the location a problem: should it be set up in Palestine, Western Europe or elsewhere. Co-operation in this matter proved impossible as the Zionists insisted on their idea of a Hebrew University located in Jerusalem, and consequently founded an independent fund for this purpose which, in fact, enabled them to purchase the land on Mount Scopus – the location of the Hebrew University today. The efforts to set up a Jewish university ended abruptly with the outbreak of World War I.[130] However, after the war, both Zionists and Liberals realised their plans: a Jewish university, the 'Institute of Higher Jewish Studies' was founded in Leningrad in 1919, as well as the Jewish University in Jerusalem in 1925.[131]

In conclusion, it would appear that organic work was heading the right way. The reform proposals brought forward by ORT and ORPE were approved by various all-Russian congresses. Reform efforts were backed up by authorities on the local level. This enabled the Jewish activists to celebrate many successes which seemed to be piecemeal, but were in fact major breaches into the traditional Jewish world. Even more, they were indicators of a rapidly modernising Jewish society: the Jewish co-operative movement, courses and institutes for vocational training and general education, the increasing numbers of Jewish students and pupils and so on. Generally speaking, organic work did not, however, achieve a breakthrough in solving the 'Jewish question' first and foremost because the regime maintained its hostile attitude towards any Jewish activity. The restrictive legislation undermined many initiatives of organic work, and thus remained an insurmountable obstacle. Nevertheless, many initiatives, such as the Jewish University, materialized when Tsarist Russia collapsed within the course of World War I. Finally, the February Revolution of 1917 granted Russian Jews legal emancipation. ORPE continued its activity in the former Soviet Union until the end of the 1920s. The Jewish Saving and Loan Associations were further developed in Israel. ORT and OZE became worldwide organizations and still exist. All these ideas and organizations were the brainchild of the Jewish activists of organic work and could have born fruit already in Tsarist Russia, had the regime not maintained its intolerance towards minorities in general and Jews in particular.

# 6 Conclusion: The Russian-Jewish Liberals and their Position in European Jewish History

Contrary to the development in the West, where they appeared first, Jewish Liberals were the last of the four major political forces of Russian Jewry to appear on the political stage. The reasons for this reversal of the 'normal' historical sequence – which were not the object of this study – lay in the historical backwardness of Russia in general and of the Jewish community in Russia in particular, partly also in the fact that Russian Jews had not been emancipated. For these reasons, a modernized Jewish middle class or Jewish middle class intelligentsia were late to appear as it remained extremely difficult for Jews in the Russian empire to pursue normal lives and normal bourgeois careers. The Jewish communities largely remained caught in the patterns of a traditional life that did not allow for a separation of secular and religious leadership and that therefore had made no room for the participation of groups of Jews that had fully accepted a modern way of life and had cut a niche for themselves in that life. Only by the end of the ninteenth century these new forces of Jewish society grew strong enough, and the communities became sufficiently touched by some modicum of modernization, that the former could organize themselves and start to make their impact felt. Until then, small layers of a Jewish intelligentsia, Socialists or Zionists, acculturated in any case, had been able to show their flags as opposed to the vast masses of an immobile Orthodoxy. However, the historical precedence of Socialists and Zionists may not have been as important as seems at first glance, because they, too, in all honesty, could not move the masses before the end of the ninteenth century, when the Liberals first appeared and soon were able to compete – or even, difficult as this remains to assess – to surpass their competitors in mass appeal. Also in contrast to the west, Jewish Liberals were also nationalists. This again has to be seen as a result of the special circumstances in the Russian Empire. Assimilation had not made major breakthroughs, due to the powers to conserve of Jewish traditionalism, which largely again was negative and mainly due to the fact that modernization and industrialization had hardly touched the *shtetl* before the turn of the century. Russian Jewish Liberals, therefore, were not 'Assimilationists', nor were they themselves 'assimilated' in the full sense of the word, rather, they were acculturated Jews – mostly, by the way, observant of the laws of religion – who saw the Jews as a nation or at least as a potential nation. The national attitudes of the Liberals were not mainly the result of anti-Jewish policies, but they stemmed from this residual national strength of certain Jewish elements that had also forced the Bundists to develop a more 'nationalistic' approach to Jewish socialism.[1] What Liberals found within the Pale of Settlement, of course, was at best a pre-modern ethnic group that could be transformed into a nation. In this work of transformation Jewish Liberals took a very active part, in fact, often were the leaders and pathbreakers.

The Liberals could unfold their activities and increase their influence not so much due to their ideology, but due to their political flexibility which arose from the fact that they were well grounded in two 'communities' or 'societies', the Russian and the Jewish. They were actors on the all-Russian political stage as well as the inner Jewish. Thus, they could operate in internal as well as external lobbies and pressure groups. While Jewish socialists might have shared this advantage, their political doctrinairism and their unwillingness to take part in something they regarded largely as *malenkie dela*, devoid of the heroic revolutionary gesture, and their disdain for 'parliamentary' tactics made them forgo the opportunities that offered themselves. As opposed to their political opponents, the Zionists and Bundists, Liberals were not restricted by party discipline or ideological blueprints, and were thus tactically and strategically more flexible. Their strength was that they adjusted their actions and policy to the political, social and economic opportunities of Tsarist Russia. The political programme of their allies, the Russian Constitutional Democrats (Kadets), was more acceptable to the Jewish masses of artisans and traders who basically looked for means and ways to make a decent living. While Zionists and Bundists were caught in the net of world wide organizations, Jewish Liberals remained – with their demands for full civil and national emancipation – within the framework of Tsarist politics, without projecting political aims onto an age of millenarianism or without adopting different geographical parameters, which within the context of the times could still seem the result of wishful thinking.

Sure enough, Jewish Liberal politics did not emerge out of the blue. It was rather the result, among others, of the more liberal policy under Tsar Alexander II, who had opened the universities to Russian Jews, and thus, created the cadres of Jewish radical activists of all colours. Furthermore,

Jewish Liberals emerged as successors to the *maskilim* at the time when the struggle between the Haskalah and Jewish traditionalism had become obsolete as the Russian government had torn up the 'emancipation pact' by reversing to a policy of excluding and separating Russian Jews by the means of a new anti-Jewish legislation. Certainly, traditional Jewish life was challenged before the involvement of Jewish Liberals. Jewish organizations such as ORPE and ORT were also founded before, and by the time Jewish Liberals became active, the traditional *shtadlanut* policy of the Jewish notables was still very much in practise. In short, Jewish politics – in terms of a non-party activity – always existed in Russia, and elsewhere.[2]

The merits of Jewish Liberal politics were to have mobilised and politicized the Jewish masses within the scope of parliamentary work in semi-constitutional Tsarist Russia, and at the same time to have offered a formula – 'organic work' – through which Jewish life in Russia could be improved independently of adverse circumstances and through which the rebirth and survival of the Jews as a nation could be made possible. Of course, Jewish Liberal politics were never expressed in as flamboyant a way as that of the Bund, with its strikes, self-defence groups and mass membership and so on, or as that of the Zionists, with their spectacular demand for a separate country for the Jews. The Liberals' politics were less visible, less spectacular, but perhaps even more effective; this is supported by the fact that the Zionists adopted their programme (that of the Soiuz polnopraviia) *in toto* as their *Programme for Today*. Liberals capitalized on the opportunities presented to them through circumstances in order to advance their demands: in the political arena, during the Duma elections, they fought shoulder to shoulder with other nationalities and Russian political parties against right-wing and ultra-conservative groups and parties. They exploited especially the freedoms which were acquired through the Revolution of 1905 such as the right to vote and the right of assembly. Vinaver and his associates made sure that their allies, the Kadets, actively adhered to their political programme concerning Jewish rights, and in 1908–09, for instance, forced the Kadets to adopt a more active defense of Russian Jews inside the Duma. Liberal tactics in terms of lobbying for Jewish rights in the Duma changed according to political circumstances. If they – for instance Vinaver – openly demanded Jewish equality in the plenum of the First Duma, they had to pursue a rather more defensive tactic, especially in the Third and Fourth Duma. Herein, they acted according to the balance of power in the Duma, the political events outside the Duma, and the tactics of their Russian political allies, the Kadets.

In their defense of Russian Jewry, Liberals successfully mobilised Russian as well as foreign public opinion by using the increasing importance of the press and printed materials. Here, they proved able to celebrate two main successes when the increasing information on the Jewish plight caused by the Russian government's policy towards the national minorities in general, and Russian Jews in particular led to the fact that foreign Jewish bankers and activists – such as Paul Nathan, Jacob Schiff, Lucien Wolf and Louis Marshall – not only lost confidence in the reform-mindedness of the Russian government, but increasingly undermined the Russian government's efforts to float loans abroad. This took place on two occasions: during the Russo-Japanese War when Jacob Schiff unsuccessfully called upon West European bankers to refuse loans to Russia, but paved the way for Japan into the international financial market, and thus supplied it with the funds needed to fight the war. The other success was evident in the fact that Louis Marshall's campaign against the extension of the Russo-American trade treaty was so successful that the American government let it lapse. During the blood accusation against Mendel Beilis, Jewish Liberals actively organized a national and international protest wave. They also provided the lawyers the intellectual, investigative and publishing capacity to reveal to the world the evidence of government involvement in stage managing the trial. In short, the Russian government's prestige became seriously damaged through the publicity offensive instigated by Jewish Liberals.

The Liberals developed a threefold approach to Jewish politics on the Imperial Russian plane: they combined political action (defense of Jewish rights in the Duma, participation in the Duma elections as a means to mobilize Jewish society beyond mere participation in the elections), the struggle against anti-Semitism (as described in the instance of the Beilis Trial) and organic work (modernization of Russian-Jewish life). Organic work had hesitantly started already immediately around the turn of the century, but really came into its own only after the failure of the Revolution of 1905 when unrealistic dreams had to be given up and when flamboyant gestures became counterproductive; at a time, in other words, when everybody in Russia had to sit down for serious thinking and serious work. It is interesting to compare this and earlier phases with the development of the non-historical nations in Eastern Europe, or with the struggle of one historical nation, the Poles, against their oppressors, Prussians and Russians. Many similarities spring to the eye: the discovery of one's history, the development of ethnography concentrating on 'Volkstradition', the importance of the intelligentsia in raising a national consciousness, and finally, the attempts to build a 'national' economy (with credit co-operatives as a corner-stone) able to stand on its own feet, in order to combat the integrating and assimilating tendencies of a capitalism dominated by the ruling nationality. The period of organic work became one of the most important chapters of modern Jewish history in general, and Russian-Jewish history in particular, as this was when most of the organizations, ideas, and ideologies took their final shape and began to modernize Russian-Jewish life to the extent possible in an autocratic state like Tsarist Russia. Jewish teachers' seminars, Jewish secular primary schools, secular structured community councils, Saving and Loan Co-operatives, Credit Co-operatives, Jewish newspapers, political parties and groups became a major factor in Russian-Jewish life.

The modernization of Jewish society also became evident in the fact that progressive rabbis with a secular education increasingly appeared – at last – in the big Jewish centres. The traditional rabbis gave up their voluntary isolation, organized themselves and appeared as the fifth political force within Russian-Jewish society. As we have seen, these rabbis naturally opposed and denied the claims of the secular elements for community leadership, but in general they were prepared to back up economic and social reforms where it seemed to be for the better of the Jewish population. Finally, they actively supported the secular political activists' struggle against blood libel and anti-Semitism.

Due to the lack of political alternatives within the period of organic work, political competition between the various Jewish political parties and groups gave way to widespread co-operation. Increasing persecution of members of oppositional parties, including the bourgeois section of Russian Zionists (RSO), forced the Jewish political activists of all colours to redirect their political activities towards organic work. In fact, all Jewish organizations at that time witnessed a mixed membership embracing Bundists (some of them, anyway), Zionists, Liberals and Autonomists. Political dissent resurfaced from time to time, for example in certain local constituencies during the elections to the Third and Fourth Duma, or when the social and educational reforms discussed within ORT and ORPE had ramifications touching on vital ideological differences. In the first case, Jewish Liberals and Zionists fought each other for no good reason – as for instance in Odessa; in the second case the struggle between Hebraists (mainly Zionists and Nationalists) and Yiddishists (mainly Bundists) became ever more intense. One should not, however, overestimate the negative impact of these 'ideological battles'. Since pragmatism as represented for instance by Jewish Liberals prevailed as a rule, these conflicts mostly had positive consequences as they induced more and more Jews to participate in organic work. This sort of conflict was a normal side effect of a political and social differentiation process within Jewish society, and proved the fact that Russian Jewry was in the midst of a modernization process. The growing industrialization of the Russian economy with all its side-effects brought about the need for a modernization and transformation of Jewish society, too, which naturally entailed new 'battlefields' such as economic and social reform, and with it the old battle over secularization of Jewish social life.

Goldscheider and Zuckerman have already pointed to the fact that competition among Jewish political parties and groups fostered clear political programmes.[3] This certainly held true for all Jewish political parties in Russia. The appearance of the Zionists forced the Bundists to clarify their national programme even further; the advent of the Liberals and Autonomists forced the Zionists to get involved in Russian politics; the competition between the former allies within the SP forced the Liberals to clarify their national standing, and to elaborate their solution of the Jewish Question, that is national-cultural autonomism. Political competition stimulates creativity, and this was exactly the reason for the success of organic work. All tendencies, activities and ideologies were continued between the two World Wars; the co-operative movement found further development in Poland, the Soviet Union and in Israel; organizations such as ORT and OZE still exist; and the ideologies developed in Russia found their ways through Jewish students into Western Europe and the United States.

We have seen that the period between 1900 and 1914 was indeed the cradle for Modern Jewish history in the Tsarist Empire. Of course, many questions remain open, especially regarding many aspects of organic work as a thorough coverage of the modernization process of Russian Jewry would have meant writing the social and economic history of Russian Jews as a modern scholarly study is waiting for its researcher. I hope to have at least painted a more rounded picture, tracing the basic outlines of Jewish politics and the efforts of major groups throughout the period. The author is, however, aware of the fact that in order to come to more explicit judgments further studies are needed such as the examination and comparison of the economic and social conditions of various Jewish centres, the study of and comparison between the various Jewish cultural and social organisations especially at the grassroots, the Jewish co-operative movement and so on. In short, further and more detailed examination of the economic situation of Russian Jewry is necessary in order to show to which extent Jewish life in Russia changed. The problem of unreliable and inconsistent statistical material on all sectors of Jewish life perhaps will never disappear. This can be overcome, however, by further studies on the local situation of Russian cities where Jews represented a major share of the population. In this context, we can only hope that the local archives and libraries in the cities of the former Pale of Settlement, which are now open to historians, will provide us with that information.

# Notes and References

## 1 THE EMERGENCE OF JEWISH LIBERALS IN RUSSIA: FROM ACCULTURATION TO REVOLUTION

1. Inge Blank has shown the extent to which Jewish society was changing in terms of, for instance, an increasing number of Jewish university students. For more detail see Inge Blank, 'Haskalah und Emanzipation. Die russisch-jüdische Intelligenz und die "jüdische Frage" am Vorabend der Epoche der "Großen Reformen" ', in Gotthold Rhode (ed.), *Juden in Ostmitteleuropa. Von der Emanzipation bis zum Ersten Weltkrieg* (Marburg/Lahn, 1989) pp. 197–231; for a brief summary of the governmental policy towards Russian Jews until 1881, see Hans Rogger, 'The Question of Jewish Emancipation', in Hans Rogger, *Jewish Policies and Right-Wing Politics in Imperial Russia* (Oxford, 1986) pp. 1–24.

2. While in 1835 eleven Jewish students were matriculated at Russian Universities, the number increased to 129 in 1863. See Blank, op. cit., pp. 211–12; in 1894, the Jewish student body had reached the number of 1,853 students (13.3 per cent of all Russian students). However, due to the introduction of the Numerus Clausus, this high percentage of Jewish students was to drop to 7 per cent in 1902. See Zvi Halevy, *Jewish University Students and Professionals in Tsarist and Soviet Russia* (Tel Aviv, 1976) pp. 43f.

3. For more details about the 'Haskalah', see Jacob Raisin, *The Haskalah Movement in Russia* (Philadelphia, 1913); Michael Stanislawski, *Tsar Nicholas I and the Jews. The Transformation of Jewish Society in Russia, 1825–55* (Philadelphia, 1983).

4. For more detail concerning ORPE, see I.M. Tcherikover, *Istoriia obshchestva dlia rasprostranenie prosveshcheniia mezhdu evreiami v Rossii* (St. Petersburg, 1913). This book, however, covers only the early period until the 1880s. For more detail concerning ORT, see Leon Shapiro, *The History of ORT: A Jewish Movement for Social Change* (New York, 1980).

5. See Michael A. Meyer, *Jewish Identity in the Modern World* (Seattle, 1990) pp. 25–6.

6. The term *Luftmenschen* described all Jews who were not regularly employed and lived in complete poverty.

7. See Gregorii Aronson, 'Ideological Trends among Russian Jews', in Jacob Frumkin, Gregorii Aronson and Alexis Goldenweiser (eds), *Russian Jewry, 1860–1917* (New York and London, 1966) pp. 145–6; Stanislawski, op. cit., pp. 187/188.

8. The *Razsvet* of 1860–61 had only 640 subscribers. The next newspaper which appeared in Odessa had not many more. See Blank, 'Haskalah und Emanzipation', pp. 224–9; Moshe Perlmann, '*Razsvet* 1860–61. The Origins of the Russian Jewish Press', *Jewish Social Studies*, no. 29, 3 (1962) pp. 162–82; and Alexander Orbach, *New Voices of Russian Jewry. A Study*

*of the Russian-Jewish Press of Odessa in the Era of the Great Reforms, 1860–1871* (Leiden, 1980) pp. 22–53.

9. See Eli Lederhendler, *The Road to Modern Jewish Politics. Political Tradition and Political Reconstruction in the Jewish Community of Tsarist Russia* (Oxford, 1989) pp. 111–53; and also Inge Blank's article quoted above.

10. The pogroms of 1881–1882 were mainly interpreted by scholars as a complex of economic and social factors. Thereby, no evidence was found for a conspiracy theory, meaning that the pogroms had been organized by the authorities. See Mina Goldberg, *Die Jahre 1881–1882 in der Geschichte der russischen Juden*. D.Phil. thesis (Berlin, 1934) pp. 8–23. She explained the pogroms as being the result of the modernization process of the Russian economy after 1861 which witnessed the emergence of the Russian bourgeoisie on the one side, and an increasing impoverishment among the peasants on the other. The Russian bourgeoisie, especially the merchants, developed anti-Jewish sentiments against its Jewish competitors. When Alexander II was murdered this propaganda activity – the Jew as the scapegoat for everything – was spread by the newspapers among the peasants. The Russian revolutionaries at that time, the narodovol'tsy, in turn hoped to succeed with the revolution by diverting the people's anger against the authorities. For Goldberg, the outcome of the pogroms was more an exploitation of the peasants' miserable economic condition by the anti-Jewish Russian bourgeois circles which met with a shift by the government towards an anti-Jewish policy; the role of the narodovol'tsy and their anti-Jewish views are covered by Stephen M. Berk, 'The Russian Revolutionary Movement and the Pogroms of 1881–1882', in *Soviet Jewish Affairs* 7, 2 (1977) pp. 22–39; Michael Aronson underlined Goldberg's views but he pointed also to the railway workers and individuals coming from the cities where the pogrom wave had started. See I. Michael Aronson, *Troubled Waters. The Origins of the 1881 anti-Jewish Pogroms in Russia* (Pittsburgh, 1990).

11. For more detail regarding the pogroms of 1881–1882, see Stephen M. Berk, *Year of Crisis, Year of Hope. Russian Jewry and the pogroms of 1881–1882* (Westport, Connecticut and London, 1986).

12. See John D. Klier, 'The Concept of "Jewish Emancipation" in a Russian Context', in Olga Crisp, Linda Edmondson (eds), *Civil Rights in Imperial Russia* (Oxford, 1989) pp. 136–9.

13. The major points of the May Laws are cited in Paul R. Mendes-Flohr and Jehuda Reinharz (eds), *The Jew in the Modern World: A Documentary History* (New York and Oxford, 1980) p. 309; for more information on the meeting of the Council of Ministers drawing the May Laws see Hans Rogger, 'Russian Ministers and the Jewish Question, 1881–1917', in Rogger, *Jewish Policies*, pp. 56–112, especially pp. 57–63.

14. For more details about the debates in this newspaper, see Jonathan Frankel, 'The crisis of 1881–82 as a turning-point in modern Jewish history', in David Berger (ed.), *The Legacy of Jewish Migration: 1881 and its Impact* (New York, 1983) pp. 9–22.

15. Ibid., pp. 14–18.

16. Pinsker's 'autoemancipation' is published in full in Helmut Heil (ed.), *Die*

*neuen Propheten. Moses Hess, Leon Pinsker, Theodor Herzl, Achad Haam* (Fürth and Erlangen, 1969).

17.  See Ellen S. Cannon, *The Political Culture of Russian Jewry during the Second Half of the Nineteenth Century*, D.Phil Thesis. (University of Massachussetts, 1974) p. 259; and Salo W. Baron, *The Russian Jew under Tsars and Soviets*, 2nd edn. (New York, 1987) p. 146.

18.  The Jewish elites were to organize a national committee which was to collect money and buy land in order to secure a politically guaranteed asylum where all the Jews willing to emigrate could turn to. See 'Autoemanzipation', pp. 128–33.

19.  For more information on Pinsker, Lilienblum, Smolenskin and so on, see David Vital, *The Origins of Zionism* (Oxford, 1980) pp. 137–8.

20.  See Shmuel Ettinger, 'The Growth of the Jewish National Movement and the Burgeoning of Independent Political Activity', in H.H. Ben-Sasson, *A History of the Jewish People* (Cambridge, Massachusetts, 1976). Details about the Zionist movement in Russia in David Vital, *Zionism. The Formative Years* (Oxford, 1982); and for the history of Zionism in general, see Walter Laqueur, *Der Weg zum Staat Israel. Geschichte des Zionismus* (Vienna, 1972).

21.  See Ettinger, 'Growth of the Jewish National Movement', pp. 894–6.

22.  For more information about the 'engagement' of Russian Jews in the Narodnaia Volia, see Norman M. Naimark, *Terrorists and Social Democrats. The Russian Revolutionary Movement under Alexander III* (Cambridge, Massachusetts and London, 1983) pp. 92–95, 202–211; and Nora Levin, *While Messiah Tarried. Jewish Socialist Movements 1871–1917* (New York, 1977).

23.  This group consisted of people like Arkadii Kremer, Tsemakh Kopelson, Samuel Gozhanskii, Joseph (John) Mill, Matle Srednitskii, Isaia Izenstat and Yulius Martov. For more detail see Henry Tobias, *The Jewish Bund in Russia. From its Origins to 1905* (Stanford, California, 1972) pp. 73–86; and Yoav Peled, *Class and Ethnicity in the Pale. The Political Economy of Jewish Workers' Nationalism in late Imperial Russia* (London, 1989) pp. 31–70. He rather focuses, however, on the evolution of the Bund's national programme in general than on the Vilna Group in particular. Thus, he illustrates the way in which national ideas spread among the Jewish workers, which in turn forced the Bund leadership to follow the national tendencies at the grassroots.

24.  Dubnov's essay 'Autonomism' and Ahad Ha'am's 'Cultural Zionism' are published in Helmut Heil, *Die neuen Propheten*. More about Dubnov's 'Autonomism' is contained in Koppel S. Pinson, 'The National Theories of Simon Dubnov', in *Jewish Social Studies*, 10 (1948) pp. 335–58; Jacob Lestschinsky, 'Dubnow's Autonomism and his "Letters on Old and New Judaism" ', in Aaron Steinberg (ed.), *Simon Dubnow. The Man and his Work* (Paris, 1963) pp. 73–91, and Koppel S. Pinson (ed.), *Nationalism and History. Essays on old and new Judaism by Simon Dubnow* (Philadelphia, 1958). As Pinson pointed out, Dubnov had taken the intermediate position between the ideas of Socialism and Zionism, and promoted the view of a 'synthesis' of the Jewish and the non-Jewish environments in the form of 'autonomism' (see p. 11); finally, for Dubnov's disputes with Ahad Ha'am,

and a brief description of his political activity, see Robert Seltzer, *Simon Dubnow. A Critical Biography of his Early Years*. PhD Columbia University (Ann Arbor and London: Universal Microfilm International, 1977) especially pp. 176–237.

25. The restrictions began to affect every sphere of Jewish life. For instance, it was forbidden for Jews to trade on Christian holy days, as a result of which the Jewish working week was diminished to five days (if one takes into account the Shabbat). This meant an extreme weakening of social and economic efficiency. Furthermore, in 1890 the Jews lost the right to participate in the elections to the municipal and rural self-government organs. In addition to this arbitrary deportation orders by rural authorities increased tremendously, and so on. See Heinz-Dietrich Löwe, *Antisemitismus und reaktionäre Utopie. Russischer Konservatismus im Kampf gegen den Wandel von Staat und Gesellschaft* (Hamburg, 1978) pp. 32–9.

26. See Baron, *The Russian Jew*, p. 48. He stated that 'the decree restricted also the admission of Muslims and Karaite lawyers to the bar, requiring in each case special permission from the minister of justice on the recommendation of the presidents of local bar associations or judicial institutions.'

27. See Alexander Orbach, 'The Jewish People's Group and Jewish Politics, 1906–1914', in *Modern Judaism*, February 1990, vol. X, p. 2.

28. Dubnov, Ahad Ha'am, Simon Frug, Sholem Aleichem, Khaim Nachman Bialik and others had organized a small informal literary circle in Odessa in the early 1890s which became known under the name National Committee. The 'chief purpose of this committee', as Pinson wrote, 'was to combat assimilation among the Jewish intelligentsia'. For more detail see Pinson, *Nationalism and History*, p. 14.

29. For more detail see Gregorii Aronson, 'Ideological Trends among Russian Jews', pp. 150–1; and Baron, *The Russian Jew*, pp. 139–40. He mentions especially the Vilna rabbinical seminary and 'Realgymnasium'. Unfortunately, no statistics are available which would give an indication of the size and percentage of these 'outbreakers'.

30. *Budushchnost* was oriented towards Zionism while *Voskhod* continued the earlier tradition of education and enlightenment. *Voskhod* showed national characteristics but without any party tendencies. See Genrikh B. Sliozberg, *Dela minuvshikh dnei. Zapiski russkago evreia*, vol. III (Paris, 1933) pp. 110–11.

31. See Pinson, *Nationalism and History*, p. 17. This call was published as an essay in *Voskhod* in 1891 under the title 'The Study of the History of Russian Jews and the Establishment of a Russian Jewish Historical Society'. This article was the result of Dubnov's research on the various communal and autonomous Jewish institutions in Eastern Europe, which he had done in various archives at this time; see also S.M. Dubnov, *Kniga Zhizni. Vospominaniia i Razmyshlenia*, vol. I (Riga, 1934) pp. 265–6.

32. See S. Levenberg, 'Simon Dubnow. Historian of Russian Jewry', *Soviet Jewish Affairs*, vol. 12, no. 1 (1982) p. 5. He mentions Isaiah Trunk's theory that 'a similar process took place among the Poles after the 1863 uprising, among the Czechs after the failure of the 1848 Revolution, and among the Ukrainians during the growth of the national movement in the second half of the 19th century'.

33. See S.V. Pozner, 'Bor'ba za ravnopravie', in Paul Milinkov et al. (eds) *M.M. Vinaver i russkaia obshchestvennost' nachala XX veka* (Paris, 1937) p. 166. A more detailed account on the activities of the committee is given in M.M. Vinaver, 'Kak my zanimalis istoriei', in *Evreiskaia Starina*, 1909, 1, pp. 41–54. In fact, this was Vinaver's speech at the opening of the Jewish Historic-Ethnographic Society on 16 November 1908; a shorter version of the speech was translated, see Maxim M. Vinaver, 'When Lawyers studied History', in Lucy S. Dawidowicz, *The Golden Tradition: Jewish Life and Thought in Eastern Europe* (New York, Chicago and San Francisco, 1967) pp. 242–8; and is briefly mentioned in Dubnov, *Kniga Zhizni*, vol. I, p. 265.

34. See Sliozberg, *Dela*, p. 111; and Simon Dubnow, *Mein Leben*, edited by Elias Hurwicz (Berlin, 1937) pp. 118–19; Ben Tsion Kats – who at that time studied at the university in St. Petersburg and later worked as a journalist at the Hebrew newspaper *Hazman* – participated also in the production of the 'regesty' by collecting historical sources at the Imperial Library in St. Petersburg. See Ben Tsion Kats, 'Zikhronut fun mein Lebn', in *Der Tag-Morgen Zhurnal* (The Day-Jewish Journal), 31 January 1954.

35. Information on these people is, unfortunately, not complete in the encyclopedias: Vinaver was born in 1863 in a small village near Warsaw, his father was a banker, and he studied in Warsaw; Sliozberg was born in 1863 in the village Miro (Gubernia Minsk), studied in St. Petersburg; Gruzenberg was born in 1866 in Ekaterinoslav, had a non-traditional education, and studied in Kiev; Kulisher's parents were colonists in the Gubernia of Volynia, he received a non-traditional education, studied in Kiev; Bramson was born in 1869 in Kovno and studied in Moscow; Passover himself was born in 1840 in Uman (Gubernia Kiev), his father was a military doctor, and studied in Moscow. See A. Garkavi and L. Katsenel'son (eds), *Evreiskaia Entsiklopediia* (St. Petersburg, 1906) [Reprinted an *Slavistic Printings and Reprintings*, edited by H. van Schooneveld, (The Hague and Paris, 1971) 16 vols]; Vinaver's wife mentions in her memoirs further members of the Historic Commission such as Arkadii Gornfeld, Leopold Sev, and Maksim Syrkin. See Roza G. Vinaver, *Vospominaniia Maksima M. Vinavera*, unpublished typescript (New York, 1944) pp. 26–7; other members of the Moscow group were M. Pozner and L. Zaidenman who both were to join the political struggle on the nationwide scale with the Revolution of 1905. See Yulii Brutskus, 'Leon Bramson – organizator russkago evreistva', in *Evreiskii Mir*, sbornik II (New York, 1944) pp. 15–17.

36. See Pozner, 'Bor'ba za ravnopravie', p. 166; and A. Litvak, *Geklibene Shriftn* (New York, 1945) p. 463. Unfortunately, neither of them mentioned details on Vinaver's activity in those organizations; Bramson apparently joined ORPE as early as 1892, in the mid-1890s got involved in EKO's work, and finally, after 1906 became one of the top ORT leaders. See G.A., 'Zhizn i deiatelnost' Leontiia Moiseevicha Bramsona', in *Evreiskii Mir*, sbornik II, pp. 8–10.

37. The professional structure of the Jewish population showed exactly the opposite structure to that of the Russian population: 74.31 per cent of the general population was working in agriculture and 14 per cent in trade, handicraft and industry. By contrast, only 3.55 per cent of the Jews were active in agriculture, but 74.08 per cent were in trade, handicraft and industry. See Löwe, *Antisemitismus*, p. 33.

38.  Baron quoted the statistics of Jewish charities which showed an increase of 'indigent Jewish families' in Russia from 1894 to 1898 of about 20 per cent. See Baron, *The Russian Jew*, pp. 95–6; and Löwe, *Antisemitismus*, p. 35.

39.  For more information about Gintsburg's struggle against anti-Jewish restrictions in general, and the May Laws in particular, see G.B. Sliozberg, 'Baron G.O. Gintsburg i pravovoe polozhenie evreev', in *Perezhitoe*, vol. II (St. Petersburg, 1910).

40.  For more information about Moshe Ginzburg's activity on behalf of Russian Jews see Moshe Ginzburg, *Sein Lebn un Tetigkait. Mit ain Forwort fun Henrik Sliosberg* (Paris, 1935).

41.  See Ginzburg, *Sein Lebn*, pp. 54–9. Herein, Sliozberg gave an example of such a delegation to Ginzburg, and described the way in which those people usually approached Ginzburg for help in a respective matter.

42.  Isaac Shneerson, a relative of the famous Hasidic dynasty of rabbis, but himself state rabbi, mentions in his memoirs that he took the St. Petersburg community as a model to reform and modernize the community of Gorodnie, and later Chernigov. See Isaac Shneerson, *Lebn un Kampf fun yidn in Rusland* (Paris, 1968) p. 175; Stanislawski called St. Petersburg 'the capital of Jewish creativity in the Russian language', and mentions Odessa as the only community which could compete with St. Petersburg until the twentieth century. See Michael Stanislawski, *For whom do I toil? Judah Leib Gordon and the Crisis of Russian Jewry* (New York and Oxford, 1988) p. 109.

43.  The name came from the fact that they offered to give juridical help to the victims of repression and arbitrariness. A brief account on the Defense Bureau's activity had also been given by the lawyer and DB member Frumkin. See Jacob Frumkin, 'Pages from the History of Russian Jewry', in Frumkin, *Russian Jewry*, pp. 32–5.

44.  The Blood Accusation resurfaced several times in this form during the nineteenth century in Russia: it claimed that the Jews would murder Christian children and drink or use their blood for religious rituals. In this case David Blondes, a Vilna barber, was put on trial. The whole affair ended after a retrial in 1902 with Blondes' acquittal. See Baron, *The Russian Jew*, p. 62; Pozner, unfortunately, did not mention any details on Vinaver's part in this trial. See Pozner, 'Bor'ba za ravnopravie', p. 169; Kats stated that Vinaver initiated the conduct of the defense, and O.O. Gruzenberg took over as Blondes' attorney. However, since Gruzenberg was not yet admitted to the Russian Bar, Mironov functioned officially as the attorney. See Ben Tsion Kats, 'Zikhronut fun mein Lebn', in *Der Tag-Morgen Zhurnal*/'The Day-Jewish Journal', 23 and 30 May 1954.

45.  See Krol, *Stranitsy*, p. 312. Krol had been sent by the Defense Bureau to Maxim Gorky, the most popular Russian writer at that time, in order to convince him to write a brochure about the pogroms. However, Krol did not meet with sympathy at Gorky's house, but with an atmosphere of hostility and indifference; in 1894, Leon Bramson had been sent to Solov'ev and Tolstoi in order to convince them (especially Tolstoi) to write some kind of protest against the government's anti-Jewish policy. Apparently, Bramson was well received, and got Tolstoi interested in Jewish organic work, such as the activities of ORPE, ORT and so on. In the following years, Bramson kept a correspondence with Tolstoi informing him about all the various

activities on behalf of Russian Jews which, finally, convinced Tolstoi to write a four-page brochure in which he expressed openly his protest against the regime. Unfortunately, the brochure was confiscated when the Okhrana searched Bramson's flat in 1905, and therefore, never reached the Russian public. See L. Bramson, 'U Tolstogo v Yasnoi Poliane', in *Evreiskii Mir*, sbornik II, pp. 355–70. During the next years, however, they won important public figures to sign or organize protest resolutions against the government's anti-Semitic course; Baron pointed to the change of view among Russian intellectuals, especially writers, from prejudice and indifference towards solidarity with the Jews. He mentioned especially Vladimir S. Soloviev, Korolenko as well as Gorky. See Baron, *The Russian Jew*, p. 51.

46. See Sliozberg's description of Baron G.O. Gintsburg interventions at all the ministers of interior from the late 1870s until 1904, in Sliozberg, 'Gintsburg', pp. 102–12.

47. See Krol, *Stranitsy*, pp. 299–300.

48. See Sliozberg, *Dela*, pp. 168–70.

49. For more details about the ideology of the Poale Zion see Ber Borochov, *Nationalism and the Class Struggle. A Marxian approach to the Jewish problems* (Westport, Connecticut, 1937, reprinted 1972); Matityahu Mintz, 'Ber Borokhov', in *Studies in Zionism*, no. 5 (April 1982) pp. 33–53; and Zeev Abramovitch, 'The Poale Zion Movement in Russia, its History and Development', in Henrik F. Infield (ed.), *Essays in Jewish Sociology, Labour and Co-operation. In memory of Dr. Noah Barou 1889–1955* (London and New York, 1961) pp. 63–72.

50. See K. Zalevskii, 'Natsional'nye partii v Rossii', in *Obshchestvennoe dvizhenie v Rossii v nachale XXgo veka*, vol. III, p. 319.

51. Paragraph 22 of their program articulated on their congress in Minsk in 1902 stated: 'The Union of the Zionists and its organs are neither dealing with general nor home or foreign affairs.' See M.N. Pokrovskii, *1905. Materialy i dokumenty. vol. V. Evreiskoe rabochee dvizhenie*, edited by A.D. Kirzhnits (Moscow, 1928) p. 64.

52. Their ideology was, like the Bund, oriented towards Marxism. As opposed to the Bund, however, they demanded a free emigration and an own territory for the Jews. The Jewish masses, they argued, were driven out of their positions by the capitalist development and economic anti-Semitism. Therefore, they could not gain a foothold in the big industry and the only solution to this would be to go for an own territory where socialism could grow in the way Marx had predicted. See *Evreiskaia Entsiklopediia*, vol. XII, pp. 590–1.

53. See Dimitry Pospielovskij, *Russian Police Trade Unionism. Experiment or Provocation* (London, 1971) p. 49.

54. As Mendelssohn has pointed out, the success of the Poalei Zion was due to the fact that the membership in the Bund had demanded from the Jewish workers to keep a distance from Jewish life and its regulations. See Ezra Mendelssohn, *Class Struggle in the Pale. The Formative Years of the Jewish Workers Movement in Tsarist Russia* (Cambridge, 1970) p. 208. Thus, an orthodox way of life could not be reconciled with a life of illegality.

55. Branches were founded in Dvinsk, Vilna, Vitebsk, Odessa, Warsaw and so on. See *Evreiskaia Entsiklopediia*, vol. XII, pp. 590–1.

56. For more details regarding the 'Zubatovshchina' and the programme of the 'Independents' see Jeremiah Schneiderman, *Sergei Zubatov and Revolutionary Marxism. The Struggle for the working class in Tsarist Russia* (London, 1976) p. 233; and the relation of the Bund to Zubatovshdina, see the respective chapters in Yoav Peled, *Class and Ethnicity in the Pale* (London, 1989).

57. See Schneiderman, *Zubatov*, p. 365.

58. Zubatov convinced the imprisoned Mania Vilbushevich, Aleksandr Khemeriskii, Josif Goldberg and Yulii Volin to support him. Ibid., p. 243.

59. The newspaper published in Yiddish was called *Arbaits-Markt*.

60. He had stood up for the workers' demands during a strike in Minsk by reproaching the employers with the fact that they were only exploiting the workers. See Schneiderman, *Zubatov*, p. 237.

61. Ibid., p. 255.

62. For more detail see Pospielovskij, *Russian Police Trade Unionism*, pp. 98–144.

63. The Bund had lost, for instance, its supremacy among the working class in Minsk. See Schneiderman, *Zubatov*, p. 255.

64. See Hans Rogger, 'Russian Ministers and the Jewish Question 1881–1917', in Rogger, *Jewish Policies*, pp. 80–1.

65. See Schneiderman, *Zubatov*, p. 283.

66. See Shmarya Levin, *The Arena* (New York, 1932) p. 254. For more detail about the Uganda crisis and the split see Shmuel Almog, *Zionism and History. The Rise of a new Jewish Consciousness* (Jerusalem, 1987) pp. 254–304; Ben Halpern and Jehuda Reinharz, 'Nationalism and Jewish Socialism: The Early Years', in *Modern Judaism*, vol. 8, no. 3 (October 1988) pp. 240/241.

67. See Jonathan Frankel, *Prophecy and Politics. Socialism, Nationalism and the Russian Jews, 1862–1917* (Cambridge, 1981) p. 154.

68. The Bund increased its number of members from 5,000 in 1900 to 30,000 in 1903. See Tobias, *The Jewish Bund*, p. 140.

69. For more detail about the first activities of the Bund see Tobias, *The Jewish Bund*, pp. 35–60; Frankel, *Prophecy and Politics*, pp. 171–258; and Peled, *Class and Ethnicity*, pp. 31–70.

70. For instance, the proposal of the organized workers to pay constantly money into the strike box, whether or not there was a strike, did not meet with understanding within the basis during the strike of the weavers in Belostok in 1895. See Mendelssohn, *Class Struggle in the Pale*, pp. 92–3.

71. The Bund complained in 1900 that the workers' movement in Belostok had grown too big to control. Ibid., p. 94.

72. Peled described this change towards a more nationally-oriented programme as the final breakthrough of nationalist ideas which were to be seen among the Bundist circles with the May Day Speeches of 1892, followed by Arkadii Kremer's pamphlet 'On Agitation' and Shmuel Gozhanskii's 'Letter to the Agitators' and Avrom Gordon's pamphlet 'Letter to the Intelligenti' (all of them written in 1893). See Peled, *Class and Ethnicity*, pp. 34–49; the importance of the Zionist/Nationalist competitor as the main cause for the Bund's move towards the inclusion of Jewish national demands in its programme is also stressed in Calvin Goldscheider and Alan S. Zuckerman, *The Transformation of the Jews* (Chicago and London, 1984) pp. 130–2.

73. See Leonard Shapiro, 'The role of the Jews in the Russian Revolutionary Movement', *The Slavonic Review*, 40 (1961) p. 158.

74. Abramovich wrote that the thirty Bundist leaders gathering at the sixth party conference in Zurich were completely surprised by the strike movement in October 1905 due to the split with the RSDRP. Thus, they had to follow the events in the foreign newspapers. See R. Abramovich, *In tsvai revolutsies*, vol. I (New York, 1944) pp. 224–5.

75. Löwe mentions a number of 50,000 Jewish industrial workers. See Löwe, *Antisemitismus*, p. 34.

76. Even if this memorandum was possibly not drafted by Pobedonostsev himself, it indicates the way of thinking in these circles: '. . . The Jews soften the orthodox religion and the moral, and they exploit the native population. Furthermore, the Jews were mainly revolutionaries and the tool of an Austrian-German expansion policy with which the Balkans as well as the Ottoman Empire should be germanized. And all this was a conspiracy of the all-mighty Kahal, the secret Jewish world government.' For more detail see Löwe, *Antisemitismus*, pp. 58–64.

77. See Krol, *Stranitsy*, vol. I, p. 299.

78. Among the founders of the Defense Bureau were G.B. Sliozberg, M.M. Vinaver, M.I. Kulisher, L.M. Bramson, L.O. Zaidenman, B.F. Brandt and A.I. Braudo. In 1902 Aizenberg, Veisenberg and M.A. Krol himself joined, followed shortly after by people such as Yu.D. Brutskus and M.B. Pozner. See Krol, *Stranitsy*, p. 299.

79. See Sliozberg, *Dela*, p. 132.

80. For more information about Paul Nathan and his activity in the Hilfsverein see Ernst Feder, *Paul Nathan. Ein Lebensbild* (Berlin, 1929); Ernst Feder, 'Paul Nathan and his work for East European and Palestinian Jewry', in *Historia Judaica*, 14 (1952) pp. 3–26; and Zosa Szajkowski, 'Paul Nathan, Lucien Wolf, Jacob Schiff and the Jewish Revolutionary Movements in Eastern Europe 1903–1917', *Jewish Social Studies*, 29 (1967) pp. 3–26.

81. See Sliozberg, *Dela*, p. 144.

82. For more information on the Anglo-Jewish Association see Zosa Szajkowski, 'Conflicts in the Alliance Israelite Universelle and the founding of the Anglo-Jewish Association, the Vienna Allianz and the Hilfsverein', *Jewish Social Studies*, 19 (1957) pp. 29–50.

83. Information about Russian Jewry in general and the anti-Semitic policy by the Russian government in particular can be found more extensively from 1904 onwards in the *Jewish Chronicle*. Wolf's 'engagement' for the Russian Jews' cause resulted some years later in the publishing of another information brochure: Lucien Wolf (ed.), *The legal sufferings of the Jews in Russia. A survey of their present situation and a summary of laws* (London, 1912).

84. See Krol, *Stranitsy*, p. 300. Here, he wrote that in many cases the Defense Bureau had no idea how Braudo succeeded in one or the other campaign in the press.

85. See Krol, *Stranitsy*, p. 302.

86. Ibid., pp. 302–3.

87. 'He did not allow this new investigation on the authorities' level as he was afraid it would lead up to the head of the "pogromshchiki", Pleve.' See

Krol, *Stranitsy*, pp. 303–4. It has to be pointed out, however, that Krol's statement mostly reflected the general view at this time – that the government and especially the minister of the interior must have known about the pogrom and, thereby, also been involved in it – and not necessarily reality. Nobody was ever able to prove that the organization of a pogrom had gone beyond the point of a governor. Therefore, there is no evidence yet that Pleve was involved or even ordered the pogrom. See John Klier and Shlomo Lambroza (eds), *Pogroms: Anti-Jewish Violence in Modern Russian History* (Cambridge and New York, 1992).

88. In this declaration the Jewish lawyers had protested against the unfairness of the conduct by the court president which did not allow them to defend their clients in an appropriate way. This conduct, they continued, had proven that an independent court was impossible under this despotic regime. See Krol, *Stranitsy*, p. 305.

89. The other lawyers were: Sliozberg, Kal'manovich, Zarudnii, Sokolov, Ganfman and Krol (St. Petersburg), M. Mandel'shtam (Moscow), Kupernik, Ratner and Margolin (Kiev). See Krol, *Stranitsy*, p. 307; In Gomel the Jewish lawyers represented Jews charged with armed self-defense. See Simon Dubnow, 'Jewish Rights between Red and Black', in Dawidowicz, *The Golden Tradition*, p. 462.

90. For more detail see Krol, *Stranitsy*, pp. 308–9. Vinaver held the declaration on the 51st day of session on 21 December 1904. See *Gomelskii Protses'. Podrobnyi otchet'* (St. Petersburg, 1907) p. 877.

91. See Pozner, 'Bor'ba za ravnopravie', p. 170; and Frumkin, 'Pages from the History of Russian Jewry', pp. 31–2.

92. For the Beilis Case see Chapter 5.

93. The term 'Liberals' were used by contemporaries referring to all the Jewish intellectuals who identified themselves with the general ideas of liberalism connected with the Russian Liberal Party, the 'Constitutional Democrats'. For their political programme see Chapter 2.


## 2   THE REVOLUTION OF 1905 AND THE STRUGGLE FOR LEGAL EMANCIPATION

1. See Miroslav Hroch, *Die Vorkämpfer der nationalen Bewegung bei den kleinen Völkern Europas. Eine vergleichende Analyse zur gesellschaftlichen Schichtung der Patriotischen Gruppen* (Prague, 1968).

2. For more information on the rapid increase and development of the press in this period, see Caspar Ferenczi, 'Freedom of the Press under the Old Regime', in Olga Crisp and Linda Edmondson (eds), *Civil Rights in Imperial Russia* (Oxford, 1989) pp. 191–214.

3. For more details see Terence Emmons, 'Russia's 'Banquet' Campaign', *California Slavic Studies*, 10 (1977) pp. 45–86; and Heinz-Dietrich Löwe, 'Die Rolle der Russischen Intelligenz in der Revolution von 1905', in *Forschungen zur Osteuropäischen Geschichte*, 32 (1983) pp. 237–43.

4. For more information about the Soiuz Soiuzov, see S.D. K(irpichnikov), *Soiuz Soiuzov* (St. Petersburg, 1906); and S.N. Dmitriev, 'Soiuz Soiuzov v

gody pervoi rossiiskoi revoliutsii', in *Istoriia SSSR* 1 (Jan./Feb.1990) pp. 40–57; and Löwe, 'Die Rolle der Russischen Intelligenz', pp. 229–56.

5. See Dmitriev, 'Soiuz Soiuzov', p. 45; Abraham Ascher, *The Revolution of 1905. Russia in Disarray* (Stanford, 1988) pp. 143–4; Sidney Harcave, *The Revolution of 1905* (London, 1970) pp. 143–5.

6. For more information on the banquet campaign see Ascher, *Revolution of 1905*, pp. 66–9.

7. See Krol, *Stranitsy*, vol. I, p. 309.

8. Therein they demanded the abolition of all restrictive laws, emancipation along with the rest of the population, freedom of movement (svoboda peredvizheniia), by abolishing the particularly oppressive Pale of Settlement, freedom of employment, and the right to obtain education and property. See *Pravo*, 1905, p. 739; all the thirty-two cities are mentioned by Sidney Harcave, *Jewish Political Parties and Groups and the Russian State Duma from 1905–1907*, unpublished DPhil thesis (Chicago, 1943) pp. 45–6.

9. See Löwe, *Antisemitismus*, p. 11.

10. The Defense Bureau members' will to approach the Jewish masses has already been documented, see chapter I, note 77.

11. The foundation of the Soiuz Polnopraviia received wide coverage in the Jewish press, see *Khronika Evreiskoi Zhizni*, no. 14, 10 April 1905, pp. 20–1, and *Voskhod*, no. 14, 6 April 1905, p. 17, as well as it found its way into the Okhrana files, see R.M. Kantor, 'Razgrom evreiskoi intelligentsii', in *Evreiskaia Letopis*, II (1924) pp. 87–95.

12. Dubnov illuminated the course of an illegal gathering like the Vilna Conference: '. . . we held closed meetings in private houses and in the course of the conference's three days and nights we changed the locus of meetings several times.' See Dubnow, 'Jewish Rights between Red and Black', p. 463.

13. Bramson had founded the Jewish Democratic Group in St. Petersburg by the end of February, 1905. See Simon Dubnow, 'Jewish Rights between Red and Black', p. 462; and S.M. Dubnov, *Kniga Zhizni. Vospominaniia i razmyshleniia*, vol. II (Riga, 1935) pp. 20–1. The other founders of the EDG were A.I. Braudo, Bikerman and Saker. Dubnov mentioned Dr. Shabad as the EDG's representative in Vilna.

14. See Dubnov, *Kniga zhizni*, p. 23; and Oscar I. Janowsky, *The Jews and Minority Rights 1898–1919* (New York, 1933, reprint 1966) p. 91. Janowsky only mentioned, however, the Liberals and Zionists as participants of the SP.

15. The national demands were: the freedom of national-cultural self-determination in all its varieties, especially the broad autonomy of the Jewish communities; the right to one's own language; and the independent regulation of schooling for Jews. In connection with the reorganisation of the Jewish communities: the abolition of all taxes – such as the Korobka and the Candle tax – which oppressed the Jews, and that all other state taxes should be given to the Jewish communities. Finally, they demanded the abolition of all special laws and decrees for Jews. See *Voskhod*, no. 14, 6 April 1905, p. 17.

16. See *Voskhod*, no. 14, 6 April 1905, p. 17.

17. According to Dmitriev the Soiuz Soiuzov had 33,000 members at its initial stage (May 1905), which increased within five months (by November 1905) to 94,000, and reached its peak in 1906 with about 300,000 members. This indicates the increasing involvement of Russian society in the Liberation Movement – even if Dmitriev's list is incomplete and, therefore, has to be dealt with with caution. See Dmitriev, 'Soiuz Soiuzov', pp. 46–7.

18. Vinaver released his definition within the scope of the elections to the Fourth. Duma and his 'engagement' in the Warsaw election campaign (see Chapter 5). For Sliozberg's statement see Henrik Sliosberg, 'A Good Russian – A Good Jew', in Dawidowicz, *The Golden Tradition*, p. 473.

19. See Simon Dubnow, *Mein Leben*, edited by Elias Hurwicz (Berlin, 1937) pp. 159–60.

20. See Dubnov, *Kniga zhizni*, pp. 24–5.

21. The congress' participants were elected by the local communities and branches of the Union. Each group of twenty-five members sent one representative. In the communities a group consisting of not less than three members set up a local committee. See *Khronika Evreiskoi Zhizni*, no. 32, 19 August 1905, pp. 1–2.

22. See Harcave, *Jewish Political Parties*, p. 47.

23. The membership fee was fixed at fifty Kopeks, but members could give more if they chose. See *Khronika Evreiskoi Zhizni*, no. 32, 19 August 1905, p. 2.

24. See *Khronika Evreiskoi Zhizni*, no. 32, 19 August, p. 3.

25. 'As an active member of the Union for the achievement of Equal Rights and the Union of Attorneys, I was a delegate to the central organ of the Union of Unions', see Arnold D. Margolin, *From a Political Diary. Russia, the Ukraine and America, 1905–1945* (New York, 1946) p. 8.

26. See S.D.K, *Soiuz Soiuzov*, p. 10; another member of the SP, the lawyer M.A. Krol, who was also sent by the SP to this congress, gives a brief account of it. See M.A. Krol, *Stranitsy moei zhizni*, vol. II, unpublished typescript, Hoover Institution Archives, Collection M.A. Krol, Box I, pp. 2–3.

27. The following statement can be read regarding the Union's further activity: 'Based on the undeniable fact that the Jewish nationality is only a small part of the huge organism called Russia, and that finally the fate of this part not only depends on the general functioning of the whole organism, but also on the general relations of the individual organs of the organism to each other, the Vilna congress considers it desirable and necessary to work in all parts of Russian society, in the city, Zemstvo and other social institutions as well as in the press and at the congresses of the various groups, so that the principle of equality before the law with regard to the Jews – supported by all the liberal circles – will be realized.' See *Khronika Evreiskoi Zhizni*, no. 32, 19 August 1905, pp. 3–4.

28. The unions affiliated to the Union of Unions were: academics, lawyers, agronomist and statisticians, medical doctors, veterinarians, railway workers, writers, Zemstvo people, the Union of the Emancipation for Women, the Union of the Full Equality for the Jews, engineers, clerks and book-keepers, teachers of the primary and middle schools, the Union of peasants and finally the pharmacists. All in all the Soiuz Soiuzov had 40–50,000

members in the summer of 1905. See S.D.K, *Soiuz Soiuzov*, pp. 21–30; for a detailed account of all the unions, see Jonathan E. Sanders, *The Union of Unions: Political, Economic, Civil and Human Rights Organizations in the 1905 Russian Revolution*, unpublished DPhil thesis, Columbia University, 1985.

29.　Sev claimed that no people, not even the least cultivated, was deprived of so many rights and freedoms as the Jewish people. He mentioned primarily the freedom of movement (*svoboda peredvizheniia*), the freedom to choose their employment and the branch of trade, as well as the right to achieve an education. Finally, he reproached the press organs with contributing to the growing belief within Russian society that the Jews would be in the public wealth's way. Thereby, an atmosphere was created within society in which the Jews were suffocating – in the real sense of the word. See 'K sez'du zhurnalistov', in *Pravo*, 1905, pp. 1222–5.

30.　Ibid., p. 1227.

31.　Ibid., p. 1226.

32.　See Ascher, *Revolution of 1905*, p. 142; and Dmitriev, 'Soiuz Soiuzov', p. 46.

33.　See L.M. Bramson, *K istorii Trudovoi Partii. Trudovaia Gruppa pervoi gosudarstvennoi Dumy*, 2nd (ed.) (Petrograd, 1917) p. 16. Here, Bramson described a meeting of this Union which took place in St. Petersburg three days before the opening of the Duma. He succeeded in pushing through a resolution in favour of equality of rights for Russian Jews against the adherents of the anti-Semite Erogin; this particular activity in the Union of Peasants is also reported by another former SP activist. See Pozner, 'Bor'ba za ravnopravie', p. 137.

34.　For more information on Gessen's activity in the Union of Zemstvo Activists, see Ascher, *Revolution of 1905*, p. 59. Ascher mentions also various talks between Gessen and Prime Minister Vitte in 1905–1906 in which the latter asked the former for political advice and co-operation.

35.　In the memorandum of 18 February 1905 to the minister of the interior, Tsar Nicholas II had promised an elected, legislative assembly. Therein the minister of the interior, Bulygin was charged with the elaboration of the right to vote. See Heinz-Dietrich Löwe, 'Bulygin Duma', in Hans-Joachim Torke (ed.), *Lexikon der Geschichte Rußlands. Von den Anfängen bis zur Oktober-Revolution* (Munich, 1985) pp. 72–73; for further information on the Bulygin Duma see Ascher, *Revolution of 1905*, pp. 177–81; and Harcave, *Revolution of 1905*, pp. 145–6.

36.　Ascher showed to which absurd results this suffrage would have led: in St. Petersburg only 7,130 out of 1,400,000 people would be able to vote for electors in the first stage of the election; in Moscow 12,000 out of 1,100,000; in Tsaritsyn 542 out of 85,000 and so on. (See Ascher, *Revolution of 1905*, p. 179.)

37.　See Harcave, *Jewish Political Parties*, p. 55; Dubnov illuminates one of those protests coming from Vilna: 'I drafted such a sharp protest in the name of the Jewish community of Vilna that many people were afraid to sign it, but we collected enough signatures and it was published in the press with other protests.' See Dubnow, 'Jewish Rights between Red and Black', p. 465; and Dubnov, *Kniga Zhizni*, p. 28.

38. The issue of participation was controversial among the radical Intelligentsia and the professional unions. The representatives of the city councillors and the Zemstva decided to participate in the Duma hoping to achieve a western type of parliament. The left-wing of the opposition in turn advocated the boycott. See Sliozberg, *Dela*, p. 173.

39. According to Krol, the SP did not want to protest publicly as this would have endangered the venture. Finally, since the regime was still strong, the SP approached the progressive governmental officials who were known to oppose the restrictive course of people such as the governor-general Trepov; see Krol, *Stranitsy*, vol. II, p. 8. Vitte having expressed his sympathy and his goodwill towards the given request, referred Sliozberg to the Minister of Finance, Kokovtsev, who gave Sliozberg and Kulisher an audience on the same day. During this audience Sliozberg was again anxious to refer to the injustice of excluding six million Jews from the elections. See Sliozberg, *Dela*, pp. 173–4.

40. Kokovtsev writes in his memoirs that Vitte was very interested to give the right to vote to the Jews. Furthermore, the majority of the meeting's participants had agreed with it. See Graf V.N. Kokovtsev, *Iz moego proshlago. Vospominania 1903–1919*, vol. I (Paris, 1933) pp. 70–1 [Reprinted 1969 in Slavic Printings and Reprintings, vol. 200/1, edited by C.H. van Schoonefeld, The Hague and Paris, 1969]; for more information on this conference see also George E. Snow, 'The Peterhof Conference of 1905 and the Creation of the Bulygin Duma', in *Russian History*, II, 2 (1975) pp. 149–62.

41. See Krol, *Stranitsy*, vol. II, pp. 9–10.

42. See Robert Weinberg, 'Workers, Pogroms, and the 1905 Revolution in Odessa', *The Russian Review*, 46 (1987) p. 46.

43. See Kantor, 'Razgrom evreiskoi intelligentsii', p. 89; according to Krol, revolutionaries of all colours extensively used the lecture halls of the universities in order to propagate the revolution and indoctrinate the audience which increasingly consisted of workers. See Krol, *Stranitsy*, vol. II, pp. 14–17.

44. The Bulygin Duma was to be elected according to curiae: the right to vote especially favoured the land-owning aristocracy and the municipal upper class, and also guaranteed a relatively strong influence to the peasants. The aristocracy was given 34 per cent, the peasants 43 per cent and the propertied bourgeoisie 23 per cent of the delegates; as the classification to some degree still followed the old 'soslovie' system, workers and the poorer intelligentsia were not even mentioned. See S.D.K, *Soiuz Soiuzov*, p. 14.

45. In many places in the Pale of Settlement the Jews proved to be the dominating group: in Kherson, of the 199 delegates one hundred were Jews. From Vinnitsa, a city in the gubernia of Podolia, it was reported that 35 per cent of the voters were Christians and 45 per cent Jews and so on. See *Voskhod*, no. 37, 16 September, p. 12. Lestschinsky talks of an absolute or relative majority (between 50 per cent and 59 per cent) of Jews in the main towns of the provinces of Minsk, Grodno, Siedltse, Vitebsk, Mogilev, Kieltse, Volynia and Radom. See Jacob Lestschinsky, 'Dubnow's Autonomism and his "Letters on Old and New Judaism"', in Aaron Steinberg (ed.), *Simon Dubnov. The Man and his Work. A memorial volume on the occasion of his birth, 1860–1960* (Paris, 1963) p. 88.

46. See Dubnow, 'Jewish Rights between Red and Black', pp. 465–66.
47. In this Manifesto, Nicholas II promised an elected assembly with legislative functions whereby no law would be enacted without the consent of the State Duma. In addition to this, the Tsar promised civil freedoms such as the freedom of meeting, speech, press and coalition, and indirectly also the emancipation of religions and nationalities, and finally, as opposed to the Bulygin Duma, an extension of the right to vote to wider strata of the population. See Heinz-Dietrich Löwe, 'Die Rolle der demokratischen Intelligenz', in M. Hellmann, K. Zernack, G. Schramm (eds), *Handbuch der Geschichte Russlands.* vol. 3/1 Von den autokratischen Reformen zum Sowjetstaat 1856–1945 (Stuttgart, 1982) p. 350.
48. The Kadets promoted a parliamentary monarchy, although they for some time left the question of the monarchy open. Originally they had strived for a Constituent Assembly, but later dropped this demand in favour of a Duma with constitutional functions. See Löwe, 'Parteien', in Torke, *Lexikon der Geschichte Rußlands*, pp. 288–91.
49. Their main argument was that 'the elections to the Duma had the only purpose of confusing the masses and diverting them from the revolutionary path'. See Ascher, *Revolution of 1905*, p. 339.
50. See Tobias, *The Jewish Bund*, p. 337.
51. In early 1906 the Soiuz Polnopraviia reached a total of 7,500 members. Unfortunately, S.D.K. did not give any account of the SP's local branches. See S.D.K, *Soiuz Soiuzov*, p. 26; the number of its branches rapidly increased from 50 (May 1905) to 163 (November 1905), and, finally, showed a slight decrease to 150 in January 1906. See Dmitriev, 'Soiuz Soiuzov', p. 47.
52. See Harcave, *Jewish Political Parties*, p. 63; Dubnov mentioned even a presence of 100 delegates. See Dubnov, *Kniga Zhizni*, p. 36; Janowsky mentioned an organizational framework of the SP with 160 'local bodies'. See Janowsky, *The Jews and Minority Rights*, p. 93.
53. A. Linden counted 660 pogroms between 18 and 29 October. See A. Linden, 'Die Dimensionen der Oktoberpogrome 1905', in *Die Judenpogrome in Russland*, vol. I (Cologne and Leipzig, 1910) p. 187. Dubnov gave the following information about the Odessa pogrom: more than three hundred people were killed, thousands were mutilated and wounded and more than 40,000 people were economically ruined. See Simon Dubnow, *Weltgeschichte des jüdischen Volkes. Vol. X. Die Neueste Geschichte* (Berlin, 1929) p. 396. *Voskhod* reported in no. 44–5 in 11 November 1905 that about eight hundred had been killed and several thousand wounded. For more detail about the background and the conditions which made the pogrom possible, see Weinberg, 'Workers, pogroms and the 1905 Revolution in Odessa', pp. 53–75; and Ascher, *Revolution of 1905*, pp. 254–62.
54. In 1904, a local SD organisation not only let a pogrom happen but did not even react to it. See Löwe, *Antisemitismus*, p. 90.
55. For more information see Löwe, 'Die Rolle der russischen Intelligenz', pp. 231–54.
56. See *Voskhod*, no. 47–8, 1 December 1905, pp. 22–3.
57. See *Voskhod*, no. 47–8, 1 December 1905, pp. 26–7.
58. Yakhnin from Igumen, Tsernovits and Ratner from Borisoglebsk and

Khoronzhitskii from St. Petersburg. See *Voskhod*, no. 49–50, 8 December, pp. 22–3.

59. The 'Autonomists' and the Zionists regarded the pogroms as a reflection of the general social anti-Semitism which they maintained could also be found in the Liberation Movement. See *Voskhod*, no. 47–48, 1 December 1905, p. 22.

60. According to Frankel, Zhabotinskii had used the demand of a National Assembly as a means to challenge the Bundists. Frankel referred to Shmarya Levin's statement: 'His [Jabotinsky',] favourite slogan was "Make the bear come out and fight", and at this time he understandably saw the Bund, the dominant force on the left, as his bear.' (see Frankel, *Prophecy and Politics*, p. 165); the Jewish national assembly was originally an idea of Dubnov's, who envisioned it as a kind of renaissance of Polish-Jewish independence in the times of the Va'ad. See Dubnov, *Kniga zhizni*, pp. 36–8; for the second congress of the SP see also Janowsky, *The Jews and Minority Rights*, p. 93. However, the course of the dispute on the October pogroms clearly showed that Janowsky was wrong when he said that the Liberals had raised the pogrom discussion in order to distract from other more controversial issues.

61. See *Voskhod*, no. 49–50, 8 December 1905, p. 29.

62. See *Voskhod*, no. 49–50, 8 December 1905, p. 30.

63. The final resolution was stated in *Voskhod*: 'In order to realise completely the civil, political and national rights of the Jewish people in Russia, the congress regards it as urgent to proceed with an all-Jewish national assembly, based on universal suffrage without any distinction of sex, with direct and secret vote; after the election by the whole Jewish people one must proceed towards the determination of the form and principles of its national self-determination and the fundament of its internal organization.' (See *Voskhod*, no. 49–50, 8 December 1905, p. 33). Apparently, Dubnov had brought up the idea that the SP should officially lean its political programme on the Kadets. See Dubnov, *Kniga zhizni*, p. 38.

64. The congress reproached count Vitte with the fact that he had tolerated the organization of the pogroms by the Black Hundreds as well as the participation of the police and the local higher administration in them. Furthermore, it claimed that he had not handed over the guilty to the court despite the general demand for it. The peak of the affair was the decoration of some administrators and Vitte's cynical answer that he can not realize the emancipation of the Jews since the population was not prepared to agree with it. See *Voskhod*, no. 49–50, 8 December 1905, pp. 35–6. However, the sharp criticism against Vitte was not justified. He had stood up for the Jews' right to vote. Furthermore, he had in fact handed over to the court the persons responsible for the pogroms. His power was not sufficient, however, for further action and thus he could not prevent acquittals. Finally, Vitte had repeatedly assured the Shtadlanim Gintsburg and Sliozberg of his intentions to solve the Jewish question, but claimed the present circumstances in Russia had hindered him from achieving a solution.

65. Concerning the question of the participation in the congresses of the Zemstva and the municipal councils, it had been decided to elect delegates for the negotiations with the Zemstvo congress. Ibid., p. 33.

66. See Dubnow, 'Jewish Rights between Red and Black', p. 467; in this context, the SP sent, for instance, Krol to Orsha in order to investigate on the background of the pogrom. See Krol, *Stranitsy*, vol. II, pp. 34–9.

67. Feder mentioned various meetings such as the ones of Paul Nathan with Vitte in 1905 and 1906, and an interview with Vitte in Portsmouth (1905) by Strauss and Schiff. See Ernst Feder, 'Paul Nathan and his work for East European and Palestinian Jewry', *Historia Judaica*, vol. XIV (April 1952) part I, pp. 10–13.

68. For more details see Zosa Szajkowski, 'Paul Nathan, Lucien Wolf, Jacob H. Schiff and the Revolutionary Movements in Eastern Europe, 1903–1917', *Jewish Social Studies*, 29 (1967) pp. 5–10.

69. Szajkowski mentioned, above all, Jacob Schiff's change of mind regarding the solution of the Jewish question. Thus, he had decided that the Jewish question could only be solved by revolutionary means. The Jewish leaders abroad concluded that the future of the Russian Jews depends on the further development of the country, and, therefore, they now regarded the Jewish struggle for emancipation as a part of the Russian Liberation Movement. See Szajkowski, 'Paul Nathan', p. 10.

70. Rothschild subsidized this newspaper until 1908. See Gary Dean Best, *To Free a People. American Jewish Leaders and the Jewish Problem in Eastern Europe, 1890–1914* (Westport, Connecticut and London, 1982) p. 167.

71. See Szajkowski, 'Paul Nathan', p. 16.

72. See Best, *To Free a People*, pp. 114–201.

73. For more information on Jacob Schiff's campaign see A.I. Sherman, 'German-Jewish bankers in World Politics: The Financing of the Russo-Japanese War', in *Yearbook of the Leo Baeck Institute*, 28 (1983) pp. 59–73.

74. See Dmitriev, 'Soiuz Soiuzov', pp. 52–3.

75. The Soiuz Soiuzov's appeal to the people was reported in *Khronika Evreiskoi Zhizni*, no. 46, 25 November 1905, pp. 16–17: '... At the same time the conference declares that the wide expansion of the Jewish pogroms and their cruel character has to be explained by the fact that the Jews have no rights which made the non-Jewish population believe that the Jews are not touched by the law. Therefore, the conference considers as necessary the immediate emancipation of the Jews with the rest of the population in the Empire and calls upon all the conscious elements of the Russian people to fight with all the means against national disunity and intolerance. Away with the restricting laws! Away with the instigators of the pogroms!'.

76. See Ascher, *Revolution of 1905*, p. 253.

77. This equality is stated in the First Paragraph, Point One of the Kadets' political programme: 'All Russian citizens irrespective of sex, religion, or nationality are equal before the law. All class distinctions and all limitations of personal and property right of Poles, Jews, and other groups of the population, should be repealed,' (see Dmytryshyn, *Imperial Russia*, p. 438); the Trudoviki had promoted civil equality as one of their primary political targets. See Bramson, *K istorii Trudovoi Partii*, p. 48.

78. See *Khronika Evreiskoi Zhizni*, no. 1, 10 January 1906, p. 34; Pozner, 'Bor'ba za ravnopravie', p. 173; Sidney Harcave, 'The Jews and the First Russian National Election', *The American Slavic and East European Review*, vol. IX, no. 1 (February 1950) p. 39.

79. In December, 1905 Lure, a Union member from Pinsk, demanded propaganda material in Yiddish for the purpose of the elections for a convocation of a Jewish national assembly in Pinsk. See *Voskhod*, no. 51–2, 30 December 1905, p. 22; brochures which were supposed to inform the population about the election system were spread by the Soiuz Polnopraviia, for instance, in Kiev; see *Voskhod*, no. 1, 6 January 1906, p. 22. Information brochures were sent to the SP's branches in the provinces. See *Voskhod*, no. 51–2, 30 December 1905, pp. 22–3; according to the Okhrana files circulars were also spread by the SP. See Kantor, 'Razgrom evreiskoi intelligentsii', pp. 87–95; regarding the election law the SP produced a brochure; *Zakon o Gosudarstvennoi Dume 11 Dekabria 1905g*, Izdanie Tsenral'nago Biuro Soiuza dlia dostizheniia polnopraviia evreiskago naroda v Rossii (St. Petersburg, 1905).

80. See Harcave, 'The Jews and the First Russian National Election', p. 36.

81. The inquiries showed mainly positive results: In Kherson one hundred out of 199 candidates were Jews; in Vinnitsa (Gub. Podolia) 35 per cent of the voters were Christians while 45 per cent were Jews, see *Voskhod*, no. 37, 16 September 1905, p. 12. In Vindavo 150 voters out of 250 were Jews; in Ekaterinoslav 40 per cent of the voters were Jews, see *Voskhod*, no. 40, 8 October 1905, pp. 14–15. According to Alexander Orbach this led to the Soiuz Polnopraviia's expectation of twenty Jewish Duma deputies. See Alexander Orbach, 'Zionism and the Russian Revolution of 1905. The Commitment to Participate in Domestic Political Life', in *Annual of Bar-Ilan University Studies in the History and Culture of East European Jewry*, vol. XXIV–XXV (Jerusalem, 1989) p. 19; Harcave even talks of an expectation of twenty-three Jewish deputies. See Harcave, 'The Jews and the First Russian National Election', p. 40.

82. Such alliances were formed in Moscow, Kharkov, Kiev, Simferopol, Odessa, Elizavetgrad, Poltava, Berdichev and Mogilev. See Harcave, *Jewish Political Parties*, p. 91; and Harcave, 'The Jews and the First Russian National Election', pp. 37–8.

83. See *Nasha Zhizn*, no. 386, 5 March 1906, p. 3.

84. See *Khronika Evreiskoi Zhizni*, 22 March 1906, p. 12.

85. See *Rech*, no. 13, 7 March 1906, p. 3.

86. See Harcave, *Jewish Political Parties*, p. 92.

87. Frankel wrote that the Bundists suffered more from the police, and the SP's speakers 'such as Jabotinsky could speak in many cities where socialists did not dare debate with him publicly.' Furthermore, the SP's congress in November 1905 could be conducted openly while the socialists' congresses had to take place secretly or alternatively abroad. See Frankel, *Prophecy and Politics*, p. 157.

88. In some places they did not inform the voters about the new election law of 11 December 1905; on several occasions Jewish candidates were arrested by the police or deleted from the election list; and finally many polling stations – in one case 50 Verst – were set up far away, so that the poor Jewish masses could not afford to exercise their right to vote. See *Voskhod*, no. 8, 23 February 1906, pp. 15–16.

89. See note 79.

90. See *Khronika Evreiskoi Zhizni*, no. 10, 15 March 1906, p. 20.

91. The following candidates were elected: Vinaver (St. Petersburg), Ostrogorskii and Yakubson (Gubernia Grodno), S. Frenkel and Chervonenkis (Province of Kiev), L.M. Bramson (Gubernia Kovno), G. Bruk (Province of Minsk), M. Sheftel (Province of Ekaterinoslav), Sh. Levin (Vilna) and N. Katsenel'son (Courland). Nine of them were Kadets and three Trudoviki. Four of the Kadets and one of the Trudoviki were also Zionists. (See Harcave, *Jewish Political Parties*, p. 96.)

92. Indifference of the Jewish population towards the SP's election campaign was reported from mainly smaller cities such as Bobruisk (Gub. Minsk), Mstislavl (Gub. Mogilev) and some other – unmentioned – places. See *Voskhod*, no. 8, 23 February 1906, p. 16.

93. There are many reports about the Bund's boycott activities but Harcave described it precisely and shortly: 'At election committees Bundists asked for the right to speak; if the request was denied, they interrupted the meetings.' (see Harcave, 'The Jews and the First Russian National Election', p. 38); similar actions were reported from Chernigov, see *Nasha Zhizn*, no. 395, 16 March 1906, p. 5; from Vilna, see Dubnov, *Kniga Zhizni*, pp. 49–50; and Cherkassy, see *Voskhod*, no. 8, 23 February 1906, p. 15; in Orsha, see Frankel, *Prophecy and Politics*, p. 162.

94. Krol mentioned alliances of Jews and peasants in the gubernii of Kovno and Grodno, and stated that the peasants as such were not anti-Semitic. Moreover, the slogan under which they were prepared to set up an alliance with the Jews was apparently: 'We ought to go with the Jews. While we give them rights, they will help us to obtain the land.' (see Krol, *Stranitsy*, vol. II, pp. 60–61.)

95. Count Pototsky was especially mentioned as a person who tried to manipulate the elections by all possible means. He promised among other things to give the people money for a new school. Furthermore, the alliance of landowners compelled the peasants to swear an oath of allegiance (by armed force?). They had to swear that they would not vote for a Jew as a Duma candidate. See *Voskhod*, no. 17, 27 April 1906, pp. 18–19.

96. The Trudovik Zabolotny, the leader of the peasants movement, did not want to form an alliance with landowners or persons who did not have the same interests as the peasants. See *Voskhod*, no. 17, 27 April 1906, p. 18.

97. For more information on the National Democrats activities, see Harcave, 'The Jews and the First Russian National Election', p. 37.

98. The Poles demanded autonomy based on the equality of all the nationalities living in Poland, and all the Polish political parties had originally this point in their programme. Finally the article mentioned the general view among Polish Jews: 'we have no reason to distrust the Poles'. See *Voskhod*, no. 15, 13 April 1906, p. 21.

99. The ND's candidate in Warsaw, Novodvorsky called for the Jews to give up Yiddish as their language, and if the Jews wanted to be treated as Poles to define themselves as Poles of mosaic faith. See *Voskhod*, no. 13, 30 March 1906, p. 22; furthermore, slogans such as 'Poland in danger! The Jew comes!', as well as statements like 'a Jewish Duma deputy from Warsaw would be a slap in the face for the entire Polish nation' were spread. See *Voskhod*, no. 16, 20 April 1906, p. 5.

100. See S. Aleksandrov, 'Evreiskii vopros v Dume i "dostigateli"', in *Nashe Slovo*, 22 June 1906, p. 4.

101. See A.K., 'K izbiratel'noi kampanii', in *Evreiskii Narod*, no. 4, 10 November 1906, cols 1–5.

102. See Shneerson, *Lebn un Kampf*, p. 278.

103. Sliozberg was deeply impressed by the interest and active participation of the Jewish voters. See Sliozberg, *Dela*, pp. 137–8. Shneerson described his activity in the election campaign to the Second Duma where he was particularly active in Chernigov and acted together with the Trudovik Bramson (see Shneerson, *Lebn un Kampf*, p. 170 and pp. 181–2).

104. Krol's statement was identical to the Bund's arguments with which it had justified its Duma boycott. For more detail on the III. Congress and its debates see also Dubnov, *Kniga zhizni*, pp. 45–7.

105. His main arguments were: '. . . we give the suppressed nation the opportunity to demand its rights in the public . . . We have to be in the Duma, as we, as a suppressed nationality, would be a lively ferment among all those rotting strata which will come into the Duma . . .'. See *Protokoly tret'ago delegatskago s'ezda Soiuza dlia dostizheniia polnopraviia evreiskago naroda v Rossii v S. Peterburge. S. 10–go po 13-oe febralia 1906g*, Izdanie Tsentral'nago Komiteta Obshchestva Polnopraviia Evreiskago Naroda v Rossii (St. Petersburg, 1906) pp. 27–8.

106. Ahad Ha'am stated that the Union would be making a mistake by formulating a fully political, instead of a purely national programme. Finally, he demanded to 'pull down the special inner Jewish wall of the prison'. See *Protokoly*, p. 65.

107. Bramson replied directly to Ahad Ha'am's statement, that 'not only the inner wall but also the external wall of the jail had to be pulled down in order to achieve freedom'. This meant to support the progressive parties and to continue the co-operation with the Russian Liberation Movement. See *Protokoly*, p. 65.

108. He suggested the imitation of the political process which was already practised by the Poles, Alsatians and Danes in the West European parliaments, in order to present themselves as a national group. See *Protokoly*, p. 88; see also Dubnov, *Kniga zhizni*, p. 46.

109. See *Protokoly*, p. 88. Bramson mentioned the problems the Jewish deputies would face in their respective Russian parties once they would emphasize Jewish national matters too strongly. See Bramson's memoirs of the First Duma, in *Novyi Put'*, no. 15, 1 May 1916, p. 8; a brief account of the disputes at the Third SP congress is also given in Krol, *Stranitsy*, vol. II, pp. 44–51.

110. See *Protokoly*, p. 90.

111. This proclamation is cited in Gregory L. Freeze, *From Supplication to Revolution. A Documentary Social History of Imperial Russia* (New York and Oxford, 1988) p. 299.

112. The left-liberal radical wing was further strengthened by two Social Democrats and 17 Social Revolutionaries. See Warren B. Walsh, 'Political Parties in the Russian Duma', *Journal of Modern History*, 22 (1950) pp. 144–145.

113. See Helmut Gross, 'Die Politik der Regierung: Kooperation mit der Gesellschaft oder Befriedung durch Gewalt?', in *Handbuch der Geschichte Russlands*, vol. III/1, pp. 377–8.

114. See Judith Elin Zimmerman, *Between Revolution and Reaction. The Constitutional Democratic Party, October 1905 to June 1907*. DPhil thesis. Columbia University (Ann Arbor, Michigan, 1969) pp. 163–70.

115. See Alexander Orbach, 'The Jewish People's Group', pp. 12–13; Bramson criticized the Kadet faction in the Duma for having acted too cautiously and, therefore, not achieving more. (See *Novyi Put'*, no. 15, 1 May 1916, p. 13). The Bundist Aleksandrov reproached the SP that it had relied too much on the Duma's power. Furthermore, it had made too many concessions and thereby had not pursued Jewish interests thoroughly enough. See Aleksandrov, 'Evreiskii vopros v Dume i "dostigateli"', pp. 4–8.

116. For more details concerning the position of the Jews in the Kadet Party, see Zimmerman, *Between Revolution and Reaction*, pp. 196–200.

117. The speech has been quoted in full length in *Voskhod*, no. 20, 19 May 1906, pp. 3–4; Dubnov also mentioned the speech in his memoirs (see Dubnov, *Kniga zhizni*, p. 53).

118. During the discussions in the committee on civil equality, Vinaver had taken the 'regesty i nadpisy' with him to the session in order to show the committee members the amount of all the restrictions. Apparently, one deputy looked at the facts and seemed to ask: 'Did we really create all these restrictions?' See Louis Greenberg, *The Jews in Russia: The Struggle for Emancipation*, vol. 2 (New York, 1976) p. 117.

119. See Sidney Harcave, 'The Jewish Question in the First State Duma', in *Jewish Social Studies*, 6 (1944) p. 161; Vinaver gave a full account of this action. See M.M. Vinaver, *Kadety i evreiskii vopros* (St. Petersburg, 1907) pp. 6/7.

120. See Löwe, *Antisemitismus*, p. 104.

121. See Harcave, 'The Jewish Question', p. 166.

122. See Bramson, *K istorii Trudovoi Partii*, p. 51; see also Krol, *Stranitsy*, vol. II, pp. 72–3. Krol – also Trudovik, but no Duma deputy – apparently served as a juridical consultant at the Trudoviki's Duma faction which meant to acquaint the peasants unexperienced in parliamentary work with the laws discussed in the Duma (see ibid., pp. 62–7).

123. See *Voskhod*, no. 19, 13 May 1906, p. 11.

124. See Orbach, 'Zionism and the Russian Revolution of 1905', p. 21.

125. Zhabotinskii was supported by the famous lawyer O.O. Gruzenberg (see *Voskhod*, no. 21, 26 May 1906, pp. 9–10).

126. See *Voskhod*, no. 21, 26 May 1906, pp. 9–10.

127. Bramson threatened the congress with the immediate departure of six Duma deputies (Ostrogorskii, Bramson, Sheftel, Chervonenkis, Vinaver and Iollos) in case the congress would agree to the Zionists' demands (see *Voskhod*, no. 21, 26 May 1906, p. 12).

128. The resolution stated: 'Regarding a common activity in all the questions affecting the Jewish equality, the Fourth Congress of the SP considers it necessary that the Jewish Duma deputies should form a Jewish group in accordance with the Vilna platform. The members of this group are not bound to a group discipline, but they are to elaborate the principles of the coordination of their activity in mutual accordance.' (See *Voskhod*, no. 19, 13 May 1906, p. 12.)

129. See *Nasha Zhizn*, no. 465, 7 June 1906, p. 1; and *Volna*, no. 19, 17 May 1906, p. 2.

130. The five Jewish deputies were Vinaver, Levin, Bramson, Ostrogorskii and Iollos. For more details, see Harcave, *Jewish Political Parties*, p. 110.

131. See Vinaver, *Kadety*, p. 7; and *Voskhod*, no. 23, 10 June 1906, p. 48; Krol who was sent by the SP to Belostok in order to inquire about the pogrom stated that the pogrom was organised by police, army and hooligans. In this context, he mentioned a speech by officer Ivanov who had, apparently, ordered his soldiers: 'the more Jews you kill, the better.' (See Krol, *Stranitsy*, vol. II, pp. 77–8.)

132. See *Gosudarstvennaia Duma: Stenograficheskie otchety 1906 god'. Sessiia Pervaia*, vol. 2 (St. Petersburg, 1906) p. 1104.

133. See *Stenograficheskie otchety*, pp. 1072–3. The Octobrist Count Geiden said that the Jewish question was too difficult to solve immeiately. Furthermore, he doubted if an immediate and complete introduction of the general principle of equality would be wise; Prince Volkonskii, however, went even further, adding to Geiden's arguments by cynically asking the Jewish Duma deputies to prove that they would not do anything evil by abolishing inequality; see also Harcave, *Jewish Political Parties*, pp. 108–9.

134. See Harcave, 'The Jewish Question', pp. 168–70.

135. Ibid., p. 166–7.

136. According to Bramson, the Trudovik leader Aladin had initiated this committee (see Bramson, *K istorii Trudovoi Partii*, p. 52). For more general information about the Trudoviki, their programme and activities in and outside the Duma see D.A. Kolesnichenko, 'Iz istorii borby rabochego klassa za krest'ianskie massy v 1906 g.', *Istoricheskie Zapiski*, 95 (1975) pp. 254–82; and D.A. Kolesnichenko, 'K voprosu o politicheskoi evolutsii trudovikov v 1906 g.', in *Istoricheskie Zapiski*, 92 (1973) pp. 84–109. However, these articles do not mention the Jewish question, and only reflect the relations between Trudoviki and Bolsheviki.

137. Harcave, 'The Jewish Question', p. 172.

138. Almost the entire Kadet and Trudovik Duma factions had gone after the dissolution of the Duma to Vyborg, Finland, in order to look for an appropriate protest action. In the end, a proclamation was issued to the Russian population in which they called upon them to refuse paying taxes and no longer to send their sons to the army. However, this action failed as it did not meet any resonance among the Russian population which was exhausted from revolutionary activities. Furthermore, the socialist parties made no efforts to support the Vyborg appeal actively. For more details on the Vyborg appeal, see 'Pervaia Gosudarstvennaia Duma v Vyborge', *Krasnyi Arkhiv*, 57 (1933) pp. 85–99; M.M. Vinaver, *Istoriia vyborgskago vozzvania* (St. Petersburg, 1917); and Bramson, *K istorii Trudovoi Partii*, pp. 77–81.

# 3 THE ROAD TOWARDS SELF-DETERMINATION: NEW ELECTIONS, THE SECOND STATE DUMA AND THE SEARCH FOR A NEW APPROACH

1. A brief description of all these parties is given in K. Zalevskii, 'Natsional'nyia partii v Rossii', in *Obshchestvennoe dvizhenie v nachale XXgo veka*, vol. III, pp. 318–44.

2.  See *Der Fraind*, no. 38, 11 September 1906, p. 1; see also the SERP organ *Di Folksshtime*, no. 1, 1 December 1906, cols 23–39. The SERP shared the re-evaluation of the Kadets among socialist circles, and promoted an alliance with the Kadets as its slogan for the election campaign; for more information on the Kadets at this time, see Bernard Pares, 'The Second Duma', *The Slavonic and East European Review*, 2 (1923) p. 44; see also K. Frumin, 'Vegn di wahlen tsu der kumender dume', *Folkstsaitung*, no. 137, 15 August 1906, pp. 1–2. Frumin also pointed out that the political arena of the election campaign should not be left to the Kadets alone, and stressed the necessity to elaborate the election tactics in the forthcoming seventh Bund Congress; Stolypin had forbidden the fourth Party congress of the Kadets which was planned for 30 August 1906, and finally took place in September 1906 in Helsingfors, Finland. See *Folkstsaitung*, no. 154, 4 September 1906, p. 1, and no. 168, 27 September 1906, p. 1.

3.  For more details see Julius Martow, *Geschichte der russischen Sozialdemokratie* (Berlin, 1926, reprint Erlangen 1973) pp. 179–90; Alfred Levin, *The Second Duma: A Study of the Social-Democratic Party and the Russian Constitutional Experiment*, 2nd. ed. (Hamden, Connecticut, 1966) pp. 42–56; R. Abramovich, *In tsvai revolsutsies. Di geshikhte fun a dor* vol. I (New York, 1944) pp. 271–2; and Herts Burgin, *Di Geshikhte fun der Yidisher Arbaiter Bewegung in Amerike, Rusland un England* (New York, 1915) pp. 539–43; the necessity for an alliance with the Kadets was justified by the Bundists with the election system which needed the combined forces of Kadets and Social Democrats in order to defeat the Octobrists. See Matvei Mates, 'Tsu fragn vegn abmakhungn', in *Folkstsaitung*, no. 193, 30 October 1906, p. 1.

4.  See *Di Folksshtime*, no. 1, 1 December 1906, cols 23–39.

5.  To mention only the main Jewish political newspapers of that time: *Svoboda i Ravenstvo* (ENG), *Evreiskii Golos* and later *Razsvet*, *Dos Yudishe Folk* (RSO); *Evreiskii Narod* (Socialist-Zionist), *Folkstsaitung, Nashe Slovo, Nasha Tribuna* (Bund), *Der Fraind* (non-party affiliated, left-wing); *Di Yudishe Virklikhkeit* (SERP); and *Di Folksshtime* (SS). For more information on the Jewish press, see Gregor Aronson, 'Jews in Russian Literary and Political Life', in Frumkin, *Russian Jewry*, pp. 253–74. For more information on the Russian press in general, see Manfred Hagen, *Die Entfaltung politischer Öffentlichkeit in Russland 1906–1914* (Wiesbaden, 1982) p. 89 and pp. 95–189.

6.  See A.K., 'K izbiratel'noi kampanii', in *Evreiskii Narod*, no. 4, 10 November 1906, cols 1–5; the importance of newspaper coverage of the Duma was especially appreciated by Lenin as it could be used for spreading revolutionary propaganda throughout the country. See Marc Ferro, *Nikolaus II. Der letzte Zar* (Zurich, 1991) p. 152.

7.  The Zionist-Socialist newspaper, *Di Yudishe Virklikhkeit*, wrote that 'the class contradiction should not prevent the proletariat from getting into closer relations with the bourgeoisie as long as it serves the common interest of the people. The elections now make such an agreement between the proletariat and the progressive part of the bourgeoisie necessary' (see *Di Yudishe Virklikhkeit*, no. 2, 10 January 1907, cols 28–30). A similar statement had been made by the S.S. organ; (see Sh.D., 'Tsu di Wahlen', in *Di Folksshtime*,

no. 3, 18 January 1907, cols 1–13). For the Bund's appeal to the Jewish voters to participate in the elections as well as to set up alliances and to vote for the Kadets in case of the danger of the election of a reactionary candidate, see I. Yudin, 'Nastoiashchii moment i ego zadachi', in *Nasha Tribuna*, no. 1, 13 December 1906, pp. 1–7.

8. See *Evreiskii Golos*, no. 3, 27 October 1906, col. 3.

9. In Kovno, the SP published an appeal to the Jewish voters to participate in the elections and to register themselves in the list of voters; in Zhitomir, SP and KD decided to set up a common list of electors. See *Evreiskii Golos*, no. 5, 10 November 1906, col. 25. Alliances with the Kadets were formed in Uman, Minsk, Kiev and Poltava. Furthermore, the SP ran a particularly active election campaign in the gubernia of Podolia, where SP candidates, especially G.B. Sliozberg, were travelling around to propagate its view. See *Evreiskii Golos*, no. 7, 24 November 1906, col. 17. The alliance with the Kadets in Poltava included also the Ukrainians; see *Evreiskii Golos*, no. 11, 22 December 1906, cols 15–17; Sliozberg pointed in his memoirs to the main problem in his election campaign, that is the decision not to set up alliances with conservative parties which made the election of a Jewish deputy from agrarian-structured Podolia impossible (see Sliozberg, *Dela*, p. 237).

10. The foundation of such election committees are reported from Minsk, Lodz, Libava, Kiev and Vilna. See *Evreiskii Golos*, no. 5, 10 November 1906, col. 23.

11. See *Evreiskii Golos*, no. 5, 10 November 1906, cols 25–37; in the gubernia Kovno the former members of the SP such as Kalmanovich, Frumkin and Khoronzhitskii ran the elections independently; in Vilna two Jewish candidates – a nationalist and a liberal – opposed each other. Temkin was represented as the Zionists' candidate in the gubernia of Kherson, and the SERP leader M.B. Ratner ran for his party in the gubernia of Vitebsk. See *Evreiskii Golos*, no. 7, 24 November 1906, col. 17.

12. For more information on the Helsingfors Congress, see Orbach, 'Zionism and the Revolution of 1905', pp. 7–23; Vital, *Zionism. The Formative Years*, pp. 467–75; Frankel, *Prophecy and Politics*, pp. 166–7; Zalevskii, 'Natsional'nyia partii v Rossii', pp. 324–8; and Janowsky, *The Jews and Minority Rights*, pp. 106–13. For the Autonomist Movement in general see Kurt Stillschweig, 'Nationalism and Autonomy among Eastern European Jewry. Origin and Historical Development up to 1939', *Historica Judaica*, 6 (1944) pp. 27–68, especially pp. 27–35, and 40–44.

13. The idea of National Jewish politics in form of an independent Jewish Duma faction was raised by the Zionist M. Shwartsman as early as October 1906. He had argued that the democratization of the country would not necessarily include the recognition of the Jewish nation and its right for national autonomy. Therefore, the future Jewish deputies were to protect solely Jewish national interests in the Duma, and should no longer rely either on Kadets or Trudoviki (see M. Shvartsman, 'Evrei-Deputaty', in *Evreiskaia Mysl'*, no. 4, 26 October 1906, cols 6–8); In November, 1906, Vladimir Zhabotinskii highlighted the basic frame for the Zionists' tactic for the elections. Thus, as a first step he recommended to set up united election committees in which the Zionists were to strive for the acceptance of their

political platform. These election committees should not, however, include Jewish political groups which either rejected the idea of special Jewish interests in principle [the Bund] or would not represent the interests of the Jewish people [the Liberals]. See Vladimir Zhabotinskii, 'Nasha positsia na vyborakh', in *Evreiskaia Mysl'*, no. 7, 16 November 1906, cols 4–6; the Zionists' refusal to co-operate in the elections with the Liberals and the Bund is also stated in Delegat, 'Gelsingforskii s'ezd o nashei predvybornoi taktike', in *Evreiskaia Mysl'*, no. 11, cols 3–5; Zhabotinskii's adherents were only prepared to set up an alliance with Dubnov's ENP as it had a similar national programme and would help to disseminate the new national approach to the intelligentsia circles. See *Evreiskaia Mysl'*, no. 12, 21 December 1906, cols 1–3.

14. Stolypin motivated his proposal with the argument that Russian Jews had always found ways and means to surpass the restrictions. Furthermore, the restrictions only served the revolutionaries' cause, and even worse, were used as a pretext for an anti-Russian propaganda campaign in America. The Tsar had argued: '. . . an inner voice prompts me more and more insistently not to take this decision upon myself.' See Alexis Goldenweiser, 'Legal Status of Jews in Russia', in Frumkin, *Russian Jewry*, pp. 92–3; and I.V. Gessen, *V dvukh vekakh. Zhiznennii otchet'* (Berlin, 1937) p. 305 [Reprinted in Arkhiv Russkoi Revoliutsii, vol. 22, The Hague and Paris, 1970]. Gessen characterized Stolypin as a man who was willing to grant Russian Jews the equality of rights but was undermined by his opponent Shcheglovitov. Gessen's interpretation is certainly influenced by Shcheglovitov's involvement in the Beilis Case. It seems to be more logical to follow Löwe's interpretation which argues that Stolypin's initiative was mainly based on the hope to calm the revolutionary spirit of Russian Jews, to show that the government was willing to compromise, and finally, to make a good impression on public opinion abroad. See Löwe, *Antisemitismus*, pp. 108–13.

15. This appeal, called 'K grazhdanam evreiam', summarized the history of the SP and held the Zionists responsible for its present state of disorganization. Furthermore, it justified the foundation of the ENG with the Zionists' decision to run Jewish politics under their own flag, and their emphasis on a Jewish Duma group with binding group discipline. Finally, it stated the ENG's main targets as being the struggle for political and national-cultural rights for Russian Jewry. This appeal was signed by M.M. Vinaver, G.B. Sliozberg, M.I. Kulisher, M. Ostrogorskii, M. Sheftel, M. Pozner, M. Goldshtein, L. Shternberg, D. Levin, L. Sev, M. Syrkin, M. Trivus, I. Gessen, A. Gornfeld, and G. Shtulman. See *Der Fraind*, no. 119, 27 December 1906, p. 3.

16. As Janowsky had pointed out: 'the ultimate goal of Zionism (Palestine) remained unaffected, only the means were altered'. Political activity in Russia was considered by the general Zionist leadership an 'invaluable instrument for the furtherance of nationalism, and the national-political programme as a sort of necessary evil'. (See Janowsky, *The Jews and Minority Rights*, pp. 112–13).

17. See *Der Fraind*, no. 119, 27 Decmber 1906, p. 3. For the Liberals' criticism of the Zionists see also Vinaver's letter in *Der Fraind*, no. 3, 4 January 1907, pp. 1–2. Here, Vinaver attacked above all the chief ideologist of the

Gegenwartsarbeit, Vladimir Zhabotinskii; the appeal 'K grazhdanam evreiam' was also published in *Evreiskii Izbiratel'*, no. 8–9, 4 January 1907, cols 25–28. It was signed by Vinaver, Sliozberg, M. Kulisher, M. Ostrogorskii, M. Sheftel, M. Pozner, M. Goldshtein, L. Shternberg, D. Levin, L. Sev, M. Syrkin, M. Trivus, A. Gornfeld, G. Shtilman, and V. Garkavi. In the same number, Vinaver published an open letter to A. Zaidenman, in which he pointed to the danger that with the slogan 'emigrants in principle', one would only encourage the anti-Semites' stand that the Jews were foreigners. See 'Otvet' na otkrytie pismo g-na Arnolda Zaidenmana', in Ibid., col. 20–23.

18. The fourth appeal was published under the title 'Kogo vybirat' v Dumu?' in *Svoboda i Ravenstvo*, no. 2, 14 January 1907, p. 16. Furthermore, it included the slogan that 'every reactionary, every opponent of the real democratic structure, Jewish or non-Jewish is our all enemy, the enemy of the fatherland and an enemy of Russian Jewry'. The second appeal was a response by Vinaver to an open letter of the editor of *Evreiskii Narod*, while the third one – 'C kem nam vstupat' v izbiratel'nyia soglasheniia?' (with whom to set up election alliances?) – was an advice given by the ENG to look for alliances with the peasants in order to defeat the conservative landowners.

19. See *Evreiskii Golos*, no. 1, 5 January 1907, col. 29. In a letter published in the Jewish press they underlined that the ENP was an independent party which neither supported Vinaver's circular, nor the ENG's programme; and *Evreiskii Izbiratel'*, no. 8–9, 4 January 1907, col. 24.

20. For more information on the ENP's programme, see *Dos Yudishe Folk*, no. 2, 17 January 1907, pp. 10–11; and Zalevskii, 'Natsional'nyia partii', pp. 328–9.

21. See Stillschweig, 'Nationalism and Autonomy', p. 34. To quote Stillschweig: 'Dubnow's thought was that no one could become a member of either this or that nation at will; one had to be born a member.' Despite the fact that all the Jewish political parties agreed to the concept of Jewish autonomy, differences occurred about the way it should take place: while the Bundists and the ENG favoured cultural autonomy, the Zionists and the Dubnovtsy advocated national autonomy for the Jews. Differences occurred also about the membership of the Jewish autonomous bodies: the ENG intended to put the membership on a voluntary basis, while the Dubnovtsy regarded these bodies as 'associations of compulsory membership'. A brief discussion on the difference between the Dubnovtsy and the Zionists is given in Janowsky, *The Jews and Minority Rights*, pp. 115–17.

22. The Zionists held the Liberals responsible for the disunity within the SP as they had refused the Zionists' demand for a national conduct of Jewish interests in the Duma. In further polemics the Liberals were reproached of being 'assimilationists' still pursuing the old 'shtadlanstvo' policy which did not allow the people to participate in running Jewish political affairs. See *Der Fraind*, no. 119, 27 December 1906, p. 1; *Dos Yudishe Folk*, no. 1, 9 January 1907, cols 3–5; *Evreiskii Golos*, no. 10, 9 March 1907, cols 10–11; *Razsvet*, no. 1, 10 January 1907, cols 5–7; see also the appeal by the Central Committee of the RSO at the Russian Jews, in *Razsvet*, no. 2, 18 January 1907, cols 1–4.

23. During the election campaign in Vilna Dr. Pasmanik, one of the Zionist leaders, used the occasion of the local gathering of voters in order to plead for the election of the nationalist-favoured candidate, the famous lawyer and former SP member O.O. Gruzenberg. In his speech he especially attacked the Bund for only protecting proletarian, and ignoring Jewish national interests. See *Razsvet*, no. 4, 31 January 1907, col. 13.

24. In this context, Medem's brochure 'Sotsialdemokratiia i natsional'nyi vopros' was mentioned in *Svoboda i Ravenstvo*, no. 28, 24 May 1907, pp. 4–6. Here, Medem underlined the fact that the Bund's main emphasis would still be the class struggle; for more details on Medem's and Litvak's views see Koppel S. Pinson, 'Arkady Kremer, Vladimir Medem, and the Ideology of the Jewish Bund', in *Jewish Social Studies*, 7 (1945) pp. 233–64. The Bund's struggle against the Nationalists/Zionists during the election campaign is also mentioned in 'Der Allgemeine Jüdische Arbeiterbund zur Zeit der russischen Revolution (1904–1907)', in *Archiv für Sozialwissenschaft und Sozialpolitik*, 36 (1913) pp. 845–7. Litvak also wrote that the Bund still fought the ENG on the ideological level, but since the ENG – like the Bund – fought the 'emigration psychology' of the Zionists, and participated in the Liberation Movement, the Bund co-operated with the Jewish Liberals whenever the prevention of the election of a conservative candidate was at stake (see A. Litvak, *Geklibene Shriftn* (New York, 1945) p. 465). An attack on the Zionists' new approach similar to Vinaver's was also launched by the Bundist F. Bogrov. He compared the Zionists with the Nationalists of the Polish Kolo who had one thing in common: both wanted to use the Russian revolutionary movement in order to achieve their national interests. Finally, he especially attacked the Zionists' election tactics of supporting a candidate solely because of the fact that he was a Jew, without any consideration of his political views. See F. Bogrov, 'Iz evreiskoi pressy', in *Nasha Tribuna*, no. 1, 13 December 1906, pp. 11–14.

25. In Minsk, the Bund at first had set up an alliance with the Zionist-Socialist parties S.S. and Poale Zion, but later shifted their support in favour of the anti-Zionist front: an alliance was set up between Bund and SP in which the Bund supported the two SP candidates Gertsyk and Gurvich (see *Evreiskii Golos*, no. 10, 15 December 1906, cols 14–25). Further arrangements between Bund and SP were made in the gubernia Volynia where the Bund supported the SP candidate Gurfinkel (see *Razsvet*, no. 8, 2 March 1907, col. 19).

26. These alliances included also the Kadets (Rostov/Don, Kremenchug), the Kadets, Ukrainians (Poltava), and Kadets, Social Revolutionaries and Social Democrats (Sevastopol') (see *Evreiskii Golos*, no. 2, 12 January 1907, cols 16–20). According to one of the Bund's leaders, Abramovich – who ran the elections in Kovno as the Bund's candidate – an alliance with the Liberals' candidate, Abramson, was formed in accordance with the Tammerfors' decision. Thereafter, a heated election campaign took place between Abramson and the Zionists' candidate, Nachman Syrkin (see Abramovich, *In tsvai revolutsies*, pp. 276–7).

27. See *Evreiskii Golos*, no. 4, 19 January 1907, cols 16–17.

28. See *Evreiskii Golos*, no. 7, 24 November 1906, col. 17.

29. According to L.Paperin, in order to win the majority in the election committee the Zionists had propagated the slogan 'only a Zionist is a real Jew' in the synagogues. See *Evreiskii Golos*, no. 10, 15 December 1906, cols 14–25; in another letter D. R-skii confirmed the Zionists' activity, and demanded the creation of a non-party-affiliated Jewish election committee in Belostok. See *Svoboda i Ravenstvo*, no. 5, 25 January 1907, pp. 11–12. Further 'battles' between 'Nationalists' and 'Internationalists' were fought in Grodno, Brest-Litovsk, Belsk and Slonim; in January 1907, the united Jewish election committee of Belostok called upon Jewish voters to fight the Zionists as they were not interested in the improvement of the situation of the Jewish masses but only aimed at emigration. Instead, the Jewish voters should vote for their list which consisted of the Christian Nikolai S. Sokolov, and the Jews Dr.Yulius Gordon, F. Kempner, Dr. Perelshtein, Dr. Rubinshtein, A. Tyktyn and Dr. Tsitron. See the leaflets 'Zapolniaite biulleteni/Shreibt an di biuletens', and 'Prosnites'/Wakht oif'('Wake up'). The Zionists reacted with a leaflet 'Tsu di Yidishe Wehler in Bialistok' in which they called on the Jewish voters to fight the alliance Bund/Liberals as both were aiming at the assimilation of Russian Jewry. See *Bund Archive. Bund and the Dumas. File MG 9–87.*

30. See L.N., 'Evreiskaia Narodnaia Gruppa i demokraticheskie elementy', in *Svoboda i Ravenstvo*, no. 7, 1 February 1907, pp. 4–5. He expressed sympathy towards the Bund because of its struggle against Zionism, and praised the Bund's realistic policy of fighting for such targets such as the liberation of the working class. Furthermore, he called the Bund the most democratic group of Russian Jewry, an ally until a certain point and a 'fellow traveller'. Finally, he said that the Bund would represent the interests of the Jewish proletariat not worse than the 'dear gentlemen' Landau, Braudo and Bramson (EDG).

31. See *Razsvet*, no. 8, 2 March 1907, col. 22. The Poalei Zion is especially mentioned here as it had supported the 'assimilationist and anti-Zionist' list in Minsk, while the SS had joined the 'Nationalist' forces.

32. Pasmanik on the one hand attacked the Bund for setting up alliances with the 'Jewish bourgeoisie' in Grodno, Minsk, Kovno and Vilna despite the fact that it still condemned them on the ideological level as the worst enemy of the Jewish people; and on the other SS and SERP for having nominated bourgeois candidates in the gubernia of Kovno (SS) and in the gubernii Volynia, Kiev and Vitebsk (SERP). See D. Pasmanik, 'Di Taktik fun dem yudishn Proletariat in der Wahl-Kampanie', in *Dos Yudishe Folk*, no. 2, 17 January 1907, pp. 1–3.

33. See *Di Folksshtime*, no. 3, 18 January 1907, cols 13–29. The author reproached the Bund that it could not serve two masters, the Jews and the RSDRP – which was the same point the bourgeois Zionists used against the Jewish Kadets. The SERPist attacked the Bund especially for its alliance tactic with the Kadets in case of a Black Hundred candidate, and he argued that with this alliance, one would not abolish the phenomenon of anti-Semitism.

34. According to Dubnov, the political court-martial which was practised from September 1906 to January 1907, 'sentenced over one thousand people to

death, among them many who were innocent or under age' (See Simon Dubnow, *History of the Jews in Russia and Poland*, vol. III (Philadelphia, 1920) pp. 140–1). For the court-martial see also Ferro, *Nikolaus II*, pp. 158–9.

35. In Samara, Jewish voters did not want to register as they feared reprisals by the Black Hundreds who agitated every gathering by accusing the Jews of being the chief culprit of the general unrest (kramola) (see *Evreiskii Golos*, no. 2, 12 January 1907, cols 25–26).

36. See *Svoboda i Ravenstvo*, no. 5, 25 January 1907, p. 16. In Zhitomir, Kishinev and Odessa the Jews were openly threatened by pogroms.

37. In Vitebsk, the former SP member S.A. Rapoport (An-skii) was arrested in his flat on the night of January 1907. See *Evreiskii Golos*, no. 3, 19 January 1907, cols 16–17; in Vilna, the secretary of the Jewish election committee, Solovei was also arrested. See *Evreiskii Golos*, no. 1, 5 January 1907, cols 28–29; Isaac Shneerson stated that he had run the elections as the Kadets' candidate in Gorodnie. However, the police arrested him as it found KD propaganda material in his house, and sent him for the time of the elections to Voronezh (see Shneerson, *Lebn un Kampf*, pp. 160–1). In Vitebsk the Jewish Duma candidate Kh. Zhitlovskii had been excluded by the gubernia election commission from the list of electors (see *Evreiskii Golos*, no. 6, 9 February 1907, col. 12). An army of spies and agents (secret police) had been sent out by the government during the election campaign in order to 'arrange' a pro-government Duma (see Sh.D., 'Tsu di Wahlen', in *Di Folksshtime*, no. 3, 18 January 1907, cols 1–13). In Smolensk, the police threatened the Jews with expulsion in case of their participation in the elections. In Odessa, Count Konovnitsin openly pursued an anti-Jewish campaign (see Sh. Lang, 'Di Wahlen un der Selbstshuts', in *Di Yudishe Virklikhkeit*, no. 1, 31 December 1906, cols 21–28). In its general analysis of the election the *Razsvet* explained the victory of many conservative candidates with the anti-Jewish agitation by landowners and clergy. See *Razsvet*, no. 6, 16 February 1907, col. 3.

38. The activities by either local aristocrats or priests followed the patterns of the elections to the First Duma. For instance, in the Gubernia Grodno, the Jewish-peasant alliance – in which the peasants had already agreed to support the Jewish candidates M. Ostrogorskii (ENG) and the Zionist N. Syrkin – was undermined by the local Russian landowners and the clergy who persuaded the peasants to renounce the already arranged alliance. In the gubernia Vitebsk, the peasants decided under the 'guidance' of the Polish landowner Serafim Polotskii that it was necessary to fight the Jews. In Volynia, the priest Vitaly led the anti-Jewish front. In the gubernia Minsk a 'block of True Russians' was formed by peasants, Czechs and Little Russians. Finally, in the gubernia Vilna, the Roman Catholic bishop Roop undermined the already fixed Jewish-peasant alliance by an anti-Semitic speech which he delivered at a gathering of peasants (see *Razsvet*, no. 6, 16 February 1907, cols 6–7).

39. See *Dos Yudishe Folk*, no. 7, 21 February 1907, col. 5. The elections in Poland ended with an overwhelming victory for the ND, which lost only five of their 34 seats, of which two went to its ally in the Kolo, the Polish Progressive Party (PPP) (see *Svoboda i Ravenstvo*, no. 28, 24 May 1907,

p. 13). Apparently, ND agitators appeared at factories in Warsaw with the slogan 'Do not buy in Jewish shops'.

40. See Sh.Lang, 'Der Resultat fun di Wahlen', in *Di Yudishe Virklikhkeit*, no. 6, 14 February 1907, cols 5–12; Dreamer, 'Der Suf fun di Wahlen', in *Dos Yudishe Folk*, no. 6, 14 February 1907, pp. 3–5; and M.N. Syrkin, 'Der Muser-Haskl fun di Wahlen', *Dos Yudishe Folk*, no. 7, 21 February 1907, pp. 3–5.

41. He described a meeting of Jewish voters in Rovno: '. . . Whom did they want to elect instead of you? Was it a Social Democrat or even a Jewish Labour Bundist who could represent the interests of those carpenters? Not at all. They supported a middle-class Kadet even less left than you, just as long as he was not a Zionist'. (See Vladimir Jabotinsky, 'Memoirs by my Typewriter', in Dawidowicz, *The Golden Tradition*, p. 395.)

42. See D. Pasmanik, 'Vos lernt uns di Wahl-Kampanie', in *Dos Yudishe Folk*, no. 4, 31 January 1907, p. 3. Pasmanik explained the Zionists' election disaster with the fact that Helsingfors had happened too late, and therefore, the principles of the new programme had not yet reached the Zionist rank-and-file. Therefore, they were not yet able to fight Vinaver's campaign in the appropriate way. On the contrary, some Zionists had even joined the 'Integrationists' alliances, for instance in Rovno.

43. See *Svoboda i Ravenstvo*, no. 6, 28 January 1907, pp. 12–13.

44. Goldshtein announced that he was neither a Zionist nor interested in a Jewish Seim, but very interested in working for the good of the Jewish people, and that was why he had joined the ENG. He pointed out that the Jewish people needed above all freedom, the whole range of freedom. Sheftel shared Vinaver's argument that the interests of Russian Jewry were closely connected to and entangled in the interests of all nationalities who were fighting in Russia. 'The Jews are interested in the general foundation of a state organism in Russia for which the Liberation Movement fights. There-fore, our main target will be Jewish equality and the development of Jewish national culture'; the Zionist Rozental had spoken in favour of unity among the Jews, and argued that since Zionism had become a political factor, it would be necessary to set up an alliance with the Zionists. Shternberg clari-fied the difference as being: the Zionists took the view of 'historical right' while the ENG favoured the view of 'natural right'. (Ibid., pp. 13–15.)

45. Other speakers were Pozner and Trivus, the latter pointing out that the organizers of the ENG had already protected Jewish national consciousness when Zionism did not yet exist. (Ibid., p. 15.)

46. Apparently 250 people attended this congress which took place in St. Petersburg on 25 January 1907. See *Svoboda i Ravenstvo*, no. 6, 28 January 1907, p. 15.

47. See *Svoboda i Ravenstvo*, no. 8, 4 February 1907, p. 11. Like Vinaver, he stated that the Zionists' decision to run politics independently, and based on purely national grounds, would endanger the struggle for political freedom of Russian Jews, and could only provoke a negative attitude towards Jewish interests.

48. Idelson stated that the ENG's only target was to fight Zionism, and there-fore, it was responsible for the inner-Jewish struggle at a moment when the Zionists were on their way to 'real' work. The Zionist Bubkov reproached

the ENG of having no principles and no programme. The Zionists in turn would show solidarity with the SP, and finally, Jewish interests could only be represented properly in the Duma through the Jewish national assembly. (See *Svoboda i Ravenstvo*, no. 8, 4 February 1907, pp. 11–12.)

49. See Shmi, 'Obshchinnaia organisatsia', in *Svoboda i Ravenstvo*, no. 8, 4 February 1907, pp. 3–5. This article was an answer to Dubnov's concept regarding the reorganization of the Jewish community. The author pointed to the basics which were needed for a reorganization, and referred to the fact that a precise regulation of the community's functions would be impossible as long as the legal foundations for this were not yet laid, that is the project about urban self-government. Finally, he rejected secularization, as it would be imposing a policy over many people's conscience; the time for the separation of church and state had not yet come for Russia. Therefore, one should not interfere now in the functions of the community.

50. Shternberg rejected the idea of a national *Seim* for various reasons: first, a *Seim* was not necessary, since a national-Jewish culture could also grow without it, as in New York; second, he mentioned the national 'egoism' of the dominating nationality in the most important spheres of economic and political life; finally, the age-old prejudices could not be swept away with the creation of separate national schools, which in turn would only create an artificial wall between the young generations of the various nationalities. Instead, he advocated the democratization of the community and its institutions. He regarded free unions as the only guarantee for the future potential of growth of the people, while the Seim would only be possible on the basis of legal guarantees and a complete democratization of the Russian self-government. See L. Shternberg, 'Natsionalniia techeniia v russkom evreistve', in *Svoboda i Ravenstvo*, no. 5, 25 January 1907, pp. 2–6.

51. See *Svoboda i Ravenstvo*, no. 8, 4 February 1907, pp. 10–15. Dubnov had argued that 'each organization needs discipline, and therefore, discipline would also apply to the organization of Russian Jewry'.

52. See 'Tsirkular No. 1: Mestnym otdelam Evreiskoi Narodnoi Gruppy', in *Svoboda i Ravenstvo*, no. 6, 28 January 1907, p. 12.

53. For the appeal see *Svoboda i Ravenstvo*, no. 12, 18 February 1907, pp. 10–11.

54. See 'Evreiskaia Narodnaia Gruppa. Vozzvanie no. 5', in *Svoboda i Ravenstvo*, no. 7, 1 February 1907, pp. 12–13.

55. See *Pervyi Uchreditelnyi s'ezd Evreiskoi Narodnoi Gruppy* (St. Petersburg, 1907) p. 4; and Zalevskii, 'Natsional'nyia partii', pp. 329–31.

56. The democratized Jewish community was to be based on a council elected by all the Community members, which was to elect its highest organ, the Executive Committee as well as the commissions which were to take over certain parts of the administration such as schools, hospitals, finances, cult and so on. See *Pervyi uchreditelnyi s'ezd*, pp. 6–7. Within the scope of the planned democratization and modernization of the Jewish community, the ENG issued in no. 23 of *Svoboda i Ravenstvo* another circular to the Jewish public in which it called for support among the Jewish social circles to reform the taxation system, and especially the Korobka tax. Since it was not yet possible to abolish the Korobka tax – as this needed legal action by the parliament – ways were to be found to reform it. Thus, the circular proposed

a taxation system based on democratic grounds, by leasing the Korobka tax to an economic council elected by the Jewish community itself instead of to private persons. This was meant to prevent further abuses of the Korobka funds by the leaseholders in general, and the administration in particular. See *Svoboda i Ravenstvo*, no. 23, 19 April 1907, pp. 22–4.

57. See Shternberg's report in *Pervyi uchreditelnyi s'ezd*, pp. 11–32.

58. See *Svoboda i Ravenstvo*, no. 28, 24 May 1907, pp. 1–4.

59. Within the framework of Jewish educational reform, the programme demanded: freedom of instruction; the opening of schools with the right to choose the language of instruction; free admission of students of all nationalities without any restrictions on all levels of school education; financial support by the various regional or urban administrations' budgets for the national community schools; instruction of subjects of Jewish learning in all school-types. Its economic demands included: a six-day working week for all the employees of trade institutions, warehouses and offices; and free choice of the day of rest according to the confession of the employees. See *Pervyi uchreditelnyi s'ezd*, pp. 7–8.

60. Every Jew, regardless of sex, who accepted the programme and subordinated to the directives of the ENG's organs could become a member. For the entire statute see *Pervyi uchreditelnyi s'ezd*, pp. 9–10.

61. See *Razsvet*, no. 7, 22 February 1907, p. 3. He asked how the ENG could convene the representatives of the Jewish communities once the SP still existed. Consequently, for him this congress was an attempt to falsify the general opinions of Russian Jewry.

62. See *Der Fraind*, no. 56, 9 March 1907, p. 1. The author asked why the ENG now raised demands similar to those of the Zionists. Therefore, he felt that the ENG should finally admit that its foundation was a mistake, and he proposed that it should either join the ENP or go back to the SP.

63. M. Kreinin (ENP) called the point of the school question in the ENG's programme superficial, and questioned the legitimacy of the ENG's congress to speak on behalf of the Jewish people as only ten provincial delegates were present. (See *Der Fraind*, no. 84, 16 April 1907, pp. 1–2.)

64. Kreinin asked how a political party, like the ENG, could plan to run educational reforms through ORPE, an antiquated organization with a bureaucratic-philanthropic character and without any influence in Jewish school affairs. (See *Der Fraind*, no. 89, 22 April 1907, pp. 1–2.)

65. The commission met on 1 April 1907, and announced the topics of the lectures: the legal situation of the Jews, the economic situation of the Jews, anti-Semitism in Western Europe, the origins of anti-Semitism in Russia, the participation of the Jews in the Liberation Movement, the epoch of emancipation of the Jews in Western Europe. See *Svoboda i Ravenstvo*, no. 21, 5 April 1907, p. 24.

66. See *Svoboda i Ravenstvo*, no. 23, 19 April 1907, p. 11.

67. See *Svoboda i Ravenstvo*, no. 27, 17 May 1907, p. 13. The audience was apparently quite big and even some Duma deputies appeared at the lecture.

68. See Pozner, 'Bor'ba za ravnopravie', p. 179; various 'Razum'' publications are mentioned in the bibliography.

69. See *Svoboda i Ravenstvo*, no. 26, 11 May 1907, pp. 1–2.

70. See *Svoboda i Ravenstvo*, no. 21, 5 April 1907, p. 24.

71. See *Svoboda i Ravenstvo*, no. 23, 19 April 1907, p. 22.
72. See *Svoboda i Ravenstvo*, no. 20, 29 March 1907, p. 22.
73. See *Svoboda i Ravenstvo*, no. 28, 24 May 1907, p. 23.
74. See *Der Fraind*, no. 115, 27 May 1907, p. 3.
75. See *Svoboda i Ravenstvo*, no. 22, 12 April 1907, p. 5–6. The author of the article expressed his hopes that all the democratic elements would join in social work in the near future.
76. See *Der Fraind*, no. 120, 28 December 1906, p. 1. At this conference, it had already been decided to publish books in Yiddish and to change the statutes in order to democratize the organization. Finally, a new committee with new people had been elected. According to *Der Fraind* these changes were due to the influx of new committee members and the influence of the public opinion which led the committee to take these steps.
77. See *Svoboda i Ravenstvo*, no. 26, 11 May 1907, p. 13.
78. See *Svoboda i Ravenstvo*, no. 28, 24 May 1907, p. 8. It was announced that ORT had officially 200 members at that time.
79. See *Svoboda i Ravenstvo*, no. 20, 29 March 1907, p. 15; according to Dubnov, the venture of the Jewish encyclopedia had already started with the formation of the editorial staff in the fall of 1906. In the preparatory meetings, intelligentsia members of various backgrounds gathered: M.I. Kulisher (ENG), Baron David Gintsburg, the historian Yulii Gessen, the Zionist Dr. L. Katsenel'son, the journalist S.L. Tsinberg, the professor for Hellenistic studies, F. Zelinskii, the philologist, Herman Henkel and so on. However, after one year, the editorial staff faced problems as Kulisher was not the most capable editor, and disputes occurred on the transcription of Jewish names in the encyclopedia. All these problems raised Dubnov's doubts about whether it was worth his time and effort to participate in this venture. See Dubnov, *Kniga zhizni*, pp. 69–71.
80. See *Svoboda i Ravenstvo*, no. 28, 24 May 1907, p. 13.
81. See *Svoboda i Ravenstvo*, no. 28, 24 May 1907, pp. 22–3.
82. In the gubernias Kiev, Chernigov, Mogilev and Vilna, EKO granted loans of 21,000 roubles and more. Furthermore, it started to support vocational education in the Pale by opening evening schools for adult workers. Such schools were in preparation for the cities Mogilev, Belostok, Minsk and Grodno. Finally, EKO opened an artisans' school in Riga, and gave 30,000 roubles to the Jewish school 'Trud' in Odessa. See *Svoboda i Ravenstvo*, no. 25, 3 May 1907, p. 11.
83. According to EKO data the amount of Loan and Saving Associations had increased after restrictions on this field had been lifted in 1905. At the end of 1906, 166 Loan and Credit Co-operatives existed in the Pale of Settlement: in the gubernias Bessarabia (21), Ekaterinoslav (8), Grodno (9), Kiev (7), Kovno (2), Courland (1), Lublin (5), Minsk (22), Mogilev (15), Poltava (9), Podolia (6), Plotsk (1), Suvalki (1), Siedlets (1), Tauria (5), Kherson (8), Chernigov (15), Warsaw (2), Vilna (12), Vitebsk (4), Volynia (11), and in the Don region (1). See *Razsvet*, no. 22, 7 June 1908, cols 10–12.
84. All the top positions in the Second Duma were held by the opposition: Golovin (KD, president), Beresin (Socialist, vice-president), Pasnanski (non-party-affiliated Socialist, vice-president), Chelnokov (KD, secretary of presidium). See *Dos Yudishe Folk*, no. 8, 28 February 1907, cols 1 and 2.

85. If one includes in the opposition parties such as the Polish Kolo (46), the Moslems' faction (30), the Kazakh Group (18), the Kadets (99), the Labour Group (98), the Peoples' Socialists (15), Social Revolutionaries (37) and Social Democrats (66), the opposition had a majority of 390 to 130 deputies, or a three-to-one majority in the parliament. See Warren B. Walsh, 'Political parties in the Russian Dumas', *Journal of Modern History*, 22 (1950) pp. 144–50. For a brief description of the various political parties and their activity in the Second Duma, see Bernard Pares, 'The Second Duma', *The Slavonic and East European Review*, 2 (1923) pp. 36–55; and Alfred Levin, *The Second Duma* (Hamden, Connecticut, 1966).

86. The Jewish Socialists considered the Duma as the tribune for political action around which the Socialists should organize the masses. See I.S., 'Di erste trit fun der Duma', in *Di Yudishe Virklikhkeit*, no. 8, 28 February 1907, cols 9–21; I. Zeiden, 'Tsu der Duma-efenung', in *Di Yudishe Virklikhkeit*, no. 7, 21 February 1907, cols 1–12; Sh.D., 'Di Duma', in *Di Folksshtime*, no. 5, 16 March 1907, cols 1–10.

87. See *Di Yudishe Virklikhkeit*, no. 7, 21 February 1907, col. 21.

88. See *Der Fraind*, no. 274, 12 December 1907, p. 3; and Gri., 'Evreiskii vopros i ego postanovka v Gosudarstvennoi Dume', in *Svoboda i Ravenstvo*, no. 20, 29 March 1907, p. 5. Jewish representation in the KD Duma faction – now standing at six Jews out of 99 Kadets, compared with a First Duma figure of nine out of 184 Kadets – had increased from 4.9 to 6.1 per cent. For more information on the Second Duma and the Kadets' attempts to pursue serious parliamentary work see I.V. Gessen, *V dvukh vekakh*, pp. 240–55. However, he did not mention any details on the Jewish question.

89. See M. Abramov, 'Di Duma un di yudishe Rekhtlosigkeit', in *Di Yudishe Virklikhkeit*, no. 12, 30 March 1907, cols 12 and 13; and *Der Fraind*, no. 274, 12 December 1907, p. 3. Here, it was reported that Abramovich was a member of three commissions, Mandelberg of one, Rabinovich of three, and Shapiro of two commissions. Apart from Mandelberg who spoke at fourteen sessions of the Duma, none of the others had raised his voice more than once. The newspaper quoted the official record of the Second Duma which had been published in December 1907.

90. The members of the first commission were the Central committee members L.M. Aizenberg, M.I. Kulisher, D.A. Levin, M.Ya. Ostrogorskii, G.B. Sliozberg, M.L. Trivus, M.I. Sheftel, as well as the lawyers Ya.M. Gal'pern, M.V. Kaplan, M.I. Mysh, I.M. Rabinovich, I.E. Fride, M.I. Shafir, L.S. El'iasson and the Duma deputy L.G. Rabinovich. See *Svoboda i Ravenstvo*, no. 21, 5 April 1907, p. 24.

91. See Gri., 'Evreiskii vopros i ego postanovka v Gosudarstvennoi Dume', in *Svoboda i Ravenstvo*, no. 20, 29 March 1907, pp. 5–6.

92. This commission consisted of thirty-three members including four SD deputies (see Gri., 'Evreiskii vopros', pp. 6–7). Sliozberg gave a report to this commission on 17 March 1907, about the various laws concerning the Jews from Catherine the Great until 1907, and in its second part about the restrictions of the Jews regarding their right of residence. In the other sessions, the commission dealt with the restrictions towards Poles and Muslims (see *Di Yudishe Virklikhkeit*, no. 12, 30 March 1907, col. 27). For the Jewish deputies', and the Kadets' work regarding the Jewish question in the Duma, see

also M.M. Vinaver, *Kadety i evreiskii vopros* (St. Petersburg, 1907) pp. 12–15.

93. So Vinaver, *Kadety*, p. 13.
94. See *Svoboda i Ravenstvo*, no. 28, 24 May 1907, p. 7.
95. See *Svoboda i Ravenstvo*, no. 27, 17 May 1907, p. 12.
96. Ibid., p. 7.
97. See Löwe, 'Staatsduma', in Torke, *Lexikon der Geschichte Rußlands*, pp. 356–7; and Pares, 'The Second Duma', pp. 53–4; and Leopold H. Haimson, 'Introduction: The Russian Landed Nobility and the System of the Third of June', in Leopold H. Haimson (ed.), *The Politics of Rural Russia 1905–1914* (Bloomington, Indiana and London, 1979) p. 15. Gessen stated that the Damocles sword of dissolution was hanging above the Second Duma from its beginning. He pointed to the fact that work in the Second Duma became more and more chaotic when the Socialists started to attack the government. In the end, the Duma's work was paralysed, see his *V dvukh vekakh*, pp. 240–4 and 248. Semen Frank, a close friend of the KD Duma deputy Petr Struve, came to the same conclusion in his biography on Struve (see S.L. Frank, *Biografiia P.B. Struve* (New York, 1956) p. 58).
98. See 'Der Tsentral-Komitet fun der Tsionistisher Organisatsie in Rusland. Finfter Tsirkular', *Dos Yudishe Folk*, no. 9, 6 March 1907, cols 1–6. For the criticism on the Bund, see M. Abramov, 'Di Duma un di yudishe Rekhtlosigkait', *Di Yudishe Virklikhkeit*, no. 12, 30 March 1907, cols 12–19. They held either the 'betrayal' of the Bund, or the inner-Jewish struggle, or anti-Semitism responsible for the small number of Jewish Duma deputies. Many articles appeared in the Jewish press under the title: 'the Duma without Jews'.
99. See M. Shalit, 'Vi sol men fervirklikhen di Gleikhberekhtigung fun di natsionen?', *Dos Yudishe Folk*, no. 15, 26 April 1907, cols 4–7. He underlined the necessity of national – as opposed to provincial – autonomy, in which every nation would have its own administration; *Evreiskii Golos*, no. 16, 19 April 1907, col. 15; *Razsvet*, no. 14, 13 April 1907, col. 1–4; *Dos Yudishe Folk*, no. 12, 5 April 1907, col. 3–4. Here, the Social Democrats were criticized that they had not mentioned the Jewish question with a single word. This would underline the fact that only Jews could represent Jewish interests properly.
100. The Zionist press propagated a reformed SP, adopting a more nationally-oriented and more democratic approach including each Jewish party. See I.L., 'Der Ferband fun Fulberekhtigung', *Dos Yudishe Folk*, no. 8, 28 February 1907, pp. 3–4.
101. Within this commission a sub-commission with Sliozberg, Bruk, and the Duma deputy Abramson was set up to advise the Jewish deputies concerning the 'shabbat rest'. The law of 15 November 1906, introduced through article 87, stipulated an obligatory Sunday rest which hampered Jewish artisans and traders because they had to conduct their business on five instead of six days a week (see *Evreiskii Golos*, no. 13, 29 March 1907, col. 9–11).
102. See *Razsvet*, no. 10, 15 March 1907, cols 30 and 31.
103. See *Evreiskii Golos*, no. 14, 5 April 1907, col. 12; for more details on the meeting see *Der Fraind*, no. 67, 27 March 1907, pp. 2–3. However, even

among the 'Nationalists' criticism occurred. For instance, Rapoport criticized the St. Petersburg branch of not having changed anything regarding the Jewish institutions. Furthermore, Bramson called on the meeting to orientate the SP more towards the left-wing parties, and said: 'Only by fighting you will achieve your rights'.

104. See L.Sh., 'Soiuz Polnopraviia', *Svoboda i Ravenstvo*, no. 21, 5 April 1907, pp. 3–7.

105. See V.Ya., 'Soiuz Polnopraviia', *Razsvet*, no. 15, 19 April 1907, cols 1–6. Here, it was stated that the Liberals were only able to fight Zionism with the help of some St. Petersburg bankers.

106. See *Der Fraind*, no. 111, 22 May 1907, pp. 1–2. Regarding this meeting see also Dubnow, 'Jewish Rights between Red and Black', in Dawidowicz, *The Golden Tradition*, pp. 461–70, especially p. 470; and Dubnov, *Kniga zhizni*, pp. 68–9.

107. See *Der Fraind*, no. 128, 12 June 1907, p. 1; and *Razsvet*, no. 16–17, 4 May 1907, cols 36 and 37. Here, a gathering of the local SP branch in Bobruisk was mentioned which spoke in favour of the preservation of the SP. Furthermore, a letter from rabbi M.A. Yoffe from Novoaleksandrovsk (gub. Kovno) was cited, which showed his distrust in the ENG and its activities in this city. Instead of the creation of a new ENG branch, Yoffe favoured the preservation of the SP as an organization embracing all the strata of Jewish society.

108. See Zhabotinskii's letter in *Razsvet*, no. 10, 15 March 1907, cols 8–11.

109. See *Der Fraind*, no. 148, 5 July 1907, p. 1.

110. See *Razsvet*, no. 44, 10 November 1907, cols 3–5.

111. The meeting's agenda included a discussion of the general political situation of Russian Jews, the struggle against anti-Semitism, directives to the Jewish deputies, the creation of an all-Jewish organization, and finally, the internal organization of Russian Jews. It eventually accepted a compromise formula regarding the elections of the electors to the congress proposed by the Nationalists (ENP): to elect the electors at the gubernias' congresses of the electors, and if this was not possible, on the level of the districts' congresses. The Zionists abstained during the ballot on the question of how to elect the participants of the congress. See *Razsvet*, no. 47, 1 December 1907, cols 11 and 12.

112. The ENG won the majority for its proposal concerning the amount of electors as the EDG abstained during the ballot on this issue (ibid., col. 12). Thereafter, the Zionist Davidson stated that the Zionists would not follow this decision as the Liberals 'did not want a real people's representation and, instead, undermined any efforts towards setting up an all-Jewish organization'. See A. Davidson, 'K s'ezdu vyborshchikov', in *Razsvet*, no. 47, 1 December 1907, cols 1 and 2. This meeting was also reported in *Der Fraind*, no. 266, 3 December 1907, p. 2.

113. See the pro-boycott article N.Sh., 'Tsu der Boikot-Frage', *Di Folksshtime*, no. 11, 11 July 1907, cols 1–12. He pointed out that the tactics pursued during the Second Duma – to organize the masses around the Duma – had not succeeded, and a boycott 'would free us from all responsibilities regarding the Duma'. Instead he favoured educational and critical work in order to raise an independent class consciousness among the masses; Borisov in

turn favoured participation in parliamentary work, as a boycott would lead to a Duma dominated by bourgeois representatives, and nobody would represent the interests of the people (see M. Borisov, 'Far vos nit Boikot', *Di Folkshtime*, no. 12, 18 July 1907, cols 1–11). For more information on the elections to the Third Duma in general, see Alfred Levin, *The Third Duma, Election and Profile* (Hamden, Connecticut, 1973).

114. For the Bund's declaration to participate in the elections. See *Evreiskii Golos*, no. 26, 28 June 1907, col. 10.

115. Election committees including non-ENG members were to mobilize the Jewish vote, to gather information on the relation between Jewish and non-Jewish voters, and to start negotiating for possible alliances. Since the new election law limited the Jewish vote to the cities one should only vote for Jewish electors, or where this was not possible, for the most desirable candidate. (See *Der Fraind*, no. 135, 20 June 1907, p. 2.)

116. See *Svoboda i Ravenstvo*, no. 39, 9 August 1907, pp. 1–2; I.L., 'Di Yudn un dos naie Wahl-Gesets', *Dos Yudishe Folk*, no. 21, 13 June 1907, cols 3–5; I. Solomonov, 'Der naier Wahl-Gesets', in *Di Folkshtime*, no. 8, 19 June 1907, cols 1–11; M. Borisov, 'Far vos nit Boikot', *Di Folksshtime*, no. 12, 18 July 1907, cols 1–11. All these newspapers described the negative aspects of the new election law, and yet called upon the Jewish voters to participate in the elections.

117. It was reported that due to the new election law the landowner curia would get one elector on the basis of 20–30 voters, while the second city curia would get one elector on the basis of 1,410 voters. Furthermore, in many cities with a big percentage of Jewish voters, many of them lost their suffrage: in Vilna 4,123, Kremenchug 3,189, Ekaterinoslav 2,500, Zhitomir 4,103, Odessa 12,000, and in Kishinev 5,000. See *Svoboda i Ravenstvo*, no. 39, 9 August 1907, pp. 4–6. I.L. illustrated the predominance given to the landowners by the new suffrage: gub. Bessarabia 115 electors (66 landowners, 23 peasants, 16 electors from the first, and 10 of the second city curia); gub. Vilna 76 electors (38 landowners, 19 peasants, 10 of the first and 18 of the second city curia, 1 worker); gub. Volynia 158 electors (83 landowners, 42 peasants, 17 of the first and 14 of the second city curia, 2 workers); gub. Voronezh 140 electors (75 landowners, 35 peasants, 15 of the first and 12 of the second city curia, 2 workers); in gub. Poltava out of 155 electors 100 were landowners and so on. Despite these changes the newspaper counted on a progressive Duma due to the fact that in the Second Duma one third of the landowners, 80–90 per cent of the city voters, and 60 per cent of the peasants belonged to the opposition. See I.L., 'Dos naie Wahl-Gesets', in *Dos Yudishe Folk*, no. 21, 13 June 1907, cols 1–3; for an analysis of the new election law and the *coup d'état* see Haimson, 'Introduction', pp. 15–20; Levin, *The Third Duma*, pp. 95–111; and Hagen, *Die Entfaltung*, pp. 307–13.

118. In Zhitomir, for instance, the first city curia consisted of 1,257 voters (491 Christians and 767 Jews), and the second of 6,369 (3,085 Christians and 3,284 Jews). The first was to elect two, and the second three electors. See *Svoboda i Ravenstvo*, no. 39, 9 August 1907, p. 9.

119. The Russian voters were given their own representatives in the gubernii Vilna and Kovno. However, hopes were kept alive that the separation of the

voters according to their nationalities would make the Jews a possible ally of other nationalities during the second phase of the elections – for instance, the Poles who were apparently prepared to set up an alliance with those Jews supporting Polish autonomy. Furthermore, it was stated that Jewish candidates would stand a good chance to be elected in the gubernii Grodno, Kiev, Minsk, Mogilev, Vitebsk, Podolia, Tauria, and in the city of Odessa; this led to an expectation of 8–10 Jewish Duma deputies. See I.L., 'Di Yudn un dos naie Wahl-Gesets', in *Dos Yudishe Folk*, no. 21, 13 June 1907, cols 3–5.

120. See I.L., 'Di drite Konstitutsie', in *Dos Yudishe Folk*, no. 20, 7 June 1907, cols 2 and 3; for more information on the elections from the Russian Nationalists' point of view see Robert Edelman, 'The Elections to the Third Duma: The Roots of the Nationalist Party', in Haimson, *The Politics of Rural Russia*, pp. 95–122.

121. As Dubnov wrote: 'Day after day the newspaper columns were crammed with reports concerning arrests of politically "undependable" persons and the executions of revolutionaries'; see Dubnow, *History of the Jews*, vol. III, p. 149.

122. Due to the initiative of some rabbis, the Jewish newspaper *Gakol* applied for permission to organize a rabbi congress of the Western gubernias in Warsaw. This congress was to discuss the present situation of the Jewish people in the Pale of Settlement. Based on this congress, the rabbis intended to make the effort to organize an all-Russian rabbi congress. (See *Evreiskii Golos*, no. 33, 18 August 1907, col. 25.)

123. The circular stated the demands: the struggle for a democratic regime, equality of rights, the recognition of the Jewish nationality and its language, the right for shabbat rest, and the convocation of the Jewish-national assembly. See *Razsvet*, no. 27, 14 July 1907, col. 6; and *Der Fraind*, no. 198, 9 September 1907, p. 3.

124. In this context, the author referred to Austria as an example where a special Jewish parliamentary group had been set up, and rejected the argument that a special group would only deal with Jewish affairs. See *Der Fraind*, no. 162, 23 July 1907, p. 1; another article pointed again to the necessity of a Jewish national Duma group, especially since ENG and Kadets had not mentioned the Jewish question in the first two Dumas. See *Der Fraind*, no. 168, 30 July 1907, p. 1. A third article defined the tasks of the 'All-Russian Jewish-National *Seim*' as the organization of education, national culture, professional education, financial aid and the creation of organizations for the Jewish working class such as Loan and Credit Co-operatives and so on, organization of the Jews for agricultural work, the production of statistics regarding all the questions of Jewish life, and finally, the organization of emigration. See M.R-R., 'Di Yudishe natsionale Avtonomie', in *Di Folksshtime*, no. 15, 10 August 1907, cols 1–7.

125. See *Svoboda i Ravenstvo*, no. 39, 9 August 1907, p. 6; alliances between Bund and ENG were also reported in *Di Folksshtime*, no. 13, 25 July 1907, col. 11; an alliance between SD [Bund], KD and the Jewish parties [ENG] was reported from Ekaterinoslav. See *Razsvet*, no. 33, 25 August 1907, col. 44. The Central Committee of the Bund had decided to set up immediately election bureaus which were to mobilize the Jewish vote together with the

professional organizations. The Bund also showed itself willing to support the neutral election committees in case they showed sympathy towards the Bund. See *Der Fraind*, no. 192, 30 August 1907, p. 2.

126. See A. Davidson, 'Politicheskiia techeniia v evreistve', in *Razsvet*, no. 26, 6 July 1907, cols 6–10. Finally, he concluded in *Razsvet*, no. 27, 14 July 1907, cols 13 and 14, that the Jews ought to shift their political direction to the left, that is to support the left-wing parties, as the Kadets had included Jewish national rights in their programme, but were not radical enough to realize them. The only way to achieve them would be the reconstruction of society along Socialist lines.

127. See *Der Fraind*, no. 213, 2 October 1907, p. 2.

128. See *Razsvet*, no. 39, 6 October 1907, cols 21–23.

129. See Vinaver's letter in *Der Fraind*, no. 214, 3 October 1907, p. 1.

130. See *Der Fraind*, no. 215, 4 October 1907, p. 1. The author of the article replied that Miliukov was not insulted by the fact that Jewish representatives had come to him in order to ask him about his opinion regarding the Jewish question. Finally, he reproached Vinaver of pursuing pure party [ENG] policy and of not having acted in the interest of the Jewish people.

131. See *Razsvet*, no. 39, 6 October 1907, col. 39. The ENG's appeal was signed by I.A. Abelson, engineer G.A. Bernshtein, M.M. Vinaver, I.I. Gessen, Baron D.G. Gintsburg, B.I. Girshovich, G.A. Goldberg, M.I. Goldshtein, I.S. Dimshits, M.V. Sev, G.M. Kabak, M.D. Kadinskii, B.A. Kaminka, M.V. Kaplan, A.A. Kaplun, Dr.S.A. Kaufman, S.I. Kopelman, M.I. Kulisher, A.M. Lesman, M.a. Lunts, M.P. Mikhelson, L.N. Niselovich, M.I. Ostrogorskii, A.G. Rabinovich, I.M. Rabinovich, V.S. Rozental, G.B. Sliozberg, G.T. Terk, D.F. Feinberg, B.E. Flaks, I.I. Fride, V.S. Fridlianskii, P.I. Hesin, M.I. Sheftel and L.S. Eliason. See *Der Fraind*, no. 215, 4 October 1907, p. 2.

132. Sliozberg rejected the questionnaire among the Jewish voters regarding the Duma candidates, as this would result in a falsified opinion, and therefore would not be representative at all. Finally, he stated that the Jewish voters had not lost confidence in the Kadets, and claimed that all the Jewish electors were Kadets, and that therefore St. Petersburg Jews should also vote for them. See *Der Fraind*, no. 219, 9 October 1907, p. 2.

133. Davidson pointed out that the ENG could not serve two masters, the Kadets and Jewish interests. See A. Davidson, 'O evreiakh i kadetakh', *Razsvet*, no. 41, 19 October 1907, col. 13; R. rejected Vinaver's criticism regarding the interviews and reproached him of pursuing a narrow-minded concurrence policy. See *Der Fraind*, no. 216, 5 October 1907, p. 1; within the scope of a election gathering, R. went so far to call Vinaver and the ENG 'the Kadets' court Jews', and *shtadlanim* who did not want to accept that the Kadets gambled away the Jews' confidence with their back-door policy in the Dumas – to deal with the Jewish question within the scope of the general Russian questions. See *Der Fraind*, no. 217, 7 October 1907, p. 1, and also *Der Fraind*, no. 219, 9 October 1907, p. 2.

134. Kreinin had to admit, however, that the Jewish masses were not interested in the Zionists and their programme despite the fact that they had worked hard in the last years. Finally, he condemned the decision by the Zionist conference in The Hague to withdraw from politics as this would damage

Zionism. See *Der Fraind*, no. 199, 12 September 1907, col. 2; for the Zionists' attacks see *Razsvet*, no. 40, 13 October 1907, col. 30.

135. In Kremenets (gub. Volynia) only 20–25 out of over one hundred invited Jews showed up for the Jewish election committee. Furthermore, some Jewish representatives who had shown a great deal of activity in the last elections, would now ignore them completely. See the letter from M. about the election campaign in Kremenets in *Razsvet*, no. 34–35, 6 September 1907, cols 40 and 41.

136. The separation into national curiae were reported from the gubernii Bessarabia, Volynia, Minsk and Poltava. See *Razsvet*, no. 36, 14 September 1907, col. 5–6. SRN activities were reported from Yaroslavl and Elizavetgrad. See *Der Fraind*, no. 146, 3 July 1907, p. 3; as well as from Minsk and Kiev. See *Der Fraind*, no. 178, 10 August 1907, p. 3.

137. See *Evreiskii Golos*, no. 26, 28 June 1907, col. 11; and *Razsvet*, no. 24, 22 June 1907, col. 29.

138. See *Der Fraind*, no. 174, 6 August 1907, pp. 1–2. They argued that the Gegenwartsarbeit was necessary in order to show the Jewish people that there was a political party which took the Jewish fate in Jewish hands and fought for their cause.

139. See Henry J. Tobias and Charles E. Woodhouse, 'Political Reaction and Reactionary Careers: The Jewish Bundists in Defeat, 1907–1910', *Comparative Studies in Society and History*, 19 (1977) pp. 367–96, especially pp. 377–391; and Zeev Abramovich, 'The Poale Zion Movement in Russia: its History and Development', in Henrik F. Infield, *Essays in Jewish Sociology, Labour and Co-operation. In Memory of Dr. Noah Barou, 1889–1955* (London and New York, 1961) pp. 63–72, especially pp. 64–6. Abramovich's accounts seem to be too high. For instance, he numbered the Bund's membership for 1906 as 80,000, the S.S.'s membership 35,000 and the SERP's 25,000. According to Abramovich, the decline of Bund and Poalei Zion movement led to a new solidarity among the Jewish and Russian Socialists which found its expression in the foundation of joint organizations embracing all the various Socialists in St. Petersburg, Chernigov, Mariopol, Kiev, Moscow and so on. For more information on the crisis of Russian and Jewish Socialism at that time see Burgin, *Di Geshikhte fun der Yidisher Arbeter Bewegung*, pp. 543–59.

140. See *Folks-Blat*, no. 1, 1 February 1908, cols 1–2. The newspaper painted a dark picture, maintaining that increasing restrictions, anti-Jewish circulars and so on had led to apathy, indifference and desperation within Jewish society.

141. Goldberg called for more patience, claiming that Jewish emancipation had only been achieved in Western Europe after a long historical process. Therefore, there was no reason to lose confidence due to the reactionary renaissance. Finally, he called for a concentration of all the Jewish forces on cultural work and for a mass emigration to Palestine as the Jewish question would no longer exist in one's own state. See B. Goldberg, 'Der politishe Moment', in *Folks-Blat*, no. 1, 1 February 1908, col. 2; furthermore, the conference of the Zionist press in April 1907 called for the organization of self-activity and self-help among Russian Jewry, such as the reorganization

and democratization of the Jewish community and its institutions alongside national self-administration. See *Razsvet*, no. 23, 15 June 1907, cols 10 and 11.

142. Grigorii Aronson confirmed this in his memoirs by calling the period between 1907 and 1914 a process towards a wide 'national concentration' which witnessed a rapprochement between Bund, SS, ENP and ENG. Aronson himself was working in many Jewish organizations such as ORT, ORPE, and SST (ssudo-sberegatil'nye tovarishchestva – Credit and Loan Cooperatives) together with liberal elements – Kadets, Radicals, Trudoviki and so on. See Grigorii Aronson, *Revoliutsionnaia Yunost'. Vospominaniia 1903–1917* (New York, 1961) p. 103. For the Bundists' move towards organic work see A. Litvak, *Vos Geven* (Vilna, 1925) pp. 248–259. Litvak argued that the decision to do organic work was forced upon the Bund by the political defeat, the increasing persecution by the police, and a general decrease of interest among the Jewish youth in political work; Abramovich confirmed Litvak's statement that many Bundists as well as their leaders were forced to enter legal work. Thus, in 1908 he started working as a teacher for Jewish history and religion at a Vilna gymnasium, and Mark Liber as a teacher for Latin and Greek – also in Vilna. See Abramovich, *In tsvai revolutsies*, pp. 319–22.

# 4  JEWISH LIBERAL POLITICS FROM 1908 TO 1911: REORGANIZATION, DETERMINATION AND THE BEGINNING OF 'ORGANIC WORK'

1. For the Poles' 'organic work', its means and aims see Rudolf Jaworski, *Handel und Gewerbe im Nationalitätenkampf. Studien zur Wirtschaftsgesinnung der Polen in der Provinz Posen, 1871–1914* (Göttingen, 1986); and Ludwig Bernhard, *Das polnische Gemeinwesen im preußischen Staat. Die Polenfrage* (Leipzig, 1907).

2. Zvi Halevy mentions some of the joint efforts regarding organic work: 'in 1907 Nomberg edited a literary collection in which articles appeared by S. Niger (S.S.), B. Vladeck (Bund) and Y. Zerubavel (Poalei Zion); in March 1908 the first issue of *Literarishe Monatsshriften* was edited by S. Gorelik (Zionist), A. Vayter (Bund) and S. Niger (S.S.)'. See Zvi Halevy, *Jewish Schools under Czarism and Communism. A Struggle for Cultural Identity* (New York, 1976) pp. 71–2.

3. See Dubnov, *Kniga Zhizni*, vol. II, p. 79–80.

4. See *Razsvet*, no. 39, 12 October 1908, col. 22.

5. See *Der Fraind*, no. 20, 24 January 1908, p. 2.

6. For Dubnov's criticism see *Kniga zhizni*, pp. 79–80. Nevertheless, Dubnov continued his lectureship in these courses throughout the next years. See Sophie Dubnov-Erlich, *The Life and Work of S.M. Dubnov. Diaspora Nationalism and Jewish History* (New York, 1991) pp. 146–62.

7. The trial took place in December 1907. For more details see *Vyborgskoe vozzvanie*. Delo o Vyborgskoe vozzvanie, stenograficheskii otchet o

zasedaniakh osobago prisutstviia S. Peterburgskoi sudebnoi palaty, 12–18 Dekabriia 1907 (St. Petersburg, 1908); Vinaver was in prison from 8 May 1908 until 6 August 1908. See Roza Vinaver, *Vospominaniia*, pp. 58–60.

8.  See *Razsvet*, no. 31, 10 August 1908, col. 21; the release was also reported in the *Jewish Chronicle*, 11 September 1908, p. 10; 18 September 1908, p. 11; and 2 October 1908, p. 11.

9.  Its first organizational congress took place in St. Petersburg on 12 October 1908. The Committee also included ENG leaders such as Kulisher, L.A. Sev and M.L. Trivus. The ELO mentioned as its first aim to concentrate its activity on St. Petersburg, to set up reading rooms and a public library, to organize discussion groups for members and public lectures as well as editorial work. See *Razsvet*, no. 40, 19 October 1908, cols 22 and 23.

10. See *Razsvet*, no. 45, 23 November 1908, col. 24; and *Der Fraind*, no. 224, 5 December 1908, p. 3. The EIO dedicated itself to collecting and editing archival material regarding Jewish history, organizing lectures on historical topics, setting up a historic archive and museum, and finally editing a historic journal; see Dubnov, *Kniga zhizni*, pp. 86–92.

11. Both, *Evreiskaia Starina* and *Evreiskii Mir* published articles on Jewish history and ethnography until the outbreak of World War I. See Dubnov, *Kniga Zhizni*, pp. 93–105. The conflict between Vinaver and the Zionists arose about Vinaver's first article in *EM*. See *Razsvet*, no. 10, 22 March 1909, col. 37.; see also Dubnov-Erlich, *The Life and Work of S.M. Dubnov*, p. 149.

12. See Isaiah Trunk, 'Historians of Russian Jewry', in Frumkin, *Russian Jewry*, pp. 465–72; and Mark Wischnitser, 'Reminiscences of a Jewish Historian', ibid., pp. 473–77.

13. See *Razsvet*, no. 16, 19 April 1909, col. 29.

14. He argued that the Committee did not yet have sufficient financial means at its disposal, and therefore was not yet able to realize all aims within the short time of the ELO's existence. See *Razsvet*, no. 48, 29 November 1909, col. 20.

15. See M. Kreinin, 'Der yetsiger Moment', in *Der Fraind*, no. 40, 17 February 1908, p. 1, and *Der Fraind*, no. 43, 20 February 1908, p. 2.

16. See *Razsvet*, no. 36, 15 September 1908, col. 20. In 1909, this organization was imitated in Odessa, see *Razsvet*, no. 18, 3 May 1909, col. 26.

17. The Society had already founded a social club (obshchestvennyi klub'), and mentioned its next targets as being the opening of schools, setting up courses for adults, libraries, reading rooms, and organizing popular lectures and scientific discussions. See *Razsvet*, no. 5, 1 February 1908, col. 9.

18. See *Razsvet*, no. 10, 8 March 1908, col. 25; *Razsvet*, no. 24, 22 June 1908, cols 28 and 31.

19. See *Razsvet*, no. 18, 10 May 1908, col. 22.

20. A gathering of twenty rabbis took place in Kiev from 9 to 11 July 1908, see *Razsvet*, no. 27, 13 July 1908, col. 26; twenty-one rabbis attended the rabbi congress of the gubernia Kherson which took place in the city with the same name, see *Razsvet*, no. 29, 27 July 1908, col. 22. The congresses in Ekaterinoslav and Vilna were mentioned only briefly and without detailed information, see *Razsvet*, no. 49, 21 December 1908, cols 26–30. The meeting of rabbis in Minsk took place from 23 to 25 December 1908 under

the chairmanship of communal rabbi Khaneles. Among other issues, special attention was paid to the education of the Jewish youth in the spirit of the Jewish religion. See *Razsvet*, no. 1, 4 January 1909, col. 29; another gathering of rabbis of the province of Taurida was reported in *Jewish Chronicle*, 8 May 1908, p. 10.

21. The Yiddish secular school movement was mainly supported by Bundists, who advocated a secular and proletarian culture with Yiddish as the language of the masses; the Zionists in turn, aimed at modernizing and natonalizing Jewish education through the reformed 'Metukan Heder' which included the teaching of Hebrew as well as general and religious subjects. For more information, see Halevy, *Jewish schools*, pp. 76–8, and 110–20.

22. The KI's programme aimed at improving the spiritual, material and legal situation of the Jews, and educating the youth on a religious basis in accordance with the principles of the purity of the morals and the love of mankind, see *Razsvet*, no. 16, 26 April 1908, cols 32 and 33.

23. See *Razsvet*, no. 50, 31 December 1908, col. 21.

24. See *Razsvet*, no. 31, 10 August 1908, col. 24.

25. See *Razsvet*, no. 29, 27 July 1908, col. 22. The result of this request was, however, never mentioned in the Jewish press.

26. In its programme the KI also demanded that the Yeshivoth should be granted – like the state schools – state subsidies, and that the law which made the teaching of general subjects in the Heders mandatory be abolished and so on. See *Razsvet*, no. 23, 15 June 1908, cols 3–6.

27. See *Razsvet*, no. 27, 13 July 1908, col. 22.

28. See *Razsvet*, no. 11, 15 March 1908, col. 27. Unfortunately, there was no detailed information mentioned.

29. See S. Gepshtein, 'K voprosu ob obshchine', in *Razsvet*, no. 15, 12 April 1908, cols 3–5. Gepshtein stated that such reports came from all over the Pale; for Vitebsk, see Gregorii Aronson, 'Dos yidishe geselshaftlikhe Lebn in Vitebsk (1913–1917)', in Gregorill Aronson, Jacob Lestchinskii and Abraham Kihn (eds), *Vitebsk amol. Geshikhte, Zikhronut, Khurbn* (New York, 1956) pp. 178–198.

30. Bernard, *Das polnische Gemeinwesen*, 1907, pp. 242–451; and Rudolf Jaworski, *Handel und Gewerbe*, p. 49f. Jaworski called the Polish economic organizations the 'real ammunition depots' for the national defense in the cities (concurrence struggle) and the countryside (struggle for land). In short, the Polish Saving and Loan Associations were founded in order to provide Polish economic organizations and peasants with cheap credit. In this context they served as a means for the Poles to fight the 'Germanization' of economic and cultural life in the province of Posen.

31. The amount of consumer co-operatives increased from 307 (1897), 996 (1904), 1,172 (1906), to 6,730 (1912); the first law on small credit of 1895 put these societies under state control, entailing an increase from 537 (1905) to 7,963 (1913); finally, the Loan and Saving Co-operatives increased from 924 (1905) to 3,053 (1913). See V.F. Totomiants, *Kooperatsiia v Rossii* (Prague, 1922) pp. 27–9 and pp. 52–5; see also Patrick J. Rollins, 'Cooperative Movement in Russia and the Soviet Union', *The Modern Encyclopedia of Russian and Soviet History*, vol. 8., pp. 53–8; the years between 1908 and 1913 witnessed – after the upswing in the 1890s – a second large

industrial up-swing, see Heiko Haumann, 'Rüstung und Monopole: Industriepolitik der Regierung und organisierte Unternehmerinteressen', *Handbuch der Geschichte Russlands*, vol. 3/1, pp. 430–7; and Hugh Seton-Watson, *The Russian Empire 1801–1917* (Oxford, 1988) pp. 649–62, here pp. 654–5. According to Seton-Watson, the co-operative credit and saving associations had eight million members throughout the Empire.

32. For the annual reports of the Loan and Saving Co-operatives of Akkerman, Smorgonsk, Lutsk for 1908 see *Razsvet*, no. 12, 22 March 1909, col. 36; for Gomel see *Razsvet*, no. 15, 12 April 1909, col. 21/22; for Koretsk see *Razsvet*, no. 16, 19 April 1909, col. 28; Cherkassy see *Razsvet*, no. 22, 31 May 1909, cols 15–17 and so on. For more information see S.O. Margolin, *Evreiskiia Kreditnyia Kooperatsii* (St. Petersburg, 1908); the EKO report for 1909–1910 stated the existence of 459 Loan and Saving Associations (1908) of which 226 were subsidized by EKO. See Hugo Nathanson, 'Die jüdischen Spar- und Darlehenskassen in Rußland und Galizien', in *Zeitschrift für Demographie und Statistik der Juden*, no. 12 (December 1910) pp. 184–9; for the general Russian co-operative movement see Totomiants', *Kooperatsiia v Rossii*, pp. 47–70.

33. See Aexander Orbach, 'The Jewish People's Group and Jewish Politics in Tsarist Russia, 1906–1914', in *Modern Judaism*, February 1990, vol. X, pp. 9–10.

34. Heinz-Dietrich Löwe, 'From charity to social policy', *Paper presented at the Deutsch-Polnische Historikertag: Deutsche – Polen – Juden*, February 1992, Freiburg/Breisgau, Germany, pp. 10–12.

35. See *Der Fraind*, no. 61, 13 March 1908, p. 1.

36. See *Der Fraind*, no. 61, 13 March 1908, p. 2. Unfortunately, the newspaper only summarized the various speeches. *Der Fraind* blamed this on the fact that no representatives of the press were admitted to the gathering. *Razsvet* did not mention the economic conference with a single word, and another newspaper, the *Lodzer Tagblat* ridiculed the initiators' attempt to work in the economic field, and called the Liberals people who were never really interested in helping the broad masses, see *Der Fraind*, no. 71, 25 March 1908, p. 3; see also Pozner, 'Bor'ba za ravnopravie', p. 179. Pozner does not, however, give any details of the conference.

37. A congress of this organization was mentioned in *Razsvet*, no. 49, 21 December 1908, cols 2–5.

38. See *Der Fraind*, no. 242, 28 December 1908, p. 1.

39. See *Der Fraind*, no. 242, 28 December 1908, p. 1; and *Der Fraind*, no. 243, 29 December 1908, pp. 1–2.

40. The Odessa evening course had 160 participants each paying 50 kopeks/month, Mogilev 100 (25 kopeks/month), Warsaw 74, and no numbers were mentioned for Vilna. See *Der Fraind*, no. 245, 31 December 1908, pp. 1–2.

41. The teachers Rein and Ber emphasized the necessity of general education in the artisans' school. Other pro-general education propagators were Mirenski (Riga) and Kaletskii (Belostok). See *Der Fraind*, no. 245, 31 December 1908, p. 2.

42. See *Novyi Voskhod*, no. 1, 6 January 1910, cols 14–17. Unfortunately, this organization and its activity cannot be traced down in the following period

as its functions were mainly carried out by ORT. The Jewish press revealed no further information.

43. See *Razsvet*, no. 15, 12 April 1908, col. 16; and *Der Fraind*, no. 78, 2 April 1908, p. 2. Here, I. Levinson held the Central Committee's insufficient activity responsible for the fact that ORT did not have any members in Poland.

44. See *Razsvet*, no. 18, 10 May 1908, cols 19–21.

45. See *Razsvet*, no. 50, 31 December 1908, cols 13–14. The growing involvement of the Jewish intelligentsia in organic work can be seen in the fact that the chairman of this congress became the former judge Ya.L. Teitel from Saratov. ORT had a kind of rotation system for the chairmanship: at the meeting in April 1908 the chairman was the Zionist Dr. V.S. Zalkind, in December it was Teitel, and the chairmen of the next congresses in March, April and May 1909 were the Liberals' leader, M.M. Vinaver, ex-Second. Duma deputy L. Rabinovich, and M.V. Kaplan respectively.

46. See *Razsvet*, no. 12, 22 March 1909, col. 37; *Razsvet*, no. 16, 19 April 1909, cols 21 and 22; *Razsvet*, no. 19, 10 May 1909, col. 23; and Shapiro, *The History of ORT*, pp. 61–3.

47. For instance, in March 1908 the ORPE activist Slepian travelled to Minsk, Smolensk and Nizhnyi-Novgorod in order to activate the local Jewish leaders. See *Razsvet*, no. 10, 8 March 1908, col. 25. A similar action by the ORPE representative Strashun was reported from Bobruisk almost a year later, in February 1909. See *Razsvet*, no. 7, 15 February 1909, col. 29.

48. See *Razsvet*, no. 45, 23 November 1908, cols 14 and 15; and *Razsvet*, no. 3, 18 January 1909, cols 24 and 25.

49. In an interview with *Der Fraind*, Vinaver stated that the congress was in planning since two years. However, due to different views about the way participants should be chosen, it did not make any progress. He believed especially that the Zionists/Autonomists' proposal to convene it out of all the former electors of the Duma elections was unrealistic, as this would have excluded the rabbis, and these electors might not be the people actually needed. Therefore, it was agreed to convene the congress from representatives of all the Jewish tendencies. The election procedure remained a problem, but Vinaver finally asked the Jewish community of Kovno to get the permission from the governor – after nothing was achieved in Kiev. See *Der Fraind*, no. 125, 5 June 1909, p. 2. Kovno was chosen by the conference's organizers because of the good relations they had with governor Kharuzin, who had shown an unusual awareness of the problems facing Jewish society. See Sliozberg, *Dela*, p. 262.

50. During the meeting, Dr. Chlenov criticized the Kadet Duma faction for not having responded to the right-wing anti-Jewish attacks. According to Chlenov, the Jewish voters would have to believe that they had no representatives in the Duma who would defend or support their case; consequently the Kadets' credibility was at stake. Vinaver spoke of the feeling in the country that the people would start to believe that there was no opposition whatsoever in the Duma. Vinaver accused the Kadets of inactivity and indifference towards the Jewish question, and he concluded that all the Jews wanted the Jewish question to be put forward in the Duma now and in the sharpest way possible. The Moscow Kadets also demanded a change of Kadet politics in the

Duma towards active oppositional politics. See *Der Fraind*, no. 16, 20 January 1909, p. 3; and *Der Fraind*, no. 18, 22 January 1909, p. 3.

51. On 22 January 1909, during the Duma's discussions of a bill about terror in the country, the Kadet Duma deputy Rodichev rejected the right-wing's statements that the Jews were at the centre of the terror, and put the blame on the government's repressive policy: 'We came here in order to defend Jewish equality. However, in a country where people have no rights, there is no order and no justice. Gentlemen, the question of equality is a basic question for Russia without which you can not start the new Russia . . .'. See *Der Fraind*, no. 19, 23 January 1909, p. 1.

52. The Kadets did not limit themselves to protest speeches but also prepared themselves for a proper representation of the Jewish question. In January 1909, the Kadet Duma deputy Maklakov went to Moscow in order to gather material concerning the Jews. He spoke with rabbi Maze as well as with V. Garkavi, the chairman of the Jewish organization, the Society for the Dissemination of True Knowledge about the Jews and Jewry. During the talk with Maze, Maklakov promised to speak on behalf of the Jews in the discussion on Stolypin's circular regarding the right of residence. While Maklakov was pessimistic about an open discussion of the Jewish question in the Duma, he was more optimistic that support regarding concessions on certain details of the Jewish question could be achieved within the political centre of the Duma. See *Der Fraind*, no. 26, 1 February 1909, p. 3.

53. At that time, Petr Struve, one of the KD's central committee, concluded his ideological shift from the 'Liberal on the Left' to the 'Liberal on the Right'. See Richard Pipes, *Struve: Liberal on the Right 1905–1944* (Cambridge, Massachusetts, 1980). Struve published several articles in the Russian press in which he not only raised the Russian national demands – for instance towards a unification of Russian language and culture in the Ukraine – but also openly supported the idea of a continuation of a unified Russian empire in its political form, and defended Stolypin's land reform project. This caused an outcry among the radical Russian intelligentsia in and outside the Kadet party. See S.L. Frank, *Biografiia P.B. Struve* (New York, 1956) pp. 72 and 96. In this context, Vinaver approached Struve with an open letter in which he defended the Jews' rights for national self-determination. See *Der Fraind*, no. 61, 15 March 1909, p. 2. For more information on this controversy see *Po vekham. Sbornik statei ob intelligentsii i natsional'nom litse: P. Boborykina, A. Vasileva, M. Vinavera et al*, 2nd ed. (Moscow, 1909) especially pp. 32–7, 42–7, 81–6; and Hagen, *Die Entfaltung*, pp. 264–5.

54. See N.M. Fridman's report about the bill at the conference in *Stenograficheskii otchet. Soveshchanie evreiskikh deiateli v Kovne 19–22 Novembria 1909* (St. Petersburg, 1910) pp. 48–52.

55. The initiators of the Conference sent letters to the leaders of the Jewish communities and other organizations, informing them of the new bill and asking them to come to Kovno to discuss the bill as well as the problems facing the Jewish communities. See *Stenograficheskii otchet*, pp. 1–10.

56. ENG leaders were reproached of exploiting the disunity among the national-social forces, and obtaining a fictive all-Jewish mandate. See *Razsvet*, no. 45, 8 November 1909, cols 1 and 2. Other Jewish organizations such as the ELO, the Emigration Society, and Choveve Sfat Eiver claimed that they had

not been invited. The Committee of the ELO sent a telegram to the Kovno protesting against the fact that the ELO as an organization was not invited, and consequently, would disregard the resolutions of this congress. See *Razsvet*, no. 47, 22 November 1909, col. 15.

57.  The community of Vologda, in fact, received an invitation from Sliozberg. However, when a local gathering was organized to elect the representative, a group which opposed the Kovno Congress won the majority, and no representative was sent. See *Razsvet*, no. 46, 15 November 1909, col. 19; and *Der Fraind*, no. 235, 21 October 1909, p. 2. The communal rabbi of Belostok, I.S. Mogilever, stated in a letter to Razsvet that no invitation was sent to his community. See *Razsvet*, no. 47, 22 November 1909, col. 14. The local community leaders of Bobruisk raised the same complaints. Nevertheless, they organized a meeting which elected and sent representatives to Kovno. See *Der Fraind*, no. 234, 20 October 1909, p. 1.

58.  Medem wrote that practical results should probably not be expected from this conference but that it might be of some use at least to discuss the problems. However, he questioned the conference's legitimacy of speaking on behalf of all Russian Jews, and he doubted whether the conference really had the mandate to do so. Finally, he attacked the ENG indirectly by pointing out that 'there are certain tendencies and people who like to tell us what to do, and they always talk in the name of Russian Jewry. These people', Medem said, 'are only to be found either in Vitte's, Miliukov's or Guchkov's chambers, and they do not really care what the Jewish masses think, and treat them only as a side-scene. From this point of view, we do not accept such a conference, and consider it as useless.' See *Der Fraind*, no. 163, 21 July 1909, p. 2; he continued his criticism in *Der Fraind*, no. 164, 22 July 1909, pp. 2–3. In principle, however, he accepted the idea of a Jewish congress as long as the participants would be elected, and called on the Bundists to participate in the congress. A. Litvak mentioned the same points as Medem, and in general came to the same conclusion, by considering the conference an important event. See *Der Fraind*, no. 232, 18 October 1909, p. 2; and *Der Fraind*, no. 233, 19 October 1909, p. 1.

59.  According to Litvak, the Bund had sent delegates to the conference in order to show that the Bund still existed. See Litvak, *Vos Geven*, pp. 286–7. Unfortunately, he did not mention the names of the other delegates.

60.  See *Razsvet*, no. 48, 29 November 1909, col. 16.

61.  *Stenograficheskii otchet*, pp. 1–15. All the congress members are listed in detail.

62.  See *Novyi Voskhod*, no. 1, 6 January 1910, p. 11. 'They would not give a kopek for Jewish community affairs.'

63.  For a detailed description of Jewish community life in Russia see Lazar Abramson, 'Die ostjüdische Gemeinde', in *Der Jude* 1 (1916–17) pp. 80–9 and Isaac Levitats, *The Jewish Community in Russia, 1844–1917* (Jerusalem, 1981) pp. 5–23. According to Silberfarb, regarding its fiscal duties to the state, the Jewish community still existed after the formal abolition of the kahal. See Moses Silberfarb, *Die Verwaltungen der jüdischen Gemeinden* (Pressburg, 1911) pp. 34–47.

64.  See Levitats, *Jewish Community*, pp. 26–7. He also quoted some examples of abuses of the Korobka tax by Jewish tax-farmers, but also of some cases of tax-farmers going bankrupt.

65. See *Razsvet*, no. 48, 29 November 1909, col. 12.
66. See *Razsvet*, no. 48, 29 November 1909, col. 11.
67. See *Stenograficheskii otchet*, p. 126.
68. Ibid., p. 82. He complained about the Jews who only appeared in the community in case of their birth or death.
69. See *Stenograficheskii otchet*, p. 69.
70. For Maze's statement, see *Stenograficheskii otchet*, pp. 78–82.
71. Ibid., p. 97. He mentioned the disputes and quarrels between the various prayer houses which could not be the basis for a unified organization.
72. Ibid., pp. 98–9.
73. Ibid., pp. 132–3.
74. As Rabbi Maze stated, 'the Korobka tax is a tax which has been introduced by the Jewish people itself and it can also be found in Jewish law ... The critics of this tax have obviously forgotten that there were also people who wanted to keep it. We must have such a tax, which we could control daily'. See *Stenograficheskii otchet*, pp. 78–9; for rabbi Aronson's statement see ibid., pp. 88–91; and rabbi Vygodskii's statement, Ibid., pp. 128–9. The pros and cons concerning the Korobka tax were also stated in Shneerson, *Lebn un Kampf*, pp. 296–7.
75. L.I. Brodskii from Kiev gave the example of the Jewish hospitals in Kiev which could no longer be financed only by the Korobka tax. See *Stenograficheskii otchet*, p. 84. For a detailed description of the Korobka and the candle tax, see Silberfarb, *Die Verwaltungen der jüdischen Gemeinden*, pp. 61–77.
76. L.G. Rabinovich quoted the following numbers from EKO statistical material. In 1898, 25–37 per cent of the Jewish population occasionally resorted to welfare. By 1908–09, this number had increased in some places to 40–45 per cent. He mentioned Odessa as an example, where 60,000 Jews – out of a total of 150,000 – had to be supported by welfare at least occasionally. See *Stenograficheskii otchet*, p. 141.
77. Ibid., p. 142.
78. Ibid., p. 145. He also mentioned in this context the 'ORT' statutes.
79. Ibid., pp. 186–7.
80. For the vote on the various points of the Kovno Conference resolutions see *Stenograficheskii otchet*, pp. 187–92.
81. For instance, Dr. Grigorii Bruk (Vitebsk), Dr. Temkin (Ekaterinoslav), Isaac Shneerson (Chernigov) and Jacob Maze who all favoured a modernization of Jewish community life. See Shneerson, *Lebn un Kampf*, pp. 295–8.
82. See Gregor Aronson, 'Ideological Trends among Russian Jews', in Frumkin, *Russian Jewry*, p. 169. The former advisory board decided to dissolve itself at its meeting of 16 January 1910. However, they made the request that the unification must take place on equal terms, meaning that they did not accept a St. Petersburg domination. See *Der Fraind*, no. 15, 18 January 1910, p. 1. According to Shneerson, the KK consisted of 36 members with an executive committee of nine members. See Shneerson, *Lebn un Kampf*, pp. 298–301; Frumkin mentions as the nine members: Sliozberg, Vinaver, Shternberg (ENG), I.A. Rozov, M.S. Aleynikov, Isaak Grunbaum (Zionists), M.N. Kreinin, Dubnov, A.V. Zalkind (ENP). The EDG was represented within the wider Kovno Komitet, see Jacob Frumkin, 'Pages from the History of Russian Jewry', in Frumkin, *Russian Jewry*, pp. 54–55.

83.  See *Der Fraind*, no. 32, 7 February 1910, p. 1; and *Der Fraind*, no. 34, 9
     February 1910, p. 1. Apparently, the questionnaire consisted of questions
     regarding the problem of the double rabbinate, the educational census for
     rabbis, the kind of education one could demand from rabbis, the number of
     rabbis necessary in one city, the people who were to elect the rabbis and
     so on.

84.  See *Der Fraind*, no. 59, 10 March 1910, p. 3.

85.  See *Jewish Chronicle*, 25 March 1910, p. 6.

86.  See *Novyi Voskhod*, no. 8, 25 February 1910, pp. 18–19.

87.  See Shneerson, *Lebn un Kampf*, pp. 339–40. According to Shneerson, the
     rabbi of Liubavich intended such a unification of the orthodox elements.

88.  During the elections of the participants of the Rabbi Commission, the rabbis
     had already sent more than 230 reports to the Ministry of Interior. These
     reports illustrated the fears among many orthodox rabbis – especially in the
     countryside – of the strong influence of the secular elements, such as the
     Jewish intelligentsia, which undermined their authority. Therefore, the fol-
     lowing issues were primarily mentioned in the reports: the permission to set
     up a Consistory in Russia, the reorganization of the Jewish prayer houses,
     the immorality of the Jewish youth, complaints about the influence of as-
     similation and the struggle between the Orthodox – religious – and the
     'Progressist' – secular elements. See *Novyi Voskhod*, no. 5, 4 February
     1910, pp. 19–20. An interview which Ahad Ha'am gave the *Jewish Chroni-
     cle* underlined the difficulties the rabbis had in playing at least an important
     role in the communities, a role which was seriously threatened by the secu-
     lar elements' influence. To the question 'what is the influence of the rabbis?',
     Ahad Ha'am replied: 'at the present moment it is very little. In the south of
     Russia, where Chassidism is still in favour, the Zaddikim have a certain vogue
     . . . but the real heads of the community are laymen, the gevirim' and 'the
     influence of the rabbis depends to a great extent on individual personality'.
     See *Jewish Chronicle*, 13 August 1909, p. 12. The struggle over the secular-
     ization of Jewish education as one of the main reasons of the emergence of
     the rabbis' activity is also stated in Shneerson, *Lebn un Kampf*, pp. 334–8.

89.  The state rabbi was appointed by the government and had administrative
     duties such as the collection of the special taxes and the registration of the
     Jews into the Metric Books, while the communal rabbi was elected by the
     community and he dealt primarily with religious questions. As Achad Ha'am
     put it: 'the Crown Rabbis [state rabbis] are generally regarded by the com-
     munity simply as officials of the government'. See *Jewish Chronicle*,
     13 August 1909, p. 12. For more information concerning the legal status
     of the community in general and the rabbis in particular see Abramson,
     'Die ostjüdische Gemeinde', pp. 80–9; and Levitats, *Jewish Community*, pp.
     5–23.

90.  Sliozberg described the role of the rabbi in the future community in a way
     acceptable to the rabbis: 'the rabbi must show love to his own people, to
     Jewry and the Jewish spirit'. (See *Novyi Voskhod*, no. 9, 4 March 1910, pp.
     15–17.)

91.  The communal rabbis Grodzenskii (Vilna), Shneerson (Liubavich), Khein
     (Nezhin) and the state rabbis Kh. Soloveichik (Brest-Litovsk), Sh.
     Polinkovskii (Odessa), Tsirelson (Kishinev), as well as the lawyer Mazor
     (Kiev). (See *Novyi Voskhod*, no. 8, 28 February 1910, pp. 18–19.)

92. Unfortunately the stenographic reports were not published. See Sliozberg, *Dela*, p. 279. The congress was opened by A.N. Kharuzin, director of the Department for Foreign Denominations. The congress itself sent telegrams to the Tsar and Stolypin assuring them of its loyalty. The government gave the congress permission to use Yiddish as well as Russian, which made the congress functionable. It has to be remembered that many rabbis, especially from the *shtetl*, could neither speak nor understand Russian. See *Novyi Voskhod*, no. 9, 4 March 1910, pp. 15–16.

93. Other issues were more concerned with religious life such as divorce, baptism, education of the youth, the registration into the Metric Books and so on. See *Novyi Voskhod*, no. 9, 4 March 1910, pp. 1–3.

94. As Jewish intelligentsia circles showed a lack of interest in these elections which took place between December 1909 and February 1910, the Orthodox were able to push their candidates through in most places. See the reports about the elections in *Novyi Voskhod*, no. 5, 4 February 1910, pp. 20–1 (Warsaw); *Novyi Voskhod*, no. 3, 21 January 1910, p. 24 (Chernigov), *Novyi Voskhod*, no. 2, 14 January 1910, p. 20 (Nel'tsy, Andreev, Pinchevo, Minsk, Mogilev, Gub. Vilna and St. Petersburg). The participants of the Rabbi Congress included five merchants, six state rabbis, 19 communal rabbis, five rabbis who were both state and communal rabbis, the lawyers Sliozberg and Mazor, Jewish community activists Gintsburg, Poliakov and Brodskii, and Dr. Kreps as the organizer of the congress. See *Razsvet*, no. 9, 28 February 1910, cols 19–22.

95. See *Novyi Voskhod*, no. 10, 11 March 1910, p. 15.

96. First Shneerson attacked the Moderates for their presence at the congress by stating: 'they have seized our prayer houses, transformed them into clubs and expelled any spirit of piety out of them', and concerning the census he said that 'they have split the Jewish people and now they are sneaking up to the rabbis. Any census is a fatal danger to Jewry'. See *Novyi Voskhod*, no. 9, 4 March 1910, pp. 15–17. Then he turned to the state rabbis, reproaching them of lacking the scholarship necessary for such a post, and calling them simple bureaucrats. According to him, a rabbi just had to know the Torah, and nothing else. See *Novyi Voskhod*, no. 11, 18 March 1910, p. 13; and Vl. Temkin, 'Na Ravvinskom s'ezde', in *Razsvet*, no. 11, 14 March 1910, cols 21 and 22. The state rabbis regarded their opponents as ivory-towered and as a 'medieval' part of the society who, as rabbi Brushtein put it, 'do not know anything about the new life. On the contrary they are sitting on mount Sinai observing the Jewish masses'. (See *Novyi Voskhod*, no. 12, 25 March 1910, p. 22.)

97. See *Novyi Voskhod*, no. 11, 18 March 1910, pp. 14 and 15.

98. Communal rabbi Rabinovich demanded that the rabbis should be elected from the prayer houses alone, and have the last word in religious affairs (*Novyi Voskhod*, no. 12, 25 March 1910, pp. 21 and 22).

99. The important role the rabbis played within the Jewish communities should not be underestimated. His advice and last word was in many cases decisive. See Sliozberg's descriptions of the part rabbis such as Shneerson, Soloveichik, Fainshtein, Kats, Temkin and Maze played in their communities. See Sliozberg, *Dela*, pp. 270–5.

100. Shneerson claimed that a reformed Jewish community would weaken religious life in the community, and a unification of all the institutions would

undermine the rabbi's authority. They agreed, however, to a unification of the welfare and educational institutions where they, of course, could still play an important role. See *Novyi Voskhod*, no. 10, 11 March 1910, p. 15; and *Novyi Voskhod*, no. 11, 18 March 1910, p. 14; and Shneerson, *Lebn un Kampf*, pp. 355–69, here pp. 360–1 and 365–6. Here, both Shneerson and Temkin argued that the rabbis had to adjust to the changed realities which needed an adaptation of the Jewish educational system according to modern and secular educational ideas, including the teaching of secular subjects.

101. See *Jewish Chronicle*, 1 April 1910, p. 9.

102. The future Jewish community would be conducted by the Council of the community elected by direct vote. The Council in turn would elect the executive of the community consisting of seven to ten members which was the governing body of the community. See *Stenograficheskii otchet. Soveshchanie evreiskikh obshchestvennykh deiateli v Kovne*, pp. 186–7. Compare this with the resolution taken by the rabbi congress (see *Novyi Voskhod*, no. 13, 1 April 1910, pp. 15–19). See also Vladimir Medem's article in which he showed understanding for the rabbi congress in supporting the Kovno resolutions. See *Evreiskaia Nedelia*, no. 3, 29 April 1910, p. 7.

103. See *Novyi Voskhod*, no. 12, 25 March 1910, p. 22. In Kovno every Jew who was older than eighteen years was a community member. See *Stenograficheskii otchet'*, pp. 186–7.

104. Mazor called the tax immoral and a heavy burden for the Jewish poor which had to pay for the right to fulfil their religious duties. See *Novyi Voskhod*, no. 12, 25 March 1910, p. 23.

105. See *Evreiskaia Nedelia*, no. 1, 15 April 1910, p. 35.

106. Shneerson called the introduction of the Russian language into the Talmud Torah and Heder schools a violation of the Torah. He held the Liberals responsible for this innovation and accused them of having betrayed the Jewish religion, see *Novyi Voskhod*, no. 11, 18 March 1910, p. 13. For the final decision see *Novyi Voskhod*, no. 13, 1 April 1910, p. 19.

107. A special court consisting of three rabbis would decide if an engagement was valid or not. This was necessary because of a general tendency to abuse the engagement regulations. The law said that an engaged person could not enter into a new relationship within one year. A violation of this law could be legally prosecuted. Rabbi Temkin, however, reported about young men who specialised in getting engaged to a girl and then blackmailing the girl's parents who were interested in dissolving the engagement. In order to prevent this kind of blackmail an engagement would have to be approved by this special court. See *Novyi Voskhod*, no. 13, 1 April 1910, pp. 17–18.

108. 'Only the children should be registered in the Metric Books on whom the ritual of the circumcision was fulfilled with the exception of the cases in which the doctor considers it as impossible to implement the procedure' (see *Novyi Voskhod*, no. 13, 1 April 1910, p. 19). For the decision not to open the Heder for Jewish girls see *Evreiskaia Nedelia*, no. 1, 15 April 1910, pp. 34–5.

109. See *Novyi Voskhod*, no. 11, 18 March 1910, pp. 15–16.

110. See A.Litvak, 'Rebnim Tsusamenfor', in *Tsaitfragen*, March 1910, vol. II, p. 10. Litvak described in detail Stolypin's attitude towards the deputation:

after he made them wait for one and a half hours, he came out of his office and ignoring the rabbis went straight to Gintsburg and Poliakov asking them: 'you are also dealing with such affairs?'. Stolypin's hostile behaviour was also reported in *Jewish Chronicle*, 8 April 1910, p. 14; *Razsvet*, no. 12, 21 March 1910, cols 28 and 29; and Shneerson, *Lebn un Kampf*, p. 374–6.

111. Litvak and *Novyi Voskhod* shared the disappointment with the minister who had completely discredited himself in the eyes of the Jewish public. See Litvak, 'Rebnim Tsusamenfor', p. 10; *Novyi Voskhod*, no. 12, 25 March 1910; and *Jewish Chronicle*, 8 April 1910, p. 14.

112. At the congress, the anti-Semitic propagandists such as Markov and Purishkevich sang their old songs: 'The fact that the Jews are mainly revolutionaries is their chief guilt' (see *Novyi Voskhod*, no. 12, 25 March 1910, p. 3).

113. See *Jewish Chronicle*, 20 May 1910, p. 10.

114. See *Jewish Chronicle*, 29 April 1910, p. 8.

115. See *Jewish Chronicle*, 16 December 1910, p. 10.

116. The Zionist Davidson criticized the fact that the KK was not elected as well as its decision to act as a non-party organization (see *Razsvet*, no. 2, 10 January 1910, cols 1–6; and no. 3, 17 January 1910, cols 1–4).

117. Vladimir Medem's statement is mentioned in *Novyi Voskhod*, no. 4, 28 January 1910, pp. 6–8; and A. Litvak's article 'Der Kovner Tsusamenfor', *Tsaitfragen*, vol. I, November 1909, pp. 1–14.

118. The proclamation stated: 'Vinaver spoke in his open letter to Struve about the right to national self-determination but if the community would be led by such persons, what will happen to all the traditionally minded institutions embodying the spirit of Judaism . . . It is impossible for a Jew to give up his religious feelings . . . The Intelligentsia, however, will expel all the Orthodox from the community and they will not only dominate the community but also destroy any sense of religion.' (See *Novyi Voskhod*, no. 5, 4 February 1910, pp. 1–3.)

119. Pointing to the worsening political and economic situation, and arguing that the Jews had no choice but to fight in a united front, the Liberals tried to allay the fears of the ultra-Orthodox and demanded from them to try to understand why the conference acted as it did: 'They [the Intelligentsia] do not want to split Jewry into two parts. Judaism is based on the Intelligentsia as well as on the advocates of the faith. The Orthodox are afraid now of the domination of the Jewish people by the Intelligentsia, but which way should we go to free it from its present predicament?' (Ibid., p. 4) The fact that the Liberals did not succeed in convincing the Hasidim to participate in the reform became evident in December 1910 when a deputation headed by rabbi Shneerson went to the Ministry of Interior 'with the object of pleading against the intention of the cabinet to subordinate the old Rabbinical qualifications to a knowledge of Russian'. (See *Jewish Chronicle*, 16 December 1910, p. 10.)

120. The Liberals rejected all criticism regarding the convocation and the composition of the conference by arguing that the political situation had forced the organizers to act in this way and that there was no justification for wasting time with long elections. The mere fact of the convocation of Jewish

activists from all over Russia was of prime importance to them. Beyond this, they valued the possibilities for propagating solutions to the main problems facing the Jewish community. The conference, in their eyes, had moved Jewish activities from the sphere of literary discussion into the realm of practical work. See A. Perelman's article, 'Kovenskii s'ezd', in *Evreiskii Mir* November–December 1909, suppl. pp. 1–9.

121. *Ha'olam* and *Razsvet* denied the rabbis' rights to act on behalf of Russian Jewry as 'the rabbis do not have any basis within Russian Jewry any more, and by striving for a way out of their illegal situation the communal rabbis only degrade themselves'. The author of this article summarized the reaction of the Jewish press and for the Zionists' reaction he quoted *Ha'olam*, no. 12, 1910, p. 5 and *Razsvet*, no. 13, 1910, p. 6. See *Evreiskaia Nedelia*, no. 3, 29 April 1910, p. 6. The Bundist A. Litvak called the rabbi congress the 'relic of Jewish Clericalism' which had put another stone on the way towards a more democratic Jewish community. He particularly criticised the Liberals' [Sliozberg] presence at the congress and their attempts to influence the rabbis' decisions: 'they [Liberals] have already pointed out their view at the Kovno Conference . . . they had again interfered in things which were none of their business'. (See Litvak, 'Rebnim Tsusamenfor', pp. 1–4, and p. 10.)

122. 'Why should it be impossible that the Kovno Conference and the rabbi congress should have the same point of view concerning the reorganization of the Jewish community?', and, 'is it unthinkable – under the present political circumstances – that the rabbis would come to conclusions similar to the Kovno resolutions, and to cooperate with the Liberals in order to achieve a unified Jewish community structure?'. Finally the Liberals pointed out that with the support of the rabbis – who were still in an influential position within Russian Jewry – these resolutions could succeed. See *Evreiskaia Nedelia*, no. 3, 29 April 1910, p. 7. Medem stated: 'until recently the Jewish community had no particular form, no organs, all was anonymous . . . Without a centre, however, it would be impossible to bring any order in our work, and as long as it is impossible to achieve the best, we must bring the Kovno programme into life'. He called passivity and the boycott movement the worst enemies of Russian Jewry. Finally, referring to Litvak, he concluded that the rabbi congress had to be regarded as the fundament for the reorganized Jewish community and not as a 'stone on the way to it'. See Vladimir Medem, 'Die Yudishe Khilo', *Tsaitfragen*, March 1910, vol. II, pp. 25–37.

123. For the reports of the delegates in Orel, see *Novyi Voskhod*, no. 6, 11 February 1910, p. 23; in Chernigov, see *Novyi Voskhod*, no. 4, 28 January 1910, pp. 33–4; in Melitopol, see *Novyi Voskhod*, no. 3, 21 January 1910, pp. 24–5; in Gomel, see *Novyi Voskhod*, no. 1, 6 January 1910, p. 20.

124. See *ORPE. Za piat'desiat' let'* (St. Petersburg, 1913); and Shapiro, *The History of ORT*, p. 68. ORT's budget showed an increase from 44,574 roubles in 1909 to 61,951 in 1911.

125. For more information see Zvi Halevy, *Jewish schools*, pp. 75–8, and 110–20.

126. See Löwe, 'From Charity to Social Policy', pp. 21–2.

127. See *Der Fraind*, no. 31, 5 February 1910, p. 2; and *Razsvet*, no. 3, 17 January 1910, cols 5 and 6.

128. In July 1908, a second course for teachers was set up at the Grodno courses indicating that the seminar was working successfully. The first course of the Grodno seminar had 80 teachers enlisted. See *Der Fraind*, no. 153, 5 July 1908, p. 2.

129. Kiev's ORPE branch questioned the St. Petersburg leadership. They arued that the edition of a journal, the production of statistics concerning educational matters as well as teachers congresses could also take place in Kiev. Therefore, they demanded more independence for the branches and a decentralization of ORPE activities. The Central Committee argued that an organization like ORPE needed a central leadership, and to decentralize the organization would result in inefficiency. See *Der Fraind*, no. 75, 29 March 1910, p. 1; *Razsvet*, no. 14, 4 April 1910, cols 13–16; and *Novyi Voskhod*, no. 13, 1 April 1910, cols 9–15.

130. The journal was called *Vestnik Obshchestva Rasprostranenia Prosveshcheniia mezhdu Evreiami v Rossii*, and appeared from November 1910 until 1913.

131. The Zionist Grinbaum argued that Russian would assimilate the teachers; Kogan (Vilna), the travelling representative of ORPE, Strashun, the delegate Goldman and others argued that there were many teachers who would not understand Russian, and therefore, demanded to add to the Russian edition a supplement in Yiddish and Hebrew. See *Der Fraind*, no. 76, 30 March 1910, p. 1; and *Novyi Voskhod*, no. 13, 1 April 1910, cols 9–15.

132. For Eiger's report see Ya. Eiger, 'Normal'nyi tip evreiskoi shkoly', in *Vestnik Obshchestva Rasprostraneniia Prosveshcheniia mezhdu Evreiami v Rossii*, no. 1 (November 1910) pp. 5–28.

133. Rozenbaum rejected the exclusion of Hebrew as it was – with Yiddish – the national language of the Jews. Syrkin (Kiev) supported the idea of a nationally-oriented school which would exclude Russian. Grinbaum (Vilna) claimed that a national school was not to include a foreign language and culture, and instead demanded the teaching of Yiddish and Hebrew. See *Der Fraind*, no. 77, 31 March 1910, p. 2; and *Razsvet*, no. 14, 4 April 1910, col. 16.

134. For the elections of the Committee in 1911, see *Der Fraind*, no. 7, 9 January 1911, p. 3; and *Der Fraind*, no. 10, 12 January 1911, p. 1. Apparently, the ENG succeeded in bringing all four of their candidates into the Committee, among them a new Committee member, the lawyer Kalmanovich.

135. The provincial delegates claimed that the planned edition of books for the schools, evening courses and the Heders was only fulfilled on paper but not in reality; they finally pressured the Committee for more education in Yiddish, such as for an edition of school books in Yiddish. See *Der Fraind*, no. 3, 4 January 1911, p. 1.

136. See S.L. Kamenetskii, 'K zakonoproektu o nachal'nykh uchilishchakh', in *Vestnik Obshchestva Rasprostraneniia Prosveshcheniia mezhdu Evreiami v Rossii*, no. 1 (November 1910) pp. 72–86; and ibid., no. 2 (December 1910) pp. 38–50.

137. Ginzburg complained that the decision of the conference of 1910 – to demand a contribution of 50 Kopeks/member by the provincial branches to ORPE's general budget – was not implemented in many branches. The *Vestnik* received therefore financial support only from the Kiev and Vilna branches. All the other branches had not sent any contributions to the correspondence section of the paper. Only one branch sent full financial aid, while nine contributed only a certain sum, and 19 did not sent a single

kopek. Some provincial delegates – whose names were not mentioned – explained the problems with the unpopularity of the St. Petersburg Committee in the provinces. See *Der Fraind*, no. 83, 13 April 1911, p. 1; and *Razsvet*, no. 16, 17 April 1911, cols 15–18.

138. The Bundist Rafes was one of the Yiddishists who rejected the teaching of Hebrew and the bible. See *Razsvet*, no. 16, 17 April 1911, col. 18.

139. Children would enter school at the age of six; training was to be for five or an optional sixth year. School fees were to be paid, but special institutions were to pay for poor children. The plan was also concerned with the improvement of hygienic conditions and the development of the physical fitness of the children. See *Der Fraind*, no. 83, 13 April 1911, p. 1; *Der Fraind*, no. 85, 15 April 1911, p. 1; and *Der Fraind*, no. 91, 22 April 1911, p. 2. For the resolutions see also *Razsvet*, no. 16, 17 April 1911, col. 18; and *Razsvet*, no. 17, 24 April 1911, cols 10 and 11.

140. See *Razsvet*, no. 17, 24 April 1911, col. 13.

141. See *Razsvet*, no. 16, 17 April 1911, col. 16; and *Der Fraind*, no. 83, 13 April 1911, p. 1.

142. See *Razsvet*, no. 4, 23 January 1911, col. 14.

143. When some governors did not allow Jewish artisans to go to St. Petersburg, ORT intervened with the committee organizing the conference. The congress sent its chairman, Loranskii, to the Minister of Interior to ensure that the Jewish artisans would receive the right of residence for the course of the conference. The final number of seventy-five Jewish delegates seemed to indicate that this met with success. See *Der Fraind*, no. 11, 13 January 1911, p. 1; and *Der Fraind*, no. 13, 16 January 1911, p. 1. The Jewish delegates were representatives of the Vilna arts and crafts school, ORT, the artisans' schools in Vilna, Mogilev and Belostok, the Saratov society for mutual help for Jewish artisans, the professional organization of the Vilna metal workers, and representatives of artisans from various cities such as Simbirsk, Romno, Kovno, Belostok, Mogilev, Polotsk, Kremenchug, Rostov/Don, Vinnitsa, Nezhin, Simferopol, Aleksandrovsk, and Riga. See also *Razsvet*, no. 4, 23 January 1911, col. 15.

144. The anti-Jewish part of the congress consisted of delegations such as the Russian artisans of Tula and Pensa, and anti-Semites like the St. Petersburg master Alekseev. Alekseev suggested to expel Jewish artisans from the city as well as the province of St. Petersburg. The Tula artisans claimed that the activity of Jewish artisans was harmful, and that therefore Jewish artisans should not be allowed to open workshops outside the Pale. Finally, the Pensa artisans proposed examinations for Jewish artisans in the cities or places where they intended to settle. As *Der Fraind* pointed out, it was obvious that in Russian reality Christian artisans would refuse a license to pursue a craft to their Jewish competitors. See *Der Fraind*, no. 13, 16 January 1911, p. 1; and *Razsvet*, no. 4, 23 January 1911, col. 15. In an interview, a former participant of the First All-Russian Artisans Conference in 1900 emphasized the difference between the First and the Second Conference: in 1900 only ten Jewish delegates from the provinces were present and the opening speech was characterized by anti-Semitic resentments. Now the anti-Semites had to face a far bigger Jewish representation which was not afraid to confront them. See *Der Fraind*, no. 14, 17 January 1911, p. 1;

and *Novyi Voskhod*, no. 4, 27 January 1911, cols 1–3. The author praised the liberal and tolerant tendency in the congress.

145. Chemeriskii justified his demand to abolish the percentage norms for Jews in schools and the Pale of Settlement claiming that these restrictions had caused the move of Russian Jews to Poland which had increased the competition among artisans in Poland, *Der Fraind*, no. 15, 18 January 1911, p. 1; *Der Fraind*, no. 23, 27 January 1911, p. 1; and *Razsvet*, no. 4, 23 January 1911, cols 16 and 17.

146. The resolution stated that the day of rest was not to be fixed and that minorities were to choose this day following their religion, *Der Fraind*, no. 26, 31 January 1911, p. 1; *Razsvet*, no. 6, 6 February 1911, cols 20–1; and *Novyi Voskhod*, no. 4, 27 January 1911, cols 1–3.

147. The St. Petersburg administration had refused to extend the right of residence to 10 of the seventy Jewish delegates. The delegates affected by the decision were: I.B. Nisinskii, A.Sh. Tarlovich (Belostok), G. Dantsis, I. Kremer (Mogilev), G.M. Burevin, A.A. Golombek (Simbirsk), H.D. Vinokirov (Mstislavl), A.S. Kheist (Vinnitsa), N.M. Taitsh (Riga), and A. Vits (Saratov). See *Der Fraind*, no. 20, 24 January 1911, p. 1.

148. Ginzburg argued that first of all Jews living outside the Pale would tend to assimilate, and second, would leave handicraft for trade. Therefore, it would be more important to disseminate technical and artistic know-how. S. Margolin opposed this from an economic point of view, stating that there was enough place within the Pale and that the amount of artisans outside was not smaller than the one inside the Pale. Finally, he accepted Ginzburg's opinion that, if Jews leave the Pale, they tend to leave the crafts. Vysotskii (Vilna) added that whoever wants to find work within the Pale would not remain without employment. See *Der Fraind*, no. 27, 1 February 1911, p. 1. For the organization of this special committee see *Razsvet*, no. 13, 27 March 1911, cols 33–34.

149. See *Der Fraind*, no. 27, 1 February 1911, p. 1.

150. See *Razsvet*, no. 16, 26 April 1908, cols 1–4; and *Jewish Chronicle*, 8 May 1908, p. 9.

151. See L.N. Niselovich, 'K zakonoproektu o ravnopravie', in *Razsvet*, no. 21, 31 May 1908, cols 1–3. Thereby, he answered Idelson's attack on the impossibility of such an action. See A. Idelson, 'K' zakonoproektu o ravnopravie', in *Razsvet*, no. 20, 24 May 1908, cols 1–4.

152. He based his optimism on various successes in the Duma commissions such as the one on the judiciary reform which decided not to make any distinction between Jews and non-Jews. Furthermore, the commission on State Defence did not exclude Jews from the army. See L.N. Niselovich, 'Evreiskii vopros v III.-ei Gosudarstvennoi Dume', in *Razsvet*, no. 34, 31 August 1908, cols 1–12. Niselovich pointed out that in the commission on the judiciary reform he was supported by the Kolo deputy Parchevskii, the Muslim representative and Kadet Adzhemov, the Nationalist Miloradovich and the Octobrist Andronov.

153. He admitted that many deputies displayed a negative attitude towards the Jews, but he maintained that this was due to a lack of knowledge and information. See L.N. Niselovich, 'Evreiskii vopros v III.-ei Gosudarstvennoi Dume', in *Razsvet*, no. 35, 7 September 1908, cols 1–9.

154. See *Razsvet*, no. 36, 15 September 1908, cols 1–4.

155. Here, he was supported by speakers of the opposition, such as the Kadet leader Rodichev. See *Razsvet*, no. 36, 15 September 1908, cols 1–4. The activity of the Jewish deputies in defending the Jewish cause towards anti-Jewish attacks by the ultra-conservatives in general were also reported in various numbers of the English-Jewish newspaper *Jewish Chronicle* in 1908 and 1909.

156. He pointed out that Russia alone applied a percentage norm for its Jewish citizens. He also condemned the practise that in spite of vacancies in Russian universities, for instance Odessa, Jewish parents would have to support nine Christian students in order to achieve the admission of one Jewish student to the university. See *Razsvet*, no. 18, 3 May 1909, col. 26.

157. See L.N. Nisselowitsch, *Die Judenfrage in Russland* (Berlin, 1909).

158. See L.N. Niselovich, 'K zakonoproektu o ravnopravii', in *Razsvet*, no. 21, 31 May 1908, cols 1–3.

159. Only the Nationalist Prince Urusov held to the slogan 'Russia to the Russians'. See *Razsvet*, no. 48, 29 November 1909, cols 6–7.

160. See *Razsvet*, no. 50, 15 December 1909, cols 5–6.

161. Niselovich attacked the Jewish Liberals' procrastinations, arguing that they rejected action earlier because of narrow party interests. He implied that the Liberals had waited until they could set up the Kovno Committee which was dominated by themselves, and thus, were more able to control it. See *Razsvet*, no. 9, 28 February 1910, cols 6 and 7. A month later, Niselovich reported again on the bill. By now he had found wider support among the participants of the Rabbi Commission and Baron Gintsburg who agreed that such a project was necessary as the Jewish masses were awaiting results from the Duma. But the KK insisted on withholding the draft bill until after Easter pointing to some anti-Jewish appearances. See *Razsvet*, no. 13, 28 March 1910, cols 6–7. However, in June 1910 the KK had still not given its approval. See *Razsvet*, no. 25, 20 June 1910, cols 3–5.

162. For more information on the discussions of this bill see Neil B. Weissman, *Reform in Tsarist Russia. The State Bureaucracy and Local Government, 1900–1914* (New Brunswick, New Jersey, 1981) especially pp. 197–201; and Manfred Hildermeier, *Die Russische Revolution 1905–1921* (Frankfurt/M., 1989) pp. 106–7.

163. See Joseph Lichten, 'Notes on the assimilation and acculturation of Jews in Poland, 1863–1943', in C. Abramsky et al. (eds), *The Jews in Poland* (Oxford, 1986) pp. 106–129; and Frumkin, 'Pages from the History of Russian Jewry', pp. 37–8. Frumkin mentions the attempts of the SP to activate Warsaw Jews during the election campaign to the First Duma, which failed due to the resistance of the Nathanson group.

164. See *Der Fraind*, no. 266, 24 November 1910, p. 2.

165. See *Der Fraind*, no. 267, 25 November 1910, p. 2. The talks took place in Nisselovich's apartment after the Duma commission had decided in principle to restrict Jewish rights. Fridman reproached the Kolo deputy Grabski for the abstention during the vote on this issue, which he regarded as the same as if Grabski had voted in favour of restrictions. Dikshtein and Nathanson not only did not support Fridman, but rejected his criticism of Grabski. Nathanson also pointed to the low level of Jewish culture in Poland and to

the difficult situation of Polish Jewry; he feared rising frictions between Poles and Jews, in the case of Jews insisting on equal rights. See *Der Fraind*, no. 268, 26 November 1910, p. 2.

166. For Vinaver it was essential to ensure that the Kolo would not be able to say that Polish Jews themselves had asked for this system of municipal self-government. See *Der Fraind*, no. 275, 5 December 1910, p. 1; no. 277, 7 December 1910, p. 1, and no. 279, 9 December 1910, p. 2. The protests from the Warsaw teachers and Samoshch, ibid., no. 294, 27 December 1910, p. 3. More information on the Polish–Jewish conflict in Grigorii Landau, *Pol'sko-Evreiskiia otnosheniia. Stati i zametki* (Petrograd, 1915). This book presents a collection of articles which appeared on the issue in various newspapers or journals.

167. See *Der Fraind*, no. 269, 28 November 1910, p. 1. The four deputies voting against were Vasilev, Beneke, Grabski and Fridman himself; despite the fact that the Duma passed the law on municipal self-government in the gubernii of the former kingdom of Poland, it was rejected by the Council of State.

168. See *Der Fraind*, no. 15, 18 January 1911, p. 3; *Der Fraind*, no. 16, 19 January 1911, p. 2; and *Der Fraind*, no. 19, 23 January 1911, p. 2.

169. See *Der Fraind*, no. 34, 9 February 1911, p. 1; and *Der Fraind*, no. 35, 10 February 1911, p. 1; for the Octobrists' view see Ben-Cion Pinchuk, *The Octobrists in the Third Duma, 1907–1912* (Seattle and Washington, 1974) p. 173. Pinchuk describes the Octobrists as being paralysed by fear of their right-wing partners, and therefore, in order to show their 'patriotism' they never really opposed the anti-Semitic outbursts of their partners – despite the fact that quite a few Octobrists probably had a more tolerant view towards Russian Jews; see also Löwe, *Antisemitismus*, pp. 117–21. He held the Octobrists' right-wing responsible which succeeded to hold the party on an indifferent course.

170. See *Der Fraind*, no. 41, 17 February 1911, p. 1.

171. These booklets were all written in the same way: first, they acquainted the commission with the history of the Pale; second, they linked it to the arbitrariness of the local authorities and pointed to the negative impact on Russian Jews and the Russian economy; third, they emphasized that the modernization of Russian economy and of trade in particular would profit from the abolition, as Russian Jews had proven to be economically useful; finally, the abolition would give the Russian government more credibility abroad. See *Materialy po voprosu o cherte evreiskoi osedlosti* (Kiev, 1911); I. Bikerman, *Materialy k zakonoproektu ob otmene cherty evreiskoi osedlosti. Ekonomicheskaia deiatelnost' evreev*, vypusk pervyi (St. Petersburg, 1911); *O cherte evreiskoi osedlosti*, produced by Obshchestvo rasprostraneniia pravil'nykh svedenii o evreiakh i evreistve, vypusk I (Moscow, 1911); and Yulii Gessen, 'Zakonodatel'stvo o zhitel'stve evreev v Rossii', in *Russkaia Mysl*, 1911, vol. 5, no. XII, pp. 82–98.

172. See *Der Fraind*, no. 49, 27 February 1911, p. 3; and Paul Miliukov, *Political Memoirs, 1905–1917*, edited by Arthur Mendel (Ann Arbor, 1967) pp. 214–5.

173. For the parliamentary action see *Razsvet*, no. 18, 1 May 1911, col. 17; and the first anti-Semitic article in connection with the Beilis Case in Russkaia Znamia see *Der Fraind*, no. 88, 19 April 1911, p. 1.

174. For instance, one hundred Jewish families were expelled from Riazan with the argument that they did not exercise their profession. In Kishinev the authorities rejected the local ORPE's request to open a Russian-Jewish library in Kishinev by referring to ORPE's statute which only allowed the Central Committee to do so. The difficulties which were reported from Kursk did not, however, prevent the local Jewish population from striving for education. See *Razsvet*, no. 11, 13 March 1911, cols 37–38.

175. ELO had founded branches in all the bigger cities of the Pale as well as in cities such as Baku, Irkutsk, and Tomsk. See *Razsvet*, no. 28, 10 July 1911, cols 3–5. Officially, the decision was justified by the argument that the Society had founded many branches in the provinces which they were not able to control, as according to various reports of the governors, these branches did not only deal with literary activity but with politics. See *Der Fraind*, no. 151, 3 July 1911, p. 1.

176. In St. Petersburg university out of 2,250 free places only 1,400 new students were admitted, and among them only sixty-seven Jews. See *Der Fraind*, no. 182, 8 August 1911, p. 3; for a summary of all these new restrictions see I. Kleinman, 'Antisemitizm v Rossii v 1911 godu', in *Ezhegodnik gazety Rech' 1912*, pp. 524–32.

177. He started his speech with the sentence 'in Kiev on 1 September 1911 the Jew Mordko Bogrov ...'. See *Razsvet*, no. 52, 23 December 1911, cols 3–4.

178. Ibid., p. 4.

## 5 THE 'DARK YEARS' AFTER STOLYPIN: ANTI-SEMITISM, CO-OPERATION AND THE PEAK OF 'ORGANIC WORK'

1. See Shapiro, *The History of ORT*, pp. 53–71.

2. In a meeting in April 1911, the Society reported that in 1910 it had organized a series of public lectures in and outside the Pale, distributed books and brochures on the Jewish question in 18,000 exemplars. See *Der Fraind*, no. 94, 26 April 1911, p. 3. Leading members of the Society were Vinaver, Sliozberg, rabbi Maze, Garkavi and Dr. Chlenov; the Society's newspaper, appearing in 1912 in Moscow, was called *Izvestiia Obshchestva rasprostraneniia pravilnykh svedenii o evreiakh i evreistve*. Its first edition (1912, no. 1) included the society's statutes which stated as its main task the struggle against false apprehension of Jews and Judaism (§1); its mode of operation would be the organization of public lectures and many further editorial activities (§2). The Izvestiia covered issues raised by anti-Semites. See for example S. An-skii, 'Otechestvennaia voina i evrei', in ibid., pp. 53–84 – describing the Jews' share in the war against Napoleon, and Mar-bad, 'Voinskaia povinnost i evrei', ibid., pp. 172–195 – both directed against the anti-Jewish misrepresentation of Jews as cowards; the latter pointed out that Jews were overrepresented in the Russian army.

3. On 21 April 1914, an EIO conference stated its activities of 1913 as: running the journal *Evreiskaia Starina*; having held seven scientific conferences,

organizing the section within the EINO for the study of Jewish law; editing the third volume of 'regesty i nadpisi'; and collecting archival material. See *Razsvet*, no. 17, 25 April 1914, cols 31 and 32.

4. The Gradonachalnik of St. Petersburg restricted the permission to activities in St. Petersburg only, and rejected the request of the new Society to open a club in St. Petersburg. See *Razsvet*, no. 49, 2 December 1911, col. 37; *Der Fraind*, no. 273, 28 November 1911, p. 3; and *Der Fraind*, no. 274, 29 November 1911, p. 3; the ENLO held its founding congress on 12 December 1911. About eighty people attended the meeting, which took place under the chairmanship of I. Gurevich. However, the congress did not discuss its further activity, and only elected a Central Committee consisting of twelve people, and fixed the organization's estimate of expenses at 3,000 roubles. See *Der Fraind*, no. 287, 14 December 1911, p. 1.

5. The Liberals met with support among well-known rabbis such as Dr. Katsenelson, Dr. Sh. Aronson (Kiev), Menahem Mendel (Nezhin), Dr. M.A. Aizenshtat (St. Petersburg) and S.M. Treinin who called on all rabbis to protest against the blood libel. See *Der Fraind*, no. 116, 23 May 1911, p. 1. The rabbis followed with telegrams expressing their disgust, see *Der Fraind*, no. 119, 26 May 1911, p. 3; one protest letter was signed by 500 rabbis, and sent to the newspapers *Rossiia* and *Novoe Vremia*, see *Der Fraind*, no. 124, 1 June 1911, p. 1; another resolution was signed by the chairman of the Rabbi Commission, L.M. Tsirelson, 297 community rabbis and 13 Zaddikim. In it they pointed out that a series of popes such as Gregor IX, Clemens VI, Siksta IV and Paul III had already condemned the blood libel in official bulls. Even Tsar Aleksander I had declared in 1817 that there was no proof for the blood libel, and that this accusation was only based on prejudices. See *Razsvet*, no. 23, 5 June 1911, cols 16–18. Another protest letter was sent in November, 1911, which carried the signatures of 800 rabbis from all parts of Russia. See *Razsvet*, no. 47, 18 November 1911, cols 12 and 13.

6. The declaration stated: 'in the name of justice, reason and humanity, we raise our voice against the blaze of fanaticism and dark untruth', and it finally called on Russian society to counteract the lie of the blood libel. See *Razsvet*, no. 49, 2 December 1911, cols 21–23; see also Mark Vishniak, 'Anti-Semitism in Tsarist Russia. A Study in Government-Fostered Anti-semitism', in Koppel S. Pinson (ed.), *Essays on Anti-semitism* (New York, 1942) pp. 108–9; for Korolenko's 'engagement' in the struggle for Jewish rights and his general view of the Jewish question see Maurice Comtet, 'V.G. Korolenko et la Question Juive en Russie', in *Cahiers du monde russe et sovietique*, 10 (1969) pp. 228–56.

7. See S. Elpatevskii, 'Evreiskii vopros', in *Russkoe Bogatstvo*, no. 10, 1913, pp. 348–59; or M. Lvovich, 'Kontr-revoliutsiia i evrei', in *Russkoe Bogatstvo*, no. 12, 1911, pp. 43–58; for Korolenko's campaign against anti-Semitism, and his activities as a correspondent for various Russian newspapers during the Beilis trial, see Frank Häusler, 'V.G. Korolenkos Kampf gegen den Antisemitismus', in *Wissenschaftliche Zeitschrift der Martin-Luther-Universität Halle-Wittenberg*, X/1 (February 1961) pp. 237–48.

8. See V. Medem, 'Evreiskii vopros v Rossii', in *Vestnik Evropy*, no. 4, 1911, pp. 271–84; V. Zhabotinskii, 'Pisma o natsional'nostiakh i oblastiakh', in *Russkaia Mysl*, no. 1, 1913, pp. 95–114.

9. The French protest was published in *Novyi Voskhod*, no. 12–13, 22 March 1912, cols 21 and 22; for the joint German–Austrian protest signed by scientists, artists, politicians and industrialists see *Novyi Voskhod*, no. 11, 15 March 1912, cols 8–10; for the English protest letter see *Novyi Voskhod*, no. 18, 4 May 1912, cols 27–31; the *Jewish Chronicle* was very well informed and reported on everything affecting Russian Jews. See the special section of the Chronicle designated to Russia in the respective years.

10. For Lucien Wolf's struggle against granting loans to the Russian government through his journal *Darkest Russia* see Zosa Szajkowski, 'Paul Nathan, Lucien Wolf, Jacob H. Schiff and the Jewish Revolutionary Movements in Eastern Europe, 1903–1917', in *Jewish Social Studies*, 29 (1967) pp. 3–26, and especially pp. 19–20; for the West European bankers' 'engagement' see C.C. Aronsfeld, 'Jewish Bankers and the Tsar', in *Jewish Social Studies*, 35 (1973) pp. 87–104; for Jacob Schiff's activity in this matter see his letter of February 20 1911 to US president Taft, in Cyrus Adler, *Jacob H. Schiff. His Life and Letters*, vol. II (New York, 1928) pp. 147–9.

11. See *Der Fraind*, no. 282, 8 December 1911, p. 1; for more details see Naomi W. Cohen, 'The Abrogation of the Russo-American Treaty of 1832', in *Jewish Social Studies*, 25 (1963) no. 1, pp. 3–41; and Best, *To Free a People*, pp. 166–201. One example for the protest campaign in the Unted States can be seen in *The United States Passport and Russia* by Hon. Rufus B. Smith, a paper read before the Temple Club of Congregation Bene Israel Cincinnati, April 5 1911, and printed by resolution of the club.

12. The trial was reported in detail in all Jewish newspapers, for instance, *Der Fraind*, no. 221, 25 September 1913, p. 1; *Novyi Voskhod*, no. 42, 16 October 1913, cols 5–33; no. 43, 24 October 1913, cols 6–26; no. 44, 31 October 1913, cols 6–57; and D. Pasmanik, 'Tragizm' malen'koi dramy', in *Razsvet*, no. 41, 9 October 1913, cols 3–5; extensive coverage of the Beilis Case was also given throughout the period in the respective numbers of the London *Jewish Chronicle*, and in its supplement *Darkest Russia*; the Beilis Case itself lies outside the scope of this study. For a detailed account see Maurice Samuel, *Blood Accusation. The Strange History of the Beiliss Case* (London, 1967); Hans Rogger, 'The Beiliss Case: Anti-Semitism and Politics in the Reign of Nicholas II', in Rogger, *Jewish Policies*, pp. 40–55; Löwe, *Antisemitismus*, pp. 134–45; and Alexander B. Tager, *The Decay of Czarism: the Beiliss Trial* (Philadelphia, 1935); and finally, see the memoirs of Beiliss lawyer O.O. Gruzenberg, *Yesterday: Memoirs of a Russian-Jewish Lawyer* (Berkeley, Los Angeles and London, 1981) pp. 104–24; a nationalist-conservative Russian Duma deputy criticized the instigators of the Beilis Case for the fact that 'they could not have given a better propaganda weapon to Russian Jews than to pursue with the blood libel'. See V.V. Shulgin, *The Years: Memoirs of a Member of the Russian Duma, 1906–1917*, translated by Tanya Davis (New York, 1984) pp. 102–23.

13. See Miliukov, *Political Memoirs*, p. 285.

14. For more information on this trial see *Razsvet*, no. 24, 13 June 1914, cols 1–3; *Novyi Voskhod*, no. 18, 8 May 1914, cols 23–4; *Novyi Voskhod*, no. 22, 5 June 1914, cols 10–16; and *Novyi Voskhod*, no. 23, 12 June 1914, cols 12–19.

15.   Jewish Liberals called on Russian Jews to prepare for the forthcoming elections to the Fourth Duma, and to inquire as early as possible among the candidates of the city curiae about their views with respect to the Jewish question; as far as the tactics in the elections were concerned, they suggested nominating Jewish electors in those constituencies where Jews would have a chance to get elected. See *Novyi Voskhod*, no. 26, 30 June 1911, cols 1–4.

16.   The prospective all-Jewish congress was to consist of the electors of all the previous Duma elections, all the former Jewish Duma deputies, community leaders, representatives of the Jewish welfare organizations, and the Jewish Loan and Saving Co-operatives. The task of this congress was to organize an election committee which would run the election campaign. Thus, Russian Jewry could be unified and organized, and would be able to finally run Jewish politics. See *Der Fraind*, no. 86, 16 April 1912, p. 2. Jewish Liberals agreed that election committees of all Jewish organizations should be organized to run the election campaign by hammering out common election tactics. These gatherings should also be used to discuss further social work, and the conditions for the convocation of an all-Jewish congress. See *Der Fraind*, no. 87, 17 April 1912, p. 2. However, the all-Jewish congress did not evolve beyond the theory stage until 1918. Only the first step, the organization of election committees, materialized.

17.   See *Der Fraind*, no. 143, 26 June 1912, p. 3, and no. 147, 1 July 1912, p. 1; the Jewish Duma candidates came from the same strata as in previous elections. To name a few candidates: the lawyers Stachunskii and Pollak (Dvinsk), Berezovskii and Polonskii (Ekaterinoslav), the doctor Yarin and the former state rabbi, the lawyer Freidenberg (Kremenchug). See *Novyi Voskhod*, no. 39, 27 July 1912, col. 20; or the lawyers Nevelshtein, doctor Khasin (Kherson), state rabbi Temkin (Elizavetgrad), engineer Liubarskii and the lawyer Burkser (Mariupol), bank director Finkelshtein and the lawyer Yudin (Vitebsk). See ibidem, no. 40, 4 October 1912, col. 13; for the Jewish election committee in Vilna see *Der Fraind*, no. 154, 9 July 1912, p. 1.

18.   In one of the police districts in Odessa, civil servants changed regulations so that in order to gain the right to vote Jews were required to have had an apartment in the city since ten years instead of one; or, in many cities, many Jewish voters were simply disfranchised, for instance in Kiev and Kherson. See *Der Fraind*, no. 148, 2 July 1912, p. 1; the editor of the Jewish newspaper *Hatsefira*, Sokolov was deleted from the electors' list by the authorities in Belostok by referring to the fact that he had the right to vote in Warsaw, but not in Belostok. See *Novyi Voskhod*, no. 29, 19 July 1912, col. 15; for more information on the elections in general, and the machinations etc. in particular see Ya.L., 'Vybory', in *Ezhegodnik gazety Rech' 1913*, pp. 198–239.

19.   For instance, in Ekaterinoslav, see *Der Fraind*, no. 190, 20 August 1912, p. 3; and Minsk, see *Der Fraind*, no. 203, 6 September 1912, p. 1.

20.   See *Der Fraind*, no. 134, 13 June 1912, p. 1; *Novyi Voskhod*, no. 25, 21 June 1912, cols 1–3; and *Der Fraind*, no. 147, 1 July 1912, p. 3.

21.   In Kremenchug, the SRN called on the local population to fight Jewish equality and the strikes which supposedly ruin trade. Therefore, one should

vote for the 'real Russian people'. See *Der Fraind*, no. 163, 19 July 1912, p. 1. In Ekaterinoslav, the governor called the local rabbi, and threatened him openly with consequences, should the Jews continue their activities in the election campaign. See *Novyi Voskhod*, no. 27, 5 July 1912, cols 1–3.

22. In the gubernia of Volynia an intensive election campaign was only reported from the cities Zhitomir and Rovno, while in all the other places a certain indifference dominated among the Jewish community activists. See *Der Fraind*, no. 136, 15 June 1912, p. 1.

23. The Octobrists withdrew their candidate in the government of Tver once they realized that their chances were deteriorating. See *Der Fraind*, no. 75, 3 April 1912, p. 1. Apparently, the Central Committee of the Octobrists increasingly received news from its provincial committees that the election prospects were not good as in many places the Octobrists did not even have enough members to set up an election committee. Therefore, they proposed to set up agreements with Nationalists and the ultra-right. The Central Committee did not agree, however, and instead proposed to await the further development of the elections. See *Der Fraind*, no. 148, 2 July 1912, p. 1. Similar statements on the Octobrists' less successful election campaign were reported in Ya.L., 'Vybory', pp. 229–32. The author especially celebrated the KD victory in Riga, Moscow and St. Petersburg; see also A.S. Izgoev, 'Ot tretei Dumy k chetvertoi', in *Ezhegodnik gazety Rech' 1913*, pp. 195–6.

24. The Jewish Nationalists anticipated that the Kadets would thereby be forced to withdraw their candidate Nikolskii. See *Der Fraind*, no. 166, 23 July 1912, p. 1; ibid., no. 170, 27 July 1912, p. 1. For the Zionists' decision to nominate Zhabotinskii, ibid., no. 137, 17 June 1912, p. 1.

25. The alliance between Kadets and ENG was confirmed in an interview of the Kadet Kolubakin with *Der Fraind*. He argued that it was impossible to run two oppositional candidates in the second curia, while in the first curia which was separated according to nationalities, the opposition's best candidate was Sliozberg. Therefore, while the ENG would support the Kadets' candidate in the second city curia, Nikolskii, the Kadets would vote for Sliozberg in the first curia. See *Der Fraind*, no. 147, 1 July 1912, p. 1; also S. Kal'manovich, 'Odesskoe evreistvo i evreiskaia kandidatury v 4-iu Gosudarstvennuiu Dumu', in *Novyi Voskhod*, no. 25, 21 June 1912, cols 4–7.

26. *Der Fraind* reproached the ENG with meddling into too many things, and called the Jewish Liberals 'St. Petersburg Monopolists', and Sliozberg's action *Shtadlanut*. It supported running its own candidate in the second curia in order 'to teach the Kadets and the "Monopolists" a lesson'. See *Der Fraind*, no. 135, 14 June 1912, p. 1.

27. Sliozberg stated in an interview with *Odesskiia Novosti* that the Jewish candidate should not be under the flag of any party but solely under that of the Jewish nation. However, as a deputy to the All-Russian Duma, the Jewish deputy had to protect both Jewish as well as general interests. He raised the autonomist demand for equality for all nationalities with autonomy regarding their own cultural activities. Sliozberg concluded that Jewish equality was a question of historical justice, and ought to be defended in public. See *Der Fraind*, no. 84, 13 April 1912, p. 1. Sliozberg's

candidature in Odessa became possible as he had bought a house in Odessa already before the end of the Third Duma. See Sliozberg, *Dela*, p. 313.

28. See *Der Fraind*, no. 242, 28 October 1912, p. 1; the SRN distributed leaflets among Jewish voters, threatening pogroms in case of the election of a Jewish deputy from Odessa. The threat proved to be effective: Dr. Himelfarb together with twenty-one other Jews sent a letter in which they assured the SRN that they would not go to the polls as 'occupation with politics was a dangerous thing'. The SRN committee printed this letter in 50,000 exemplars and distributed them at the polling stations. See *Der Fraind*, no. 193, 23 August 1912, p. 1. Sliozberg accused the election commission in Odessa – which was headed by the anti-Semite Sosnovskii, and consisted exclusively of members of the SRN – of manipulating the elections; See Sliozberg, *Dela*, p. 314. The final result of the Odessa elections showed for the First City Curia: 763 votes for Sliozberg, 976 for Professor Levashev; the Second Curia: 5207 for the Kadet Nikolskii, 1163 for the worker Romanovskii, and 10,283 votes for Bishop Anatoli. See *Novyi Voskhod*, no. 44, 1 November 1912, col. 26; and 'Sionisty i odesskie vybory', in *Evreiskaia Khronika* [Kishinev], no. 40, 10 October 1912, cols 15–19.

29. See *Der Fraind*, no. 178, 6 August 1912, p. 2; and *Evreiskaia Khronika*, no. 40, 10 October 1912, col. 22f.

30. See *Der Fraind*, no. 205, 10 September 1912, p. 2; and Sliozberg, *Dela*, p. 316. For more detail on the Polish-Jewish relations in general, and the Warsaw elections in particular see Frank Golczewski, *Polnisch-Jüdische Beziehungen, 1881–1922. Eine Studie zur Geschichte des Antisemitismus in Osteuropa* (Wiesbaden, 1981) pp. 90–120.

31. *Der Fraind*, no. 223, 5 October 1912, p. 2; I.A. Kleinman, 'Pered vyborami v Pol'she', in *Novyi Voskhod*, no. 24, 15 June 1911, cols 5–7, and no. 33, 16 August 1911, cols 5–7.

32. *Der Fraind*, no. 237, 22 October 1912, p. 1; and *Novyi Voskhod*, no. 43, 25 October 1912, col. 11–14; Dubnov shared the general opinion – to vote for the Polish-Socialist candidate – but like Vinaver made it dependent on the candidate's recognition of Jewish autonomy rights, see Dubnov, *Kniga Zhizni*, p. 138.

33. For more information on the anti-Jewish boycott movement following the elections, see Golczewski, *Polnisch-Jüdische Beziehungen*, pp. 106–21.

34. The election of Dr. Bomash in Lodz was no surprise as the Jews commanded the majority in four of six districts. See S. Galperin, 'Predvyborniia perspektivy', in *Novyi Voskhod*, no. 31, 2 August 1912, pp. 14–16. Dr. Bomash was born in Kovno in 1861, finished the local gymnasium, and finished his study in Moscow in 1885. He lived in Lodz since 1892. Despite the fact that he did not belong to any party, later in the Duma he joined the Kadets' faction. See *Der Fraind*, no. 241, 26 October 1912, p. 1. Der Fraind was not particularly pleased about the election of Dr. Gurevich and Dr. Bomash, arguing that both were unknown in Jewish society. See *Der Fraind*, no. 242, 28 October 1912, p. 1.

35. The right-wing seats increased from 50 to 64. See Hagen, *Die Entfaltung*, pp. 312–17.

36. See *Der Fraind*, no. 260, 18 November 1912, p. 2. For Gurevich's statement see *Der Fraind*, no. 265, 23 November 1912, p. 1.

37. See *Der Fraind*, no. 262, 20 November 1912, p. 1.

38. See *Der Fraind*, no. 277, 7 December 1912, p. 3.

39. See *Der Fraind*, no. 284, 16 December 1912, p. 1; and *Der Fraind*, no. 287, 19 December 1912, p. 1. He referred to the expulsions of Jewish artisans and students, and especially to the expulsions of Jews from the countryside in the gubernia of Poltava. See *Der Fraind*, no. 288, 20 December 1912, p. 3.

40. Makarov had asked the rabbis to send him reports on problems among the Jewish communities, and the rabbis had already started preparing the elections to the commission. See *Der Fraind*, no. 58, 8 March 1913, p. 3.

41. During the tricentenary of the Romanov dynasty Sliozberg had asked state rabbi Shneerson to use his connections to Maklakov to present the request, which was turned down with the argument that the Jews would always use such a gathering to discuss politics. See Shneerson, *Lebn un Kampf*, pp. 437–55.

42. See *Der Fraind*, no. 51, 28 February 1913, p. 1. It was also reported that at the last Kadet conference, the Jewish question was not discussed. This foreshadowed Kadet tactics regarding the Jewish question, which were dominated by fear of anti-Jewish outrages in the Duma. See *Der Fraind*, no. 35, 10 February 1913, p. 3.

43. This article 87 gave the Prime Minister the right to pass laws in an emergency when Duma and State Council were not in session. Sliozberg was also frustrated because his complaint against the irregularities during the Odessa elections was buried in the Duma. See *Der Fraind*, no. 247, 2 November 1912, p. 1; and *Der Fraind*, no. 248, 4 November 1912, p. 1; ibid., no. 68, 20 March 1913, p. 2. Kokovtsev's shares anyway declined after the summer of 1912, when the Tsar had 'shocked' him by offering Kokovtsev the post as Russian ambassador to Berlin. This may have resulted from Kokovtsev's refusal to follow Stolypin's policies. See Miliukov, *Political Memoirs*, pp. 283–4; Löwe, *Antisemitismus*, p. 145.

44. See *Razsvet*, no. 11, 14 March 1914, col. 31.

45. The bill demanded: first, that the citizens of all nationalities in Russia should be equal before the law; second, no Russian citizen, regardless of sex and confession could be limited in any laws on the basis of his origin or affiliation to any nationality; third, all the laws, central regulations and supplements to laws which restricted the Jews in any sphere of social and state life should be abolished. See *Razsvet*, no. 14–15, 11 April 1914, col. 22; the Social Democrats' action is briefly mentioned in Nora Levin, *The Jews in the Soviet Union since 1917. Paradox of Survival*, vol. I (New York and London, 1990) p. 21.

46. To put it in Hildermeier's terms: 'Social and political change in Russia surpassed the development of the political-administrative institutions'. See Manfred Hildermeier, *Die Russische Revolution 1905–1921* (Frankfurt/M., 1989) pp. 33–50).

47. Löwe described the roots of late Tsarist Russian anti-Semitism as the struggle over the modernization of Russia between more reform-oriented and conservative elements within the government. The first became identified with the ministry of finance which favoured general economic reforms for the sake of a freely-developing economy; the latter with the conservative

ministry of interior which opposed the modernization process, regarding it as the work of revolutionaries – above all Jews – whose overall aim was the overthrow of the regime and the ruling classes. See Löwe, *Antisemitismus*.

48. See Totomiants, *Kooperatsiia*, pp. 25–70.

49. Löwe mentioned energetic protests of Russian economic bodies such as stock exchange committees, chairmen of the fairs, and entrepreneurs' organizations, as they were afraid that the nationalization of trade and industry would seriously damage Russian economy. See Löwe, *Antisemitismus*, p. 140; in 1912, the Moscow Manufacturers' Association submitted a memorandum to the Council of Ministers which pointed to the fact that anti-Jewish restrictions also damage the economic situation of the non-Jewish population. See I.M. Dijur, 'Jews in the Russian Economy', in Frumkin, *Russian Jewry*, pp. 142–3.

50. This demand was energetically pushed forward by the Nationalist Party. See Löwe, *Antisemitismus*, p. 131.

51. See Arcadius Kahan, 'The Impact of Industrialization in Tsarist Russia on the Socioeconomic Conditions of the Jewish Population', in Roger Weiss (ed.), *Essays in Jewish Social and Economic History: Arcadius Kahan* (Chicago and London, 1986) pp. 1–69; here p. 10.

52. Between 1905 and 1909, the information bureau for emigration of the EKO had increased the number of bureau from 122 to 433, which served 23.5 per cent of the 1,846 localities where Jews were allowed to live. These bureau provided the would-be emigrants with technical information, such as where to buy the cheapest ship tickets, which ship to take, which country to go to and so on. They distributed brochures and leaflets in Yiddish and Russian. In 1909, a total of 12,895 Jews emigrated out of which were 5,929 Russian [of which 4,325 (around 72 per cent) were artisans and 1,604 merchants and employees] and 6,966 Polish Jews [5,871 artisans (84.7 per cent) and 1,095 merchants and employees]. See Jakob Lestschinsky, 'Die Tätigkeit des Informationsbureaus der 'Jewish Colonisation Association' in Rußland', in *Zeitschrift für Demographie und Statistik der Juden*, no. 2 (February 1911) pp. 21–2; according to a report of the Odessa branch from 1907, out of 4,507 Jewish emigrants, 427 were afraid to live in Odessa, 396 had invitations from American relatives, 211 were unemployed, 552 justified it with the will to engage themselves in agriculture; the rest (2,921) went for a variety of other reasons. See *Zeitschrift für Demographie und Statistik der Juden*, no. 5 (May 1908) pp. 78–9. These numbers indicate that Jews did not only emigrate because of anti-Semitism or unemployment, but for all sorts of reasons.

53. To mention some main Jewish centres: Odessa's Jewish population grew from about 20,000 (1850) to 160,000 (1910); Ekaterinoslav's from 2,000 to 70,000 (1910); Lodz from 2,000 (1850) to 100,000 (1897) to decrease due to emigration to 80,000 (1910); Vilna from 15,000 (1850) to 70,000 (1910), and finally, Warsaw became the biggest Jewish centre with 280,000 Jewish inhabitants in 1910. See Baron, *The Russian Jew*, pp. 65–8; Lestschinsky mentioned slightly different data, but the trend remains the same. See Jacob Lestschinsky, *Dos Yudishe Folk in Tsiffern* (Berlin, 1922) p. 71. For data on the urbanization process in the gubernii of the Pale see pp. 52–64.

54. See Arcadius Kahan, 'Notes on Jewish Entrepreneurship in Tsarist Russia',

in Weiss, *Essays in Jewish Social and Economic History*, pp. 82–100; and B. Brutskus, 'Die sozial-ökonomische Lage der Juden in Rußland von 1905 bis jetzt', in *Zeitschrift für Demograpie und Statistik der Juden*, no. 1 (January–February 1924) pp. 4–10; no. 2 (March–April 1924) pp. 42–51; and no. 3–4 (May–July 1924) pp. 83–5; these positive signs for Jewish handicraft were already reported for 1906, see S. Margolin, 'Die Entwicklung des jüdischen Handwerks in Russland', in *Zeitschrift für Demographie und Statistik der Juden*, no. 4 (April 1906) pp. 148–51.

55. For the Kishinev cooperative see *Der Fraind*, no. 232, 11 October 1911, p. 3; for Zhitomir see ibid., no. 255, 7 November 1911, p. 3.

56. See *Razsvet*, no. 38–9, 18 September 1911, col. 53; and *Der Fraind*, no. 213, 15 September 1911, p. 3.

57. L. Zak was the author of a Russian version of one of those books with the title 'Forms of Economic Self-Help among Artisans'. It touched upon various topics such as the credit co-operatives, cooperative enterprises, purchase of raw materials and so on. See Shapiro, *History of ORT*, p. 66.

58. See *Der Fraind*, no. 236, 16 October 1911, p. 3.

59. See *Razsvet*, no. 41, 9 October 1911, cols 24–5; and *Novyi Voskhod*, no. 40, 6 October 1911, cols 16–20.

60. For the foundation of the Society in Belostok see *Der Fraind*, no. 209, 8 September 1910, p. 3; and for Dvinsk see *Der Fraind*, no. 167, 21 July 1911, p. 3. Apparently, the foundation of the Society in Dvinsk was encouraged by EKO which had promised financial aid and materialized by local communal activists.

61. The EKO was founded by Baron de Hirsch in 1891 with the intention of solving the Jewih problem by resettling Russian Jews in Argentine. EKO switched to training of artisans and education of Jewish farmers. Therefore, since the second half of the 1890s EKO became increasingly involved in Russian-Jewish affairs. For more general information on the EKO see Theodore Norman, *An Outstretched Arm. A History of the Jewish Colonization Association* (London, Boston and Melbourne, 1985).

62. For the opening of the new section at the Vilna school see *Der Fraind*, no. 167, 21 July 1911, p. 3. Apparently thirteen students had finished the course by the end of August, 1911, and even found employment in the factories. See *Der Fraind*, no. 200, 29 August 1911, p. 3. According to Shapiro, the 'drivers project was privately founded by M. Ginzburg'. See Shapiro, *History of ORT*, pp. 64–6; for a very brief description of ORT activity in this period see Jack Rader, *By the Skill of their Hands. The Story of ORT* (Geneva, 1970) pp. 14–16.

63. See *Der Fraind*, no. 35, 9 February 1912, p. 3.

64. See *Der Fraind*, no. 214, 16 September 1911, p. 4.

65. According to his report, the artisans' schools were attended by 2,391 apprentices. The schools were lacking a unified school type as some of them had secular and others religious character, the masters to whom the apprentices were given were not selected due to their skills but to their need of apprentices. In some schools no apprentices of the second or third year of training were registered. Furthermore, a control organ was to be set up for the training of the apprentices in the workshops. Finally, additional schools which were to be free of charge, and were to improve the general education

and technical training of the apprentices, were to be organized. Apart from general subjects, the syllabus would consist of the teaching of graphic skills and the most important aspects of the respective handicraft. See *Razsvet*, no. 42, 14 October 1911, col. 17/18; and *Novyi Voskhod*, no. 40, 6 October 1911, col. 19/20. The chairman of the meeting was M.B. Gurevich; present was the Committee member Sliozberg.

66. See Löwe, 'From Charity to Social Policy', pp. 17–18; the statistics on the Jewish artisans' schools showed the following dates: in 1910, the schools saw an increase of 100 apprentices – in comparison to 1909 – and a total number of 1,470 apprentices of whom, however, only 164 finished the course, and 348 left the schools before the end of the course. According to the report the low percentage of graduates were caused by: first, the poverty among Russian Jews which forced the children to make money earlier; second, they joined private workshops as they were free of charge and guaranteed a certain income; third, emigration; and finally some apprentices proved incapable for certain handicraft. However, the majority of the graduates of the courses found employment quickly. The eighteen schools cost 200,000 roubles per year out of which 90,000 roubles were paid for material and wages in the workshops. The statistics mentioned a turnover of the workshops of 105,000 roubles per year. The sixteen professional schools for girls had 3,118 apprentices, of whom 151 had finished the course and 738 had left before the end. Ninety per cent of the graduates found, however, employment in the field. The costs were 115,000 roubles per year, and the turnover of the workshops was 10–15,000 roubles per year. See *Der Fraind*, no. 297, 26 December 1911, p. 2; one year later the artisans' schools showed only a slight increase as the report on 1912 mentioned the existence of nineteen professional schools for boys numbering 1,935, and thirteen for girls numbering 1,060. While 181 boys had finished the course, only 135 girls did so. However, the great majority continued to work in the profession, while most found employment in big factories and only 14.9 per cent joined small handicraft workshops. See *Der Fraind*, no. 233, 17 October 1912, p. 3.

67. According to a survey organized by ORT and carried out by Margolin among 1,223 Jewish tailors in Vilna, Warsaw, Berdichev and Busin (Poland) showed that especially the seamstresses profited from the evening courses as 56.1 per cent (as opposed to 53.8 per cent among the tailors) of all seamstresses in Vilna knew how to write and read Russian and Yiddish, 30.2 per cent in Warsaw, 27.7 per cent in Berdichev, and 16.4 per cent in Busin. See Sara Rabinovitsch-Margolin, 'Zur Bildungsstatistik der jüdischen Arbeiter in Rußland', *Zeitschrift für Demographie und Statistik der Juden*, no. 11 (November 1913) pp. 153–60.

68. For the credit co-operatives see Wlad. W. Kaplun-Kogan, 'Jüdische Kreditgesellschaften auf Gegenseitigkeit in Rußland', in *Zeitschrift für Demographie und Statistik der Juden*, no. 6 (June 1913) pp. 89–92. He basically summarized what Moses Silberfarb had written on the Credit Co-operatives in Razsvet. See Dr.M. Zilberfarb, 'Evreiskiia obshchestva vzaimnago kredita', in *Razsvet*, no. 6, 8 February 1913, pp. 5–8; no. 7, 15 February 1913, pp. 15–16; no. 8, 22 February 1913, pp. 2–4; no. 10, 8 March 1913, pp. 7–10.

69. See S.O.M. [Margolin?], 'S'ezd deiateli po melkomu kreditu i sel'sko-khoziaistvennoi kooperatsii', in *Novyi Voskhod*, no. 11, 15 March 1912, col. 11; see also the following reports S.O.M.'s in *Novyi Voskhod*, no. 12–13, 22 March 1912, cols 18–22, no. 14, 5 April 1912, cols 13–20.

70. More than forty representatives of Jewish Loan and Saving Co-operatives were present at this congress. See *Der Fraind*, no. 62, 13 March 1912, p. 3. The total number of participants was 700, of whom 100 were Jewish. The Jewish participants were represented in the 'legislative commission' by the ORT activists I.A. Blium, L.S. Zak and S.B. Ratner. See S. Segal', 'Itogi kooperativnago s'ezda', in *Novyi Voskhod*, no. 12–13, 22 March 1912, cols 10–13.

71. See S. Segal, 'Itogi kooperativnaia s'ezda', in *Novyi Voskhod*, no. 12–13, 22 March 1912, cols 10–13.

72. Consumer unions existing in 1916 included: 'Kooperatsiia' (Moscow – 90,000 members); 'Vpered' (St. Petersburg – 502,000); 'Solidarnost' (Kharkov – 18,000); 'Samopomoshch' (Samara – 17,000); 'Osnova' (Ekaterinodar – 16,000); 'Trudovaia Kopeika' (Nikolaev – 14,000); 'V Edinenii Sila' (Ivanovo-Voznesensk – 23,000); and 'Zhizn' (Kiev – 11,000). For more information see Totomiants, *Kooperatsiia*, pp. 25–70.

73. In Lodz, the Jewish textile entrepreneurs, Markus Kutner & Son and Zilberblat agreed to engage Jewish weavers at the mechanized looms; in Tomashevo, the Jewish entrepreneur Borenshtein had set up a factory employing exclusively Jewish work force; and in Zdunskaia Volia, 2,000 Jewish women and children were already working at mechanized looms. See Kh.D. Gurevich, 'Chto dal nam 1911 god v sotsial'no-ekonomicheskoi oblasti?', in *Novyi Voskhod*, no. 1, 5 January 1912, cols 7–8.

74. See *Novyi Voskhod*, no. 15, 12 April 1912, col. 15.

75. Brutskus stated that the tobacco industry of Bessarabia was in Jewish hands; that the peasants in the governments of Minsk and Grodno complained about a Jewish monopoly in vegetable gardening; and that the Jews took the leading role in hop-culture in Volynia. See N. Dain, 'V Obshchestve remeslennago i zemledel'cheskago Truda', in *Novyi Voskhod*, no. 40, 4 October 1912, pp. 7–11; these successes in agriculture were also reported in Gurevich's annual report on the economic situation of Russian Jewry in 1912 in *Novyi Voskhod*. According to him, the successes in many fields were based on innovations introduced by the Jews: in viticulture the Jews secured a bigger harvest by introducing measures against the vine-louse; the farmers' co-operatives had provided the farmers with seeds, tools and dairy cattle, taken care of leasing land and the sale of agricultural products. Success in Jewish agricultural colonies was based on the intensification of farming. In vegetable gardening a new method for preserving vegetables had opened up markets far away. See Dr. Kh.D. Gurevich, 'Ekonomicheskaia zhizn' russkago evreistva v 1912 godu', in *Novyi Voskhod*, no. 3, 17 January 1913, pp. 12–16. For more information on the history of the Jewish agricultural colonies in Russia, and the various fields of activity – mentioned above – see J.M. Isler, *Rückkehr der Juden zur Landwirtschaft. Beitrag zur Geschichte der Landwirtschaftlichen Kolonisation der Juden in verschiedenen Ländern* (Frankfurt/M., 1929) pp. 14–36.

76. According to Kahan, the dietary laws were not the main reason for the

preference of Jewish entrepreneurs to employ non-Jews. He gave four reasons which determined this behaviour: non-Jewish workers were cheaper; non-Jewish skilled workers resisted the admission of Jewish workers; entrepreneurs feared possible competition of journeymen who after their vocational training might use this know how to set up their own enterprise; and finally, 'the fear of infusing a radical ferment into the labour force'. See Arcadius Kahan, 'The Impact of Industrialization', p. 41. However, Kahan pointed to the fact that Jewish factory labour in the Pale of Settlement grew, above all, due to the Jewish entrepreneurs. Ibidem, 'Notes on Jewish Entrepreneurship in Tsarist Russia', p. 98.

77. See *Novyi Voskhod*, no. 21, 30 May 1914, pp. 3–5; see also *Otchet' Obshchestva Remeslennago i Zemledelel'cheskago Truda sredi Evreev v Rossii za 1913* (St. Petersburg, 1914) pp. 60–63; since 1910, ORT had continuously invested in surveys of the economic situation which were, however, mainly assigned to ORT's travelling agents. See *Otchet za 1910*, p. 35 (3,256 roubles); and *Otchet za 1912*, p. 53 (2,000 roubles).

78. The new society specified its activity as being the collection of statistic material, which it intended to gather from various archives, such as official (that is governmental, public or city administration) or archives of the artisans' administrations and institutions which were in charge of the Korobka and other taxes. The collected material was to be scientifically examined, presented and discussed in public lectures and on conferences. See *Der Fraind*, no. 95, 26 April 1913, p. 2.

79. See *Der Fraind*, no. 109, 13 May 1913, p. 3.

80. See *Der Fraind*, no. 117, 22 May 1913, p. 3; and *Der Fraind*, no. 149, 1 July 1913, p. 3.

81. Another section was the one on the co-operative societies. The congress' chairman was Count Geiden who had opened the congress by calling on the participants not to hold any political or national speeches. See *Der Fraind*, no. 178, 4 August 1913, p. 3; for the resolution see *Der Fraind*, no. 179, 5 August 1913, p. 1.

82. See Löwe, 'From Charity to Social Policy', p. 14; and Norman, *An Outstretched Arm*, pp. 46–7. Norman gives an account of the kassa movement for 1913 based on the annual EKO report.

83. Leshchinskii pointed out that the co-operatives did not intend to follow the EKO's guidance any more, and at the same time attacked EKO's 'bureaucratism'. Leshchinskii concluded his speech by stating that the co-operative movement had grown up, and no longer needed EKO. On the contrary, EKO hindered a normal development of the Jewish co-operative movement as it did not always show an understanding for the local community activists. The EKO delegates Kh. Blum and Zak in turn rejected the reproaches, and argued that EKO had tried to reorganize the co-operatives but the co-operatives themselves did not develop enough activity. See *Der Fraind*, no. 183, 9 August 1913, p. 2. These disputes were also reported in 'Kievskii kooperativnyi s'ezd', in *Razsvet*, no. 33, 16 August 1913, col. 21–22. The committee consisted of three representatives of the four regions of the Pale of Settlement, and a special representative of the Jewish colonies. See *Der Fraind*, no. 184, 11 August 1913, p. 2.

84. See *Der Fraind*, no. 188, 15 August 1913, p. 3.

85. The resolution suggested organizing co-operatives on district levels. Special societies were to propagate the co-operative idea, collect statistics about co-operatives on the basis of statistics, and assist in the organization of a district co-operative bank. The resolution, however, also stated that such an organization should be based on the principle of legal and social equality without a distinction of nationality or religion. See *Der Fraind*, no. 184, 11 August 1913, p. 2.

86. More than half of the fifty participants came from the provinces, such as ORT's branches in Odessa, Moscow, Ekaterinoslav, Mogilev and Minsk. Brutskus suggested that ORT's efforts towards productivization of Jewish handicraft should aim at the dissemination of professional training with the aim of lifting the standard of the Jewish handicraft technique; and at the improvement of the economic conditions of production. ORT must strive in its economic activity for a further development of the artisans' co-operatives. It should, however, only initiate the co-operatives while the co-operatives themselves were to run independently. See *Razsvet*, no. 8, 21 February 1914, cols 27–8; and *Novyi Voskhod*, no. 8, 27 February 1914, cols 17–20; *Novyi Voskhod*, no. 9, 6 March 1914, cols 20–25; a full report on this ORT conference was published as a supplement to the annual report for 1914. See *Otchet' Obshchestva Remeslennago i zemledel'cheskago Truda sredi Evreev v Rossii za Rossii. Prilozhenie* (Petrograd, 1915) pp. 1–136.

87. See *Razsvet*, no. 9, 28 February 1914, cols 16–19.

88. He proposed to intensify Jewish self-initiative, and base future efforts on the study of the general conditions of small production. In order to inquire about the small production, statistical material was to be collected by surveys in as many places as possible, and should be run by local forces under the assistance of ORT. Thereafter, a person competent in statistical-economic questions would evaluate them, and the Central Committee, or if the local conditions allowed it, the local branches, should take final action. Ibid., cols 19–20.

89. The congress agreed that efforts to promote products to far away markets must be accompanied by the adaptation of local handicrafts to the needs of broader markets. Ibid., col. 20.

90. The congress prepared the budget for 1914 and discussed ORT's activity in 1913. Here, the opposition within ORT once again raised complaints against the general conduct of the organization. G.S. Voltke criticized that ORT had paid little attention to the legal situation of the artisans, and was too occupied with Jewish handicraft and the training of apprentices. While E.S. Lure underlined the importance of the two major components of ORT activity, professional training and statistical inquiries, D.S. Pasmanik demanded once again a discussion on the artisans' schools and on the fact that many apprentices left the school before the end. Sliozberg, speaking in the name of the Committee, rejected the reproaches as the Committee alone would not be able to organize the training of apprentices, and neither could it take care of all of Russia alone. See *Razsvet*, no. 22, 30 May 1914, cols 21–2.

91. See Goldscheider/Zuckerman, *The Transformation*, pp. 8–10. For the Poles' struggle against the German authorities, see Jaworski, *Handel und Gewerbe*, pp. 18–35.

92. Due to bad health, Vinaver temporarily left his post in the committee, but with Dr. L. Katsenelson, Dr. Botvinik and M.I. Sheftel, the Liberal/Autonomist wing was still dominating the Central Committee. See *Der Fraind*, no. 71, 29 March 1912, p. 2.

93. For more information on these libraries, see David Shavit, 'The Emergence of Jewish Public Libraries in Tsarist Russia', in *Journal of Library History*, 20, 3 (1985) pp. 239–52.

94. Dr. Zalkind reported that ORPE had drafted a model catalogue for Jewish and Yiddish books, published manuals giving instructions and recommendations about how to set up a library. He also reported that the insecure legal situation and the difficulties of opening a legal library had led to the organization of a new type of library: the private-social (*chastno-obshchestvennyi*) library, that is a library which officially was private. This unfortunately did not allow the libraries to become real social centres. Finally, he pointed to other grievances such as the inadequate technical facilities of many libraries, the unfortunate selection policy, as most of the newly-published books in Yiddish were 'penny dreadfuls'. See *Razsvet*, no. 2, 12 January 1914, col. 26.

95. See Totomiants, *Kooperatsiia*, pp. 120–41. He mentioned many examples where Russian Saving and Loan Co-operatives and Credit Associations contributed financially to the setting up of peoples' houses, libraries in the countryside, or donated money to the university of Moscow and so on. According to Totomiants, the Consumer Co-operatives gave about 100,000 roubles annually for national education; for examples see the Jewish Saving and Loan association of the artisans and petty traders in Kishinev, and of Zlatopol (Gub. Kiev). Both spent parts of their surplus on welfare and educational institutions. See *Razsvet*, no. 16, 19 April 1913, cols 28–9.

96. In June, 1914, the library commission of the ORPE branch in Vilna reported a constant increase of readers of the Vilna library for the past four years: 400 (1910), 900 (1911), 1,400 (1912), and 1,800 (1913). The percentage of female readers increased within this period from 20 per cent to 33 per cent of the total number of readers. See *Razsvet*, no. 23, 6 June 1914, cols 35–6; for the St. Petersburg library see *Kratkii ocherki istorii S.-Peterburgskoi biblioteki Obshchestva rasprostraneniia prosveshcheniia mezhdu evreiami v Rossii za 1872–1912 g.* (St. Petersburg, 1913); furthermore, the Moscow ORPE branch was subsidizing libraries in the gubernii Vitebsk, Mogilev and Minsk with the result that the number of readers increased, and the fees for reading decreased. See *Razsvet*, no. 2, 12 January 1914, col. 28.

97. By the end of 1913 ORPE had thirty-two branches, including branches far outside the Pale such as Irkutsk, Perm, Tula, Tomsk, Samara, Kazan and Tsaritsyn. ORPE membership increased from 227 (1864) to 677 (1890) to 3,010 (1900) to 4,650 (1909) to finally reach 7,000 in 1911. See *Obshchestvo dlia Rasprostraneniia Prosveshcheniia mezhdu Evreiami v Rossii za piat'desiat' let'. Kratkii istoricheskii ocherk* (St. Petersburg, 1913) pp. 27, 14, 31; the overall spending of all the ORPE branches rose from 821,856 roubles in 1907 to 948,796 in 1910, and by the end of 1913 finally reached 1,327,603 roubles. See *Otchet' Obshchestva dlia Rasprostraneniia Prosveshcheniia mezhdu Evreiami v Rossii za 1907* (St. Petersburg, 1908);

*Otchet' za 1910* (St. Petersburg, 1911); and *Kassovyi Otchet' Obshchestva dlia Rasprostraneniia Prosveshcheniia mezhdu Evreiami v Rossii za 1913* (St. Petersburg, 1914).

98.  The struggle of the Orthodox – mainly Hasidim – in alliance with the melameds of the traditional schools against the reform efforts of the Jewish secular elements quite often involved co-operation with the authorities, aiming at suppressing the setting up of new and modernized Jewish schools. See Löwe, 'From Charity to Social Policy', p. 21.

99.  The schools were shut down. See *Vestnik Obshchestva Rasprostraneniia Prosveshcheniia mezhdu Evreiami v Rossii*, 1911, no. 11, p. 113; for similar cases see ibid., 1912, no. 12, p. 117–18; or 1912, no. 14, p. 114. The instrumentalization of the authorities as a means of fighting the reformers had already been a pattern of the Orthodox or Hasidic Rabbis' struggle against the State Rabbis in the nineteenth century. See Levitats, *The Jewish Community*, pp. 87–8.

100. See the correspondence between the ORPE branch in Vilna and the governor which dealt with lectures on various topics of Jewish culture and history, the setting up of a reading hall in Vilna, and the organization of summer courses for Jewish pupils according to a reformed syllabus including secular and general subjects. All three requests were granted, but ORPE activists had to apply for the lectures, the reading hall and the summer courses separately; programmes and statutes had to be worked out in each case and approved by the authorities. This was a time- consuming venture, and not favourable to fast and efficient changes. See the correspondence in January, February and March 1910 (lectures), January 1911 (summer courses), and February 1912 and January 1913 (reading hall) in *Archives of the YIVO Institute. New York. Records of Khevra Mefitzei Haskole. ORPE, Vilna. Record Group No.22. Folder 13.*

101. Conflicts on educational reform between Hebraists and Yiddishists were reported from many localities such as from Vitebsk. See A. Golomb, 'Yidishe Shuln in Vitebsk for der ershter Welt-Milkhome', in *Vitebsk amol*, pp. 469–70.

102. See Löwe, 'From Charity to Social Policy', pp. 21–2.

103. For more information see Steven J. Zipperstein, 'Transforming the Heder: Maskilic Politics in Imperial Russia', in Ada Rapoport-Albert and Steven J. Zipperstein (eds), *Jewish History: Essays in honour of Chimen Abramsky* (London, 1988) pp. 87–109. Here, Zipperstein describes the former announcements as part of early ORPE activity aiming at secularizing and modernizing the Heder; however, further efforts were either blocked by the government or failed due to the fact that ORPE leadership did not yet command wider support within Jewish society.

104. Löwe, 'From Charity to Social Policy', p. 20.

105. In 1898, there were 30,000 Heders in Russia and Poland with 350,000 pupils; and 500 Talmud Torahs with 20,000 pupils (1904) in all of Russia. See Levitats, *The Jewish Community*, pp. 118–21.

106. See Golomb, 'Yidishe Shuln in Vitebsk', p. 468.

107. The 1910 official report of the ministry of education mentioned 68,816 Jewish pupils at Russian primary schools, 49,691 Jewish students at Russian secondary schools (gymnasia and pro-gymnasia – 11.4 per cent), 13,843 at

Russian trade schools (32.4 per cent), 4,244 University students (10.3 per cent), 1,901 at Technical Universities (around 10 per cent) and so on. The amount of officially registered Heders decreased from 25,540 (1897) to 7,743. Despite the fact that these official data did not include the large number of unregistered Heders, the trend of a growth of Jewish students in all kinds of general schools can not be denied. See B. Goldberg, 'Unterrichtsstatistik für das Jahr 1910 in Russland', in *Zeitschift für Demographie und Statistik der Juden*, no. 2 (February 1913) pp. 24–40. The trend towards a decrease of traditional Heders was already reported in 1908 for the Gubernia Vilna. Here, while the Heders decreased from 595 (1899) to 255 (1908), the secular Jewish schools increased from 17 to 74. See S.M., 'Der Anteil der Juden im Unterrichtswesen im Gouvernement Vilna', in ibid., no. 11, November 1910, p. 166. For more detailed data on statistics including universities, primary and secondary schools of all types from the mid-1860s until 1910, see S.V. Pozner, *Evrei v obshchem shkole* (St. Petersburg, 1914) prilozhenie 2–24, pp. 54–112.

108. Ratner had demanded to reject a reform of the Heder, as it was an institution for religious education, and favoured instead a secular Jewish elementary school. He was supported by all Jewish elementary school teachers present, with the exception of Shapiro. The majority of the meeting agreed with Bikerman's statement that 'hundreds of thousands of Jewish children were passing the Heder, and with the reform of the Heder, the elementary school would also profit and be improved. Since the Heder was doing useful work, it must have a future within Jewish life.' See *Der Fraind*, no. 3, 3 January 1913, p. 2. For ORPE's final decision for the Heder reform see also Dubnov, *Kniga Zhizni*, vol. II, p. 139.

109. ORPE had published a curriculum of general and Jewish subjects for girls' and boys' schools in the ORPE organ *Vestnik ORPE*. Furthermore, statistics on new summer teachers' courses – founded by ORPE in Odessa – were published which showed that ORPE was able to keep the number of participants on the same level: 1912 (128 teachers and 118 lady teachers) and 1913 (105 teachers and 135 lady teachers). Moreover, ORPE's expertise on educational matters was greatly appreciated, and ORPE's information bureau received more than a thousand letters from teachers asking about various issues of the school question. See *Razsvet*, no. 1, 5 January 1914, cols 25–26.

110. Slutskii accused the Central Committee that it had not included the teaching of Yiddish in the Grodno pedagogical courses, had refused to subsidize schools where Yiddish was taught, and had not edited school books in Yiddish. Levitan rejected the inclusion of Hebrew into the syllabus, claiming that it was of no use since one needed the culture of today, and not the one of the past. Regarding the language dispute Fialkov said that the parents of many girls' schools were asked which subject of teaching they preferred, and they all voted for Hebrew. See *Razsvet*, no. 1, 5 January 1914, cols 27–28.

111. See *Razsvet*, no. 2, 12 January 1914, col. 29.

112. Goldberg pointed out that in many places, although they were in the majority, Jewish children were not admitted to the general elementary schools. The only place remaining was the Jewish Heder school which did not,

however, fulfil even the most modest requirements. He also pointed to the injustice that in many localities only one-tenth of the Korobka tax, which only Jews had to pay and which was originally assigned to and actually used for the maintenance of Jewish educational and welfare institutions, were still used for this purpose. The rest was swallowed for the maintenance of the police, the reconstruction of bridges, governmental administration, the covering of the debts of churches and monasteries and so on. Furthermore, the authorities increasingly tried to keep the growing numbers of Jewish students in middle schools low by circulars and regulations, higher demands in the exams for Jews, and obstacles regarding the opening of Jewish middle schools. See *Razsvet*, no. 2, 12 January 1914, col. 32; for Fialkov's resolution which was fully accepted by the congress, see *Razsvet*, no. 1, 5 January 1914, col. 29; and *Novyi Voskhod*, no. 52, 31 December 1913, cols 24–25.

113. See Ilya Trotsky, 'Jews in Russian Schools', in Frumkin, *Russian Jewry*, p. 415.

114. In co-ordination with Chernigov's mayor Versilov (a Kadet), Jewish organizations and the gubernia administration, Shneerson managed to get the farming out of the Korobka tax into the hands of the Jewish community; within the scope of his struggle against beggars, he set up a welfare system (with a pensioners' home for old beggars, vocational schools and modernized Talmud Torah for the youngsters and attempts to employ adult beggars as servants) which aimed at re-socializing the poor into community life; with the help of ORPE and local Jewish activists, he modernized the local Jewish school system, by exchanging the *melameds* with teachers trained in the Grodno teachers courses, introducing secular subjects and improving the hygienic situation by building a new school with new furniture. Finally, he set up an artisan school, helped to found a saving and loan association and vocational evening courses for adults. See Shneerson, *Lebn un Kampf*, pp. 213–270.

115. See *Der Fraind*, no. 220, 26 September 1911, p. 3.

116. The success of the Kiev community was reported at an ORPE meeting in February 1912. The report also mentioned a successful activity of the Moscow branch, while generally it criticized the lack of support from other ORPE branches. Therefore, it suggested that the central ORPE Committee work out a new programme for the branches, organize visitations of the provinces more frequently, and pay more attention to smaller cities and towns. See *Der Fraind*, no. 45, 22 February 1912, p. 3.

117. Despite the fact that the Jewish community pleaded against this decision and asked for the right to take over the Korobka tax by promising the authorities the collection of up to 150,000 roubles – which it indeed obtained from various persons – the administration did not alter its decision. See *Der Fraind*, no. 26, 30 January 1912, p. 3.

118. See *Der Fraind*, no. 24, 27 January 1912, p. 3.

119. See *Der Fraind*, no. 28, 1 February 1912, p. 3. For the Mogilev administration's action see *Der Fraind*, no. 32, 6 February 1912, p. 3.

120. OZE was founded by Dr. M. Shvartsshtein in St. Petersburg in 1912. It found widespread support among Russian Jews, and became particularly active during World War I. Its aims -- to improve Jewish medical institutions, to disseminate medical knowledge among Jews, to set up branches

and edit a journal – responded to the needs for hygiene and were a means for the information mentioned above. See *Der Fraind*, no. 192, 22 August 1912, p. 3. For a brief description of OZE's activity see Ilya Trotsky, 'Jewish Institutions of Social Welfare, Education, and Mutual Assistance', in Frumkin, *Russian Jewry*, pp. 426–8; briefly after its foundation, OZE published an appeal to Russian Jews to join the organization as it was granted to open branches nationwide. See *Evreiskaia Khronika*, no. 42, 24 October 1912, cols 27–28.

121. In Kovno, an OZE branch was founded in March, 1914. Its administration started by setting up a gymnastic club and organising courses in hygiene for students of the local Jewish schools. See *Razsvet*, no. 12, 14 March 1914, col. 34. OZE branches were also founded in Brest-Litovsk, Kiev, Vitebsk, Feodosiia, Moscow, Odessa and Kharkov where they showed a great deal of activity which included the foundation of gymnastic clubs, the organization of lectures concerning the hygiene and nursing. The central OZE organized a touring exhibition on hygiene and nursing. See *Razsvet*, no. 22, 30 May 1914, col. 24.

122. For more information on EKOPO, see Steven J. Zipperstein, 'The Politics of Relief: The Transformation of Russian Jewish Communal Life during the First World War', *Studies in Contemporary Jewry*, 4 (1987).

123. See *Razsvet*, no. 28, 10 July 1911, col. 36.

124. In 1913 there were 2,505 Jewish university students in Russia, which equalled 7.3 per cent of the total student body. Between 1895 and 1902 there were 2,405 Russian Jews studying in Germany, Austria, Switzerland and France. Many Jewish students, however, also took the option of studying at private institutions of higher learning such as the Psycho-Neurological Institute in St. Petersburg (founded 1907 – no number mentioned), or the Kiev Commercial Institute (founded in 1912 – 1,875 students). See Zvi Halevy, *Jewish University Students and Professionals in Tsarist and Soviet Russia* (Tel Aviv, 1976), p. 50f; Goldberg mentioned the official report of the ministry for education for 1910, according to which 4,244 Jews studied at Russian Universities (10.3 per cent), 1,901 at Technical Universities (10.3 per cent), 1,027 at Higher Courses for Commerce (42.4 per cent) and 69 at veterinary institutes (4.7 per cent). Goldberg believed that Jewish students were, in fact, more numerous as the Ministry did not release statistics for the universities for music and art, higher courses for medicine and pedagogics, nor on Jewish students abroad – whose number he estimated at 2,000. See B. Goldberg, 'Unterrichtsstatistik für das Jahr 1910 in Rußland', in *Zeitschrift für Demographie und Statistik der Juden*, no. 2 (February 1913) pp. 24–30.

125. See *Razsvet*, no. 48, 25 November 1911, cols 8–9.

126. See Jack Wertheimer, 'Between Tsar and Kaiser. The Radicalization of Russian-Jewish University Students in Germany', in *Leo Baeck Institute Year Book*, 28 (1983) pp. 329–49; the campaign against Russian Jews in Germany reached its peak in 1913, when Prussia and Bavaria introduced a numerus clausus, and even liberal Baden restricted the admission of Russian-Jewish students slightly. In March 1913, some French students directed an appeal to the university administration in which they demanded not to admit Jewish students to the medical faculties. See Jack Wertheimer, 'The "Ausländerfrage" at Institutions of Higher Learning. A Controversy over

Russian-Jewish Students in Imperial Germany', in *Leo Baeck Institute Year Book*, 27 (1982) pp. 187–215.

127. See *Der Fraind*, no. 166, 21 July 1913, p. 1; and *Razsvet*, no. 30, 26 July 1913, col. 13.

128. See St., 'Ideia evreiskago universiteta', in *Novyi Voskhod*, no. 12, 21 March 1913, cols 1–3. The idea of a Jewish University had first been advanced by Professor Hermann Schapiro in 1887, but never got off the ground until Menahem Ussishkin convinced the Eleventh Zionist Congress in 1913 to set up a University Fund. See Simcha Kling, *The Mighty Warrior. Menahem Ussishkin* (New York, 1965) pp. 54–6; and Joseph Klausner, *Menahem Ussishkin. His Life and Work* (London, n.d.) pp. 53–4.

129. See Dubnov, *Kniga Zhizni*, pp. 153–4.

130. See *Der Fraind*, no. 87, 17 April 1913, p. 2; and I. Levin's article on the plan of a Jewish university in *Der Fraind*, no. 88, 18 April 1913, p. 2. He agreed to the idea, but rejected Russia as the location as it did not make sense to set up a university in a country where Jews had no rights. For the KK's action see Sliozberg, *Dela*, pp. 299–311; for Jacob Teitel's – former judge of the Saratov district court – 'engagement' on behalf of Jewish students, see A. Goldenveizer, 'Ya.L. Teitel', in *Evreiskii Mir*, sbornik II, p. 307.

131. See Mikhail Beizer, *The Jews of St. Petersburg* (Philadelphia and New York, 1989) p. 301.

## 6 CONCLUSION: THE RUSSIAN-JEWISH LIBERALS AND THEIR POSITION IN EUROPEAN JEWISH HISTORY

1. Such a hypothesis with respect to Jewish workers is advanced by Y. Peled, *Class and Ethnicity*.

2. See David Biale, *Power and Powerlessness in Jewish History* (New York, 1987).

3. To quote Goldscheider and Zuckerman: '. . . they [Jewish political organizations – C.G.] developed in competitive response to the claims of others in their political arenas. The more competitors present, the more elaborate is each ideology . . .' Here, they referred to the mutual influence of Russian Zionists and Bundists, which let them adopt political efforts or national demands, respectively. Unfortunately, Goldscheider and Zuckerman compare Russian Zionists and Socialists with German-Jewish Liberals. Therefore, they could not mention the Russian-Jewish Liberals' impact on these two groups. See Goldscheider and Zuckerman, *The Transformation*, pp. 127–35.

# Bibliography

## NEWSPAPERS AND JOURNALS

*Darkest Russia*
*Delo Naroda* (1905–1906)
*Der Fraind* (1905–1914)
*Di Folksshtime* (1907)
*Di Yudishe Virklikhkeit* (1906–1907)
*Dos Yudishe Folk* (1907)
*Evreiskaia Khronika* (Kishinev, 1912)
*Evreiskaia Nedelia* (1910)
*Evreiskaia Niva* (1913)
*Evreiskaia Starina* (1909–1914)
*Evreiskii Golos* (Belostok, 1906)
*Evreiskii Golos* (Odessa, 1906–1907)
*Evreiskii Izbiratel* (1907)
*Evreiskii Mir* (1910–1914)
*Evreiskii Narod* (1906)
*Folks-Blat* (1908)
*Folkstsaitung* (1906–1907)
*Izvestiia Obshchestva rasprostraneniia pravil'nykh svedenii* (1912)
*Jewish Chronicle* (1905–1914)
*Khronika Evreiskoi Zhizni* (1905–1906)
*Nasha Zhizn'* (1905–1906)
*Novaia Iudeia* (1908)
*Novyi Voskhod* (1910–1915)
*Poslednia Novosti* (1904–1905)
*Pravo* (1905)
*Razsvet* (1907–1914)
*Rech'* (1905–1906)
*Rus'* (1905–1906)
*Svoboda i Ravenstvo* (1907)
*Tsait-Fragen* (1910)
*Vestnik Bunda* (1904–1905)
*Vestnik Evreiskoi Obshchiny* (1913)
*Vestnik Obshchestva raprostraneniia prosveshcheniia mezhdu evreiami* (1910–1913)
*Volna* (1906)
*Voskhod* (1905–1906)
*Zeitschrift für Demographie und Statistik der Juden* (1905–1924)

PRIMARY SOURCES OR SOURCES USED AS PRIMARY
DOCUMENTS

Abram der Tate (Leib Blechman), *Bleter fun main iugnt* (New York: Ferlag Unser Tsait, 1959).

Abramovich, R., *In Tsvai Revolutsies*, 2 vols (New York: Ferlag Arbeter-Ring, 1944).

Akvilonov, E., *Judeiskii vopros. O nevozmozhnosti predostavleniia polnopraviia russkim grazhdanam iz iudeiskago naroda* (St. Petersburg: Tipografiia M. Merkusheva, 1907).

Aleksandrov, S., 'Evreiskii vopros v Dume i "dostigateli" ', *Nashe Slovo*, 22 June 1906, pp. 4–8.

Aronson, Gregorii, *Revoliutsionnaia Iunost'. Vospomonaniia 1903–1917*, Inter-University Project on the History of the Menshevik Movement, Paper no. 6, New York, August 1961.

Berlinraut', L.Ya. and Raskin, M.S., *Evreiskoe naselenie goroda Vologdy. Opyt' statisticheskago obsledovaniia ekonomicheskago, pravovogo i kul'turnago sostoianiia evreiskago naseleniia vnutrennikh gubernii Rossii* (Moscow: Tovarishchestvo Tipografii A.I. Mamontova, 1911).

Berman, Leib, *In loif fun di yorn* (New York: Ferlag Unser Tseit, 1945).

Bernstein, L., *La Première Douma* (Paris, 1908) [Reprinted in Seeds of Conflict. Series I: Irredentist and Nationalist Questions in Central Europe 1913–1919 USSR. Nendeln, 1973].

Bikerman, I., *Materialy k zakonoproektu ob otmene cherty evreiskoi osedlosti. Ekonomicheskaia deiatel'nost' evreev*. Vypusk pervyi. 'Evreiskaia eksplotatsiia', 'evreiskiia bogatstva', 'rol' evreev v khlebnoi torgovle' (St. Petersburg: Tipografiia L.Ya. Ganzburga, 1911).

Bramson, L.M., *K istorii Trudovoi Partii. Trudovaia Gruppa pervoi gosudarstvennoi Dumy*, 2nd (ed.) (Petrograd: Izdatel'stvo Edinenie, 1917).

——, 'Memoirs of the First Duma', *Novyi Put'*, no. 15, 1 May 1916, pp. 6–15.

Braudo, Aleksandr I., *Ocherki i vospominaniia*. Edited by L.M. Bramson *et al.* (Paris: Izdanie Kruzhka Russko-Evreiskoi Intelligentsii v Parizhe, 1937).

Chazan, Robert and Raphael, Marc Lee (eds), *Modern Jewish History: A Source Reader* (New York: Schocken Books, 1974).

*Chleny Pervoi Gosudarstvennoi Dumy. Biografii, kharakteristiki, politicheskie vzgliady, obshchestvennaia deiatel'nost', vybory i prochee* (Moscow: Tipografiia Pechat' i Graviura, 1906).

Dmytryshyn, Basil (ed.), *Imperial Russia. A Source Book, 1700–1917*, 3rd ed. (Chicago: The Dryden Press, 1990).

Dubnow, Simon, *Mein Leben*. Edited by Elias Hurwicz (Berlin: Jüdische Buchvereinigung, 1937).

——, 'Jewish Rights between Red and Black', in Lucy S. Davidowicz, *The Golden Tradition: Jewish Life and Thought in Eastern Europe* (New York, Chicago and San Fransisco: Holt, Rinehart & Winston, 1967) pp. 461–70.

——, *Kniga zhizni. Vospominaniia i razmyshlenia*, vols 1 and 2 (Riga: Izdatelstvo Jaunates Gramata, 1934–35).

Elpat'evskii, S., 'Evreiskii vopros', in *Russkoe Bogatstvo*, 10 (1913) pp. 348–59.

Feder, Ernst, *Paul Nathan. Ein Lebensbild* (Berlin, 1929).

Frank, S.L., *Biografiia P.B. Struve* (New York: Chekhov Publishing House, 1956).

Freeze, Gregory L., *From Supplication to Revolution: A Documentary Social History of Imperial Russia* (New York and Oxford: Oxford University Press, 1988).

Gessen, Iosif V., *V dvukh vekakh. Zhiznennyi otchet'* (Berlin, 1937. Reprinted in Arkhiv Russkoi Revoliutsii, vol. 22, The Hague and Paris, 1970).

Gessen, Yulii, 'Zakonodatel'stvo o zhitel'stve evreev v Rossii', in *Russkaia Mysl'*, 1911, vol. 5, no. XII, pp. 82–98.

——, *K istorii korobochnago sbora v Rossii* (St. Petersburg: Tipografiia I. Lur'e, 1911).

——, *O zhizni evreev v Rossii. Zapiska v Gosudarstvennuiu Dumu* (St. Petersburg: Tipografiia tovarishchestva 'Obshchestvennaia Pol'za', 1906).

Gintsburg, Saul, *Amolike Petersburg. Forshungen un zikhroines vegn yidishe Lebn in der residenz-stat fun tsarishn Rusland* (New York: Posy-Shoulson Press, 1944).

Ginzburg, Moshe, *Sain Lebn un Tetigkait. Mit ain Forwort fun Henrik Sliozberg.* (Edited by the friends of Moshe Ginzburg.) (Paris, 1935).

Goldberg, M.L., *Chego zhdam nam Russkim Evreiam ot ravnopraviia*, 2nd ed. (Elets: Tipografiia Z.P. Zalkinda, 1908).

*Gosudarstvennaia Duma. Stenograficheskie otchety*, 3 vols (St. Petersburg, 1906).

Gruzenberg, O.O., *Yesterday: Memoirs of a Russian-Jewish Lawyer*, edited and with an introduction by Don C. Rawson (Berkeley, Los Angeles and London: University of California Press, 1981).

Hillmann, Anselm, *Jüdisches Genossenschaftswesen in Rußland* (Berlin: Veröffentlichungen des Bureaus für Statistik der Juden, 1911).

Izgoev, A.S., 'Ot tret'ei Dumy k chetvertoi', in *Ezhegodnik gazety Rech na 1913*, pp. 186–97.

Kantor, R.M., 'Razgrom evreiskoi intelligentsii', in *Evreiskaia Letopis*, II, 1924, pp. 87–95.

Kats, Ben Tsion, 'Zikhronut fun mein Lebn', in *Der Tag-Morgen Zhurnal/The Day-Jewish Journal* (Buenos Aires, 1953–55).

K(irpichnikov), S.D., *Soiuz Soiuzov* (St. Petersburg, 1906).

Kirzhnic, A.D., *Evreiskoe rabochee dvizhenie 1905. Materialy i dokumenty*, vol. 5, edited by M.N. Pokrovskii (Moscow and Leningrad, 1928).

Kleinman, I., 'Antisemitizm v Rossii v 1911 godu', in *Ezhegodnik gazety Rech na 1912*, pp. 524–32.

Kokovtsov, Graf V.N., *Iz moego proshlago. Vospominaniia 1903–1919*, 2 vols (Paris, 1933. Reprinted in Slavistic Printings and Reprintings, vol. 200/1. The Hague and Paris, 1969).

*Kratkii ocherk' istorii S.-Peterburgskoi biblioteki*, edited by Obshchestvo rasprostraneniia prosveshcheniia mezhdu evreiami v Rossii za 1872–1912 gg. (St. Petersburg, 1913).

Krol, M.A., *Stranitsy moei zhizni*, vol. I (New York: Izdanie Soiuza Russkikh Evreev v N'iu Yorke, 1944).

——, *Stranitsy moei zhizni*, vol. II. Typescript, 1941, in Hoover Institution Archives, Collection M.A. Krol', Box 1, Folder 'Stranitsy Moei Zhizni', vol. II.

L., Ya., 'Vybory', in *Ezhegodnik gazety Rech na 1913*, pp. 198–239.

Landau, B., 'Evreiskii vopros', in *Ezhegodnik gazety Rech na 1914*, pp. 276–83.

Landau, Grigorii, *Pol'sko-Evreiskiia Otnosheniia. Stat'i i zametki* (Petrograd: Tip. Petr. T-va Pech. i Izd. dela 'Trud', 1915).

Levin, Shmarya, *The Arena* (New York: Arno Press, 1932).
——, *Kindheit im Exil* (Berlin: Ernst Rohwolt Verlag, 1935).
Levin, Sh.E., *O korobochnom' i svechnom' sborakh'. Ikh istoricheskoe proiskhozhdenie, kriticheskie otzyvy, deistvovavshiia i nyne deistvuiushchiia zakonopolozheniia o nikh* (St. Petersburg: Elektro-Tipografiia Sh.I. Likhtmakhera, 1910).
Liberman, Ya.M., *K voprosu o evreiskom i zhargonnom' yazykakh' v evreiskoi narodnoi shkole* (Kiev: Elektropechatnia I. Shenfel'da, 1910).
Linden, A., 'Die Dimensionen der Oktoberpogrome 1905', in *Die Judenpogrome in Russland*, vol. I (Cologne and Leipzig, 1910).
Litvak, A., *Vos geven. Etiuden un Zikhroines* (Vilna: Ferlag B. Kletskin, 1925).
——, *Geklibene Shriftn* (New York: Bildungs-Komitet fun Arbeter-Ring, 1945).
L'vovich', M., 'Kontr'-revoliutsiia i evrei', in *Russkoe Bogatstvo*, 1911, no. 12, II, pp. 43–58.
Maklakov, V.A., *Iz Vospominanii* (New York: Chekhov Publishing House, 1954).
Margolin, Arnold D., *From a Political Diary. Russia, the Ukraine and America 1905–1945* (New York: Columbia University Press, 1946).
Margolin, M.M., *Natsional'noe dvizhenie v evreistve 1881–1913* (Petrograd: Knigoizdatel'stvo Vostok, 1917).
Margolin, Salomon O., 'Die wirtschaftliche Lage der jüdischen arbeitenden Klassen in Russland', in *Archiv für Sozialwissenschaft und Sozialpolitik*, 26 (1908) pp. 240–69.
——, *Evreiskiia Kreditnyia Kooperatsii. Evreiskoe Kolonizatsionnoe Obshchestvo. Statistiko-ekonomicheskie ocherki i izsledovaniia*, vypusk I (St. Petersburg, 1908).
Martow, Julius, *Geschichte der russischen Sozialdemokratie*. Mit einem Nachtrag von Th. Dan: Die Sozialdemokratie Rußlands nach dem Jahre 1908 (Berlin: J.H.W. Dietz Nachfolger, 1926. Reprint Erlangen, 1973).
*Material and Memoirs. Chapters for the History of ORT* (Geneva, 1955).
*Materialy po voprosu o cherte evr. osedlosti* (Kiev: Tipografiia 'Trud', 1911).
Medem, Vladimir, 'Evreiskii vopros v Rossii', *Vestnik Evropy* 1911, no. 4, pp. 271–84.
——, *The Life and Soul of a Legendary Jewish Socialist*, introduced and translated by Samuel A. Portnoy (New York: Ktav Publishing House Inc., 1978).
Meier, F., *Nesostoiatel'nost' zakona o cherte evreiskoi osedlosti* (Vilna: Tipografiia Artel' Pechatnago Dela, 1910).
Mendel, Hersch, *Erinnerungen eines jüdischen Revolutionärs* (Berlin: Rotbuch Verlag, 1979).
Mendes-Flohr, Paul R./Reinharz, Jehuda (eds), *The Jew in the Modern World. A Documentary History* (New York and Oxford: Oxford University Press, 1980).
Menes, Abraham (ed.), *Der yidisher gedank in der nayer tsait* (New York: Alweltlikhe Yidishe Kultur-Kongres, 1957).
Miliukov, Paul, 'Politicheskiia partii v Gosudarstvennoi Dume za piat' let', in *Ezhegodnik gazety Rech na 1912*, pp. 77–96.
——, *Vospominaniia* (New York, 1955).
——, *Political Memoirs, 1905–1917*, edited by Arthur P. Mendel (Ann Arbor: University of Michigan Press, 1967).
M.V.D. [Ministerstvo Vnutrennykh Del'], *Vybory v Gosudarstvennuiu Dumu Tret'iago Szyva. Statisticheskii otchet Osobago Deloproizvotstva* (St. Petersburg: Tipografiia Ministerstva Vnutrennykh Del', 1911).

Nemanov, L., 'Itogi deiatel'nosti tret'ei Gosudarstvennoi Dumy', in *Ezhegodnik gazety Rech na 1912*, pp. 97–117.

——, 'Evreiskii vopros', in *Ezhegodnik gazety Rech na 1913*, pp. 325–33.

Nisselowitsch, L.N., *Die Judenfrage in Russland* (Berlin: Verlag Jüdische Rundschau, 1909).

Obshchestvo rasprostranennia pravil'nikh' svedenii o evreiakh' i evreistve (ed.), *O cherte evreiskoi osedlosti*, vypusk 1 (Moscow: Tovarishchestvo A.I. Mamontova, 1911).

Obshchestvo dlia rasprostraneniia prosveshcheniia mezhdu evreiami v Rossii za piat'desiat' let'. Kratkii istoricheskii ocherk (St. Petersburg, 1913).

Oppenheimer, Franz, 'Nationale Autonomie für die Ostjuden', in *Ostjuden. Süddeutsche Monatshefte*, February 1916, pp. 721–730.

*ORT: The Society for the Promotion of Trades and Agriculture among the Jews in Russia* (London, 1921).

ORT Union Geneva (ed.), *80 Years of ORT. Historical Materials, Documents and Reports* (Geneva, 1960).

*Otchet' Obshchestva Remeslenago i Zemledel'cheskago Truda sredi evreev v Rossii, 1907–1914* (St. Petersburg, 1908–1915).

*Otchet' Obshchestva dlia rasprostraneniia prosveshcheniia mezhdu evreiami v Rossii. 1907–1914* (St. Petersburg, 1908–1915).

'Pervaia Gosudarstvennaia Duma v Vyborge', in *Krasnyi Arkhiv*, 57 (1933) pp. 85–99.

Pinson, Koppel S. (ed.), *Nationalism and History. Essays on old and new Judaism by Simon Dubnow* (Philadelphia: The Jewish Publication Society of America, 1958).

*Po vekham. Sbornik statei ob intelligentsii i 'natsional "nom" ' litse: P. Boborykina, A. Vasil'eva, M. Vinavera, V. Golubeva et al.*, 2nd ed. (Moscow, 1909).

Pozner, S.V., 'Bor'ba za ravnopravie', in *M.M. Vinaver i russkaia obshchestvennost' nachala XX veka. Sbornik statei* (Paris, 1937).

——, *Evrei v obshchei shkole. K istorii zakonodatel'stva i pravitel'stvennoi politiki v oblasti evreiskago voprosa* (St. Petersburg: Izdatelstvo 'Razum', 1914).

*Protokoly tret'ago delegatskago s'ezda Soiuza dlia dostizheniia polnopraviia evreiskago naroda v Rossii v S.-Peterburge. S.10-go po 13-oe febralia 1906g* (St. Petersburg: Izdanie Central'nago Komiteta Obshchestva Polnopraviia Evreiskago Naroda v Rossii, 1906).

Prylucki, Noah, *Natsionalism un democratism* (Warsaw: Ferlag Ieshurun', 1907).

Ratner, M.B., *O natsional'noi i territorial'noi avtonomii* (Kiev and St. Petersburg, 1906).

Records of Khevra Mefitzei Haskole. ORPE Vilna. Archives of the YIVO Institute, New York. Record Group no. 22. Folder 13.

Rosenbaum, M.M., *Erinnerungen fun a sotsialist-revolutsioner*, 2 vols (New York and Warsaw: H. Zhitlovski Farlag, 1924).

Rubinow, Isaac B., *Economic Condition of the Jews in Russia* (New York: Arno Press, 1907. Reprinted in New York, 1975).

Sheinis', D.I., *Evreiskoe studenchestvo v tsifrakh. Po dannym' perepisi v 1909 g. v Kievskom' universitet i Politichnicheskom' Institute* (Kiev: Pechatnia Iosifa Shenfelda, 1911).

Shneerson, Isaac, *Lebn un Kampf fun yidn in tsarishn Rusland* (Paris: Les Editions Polyglottes, 1968).

Shulgin, V.V., *The Years: Memoirs of a Member of the Russian Duma, 1906–1917*, translated by Tanya Davis (New York: Hippocrene Books, 1984).

Silberfarb, Moses, *Die Verwaltungen der jüdischen Gemeinden in Russland* (Pressburg: Adolf Alkalay & Sohn Publishers, 1911).

Sliozberg, G.B., *Dela minuvshikh dnei. Zapiski russkago evreia*, 3 vols (Paris, 1933).

——, *Sbornik deistvuiushchikh zakonov o evreiakh* (St. Petersburg: Tsentral'naia Tipografiia M.Ya. Minkova, 1909).

——, *Pravovoe i ekonomicheskoe polozhenie* (St. Petersburg: Elektropechatnia Ya. Levenshtein, 1907).

——, 'Baron G.O. Gintsburg i pravovoe polozhenie evreev', in *Perezhitoe*, vol. II (St. Petersburg, 1910).

Smith, Rufus B., *The United States Passport and Russia*. Paper read before the Temple Club of Congregation Bene Israel Cincinna Ti, 5 April 1911, and printed by resolution of the Club.

*Stenograficheski otchet' Soveshchaniia evreiskikh obshchestvennykh deiateli v g. Kovne* (St. Petersburg, 1910).

Teitel, Jacob, *Aus meiner Lebensarbeit. Erinnerungen eines jüdischen Richters im alten Russland* (Frankfurt/M.: J. Kauffman Verlag, 1929).

Tolstoi, Graf Iv.Iv. and Gessen, I.I., *Fakty i mysli. Evreiskii vopros v Rossii* (St. Petersburg: Tipografiia tovarishchestva 'Obshchestvennaia Pol'za', 1907).

Tsinberg, S.L., *Istoriia evreiskoi pechati v Rossii v sviazi s obshchestvennymi techeniami* (St. Petersburg, 1915).

Usov, M.L., *Predanie i fakty. K evreiskomu voprosu* (St. Petersburg: Tipografiia Busselia, 1908).

——, *Evrei v Armii* (St. Petersburg: Izdatel'stvo Razum, 1911).

Vinaver, M.M., *Kadety i evreiskii vopros* (St. Petersburg, 1907).

——, *Konflikty v pervoi dume* (St. Petersburg: Tsentral'naia Tipo-Lit. M.Ya. Minkova, 1907).

——, *Nedavnee. Vospominaniia i kharakteristiki*, 2nd ed. (Paris, 1926).

——, *Istoriia vyborgskaia vozzvania* (St. Petersburg, 1917).

*M.M. Vinaver i russkaia obshchestvennost' nachala XX veka. Sbornik statei*, edited by P.N. Miliukov *et al.* (Paris, 1937).

Vinaver, Roza G., *Vospominaniia Maksima M. Vinavera*. Typescript (New York, 1944) in New York Public Library, Department of Slavic Languages.

*Vitebsk amol. Geshikhte, zikhroinut, khurbn*, edited by Grigorii Aronson, Yakob Leshchinskii, Abraham Kihn (New York: Waldon Press, 1956).

Vitte, Graf S.Iu., *Vospominaniia. Tsarstvovanie Nikolaia II*, vol. II, 2nd ed. (Berlin, 1922).

Wolf, Lucien (ed.), *The legal sufferings of the Jews in Russia: A survey of their present situation and a summary of laws* (London, 1912).

*Zakon o Gosudarstvennoi Dume 11 Dekabria 1905 g* (St. Petersburg: Izdanie Tsentral'nago Biuoro Soiuza dlia dostizheniia polnopraviia evreiskago naroda v Rossii, 1905).

Zalevskii, K., 'Natsional'naia partii v Rossii', in *Obshchestvennoe dvizhenie Rossii v nachale XX veka*, vol. III (St. Petersburg, 1914).

Zhabotinskii [Jabotinsky], Vladimir, 'Pis'ma o natsional'nostiakh i oblastiakh. Evreistvo i ego nastroeniia', in *Russkaia Mysl'*, 1913 , no. 1, pp. 95–114.

——, 'Memoirs by my Typewriter', in Lucy S. Dawidowicz, *The Golden Tradition. Jewish Life and Thought in Eastern Europe* (New York, Chicago and San Francisco, 1967) pp. 394–401.


## SECONDARY SOURCES

Abramovitch, Zeev, 'The Poale Zion Movement in Russia, its history and development', in Henrik F. Infield (ed.), *Essays in Jewish Socialism, Labour and Cooperation in Memory of Dr. Noah Barou, 1899–1955* (London and New York: Thomas Yoseloff, 1961) pp. 63–72.

Almog, Shmuel, *Zionism and History. The Rise of a new Jewish Consciousness* (Jerusalem: The Magnes Press, 1987).

Alston, P.L., *Education and the State in Tsarist Russia* (Stanford, California: Stanford University Press, 1969).

Anweiler, Oskar, 'Die russische Revolution von 1905', in *Jahrbücher für die Geschichte Osteuropas*, 3 (1955) pp. 161–93.

Aronsfeld, C.C., 'Jewish Bankers and the Tsar', in *Jewish Social Studies*, 35 (1973) pp. 87–104.

Aronson, Gregorii, 'Ideological Trends among Russian Jews', in Jacob Frumkin, Gregor Aronson, Alexis Goldenweiser (eds), *Russian Jewry, 1860–1917* (New York and London: Thomas Yoseloff Publishers, 1966).

Aronson, I.M., 'Geographical and Socioeconomic Factors in the 1881 Anti-Jewish Pogroms in Russia', *The Russian Review*, 39 (1980) pp. 18–31.

——, 'Russian Commissions on the Jewish Question in the 1880s', *East European Quarterly*, 14 (1980) pp. 59–74.

——, 'The Attitudes of Russian Officials in the 1880s toward Jewish Assimilation and Emigration', *Slavic Review*, 34 (1975) pp. 1–18.

——, 'The Prospects for the Emancipation of Russian Jewry during the 1880s', *Slavonic and East European Review*, 55 (1977) pp. 348–69.

——, *Troubled Waters: The Origins of the 1881 Anti-Jewish Pogroms in Russia* (Pittsburgh: University of Pittsburgh Press, 1990).

Ascher, Abraham, *The Russian Revolution of 1905: Russia in Disarray* (Stanford, California: Stanford University Press, 1988).

Baron, Salo W., *The Russian Jew under Tsars and Soviets*, 2nd ed. (New York: Schocken Books, 1987).

——, 'Ghetto and Emancipation. Shall we revise the Traditional View?', in *The Menorah Journal*, vol. XIV, no. 6 (June 1928) pp. 515–27.

——, 'The Modern and Contemporary Periods: Review of the History', in Salo W. Baron and George S. Wise (eds), *Violence and Defense in the Jewish Experience*. Papers prepared for a seminar on violence and defense in Jewish history and contemporary life. Tel Aviv University, 18 August–4 September 1974 (Philadelphia: The Jewish Publication Society, 1977). pp. 163–90.

Beizer, Mikhail, *The Jews of St. Petersburg. Excursions through a noble past*. Translated by Michael Sherbourne. Edited by Martin Gilbert (Philadelphia: The Jewish Publication Society, 1989).

Berk, Stephen M., 'The Russian Revolutionary Movement and the Pogroms of 1881–1882', *Soviet Jewish Affairs*, vol. 7, no. 2 (1977) pp. 23–39.

——, *Year of Crisis, Year of Hope: Russian Jewry and the Pogroms of 1881–1882* (Westport, Connecticut and London: Greenwood Press, 1986).

Bernhard, Ludwig, *Das polnische Gemeinwesen im preußischen Staat. Die Polenfrage* (Leipzig: Duncker und Humblot Verlag, 1907).

Best, Gary Dean, *To Free a People. American Jewish Leaders and the Jewish Problem in Eastern Europe, 1890–1914* (Westport, Connecticut and London: Greenwood Press 1982).

Biale, David, *Power and Powerlessness in Jewish History* (New York: Schocken Books, 1987).

Birth, E., *Die Oktobristen* (Stuttgart: Ernst Klett Verlag, 1974).

Blank, Inge, 'Haskalah und Emanzipation. Die russisch-jüdische Intelligenz und die "jüdische Frage" am Vorabend der Epoche der "Großen Reformen"', in Gotthold Rhode (ed.), *Juden in Ostmitteleuropa. Von der Emanzipation bis zum Ersten Weltkrieg* (Marburg/Lahn: Herder Institut, 1989).

Blau, Bruno, 'Sociology and Statistics of the Jews', *Historica Judaica*, 11 (1949) pp. 145–62.

Bonnell, V.E., *Roots of Rebellion. Workers' Politics and Organizations in St. Petersburg and Moscow 1900–1914* (Berkeley: University of California Press, 1983).

Borochov, Ber, *Nationalism and the Class Struggle. A Marxian approach to the Jewish Problems* (1937. Reprinted Westport, Connecticut: Greenwood Press, 1972).

Brooks, J., *When Russia Learned to Read. Literacy and Popular Literature 1861–1917* (Princeton: Princeton University Press, 1985).

Brym, Robert J., *The Jewish Intelligentsia and Russian Marxism: A Sociological Study of Intellectual Radicalism and Ideological Divergence* (London: The Macmillan Press, 1978).

Cannon, Ellen S., *The Political Culture of Russian Jewry during the Second Half of the Nineteenth Century*. DPhil thesis (University of Massachusetts, 1974).

Clowes, N., Kassow, S. and West, J. (eds), *Between Tsar and People: Educated Society and the Quest for Public Identity in Late Imperial Russia* (Princeton: Princeton University Press, 1991).

Cohen, Israel, *History of the Jews in Vilna* (Philadelphia: The Jewish Publication Society of America, 1943).

Cohen, Naomi, 'The Abrogation of the Russo-American Treaty of 1832', in *Jewish Social Studies*, 25, no. 1 (1963) pp. 3–41.

Comtet, Maurice, 'V.G. Korolenko et la Question Juive en Russie', in *Cahiers du monde russe et sovietique*, 10 (1969) pp. 228–256.

Coquin, François-Xavier and Gervais-Francelle, Céline (eds), *1905: La Première Révolution Russe* (Paris: Publications de la Sorbonne, 1986).

Davies, Norman, *God's Playground. A History of Poland*, 2 vols (New York: Columbia University Press, 1982).

Deutscher, Isaac, *Die ungelöste Judenfrage* (Berlin: Rotbuch Verlag, 1977).

Dmitriev, S.N., 'Soiuz Soiuzov v gody pervoi rossiiskoi revoliutsii', in *Istoriia SSSR*, Jan.–Feb. 1990, pp. 40–57.

Dubnow, Simon M., *History of the Jews in Russia and Poland. From the Earliest Times until the Present Day*, 3 vols (Philadelphia: The Jewish Publication Society of America, 1918).

——, *Weltgeschichte des jüdischen Volkes. vol. 7: Die Neuzeit* (Berlin, 1928) and vol. *10: Die Neueste Geschichte* (Berlin: Jüdischer Verlag, 1929).

Dubnow-Erlich, Sofie and S.M. Dubnow, *Diaspora Nationalism and Jewish History*, edited by Jeffrey Shandler (Bloomington, Indiana: Indiana University Press, 1991).

Elk, Julius, *Die jüdischen Kolonien in Rußland. Kulturhistorische Studie und Beitrag zur Geschichte der Juden in Rußland* (Frankfurt/M.: I. Kauffmann Verlagsbuchhandlung, 1886. Reprinted Hildesheim and New York: Georg Olms Verlag, 1970).

Emmons, Terence, *The Formation of Political Parties and the First National Elections in Russia* (Cambridge, Massachusetts: Harvard University Press, 1983).

——, 'Russia's Banquet Campaign', *California Slavic Studies*, 10 (1977) pp. 45–86.

Ettinger, Shmuel, 'The Growth of the Jewish National Movement and the Burgeoning of Independent Political Activity', in H.H. Ben-Sasson, *A History of the Jewish People* (Cambridge, Massachusetts: Harvard University Press, 1976).

——, 'Russian Society and the Jews', *Bulletin on Soviet Jewish Affairs*, 5 (1970) pp. 36–42.

Feder, Ernst, 'Paul Nathan and his work for East-European and Palestinian Jewry', *Historia Judaica*, vol. XIV, April 1952, part I, pp. 3–26.

Ferenczi, Caspar, 'Freedom of the Press under the Old Regime', in Olga Crisp and Linda Edmondson (eds), *Civil Rights in Imperial Russia* (Oxford: Clarendon Press, 1989) pp. 191–214.

Ferro, Marc, *Nikolaus II. Der letzte Zar. Eine Biographie* (Zurich: Benziger Verlag Zurich, 1991).

Frankel, Jonathan, *Prophecy and Politics: Socialism, Nationalism and the Russian Jews, 1862–1917* (Cambridge: Cambridge University Press, 1981).

——, 'The crisis of 1881–82 as a turning-point in modern Jewish history', in David Berger (ed.), *The Legacy of Jewish Migration: 1881 and its Impact* (New York: Columbia University Press, 1983) pp. 9–22.

Frankel, Jonathan and Zipperstein, Steven (eds), *Assimilation and Community in European Jewry, 1815–1881* (Cambridge: Cambridge University Press, 1989).

Fröhlich, Klaus, *The Emergence of Russian Constitutionalism 1900–1914: The Relationship between Social Mobilization and Political Group Formation in Pre-revolutionary Russia* (The Hague: Martinus Nijhoff Publishers, 1981).

Galai, Shmuel, 'The Role of the Union of Unions in the Revolution of 1905', in *Jahrbücher für die Geschichte Osteuropas*, 24 (1976) pp. 512–25.

Gatrell, P., *The Tsarist Economy 1850–1917* (London: B.T. Batsford Ltd., 1986).

Geyer, Dietrich (ed.), *Wirtschaft und Gesellschaft im vorrevolutionären Rußland* (Cologne: Kiepenheuer & Witsch, 1975) [Published as Neue Wissenschaftliche Bibliothek Geschichte vol. 71].

Golczewski, Frank, *Polnisch-Jüdische Beziehungen, 1881–1922. Eine Studie zur Geschichte des Antisemitismus in Osteuropa* (Wiesbaden: Franz Steiner Verlag, 1981).

Goldberg, Mina, *Die Jahre 1881–1882 in der Geschichte der russischen Juden.* DPhil thesis (Berlin: Paul Brandel Verlag, 1934).

Goldscheider, Calvin and Zukerman, Alan S., *The Transformation of the Jews.* Published as part of the series Chicago Studies in the History of Judaism edited by Jacob Neusner (Chicago and London: University of Chicago Press, 1984).

Goldstein, J., 'The Attitude of the Jewish and Russian Intelligentsia to Zionism in the Initial Period (1897–1904)', *Slavonic and East European Review*, 64 (1986) pp. 546–56.

Greenberg, Louis, *The Jews in Russia. The Struggle for Emancipation*, 2 vols (New York: Schocken Books, 1944/1951. Reprint 1976).

Hagen, Manfred, *Die Entfaltung Politischer Öffentlichkeit in Rußland, 1906–1914* (Wiesbaden: Franz Steiner Verlag, 1982).

Haimson, Leopold (ed.), *The Politics of Rural Russia 1905–1914* (Bloomington and London: Indiana University Press, 1979).

Halevy, Zvi, *Jewish Schools under Czarism and Communism: A Struggle for Cultural Identity* (New York: Springer Publishing Company, 1976).

——, *Jewish University Students and Professionals in Tsarist and Soviet Russia*. Publications of the Diaspora Research Institute. Edited by Shlomo Simonsohn (Tel Aviv: Internal Publication Book IV, 1976).

Halpern, Ben and Reinharz, Jehuda, 'Nationalism and Jewish Socialism: The Early Years', *Modern Judaism*, vol. 8, no. 3 (October 1988) pp. 217–48.

Hamburg, G. M., 'The Russian Nobility on the Eve of the 1905 Revolution', *Russian Review*, 38 (1979) pp. 323–38.

Harcave, Sidney, *Jewish Political Parties and Groups and the Russian State Dumas from 1905–1907*. Unpublished DPhil thesis (Chicago, 1943).

——, 'The Jews and the First National Election', *The American Slavic and East European Review*, 9 (1950) pp. 33–41.

——, 'The Jewish Question in the First Russian Duma', *Jewish Social Studies*, 6 (1944) pp. 155–76.

——, *The Russian Revolution of 1905* (London: Macmillan, 1970).

Haumann, Heiko, *Geschichte der Ostjuden* (Munich: Deutscher Taschenbuch Verlag, 1990).

——, 'Rüstung und Monopole: Industriepolitik der Regierung und organisierte Unternehmerinteressen', in Manfred Hellmann, Gottfried Schramm and Klaus Zernack (eds), *Handbuch der Geschichte Russlands*, vol. 3/1 (Stuttgart: Hiersemann Verlag, 1983) pp. 430–7.

Häusler, Frank, 'V.G. Korolenkos Kampf gegen den Antisemitismus', in *Wissenschaftliche Zeitschrift der Martin-Luther-Universität Halle-Wittenberg*, X/1, February 1961, pp. 237–48.

Healy, Ann Erickson, *The Russian Aristocracy in Crisis 1905–1907* (Hamden, Connecticut: Archon Books, 1976).

——, 'Tsarist Anti-Semitism and Russian American Relations', *Slavic Review*, 3 (1983) pp. 408–25.

Heil, Helmut J. (ed.), *Die neuen Propheten. Moses Hess, Leon Pinsker, Theodor Herzl, Achad Haam* (Fürth and Erlangen: Ner-Tamid-Verlag, 1969).

Heilbronner, Hans, 'Count Aehrenthal and Russian Jewry 1903–1907', *Journal of Modern History*, 38 (1966) pp. 394–406.

Hildermeier, Manfred, 'Die jüdische Frage im Zarenreich. Zum Problem der unterbliebenen Emanzipation', in *Jahrbücher für die Geschichte Osteuropas*, 32 (1984) pp. 321–57.

——, *Die Russische Reolution 1905–1921* (Frankfurt/M.: Edition Suhrkamp, 1989) [Published as Neue Historische Bibliothek. Neue Folge Band 534].

Hosking, Geoffrey A., *The Russian Constitutional Experiment. Government and Dumas 1907–1914* (Cambridge: Cambridge University Press, 1973).

Hroch, Miroslav, *Die Vorkämpfer der Nationalen Bewegung bei den kleinen Völkern Europas. Eine vergleichende Analyse zur gesellschaftlichen Schichtung der Patriotischen Gruppen* (Prague, 1968) [Published as Acta Universitatis Carolinae Philosophica et Historica. Monographia 24].

Ingold, F.P., 'M.I. Saltykov-Shchedrin und die Russische Judenfrage', in *Zeitschrift für Religions und Geistesgeschichte*, 30, 4 (1978) pp. 328–36.

Isler, J.M., *Rückkehr der Juden zur Landwirtschaft. Beitrag zur Geschichte der Landwirtschaftlichen Kolonisation der Juden in verschiedenen Ländern* (Frankfurt/M.: J. Kauffmann Verlag, 1929).

Janowsky, Oscar I., *The Jews and Minority Rights 1898–1919. Studies in History, Economics and Public Law*, no. 384, edited by the Faculty of Political Science of Columbia University (New York, 1933. Reprint 1966).

Jaworski, Rudolf, *Handel und Gewerbe im Nationalitätenkampf: Studien zur Wirtschaftsgesinnung der Polen in der Provinz Posen 1871–1914*, Kritische Studien zur Geschichtswissenschaft, vol. 70 (Göttingen: Vandenhoeck und Ruprecht, 1986).

Kahan, Arcadius, 'The Impact of Industrialization in Tsarist Russia on the Socioeconomic Conditions of The Jewish Population', in Roger Weiss (ed.), *Essays in Jewish Social and Economic History: Arcadius Kahan* (Chicago and London: University of Chicago Press, 1986) pp. 1–69.

——, 'Notes on Jewish Entrepreneurship in Tsarist Russia', ibid., pp. 82–100.

Kappeler, Andreas, *Russland als Vielvölkerreich. Entstehung, Geschichte, Zerfall* (Munich: Verlag C.H. Beck, 1992).

Keep, John L., 'Russian Social Democracy and the First State Duma', *Slavonic and East European Review*, 34 (1955) pp. 180–99.

Kiel, Mark W., 'The Ideology of the Folks-Party', *Soviet Jewish Affairs*, vol. 5, no. 2 (1975) pp. 75–89.

Kieval, Hillel J., *The Making of Czech Jewry: National Conflict and Jewish Society in Bohemia, 1870–1914* (New York and Oxford: Oxford University Press, 1988).

Klausner, Joseph, *Menahem Ussishkin. His Life and Work* (London: Joint Zionist Publication Committee, n.d.).

Klier, John D., 'The Ambiguous Legal Status of Russian Jewry in the Reign of Catherine II', *Slavic Review*, 35 (1976) pp. 504–17.

——, and Shlomo Lambroza (ed.), *Pogroms: Anti-Jewish Violence in Modern Russian History* (Cambridge: Cambridge University Press, 1992).

Kling, Simcha, *The Mighty Warrior. Menahem Ussishkin* (New York: Jonathan David Publishers, 1965).

Kolesnichenko, D.A., 'K voprosu o politicheskoi evolutsii trudovikov v 1906 g.', in *Istoricheskie Zapiski*, 92 (1973) pp. 84–109.

——, 'Iz istorii borby rabochego klassa za krest'ianskie massy v 1906 g.', in *Istoricheskie Zapiski*, 95 (1975) pp. 254–82.

Korzec, P., 'Three Documents of 1903–1906 on Russian-Jewish Affairs', in *Soviet Jewish Affairs*, 2 (1972) pp. 75–95.

Krupnik, Baruch, Die jüdischen Parteien. Ein Überblick zur Orientierung (Berlin, 1919) [Seeds of Conflicts II. Palestine, Zionism and the Levant 1912–1946. The Debate I. Nendeln 1974].

Kucherov, Samuel, *Courts, Lawyers and Trials under the last Three Tsars* (New York: Greenwood Press, 1953).

Lamberti, Majorie, *Jewish Activism in Imperial Germany. The Struggle for Civil Equality* (New Haven and London: Yale University Press, 1978).

Lambroza, Shlomo, 'Plehve, Kishinev and the Jewish Question: A Reappraisal', *Nationalities Papers*, 12, no. 1 (1984) pp. 117–27.

——, *The Pogrom Movement in Tsarist Russia, 1903–1906*. DPhil thesis. Rutgers University, 1981.

Laqueur, Walter, *Der Weg zum Staat Israel. Geschichte des Zionismus* (Vienna: Europa Verlag, 1972).

Lederhendler, Eli, *The Road to Modern Jewish Politics: Political Tradition and Political Reconstruction in the Jewish Community of Tsarist Russia* (Oxford: Oxford University Press, 1989).

Leontovitsch, Victor, *Geschichte des Liberalismus in Rußland*, 2nd ed. (Frankfurt/M.: Vittorio Klostermann Verlag, 1974).

Lestschinsky, Jacob, 'Dubnow's Autonomism and his "Letters on Old and New Judaism"', in Aaron Steinberg (ed.), *Simon Dubnow: The Man and his Work* (Paris, 1963) pp. 73–91.

——, 'The Anti-Jewish Pogrom: Tsarist Russia, the Third Reich, and Independent Poland', in *Jewish Social Studies*, 3 (1941) pp. 141–58.

——, *Dos Yidishe Folk in Tsifern* (Berlin: Kalal Farlag, 1922).

Levenberg, S., 'Simon Dubnow: Historian of Russian Jewry', in *Soviet Jewish Affairs*, vol. 12, no. 1 (1982) pp. 3–17.

Levin, Alfred, 'The Russian Voter in the Elections to the Third Duma', *Slavic Review*, 21, 4 (1962) pp. 660–77.

——, *The Second Duma: A Study of the Social-Democratic Party and the Russian Constitutional Experiment*, 2nd ed. (Hamden, Connecticut: Archon Books, 1966).

——, *The Third Duma. Election and Profile* (Hamden, Connecticut: Archon Books: 1973).

Levin, Nora, *While Messiah Tarried. Jewish Socialist Movements 1871–1917* (New York: Schocken Books, 1977).

——, *The Jews in the Soviet Union since 1917. Paradox of survival*, 2 vols (New York: New York University Press, 1990).

Levitats, Isaac, *The Jewish Community in Russia 1844–1917* (Jerusalem: Posner and Sons Ltd., 1981).

Lichten, Joseph, 'Notes on the assimilation and acculturation of Jews in Poland, 1863–1943', in C. Abramsky, M. Jachimczyk and A. Polonsky (eds), *The Jews in Poland* (Oxford: Basil Blackwell, 1986) pp. 106–29.

Löwe, Heinz-Dietrich, *Antisemitismus und reaktionäre Utopie. Russischer Konservatismus im Kampf gegen den Wandel von Staat und Gesellschaft* (Hamburg: Hoffmann und Campe Verlag, 1978) [Historische Perspectiven, vol. 13. Edited by Bernd Martin *et al.*].

——, 'Die Rolle der russischen Intelligenz in der Revolution von 1905', in *Forschungen zur osteuropäischen Geschichte*, 32 (1983) pp. 231–254.

——, 'Die Rolle der demokratischen Intelligenz', in M. Hellmann, K. Zernack and G. Schramm (eds), *Handbuch der Geschichte Russlands*. Vol. 3/1. Von den autokratischen Reformen zum Sowjetstaat 1856–1945 (Stuttgart: Hiersemann Verlag, 1982).

——, 'From Charity to Social Policy: The Emergence of Jewish Self-Help Organizations in Imperial Russia, 1800–1914', paper given at the Deutsch-Polnische Historikertagung: 'Deutsche – Polen – Juden', February 1992, Freiburg/Breisgau, Gemany.

McReynolds, Louise, 'Imperial Russia's Newspaper Reporters: Profile of a Society in Transition, 1865–1914', in *Slavonic and East European Review*, vol. 68, no. 2 (April 1990) pp. 277–93.

Meisl, Josef, *Haskalah. Geschichte der Aufklärungsbewegung unter den Juden in Russland* (Berlin: Schwetschke & Sohn Verlagsbuchhandlung, 1919).

——, *Geschichte der Juden in Polen und Rußland*, vol. III (Berlin: C.A. Schwetschke & Sohn Verlagsbuchhandlung, 1922).

Mendelsohn, Ezra, *Class Struggle in the Pale. The Formative Years of the Jewish Workers' Movement in Tsarist Russia* (Cambridge: Cambridge University Press, 1970).

——, *The Jews of East Central Europe between the Two World Wars* (Bloomington, Indiana: Indiana University Press, 1983).

Meyer, Michael A., *Jewish Identity in the Modern World* (Seattle and London: University of Washington Press, 1990).

Mintz, Matityahu, 'Ber Borokhov', *Studies in Zionism*, no. 5 (April 1982) pp. 33–53.

Naimark, Norman M., 'The Workers' Section and the Challenge of the "Young": Narodnaia Volia, 1881–1884', *The Russian Review*, 37 (1978) pp. 273–97.

——, *Terrorist and Social Democrats. The Russian Revolutionary Movement under Alexander III* (Cambridge, Massachusetts and London: Harvard University Press, 1983).

Norman, Theodore, *An Outstretched Arm. A History of the Jewish Colonization Association* (London: Routledge and Kegan Paul, 1985).

Ochs, Michael, *St. Petersburg and the Jews of Russian Poland, 1862–1905*. Unpublished DPhil thesis (Harvard University, 1986).

Orbach, Alexander, 'The Jewish People's Group and Jewish Politics, 1906–1914', *Modern Judaism*, February 1990, vol. X, pp. 1–15.

——, 'Zionism and the Russian Revolution of 1905. The commitment to participate in Domestic Political Life', in *Annual of Bar-Ilan University Studies in the History and Culture of East European Jewry*, vol. XXIV–XXV (Jerusalem, 1989).

——, 'The Saul Ginsburg Archival Collection: A Major Source for the Study of Russian-Jewish Life and Letters', *Soviet Jewish Affairs*, no. 2 (1981) pp. 39–51.

——, *New Voices of Russian Jewry. A Study of the Russian Jewish Press of Odessa in the Era of the Great Reforms 1860–1871* (Leiden: E.J. Brill, 1980) [Published as Studies in Judaism in Modern Times. Edited by Jakob Neusner, vol. IV].

——, 'Jewish Intellectuals in Odessa in the Late 19th Century: The Nationalist Theories of Ahad Ha'am and Simon Dubnow', *Nationalities Papers*, 6, no. 2 (1978) pp. 109–23.

Pares, Bernard, 'The Second Duma', *The Slavonic and East European Review*, 2 (1923) pp. 36–55.

Peled, Yoav, *Class and Ethnicity in the Pale. The Political Economy of Jewish Workers' Nationalism in late Imperial Russia* (London: The Macmillan Press, 1989).

Perlmann, Moshe, '*Razsvet* 1860–61. The Origins of the Russian Jewish Press', in *Jewish Social Studies*, 29 (1962) pp. 162–182.

Pinchuk, B.C., *The Octobrists in the Russian State Duma* (Seattle and London: University of Washington Press, 1974).

Pinson, Koppel S., 'The National Theories of Simon Dubnow', *Jewish Social Studies*, 10 (1948) pp. 335–58.

——, 'Arkady Kremer, Vladimir Medem, and the Ideology of the Jewish Bund', *Jewish Social Studies*, 7 (1945) pp. 233–264.

Pipes, Richard, *Struve: Liberal on the Right 1905–1944* (Cambridge, Massachusetts: Harvard University Press, 1980).

——, *The Russian Revolution 1899–1919* (London: Fontana Press, 1990).

Pospielovsky, Dmitry, *Russian Police Trade Unionism. Experiment or Provocation?* (London: Weidenfeld and Nicolson, 1971).

Rader, Jack, *By the Skill of their Hands. The Story of ORT* (Geneva: World ORT Union, 1970).

Raeff, Marc, 'Some Reflections on Russian Liberalism', *Russian Review*, 18 (1959) pp. 218–30.

Raisin, Jacob S., *The Haskalah Movement* (Philadelphia: The Jewish Publication Society of America, 1913).

Reinharz, Jehuda, *Fatherland or Promised Land. The Dilemma of the German Jew, 1893–1914* (Ann Arbor: University of Michigan Press, 1975).

——, (ed.), *Living with Antisemitism. Modern Jewish Responses* (Hanover and London: University Press of New England, 1987).

Rexheuser, R., *Dumawahlen und lokale Gesellschaft. Studien zur Sozialgeschichte der russischen Rechten vor 1917* (Cologne and Vienna: Böhlau Verlag, 1980).

Rieber, A.J., *Merchants and Entrepreneurs in Imperial Russia* (Chapel Hill: University of North Carolina Press, 1982).

Riha, Thomas, *A Russian European. Paul Miliukov in Russian Politics* (London: University of Notre Dame Press, 1969).

——, '*Riech*. A Portrait of a Russian Newspaper', *Slavic Review*, 22 (1963) pp. 663–82.

Rodichev, I., 'The Liberal Movement in Russia 1891–1905', *The Slavonic and East European Review*, 2 (1923) pp. 249–62.

Rogger, Hans, *Jewish Policies and Right-Wing Politics in Imperial Russia* (Oxford: The Macmillan Press, 1986).

——, *Russia in the Age of Modernisation and Revolution 1881–1917*. Volume in the Longman History of Russia edited by Harold Shukman (New York, 1983).

Rogger, Hans and Weber, Eugen (eds), *The European Right. A Historical Profile* (Berkeley and Los Angeles, 1965).

Rollins, Patrick J., 'Cooperative Movement in Russia and the Soviet Union', *The Modern Encyclopedia of Russian and Soviet History*, vol. 8. Edited by Joseph L. Wieczynski (Academic International Press, 1978) pp. 53–58.

Rowland, Richard H., 'Geographical Patterns of the Jewish Population in the Pale of Settlement of Late Nineteenth Century Russia', *Jewish Social Studies*, 48 (1986) pp. 207–34.

Rozenblit, Marsha L., *The Jews of Vienna, 1867–1914. Assimilation and Identity* (Albany, NY: State University of New York Press, 1983).

Sacher, Henry (ed.), *Zionist Portraits and other essays* (Oxford, 1959).

Samuel, Maurice, *Blood Accusation. The Strange History of the Beiliss Case* (London: Weidenfeld and Nicolson, 1967).

Schapiro, Leonard, 'The Role of the Jews in the Russian Revolutionary Movement', *Slavonic and East European Review*, 40 (1961) pp. 148–67.

Schechtman, Joseph B., *Rebel and Statesman. The Vladimir Jabotinsky Story. The early years* (New York, 1956).

Scheibert, Peter (ed.), *Die russischen politischen Parteien von 1905 bis 1917. Ein Dokumentationsband* (Darmstadt: Wissenschaftliche Buchgemeinschaft, 1983).

——, 'Über den Liberalismus in Rußland', in *Jahrbücher für die Geschichte Osteuropas*, Neue Folge, 7 (1959) pp. 34–48.

Schlögel, Karl, *Wegzeichen. Zur Krise der russischen Intelligenz. Essays von Nikolaj Berdjaev etc.* (Frankfurt/M.: Eichborn Verlag, 1990).

Schmidt, Christoph, 'Zur politischen Topographie St. Petersburgs. Zeitungsabsatz und Wahlausgang 1890–1917', in *Jahrbücher für Geschichte Osteuropas*, Neue Folge, 36 (1988) pp. 37–56.

Schneiderman, Jeremiah, *Sergei Zubatov and Revolutionary Marxism. The struggle for the working class in Tsarist Russia* (London: Cornell University Press, 1976).

Scholem, Gershom, *Die jüdische Mystik in ihren Hauptströmungen* (Frankfurt/M.: Suhrkamp Taschenbuch Wissenschaft, 1980).

Schorsch, Ismar, *Jewish Reaction to German Anti-Semitism 1870–1914* (New York and London: Columbia University Press, 1972).

Seltzer, Robert, *Simon Dubnow. A critical biography of his early years.* PhD dissertation Columbia University. Published by University Microfilm International (Ann Arbor and London, 1977).

Seraphim, Peter-Heinz, *Das Judentum im osteuropäischen Raum* (Essen, 1938).

Seton-Watson, Hugh, *The Russian Empire, 1801–1917* (Oxford: Oxford University Press, 1967. Reprint 1988).

Shapiro, Leon, *The History of ORT: A Jewish Movement for Social Change* (New York: Schocken Books, 1980).

Shavit, Simon, 'The Emergence of Jewish Public Libraries in Tsarist Russia', *Journal of Library History*, 20, no. 3 (1985) pp. 239–52.

Sherman, A.I., 'German-Jewish bankers in World Politics: The Financing of the Russo-Japanese War', in *Yearbook of the Leo Baeck Institute*, 28 (1983) pp. 59–73.

Snow, George E., 'The Peterhof Conference of 1905 and the Creation of the Bulygin Duma', in *Russian History*, II, 2 (1975) pp. 149–62.

Sorkin, David, 'Emancipation and Assimilation. Two Concepts and their Application to German-Jewish History', in *Yearbook of the Leo Baeck Institute*, 35 (1990) pp. 17–33.

Springer, A., 'Enlightened Absolutism and Jewish Reform: Prussia, Austria and Russia', *California Slavic Studies*, 11 (1980) pp. 237–67.

Stanislawski, Michael, *For whom do I toil? Judah Leib Gordon and the Crisis of Russian Jewry* (Oxford: Oxford University Press, 1988).

——, *Tsar Nicholas I and the Jews. The Transformation of Jewish Society in Russia 1852–1855* (Philadelphia: The Jewish Publication Society of America, 1983).

Steinberg, Aaron, *Simon Dubnow: The Man and his Work.* Published by the French Section of the World Jewish Congress (Paris, 1963).

Swietochowski, T., *Russian Azerbaijan 1905–1920: The Shaping of National Identity in a Muslim Community* (Cambridge: Cambridge University Press, 1985).

Syrkin, Marie, *Nachman Syrkin. Socialist Zionist. A Biographical Memoir* (New York, 1961).

Szajkowski, Zosa, 'Paul Nathan, Lucien Wolf, Jacob Schiff and the Jewish Revolutionary Movements in Eastern Europe 1903–1917', in *Jewish Social Studies*, 29 (1967) pp. 3–26.

——, 'Conflicts in the Alliance Israelite Universelle and the founding of the Anglo-Jewish Association and the Hilfsverein', *Jewish Social Studies*, 19 (1957) pp. 29–50.

Tager, Alexander B., *The Decay of Czarism. The Beiliss Trial. A contribution to the history of the political reaction during the last years of Russian Czarism* (Philadelphia: The Jewish Publication Society of America, 1935).

Tobias, Henry J., *The Jewish Bund in Russia. From its Origins to 1905* (Stanford, California: Stanford University Press, 1972).

Tobias, Henry J. and Woodhouse, Charles E., 'Political Reaction and Revolutionary Careers. The Jewish Bundists in Defeat, 1907–1910', in *Comparative Studies in Society and History*, 19 (1977) pp. 367–96.

Toury, Jacob, 'Troubled Beginnings: The Emergence of the Österreichisch-Israelitische Union', in *Leo Baeck Institute Year Book*, 30 (1985) pp. 457–75.

——, 'Years of Strife. The Contest of the Österreichisch-Israelitische Union for the Leadership of Austrian Jewry', in *Leo Baeck Institute Year Book*, 33 (1988) pp. 179–99.

——, 'Defense Activities of the Österreichisch-Israelitische Union before 1914', in Jehuda Reinharz (ed.), *Living with Antisemitism. Modern Jewish Responses* (Hanover and London: University Press of New England, 1987) pp. 167–92.

Ussoskin, Moshe, *Struggle for Survival. A History of Jewish Credit Co-operatives in Bessarabia, Old Rumania, Bukovina and Transylvania* (Jerusalem: Jerusalem Academic Press, 1975).

Vishniak, Mark, 'Anti-Semitism in Russia', in Koppel S. Pinson (ed.), *Essays on Anti-Semitism*. Jewish Social Studies Publications no. 2 (New York, 1942) pp. 130–41.

Vital, David, *The Origins of Zionism* (Oxford: Oxford University Press, 1975).

——, *Zionism: The Formative Years* (Oxford: Oxford University Press, 1982).

Walsh, Warren B., 'Political Parties in the Russian Dumas', in *Journal of Modern History*, 22 (1950) pp. 144–75.

Weinberg, Robert D., 'Workers, pogroms and the 1905 Revolution in Odessa', *Russian Review*, 46 (1987) pp. 53–75.

Weinryb, Bernard D., *Neueste Wirtschaftsgeschichte der Juden in Russland und Polen. Von der 1. polnischen Teilung bis zum Tode Alexanders II 1772–1881* (Breslau, 1934. Reprinted Hildesheim and New York, 1972).

Weissman, Neil B., *Reform in Tsarist Russia. The State Bureaucracy and Local Government, 1900–1914* (New Brunswick, New Jersey: Rutgers University Press, 1981).

Wertheimer, Jack, 'Between Tsar and Kaiser. The Radicalization of Russian-Jewish University Students in Germany', in *Leo Baeck Institute Year Book*, 28 (1983) pp. 329–49.

Wistrich, Robert S., *Socialism and the Jews. The Dilemmas of Assimilation in Germany and Austria-Hungary* (London and Toronto: Fairleigh Dickinson University Press, 1982).

Wolfe, Bertram D., 'Gapon and Zubatov: An Experiment in Police Socialism', *Russian Review*, 2 (1948) pp. 53–61.

Zimmerman, Judith Elin, *Between Revolution and Reaction. The Russian Constitutional Democratic Party – October 1905 to June 1907*. DPhil thesis. Columbia University (Ann Arbor, Michigan: University Microfilms, 1969).

——, 'The Kadets and the Duma 1905–1907', in Ch.E. Timberlake (ed.), *Essays in Russian Liberalism* (Columbia, Mo.: University of Missouri Press, 1972) pp. 119–38.

Zipperstein, Steven J., *The Jews of Odessa: A Cultural History, 1794–1881* (Stanford, California: Stanford University Press, 1985).

——, 'Transforming the Heder: Maskilic Politics in Imperial Russia', in Ada Rapoport and Steven J. Zipperstein, *Jewish History: Essays in Honour of Chimen Abramsky* (London: Peter Halban Publishers Ltd., 1988) pp. 87–109.

——, 'The Politics of Relief: The Transformation of Russian Jewish Communal Life during the First World War', in *Studies in Contemporary Jewry*, 4 (1988) pp. 22–40.

# Index